Lecture Notes in Computer Science 3466

Commenced Publication in 1973
Founding and Former Series Editors:
Gerhard Goos, Juris Hartmanis, and Jan van Leeuwen

Stefan Leue   Tarja Johanna Systä (Eds.)

Scenarios: Models, Transformations and Tools

International Workshop
Dagstuhl Castle, Germany, September 7-12, 2003
Revised Selected Papers

 Springer

Volume Editors

Stefan Leue
University of Konstanz
Department of Computer and Information Science
78457 Konstanz, Germany
E-mail: Stefan.Leue@uni-konstanz.de

Tarja Johanna Systä
Tampere University of Technology
Institute of Software Systems
33101 Tampere, Finland
E-mail: cstasy@cs.uta.fi

Library of Congress Control Number: 2005928335

CR Subject Classification (1998): F.3.1-2, C.2.4, D.2.1, D.2.4-5, D.3.1, K.6.5

ISSN   0302-9743
ISBN-10   3-540-26189-3 Springer Berlin Heidelberg New York
ISBN-13   978-3-540-26189-6 Springer Berlin Heidelberg New York

Springer is a part of Springer Science+Business Media

springeronline.com

© Springer-Verlag Berlin Heidelberg 2005
Printed in Germany

Typesetting: Camera-ready by author, data conversion by Scientific Publishing Services, Chennai, India
Printed on acid-free paper   SPIN: 11495628   06/3142   5 4 3 2 1 0

Preface

Visual notations and languages continue to play a pivotal rôle in the design of complex software systems. In many cases visual notations are used to describe usage or interaction scenarios of software systems or their components. While representing scenarios using a visual notation is not the only possibility, a vast majority of scenario description languages is visual. Scenarios are used in telecommunications as Message Sequence Charts, in object-oriented system design as Sequence Diagrams, in reverse engineering as execution traces, and in requirements engineering as, for example, Use Case Maps or Life Sequence Charts. These techniques are used to capture requirements, to capture use cases in system documentation, to specify test cases, or to visualize runs of existing systems. They are often employed to represent concurrent systems that interact via message passing or method invocation. In telecommunications, for more than 15 years the International Telecommunication Union has standardized the Message Sequence Charts (MSCs) notation in its recommendation Z.120. More recently, with the emergence of UML as a predominant software design methodology, there has been special interest in the development of the sequence diagram notation. As a result, the most recent version, 2.0, of UML encompasses the Message Sequence Chart notation, including its hierarchical modeling features. Other scenario-flavored diagrams in UML 2.0 include activity diagrams and timing diagrams.

To a large extent the attractiveness of visual scenario notations stems from the ease with which these diagrams can be recognized and understood. On the other hand, the ease of use of these diagrams brings with it the danger that system specifications and designs understate the inherent system complexity and lead to incomplete system models. A research focus is therefore directed at making scenario notations amenable to formal treatment – this includes models for their formal representations, transformations between different notations and abstraction levels, and tools that support editing, analysis and synthesis for scenario notations.

The seminar on which this proceedings volume reports was entitled *Scenarios: Models, Transformations and Tools* and was held as Seminar Number 03371 during September 7–12, 2003, at Schloss Dagstuhl, Germany. It was organized as a continuation of a series of workshops that have been co-located with larger conferences such as the International Conference on Software Engineering (ICSE) and the Conference on Object-Oriented Programming, Systems, Languages, and Applications (OOSPLA) since 2000. This volume is a post-event proceedings volume and contains selected papers based on presentations given during the seminar. All included papers were thoroughly peer-reviewed in two rounds of reviewing.

The paper by Haugen, Husa, Runde and Stølen opens the first section of papers that deal with the semantics and analysis of scenario notations. The authors of this paper argue for the need to use a three-event semantics which distinguishes the sending event, the receiving event and the consumption event in timed sequence diagrams. An interactive scenario design process by which the system synthesizes a design model by learning from sets of positive and negative scenarios, represented as sequence diagrams, is described in the paper by Harel, Kugler and Weiss. An analysis tool stands at the end of their tool chain. When analyzing Scenario specifications it is important to recognize the limits of decidability. The paper by Muscholl and Peled reviews important decidability results regarding Sequence Diagrams and Message Sequence Charts, another popular visual scenario notation. It is frequently observed that the application of modeling formalisms in specific application domains requires dedicated semantics. Cremers and Mauw propose in their paper an operational semantics for Messages Sequence Charts applied in the domain of security protocols.

One objective of the Dagstuhl seminar was to entice practical work that assesses the suitability of different scenario design approaches to a common case study. Two half-days during the seminar were devoted to modeling the case study known as the *Autonomous Shuttle System* using different design approaches and tools. The paper by Giese and Klein describe this case study. Some of the subsequent papers in this volume refer to it.

We mentioned above that many but not all scenario formalisms are visual. In his paper, Dromey introduces a textual scenario description language called Design Behavior Trees and exemplifies this design notation by application to the Early Warning System case study proposed by Harel and Politi.

The paper by Diethelm, Geiger and Zündorf offers a thorough treatment of the Autonomous Shuttle System case study using the Story Driven Modeling design approach. The CASE tool Fujaba, which underlies this study, enables editing, analysis and synthesis based on a collection of scenarios. The Use Case Maps notation has recently evolved as a new visual requirements notation that focusses on expressing the causalities of events happening along use cases. In their paper, Petriu, Amyot, Woodside and Jiang illustrate the use of the Use Case Maps notation by applying it to capturing requirements for the Autonomous Shuttle System case study.

It has long been recognized that Message Sequence Charts and related scenario notations can prove helpful in software testing. The paper by Beyer and Dulz suggests the use of collections of scenarios in the synthesis of a stochastic usage model, called Markov Chain Usage Models. These models are later used as the basis for testing stochastic properties of real-time systems.

Both the formal analysis of variants of Message Sequence Chart models and the synthesis of correct executable code from these models are at the heart of the paper by Bontemps, Heymans and Schobbens. Since both problems are either computationally expensive or intractable, the authors propose sound and complete "lightweight" approximations of the original problems. The synthesis problem is also the subject of the paper by Giese, Klein and Burmester. The authors suggest the derivation of behavior patterns from scenario specifications. The patterns will later be used for compositional system verification.

The modeling of mobile systems is addressed in the paper by Kosiuczenko. The author suggests a graphical scenario notation to represent object mobility as an extension of UML Sequence Diagrams and suggests a semi-formal interpretation for this notation.

Message Sequence Charts are frequently used at the early stages of the software design process, and it is desirable to derive executable design models from them. The MSC2SDL tool that Khendek and Zhang describe synthesizes SDL models from collections of MSC specifications. The authors illustrate their approach by using the Autonomous Shuttle System case study as a reference.

Object-oriented systems tend to be described by the services that the object instances can provide, and often assume that an object may provide different services as it plays different rôles. The paper by Krüger and Mathews illustrates the use of Scenario Diagrams in describing the different services that object instances may provide. They also show how a complete system view can be derived from this model. The authors exemplify the use of their notation by applying it to the Center TRACON Automation System (CTAS) case study, another benchmark case study for scenario-based system-design.

The collection of papers included in this volume covers a major portion of the discussions that took place during the seminar. More information, including the program, transparencies of the presentations, and a summary of the outcome of the seminar, is available online under the URL http://www.dagstuhl.de/03371/

Acknowledgements. We thank Francis Bordeleau for co-organizing this seminar with us and for helping us in the initial phases of the editing of this volume. We are truly grateful to Schloss Dagstuhl and its staff for providing us with the very pleasant atmosphere that made a very productive seminar come about. The permission to use the Springer LNCS online reviewing system helped us a lot in the compilation of this volume, and we wish to thank Tiziana Margaria and Martin Karusseit for their support.

March 2005

Tarja Systä (Tampere)
Stefan Leue (Konstanz)

Organization

Seminar Organizers

F. Bordeleau
S. Leue
T. Systä

Referees

D. Amyot
Y. Bontemps
F. Bordeleau
J.P. Corriveau
H. Giese
M. Glinz
S. Graf
R. Grosu
Ø. Haugen

K. Heljanko
F. Khendek
A. Knapp
H. Kugler
S. Leue
C. Lohr
E. Mäkinen
S. Mauw
D. Peled

I. Schieferdecker
S. Somé
T. Systä
S. Uchitel
G. Weiss
M. Woodside
A. Zündorf

Table of Contents

Why Timed Sequence Diagrams Require Three-Event Semantics

Øystein Haugen[1], Knut Eilif Husa[1,2], Ragnhild Kobro Runde[1],
and Ketil Stølen[1,3]

[1] Department of Informatics, University of Oslo
[2] Ericsson
[3] SINTEF ICT, Norway

Abstract. STAIRS is an approach to the compositional development of
sequence diagrams supporting the specification of mandatory as well as
potential behavior. In order to express the necessary distinction between
black-box and glass-box refinement, an extension of the semantic framework with three event messages is introduced. A concrete syntax is also
proposed. The proposed extension is especially useful when describing
time constraints. The resulting approach, referred to as Timed STAIRS,
is formally underpinned by denotational trace semantics. A trace is a
sequence of three kinds of events: events for transmission, reception and
consumption. We argue that such traces give the necessary expressiveness to capture the standard UML interpretation of sequence diagrams
as well as the black-box interpretation found in classical formal methods.

1 Introduction to STAIRS

Sequence diagrams have been used informally for several decades. The first standardization of sequence diagrams came in 1992 [ITU93] – often referred to as
MSC-92. Later we have seen several dialects and variations. The sequence diagrams of UML 1.4 [OMG00] were comparable to those of MSC-92, while the
recent UML 2.0 [OMG04] has upgraded sequence diagrams to conform well to
MSC-2000 [ITU99].

Sequence diagrams show how messages are sent between objects or other
instances to perform a task. They are used in a number of different situations.
They are for example used by an individual designer to get a better grip of a
communication scenario or by a group to achieve a common understanding of
the situation. Sequence diagrams are also used during the more detailed design
phase where the precise inter-process communication must be set up according to
formal protocols. When testing is performed, the behavior of the system can be
described as sequence diagrams and compared with those of the earlier phases.

Sequence diagrams seem to have the ability to be understood and produced
by professionals of computer systems design as well as potential end-users and
stakeholders of the (future) systems. Even though sequence diagrams are intuitive – a property which is always exploited, it is not always obvious how one goes

S. Leue and T.J. Systä (Eds.): Scenarios, LNCS 3466, pp. 1–25 , 2005.

about making the sequence diagrams when a certain situation is analyzed. It is also the case that intuition is not always the best guide for a precise interpretation of a complicated scenario. Therefore we have brought forth an approach for reaching a sensible and fruitful set of sequence diagrams, supported by formal reasoning. We called this approach STAIRS – Steps To Analyze Interactions with Refinement Semantics [HS03].

STAIRS distinguishes between positive and negative traces and accepts that some traces may be inconclusive meaning that they have not yet or should not be characterized as positive or negative. STAIRS views the process of developing the interactions as a process of learning through describing. From a fuzzy, rough sketch, the aim is to reach a precise and detailed description applicable for formal handling. To come from the rough and fuzzy to the precise and detailed, STAIRS distinguishes between three sub-activities: (1) supplementing, (2) narrowing and (3) detailing.

Supplementing categorizes inconclusive behavior as either positive or negative. The initial requirements concentrate on the most obvious normal situations and the most obvious exceptional ones. Supplementing supports this by allowing less obvious situations to be treated later. Narrowing reduces the allowed behavior to match the problem better. Detailing involves introducing a more detailed description without significantly altering the externally observable behavior.

STAIRS distinguishes between potential alternatives and mandatory or obligatory alternatives. A special composition operator named xalt facilitates the specification of mandatory alternatives.

Figure 1 shows our STAIRS example – an interaction overview diagram description of the making of a dinner at an ethnic restaurant.

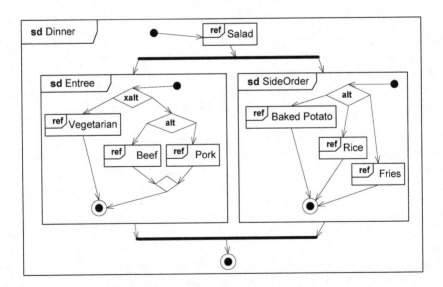

Fig. 1. Interaction overview diagram of a dinner

The dinner starts with a salad and continues with a main course that consists of an entree and a side order, which are made in parallel. For the side order there is a simple choice between three alternatives and the restaurant is not obliged to have any particular of them available. Supplementing side orders could be to offer soya beans in addition, while narrowing would mean that the restaurant could choose only to serve rice and never potatoes nor fries. It would still be consistent with the specification and a valid refinement. On the other hand, the entree has more absolute requirements. The restaurant is obliged to offer vegetarian as well as meat, but it does not have to serve both beef and pork. This means that Indian as well as Jewish restaurants are refinements (narrowing) of our dinner concept, while a pure vegetarian restaurant is not valid according to our specification.

The remainder of the paper is divided into six sections: Section 2 motivates the need for a three event semantics for sequence diagrams. Section 3 introduces the formal machinery; in particular, it defines the syntax and semantics of sequence diagrams. Section 4 defines two special interpretations of sequence diagrams, referred to as the standard and the black-box interpretation, respectively. Section 5 demonstrates the full power of Timed STAIRS as specification formalism. Section 6 introduces glass-box and black-box refinement and demonstrates the use of these notions. Section 7 provides a brief conclusion and compares Timed STAIRS to other approaches known from the literature.

2 Motivating Timed STAIRS

STAIRS works well for its purpose. However, there are certain things that cannot be expressed within the framework as presented in [HS03]. For instance time constraints and the difference between glass-box and black-box view of a system. This section motivates the need for this extra expressiveness.

Let us now look closer at the details of making the Beef in Figure 1.[1] From Figure 2 it is intuitive to assume that the working of the Cook making Beef can be explained by the following scheme: The Cook receives an order for main dish (of type Beef) and then turns on the heat and waits until the heat is adequate. Then he fetches the sirloin meat from the refrigerator before putting it on the grill. Then he fetches the sirloin from the stove (hopefully when it is adequately grilled). He then sends the steak to the customer.

We reached this explanation of the procedures of the cook from looking locally at the cook's lifeline in the Beef diagram. The input event led to one or more outputs, before he again would wait for an input. We found it natural to assume that the input event meant that the cook handled this event, consumed it and

---

[1] This sequence diagram is not a complete specification of Beef. The supplementing has not yet been finished. From a methodological point of view, the diagram should be "closed" with an assert when the supplementing has been finished. This to state that what is still left as inconclusive behavior should from now on be understood as negative. Otherwise, we do not get the semantics intended by Figure 1.

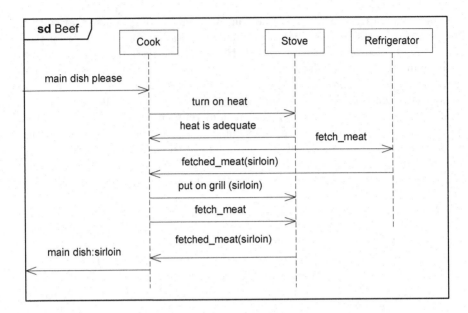

Fig. 2. Sequence diagram of Beef

acted upon it. This intuition gives rise to what we here will call the standard interpretation of sequence diagrams where an input event is seen as consumption of the event, and where the directly following output events of the trace are causally linked to the consumption. Thus, we can by considering each separate lifeline locally determine the transitions of a state machine describing the lifeline.

Our description of how the beef is made comes from a quiet day, or early in the evening when there were not so many customers and the kitchen had no problems to take care of each order immediately. Furthermore our description was probably made for one of those restaurants where the customers can look into the kitchen through glass. It was a glass-box description. We want, however, to be able to describe the situation later in the evening when the restaurant is crammed with customers and in a restaurant where there is only a black door to the kitchen. We would like to assume that even though the restaurant is full, the kitchen will handle our order immediately, but alas this is of course not the case. We can only observe the kitchen as a black-box. We observe the waiters coming through the door as messengers – orders one way and dishes the other. From these observations we could make estimates of the efficiency of the kitchen. Notice that the efficiency of the kitchen cannot be derived from when the customers placed the orders because the waiters may stop at several tables before they enter the kitchen. Comparing black-box observations of the kitchen with our glass-box one, we realize that in the glass-box description no event was attached to passing through the door. The order was sent by the customer and consumed by the chef. The passing through the door represents that the kitchen is receiving the message but not necessarily doing something with it. As long as you are not interested in timing matters, the difference is seldom practically significant, but when time matters, the difference between when a message is received and when it is consumed is crucial. How is the kitchen organized to handle the orders in a swift and fair manner?

Motivated by this we will use three events to represent the communication of a message: the sending event, the receiving event and the consumption event, and each of these events may have a timestamp associated. We will introduce concrete syntax for sequence diagrams to capture this and the distinction is also reflected in the semantics. This will give us sufficient expressiveness to describe a black-box interpretation as well as the standard glass-box interpretation.

3 Formal Foundation

In the following we define the notion of sequence diagram. In particular, we formalize the meaning of sequence diagrams in denotational trace semantics.

3.1 Syntax of Sequence Diagrams

A message is a triple (s, tr, re) of a signal s, a transmitter tr, and a receiver re. M denotes the set of all messages. The transmitters and receivers are lifelines. L denotes the set of all lifelines.

We distinguish between three kinds of events; a transmission event tagged by an exclamation mark "!", a reception event tagged by a tilde "∼", or a consumption event tagged by a question mark "?". K denotes $\{!, \sim, ?\}$.

Every event occurring in a sequence diagram is decorated with a unique timestamp. T denotes the set of timestamp tags. We use logical formulas with timestamp tags as free variables to impose constraints on the timing of events. By $\mathbb{F}(v)$ we denote the set of logical formulas whose free variables are contained in the set of timestamp tags v.

E denotes the set of all events. Formally, an event is a triple of kind, message and timestamp tag

$$E = K \times M \times T$$

We define the functions

$$k._- \in E \to K, \quad m._- \in E \to M, \quad t._- \in E \to T, \quad tr._-, re._- \in E \to L$$

to yield the kind, message, timestamp tag, transmitter and receiver of an event, respectively.

$\mathbb{N}$ denotes the set of natural numbers, while $\mathbb{N}_0$ denotes the set of natural numbers including 0.

The set of syntactically correct sequence diagrams D is defined inductively. D is the least set such that:

- $E \subset D$
- $d \in D \Rightarrow \mathsf{neg}\, d \in D \land \mathsf{assert}\, d \in D$

- $d_1, d_2 \in D \Rightarrow d_1 \text{ alt } d_2 \in D \wedge d_1 \text{ xalt } d_2 \in D \wedge d_1 \text{ seq } d_2 \in D \wedge d_1 \text{ par } d_2 \in D$
- $d \in D \wedge C \in \mathbb{F}(tt(d)) \Rightarrow d \text{ tc } C \in D$

where $tt(d)$ yields the set of timestamp tags occurring in d. The base case implies that any event is a sequence diagram. Any other sequence diagram is constructed from the basic ones through the application of operators for negation, assertion, potential choice, mandatory choice, weak sequencing, parallel execution and time constraint. The full set of operators as defined by UML 2.0 [OMG04] is somewhat more comprehensive, and it is beyond the scope of this paper to treat them all. We focus on the operators that we find most essential.

We define the function

$$ll \in D \rightarrow \mathbb{P}(L)$$

to yield the set of lifelines of the sequence diagram constituting its argument.

3.2   Representing Executions by Traces

We will define the semantics of sequence diagrams by using sequences of events.

By A^∞ and A^ω we denote the set of all infinite sequences and the set of all finite and infinite sequences over the set A, respectively. We define the functions

$$\#_- \in A^\omega \rightarrow \mathbb{N}_0 \cup \{\infty\}, \quad \_[\_] \in A^\omega \times \mathbb{N} \rightarrow A$$

to yield the length and the nth element of a sequence. Hence, $\#a$ yields the number of elements in a, and $a[n]$ yields a's nth element if $n \leq \#a$.

We also need functions for concatenation, truncation and filtering:

$$\_\frown\_ \in A^\omega \times A^\omega \rightarrow A^\omega, \quad \_|\_ \in A^\omega \times \mathbb{N}_0 \rightarrow A^\omega,$$
$$\_\circledS\_ \in \mathbb{P}(A) \times A^\omega \rightarrow A^\omega, \quad \_\circledT\_ \in \mathbb{P}(A \times B) \times (A^\omega \times B^\omega) \rightarrow A^\omega \times B^\omega$$

Concatenating two sequences implies gluing them together. Hence, $a_1 \frown a_2$ denotes a sequence of length $\#a_1 + \#a_2$ that equals a_1 if a_1 is infinite, and is prefixed by a_1 and suffixed by a_2, otherwise. For any $0 \leq i \leq \#a$, we define $a|_i$ to denote the prefix of a of length i.

The filtering function $\circledS$ is used to filter away elements. By $B \circledS a$ we denote the sequence obtained from the sequence a by removing all elements in a that are not in the set of elements B. For example, we have that

$$\{1,3\} \circledS \langle 1,1,2,1,3,2 \rangle = \langle 1,1,1,3 \rangle$$

The filtering function $\circledT$ may be understood as a generalization of $\circledS$. The function $\circledT$ filters pairs of sequences with respect to pairs of elements in the same way as $\circledS$ filters sequences with respect to elements. For any set of pairs of elements P and pair of sequences t, by $P \circledT t$ we denote the pair of sequences obtained from t by

- truncating the longest sequence in t at the length of the shortest sequence in t if the two sequences are of unequal length;
- for each $j \in [1 \ldots k]$, where k is the length of the shortest sequence in t, selecting or deleting the two elements at index j in the two sequences, depending on whether the pair of these elements is in the set P.

For example, we have that

$$\{(1,f),(1,g)\} \oplus (\langle 1,1,2,1,2 \rangle, \langle f,f,f,g,g \rangle) = (\langle 1,1,1 \rangle, \langle f,f,g \rangle)$$

For a formal definition of $\oplus$, see [BS01].

We are mainly interested in communication scenarios. The actual content of messages is not significant for the purpose of this paper. Hence, we do not give any semantic interpretation of messages as such. The same holds for events except that the timestamp tag is assigned a timestamp in the form of a real number. $\mathbb{R}$ denotes the set of all timestamps. Hence:[2]

$$[\![E]\!] \stackrel{\text{def}}{=} \{(k,m,t \mapsto r) \mid (k,m,t) \in E \wedge r \in \mathbb{R}\} \tag{1}$$

We define the function

$$r._{\_} \in [\![E]\!] \to \mathbb{R}$$

to yield the timestamp of an event. Moreover, for any lifeline l and kind s, let $E(l,s)$ be the set of all events $e \in [\![E]\!]$ such that $tr.e = l$ and $k.e = s$.

A trace h is an element of $[\![E]\!]^{\omega}$ that satisfies a number of well-formedness conditions. We use traces to represent executions. By an execution we mean the trace of events resulting from an execution of the specified system. We require the events in h to be ordered by time: the timestamp of the ith event is less than or equal to the timestamp of the jth event if $i < j$. Formally:

$$\forall i,j \in [1..\#h] : i < j \Rightarrow r.h[i] \le r.h[j]$$

This means that two events may happen at the same time.

The same event takes place only once in the same execution. Hence, we also require:

$$\forall i,j \in [1..\#h] : i \ne j \Rightarrow h[i] \ne h[j]$$

The following constraint makes sure that time will eventually progress beyond any finite point in time:

$$\#h = \infty \Rightarrow \forall t \in \mathbb{R} : \exists i \in \mathbb{N} : r.h[i] > t$$

That is, for any timestamp t in an infinite trace h there is an event in h whose timestamp t' is greater than t.

---

[2] The functions k, m, t, tr, re on E are lifted to $[\![E]\!]$ in the obvious manner.

For any single message, transmission must happen before reception, which must happen before consumption. However, in a particular sequence diagram we may have only the transmitter or the receiver lifeline present. Thus we get the following well-formedness requirements on traces, stating that if at any point in the trace we have a transmission event, up to that point we must have had at least as many transmissions as receptions of that particular message, and similarly for reception events with respect to consumptions:

$$\forall\, i \in [1..\#h] : k.h[i] = ! \Rightarrow \tag{2}$$

$$\#(\{\,!\,\} \times \{m.h[i]\} \times U) \circledS h|_i > \#(\{\sim\} \times \{m.h[i]\} \times U) \circledS h|_i$$

$$\forall\, i \in [1..\#h] : k.h[i] = \sim \Rightarrow \tag{3}$$

$$\#(\{\sim\} \times \{m.h[i]\} \times U) \circledS h|_i > \#(\{?\} \times \{m.h[i]\} \times U) \circledS h|_i$$

where $U \stackrel{\text{def}}{=} \{t \mapsto r \mid t \in T \wedge r \in \mathbb{R}\}$. H denotes the set of all well-formed traces.

We define three basic composition operators on trace sets, namely parallel execution, weak sequencing, and time constraint denoted by $\parallel$, $\succsim$, and $\wr$, respectively.

Informally, $s_1 \parallel s_2$ is the set of all traces such that

– all events from s_1 and s_2 are included (and no other events),
– the ordering of events from s_1 and from s_2 is preserved.

Formally:

$$s_1 \parallel s_2 \stackrel{\text{def}}{=} \{h \in H \mid \exists\, p \in \{1,2\}^\infty : \tag{4}$$

$$\pi_2((\{1\} \times [\![\, E \,]\!]) \circledT (p,h)) \in s_1 \wedge$$

$$\pi_2((\{2\} \times [\![\, E \,]\!]) \circledT (p,h)) \in s_2\}$$

In this definition, we make use of an oracle, the infinite sequence p, to resolve the non-determinism in the interleaving. It determines the order in which events from traces in s_1 and s_2 are sequenced. π_2 is a projection operator returning the second element of a pair.

For $s_1 \succsim s_2$ we have the constraint that events on a lifeline from s_1 should come before events from s_2 on the same lifeline:

$$s_1 \succsim s_2 \stackrel{\text{def}}{=} \{h \in H \mid \exists\, h_1 \in s_1, h_2 \in s_2 : \forall\, l \in L : \tag{5}$$

$$e.l \circledS h = e.l \circledS h_1 \frown e.l \circledS h_2\}$$

$e.l$ denotes the set of events that may take place on the lifeline l. Formally:

$$e.l \stackrel{\text{def}}{=} \{e \in [\![\, E \,]\!] \mid (k.e = ! \wedge tr.e = l) \vee (k.e \in \{\sim, ?\} \wedge re.e = l)\} \tag{6}$$

Time constraint is defined as

$$s \wr C \quad \overset{\text{def}}{=} \quad \{h \in s \mid h \models C\} \tag{7}$$

where $h \models C$ holds if for all possible assignments of timestamps to timestamp tags done by h, there is an assignment of timestamps to the remaining timestamp tags in C (possibly none) such that C evaluates to true. For example, if

$$h = \langle (k_1, m_1, t_1 \mapsto r_1), (k_2, m_2, t_2 \mapsto r_2), (k_3, m_3, t_2 \mapsto r_3) \rangle, \qquad C = t_1 < t_2$$

then $h \models C$ if $r_1 < r_2$ and $r_1 < r_3$.

3.3   Interaction Obligations

An interaction obligation is a pair (p, n) of sets of traces where the first set is interpreted as the set of positive traces and the second set is the set of negative traces. The term obligation is used to explicitly convey that any implementation of a specification is obliged to fulfill each specified alternative.

O denotes the set of interaction obligations. Parallel execution, weak sequencing and time constraint are overloaded from sets of traces to interaction obligations as follows:

$$(p_1, n_1) \parallel (p_2, n_2) \quad \overset{\text{def}}{=} \quad (p_1 \parallel p_2, (n_1 \parallel (p_2 \cup n_2)) \cup (n_2 \parallel p_1)) \tag{8}$$

$$(p_1, n_1) \succsim (p_2, n_2) \quad \overset{\text{def}}{=} \quad (p_1 \succsim p_2, (n_1 \succsim (n_2 \cup p_2)) \cup (p_1 \succsim n_2)) \tag{9}$$

$$(p, n) \wr C \quad \overset{\text{def}}{=} \quad (p \wr C, n \cup (p \wr \neg C)) \tag{10}$$

An obligation pair (p, n) is contradictory if $p \cap n \neq \varnothing$.

The operators for parallel execution, weak sequencing and time constraint are also overloaded to sets of interaction obligations:

$$O_1 \parallel O_2 \quad \overset{\text{def}}{=} \quad \{o_1 \parallel o_2 \mid o_1 \in O_1 \wedge o_2 \in O_2\} \tag{11}$$

$$O_1 \succsim O_2 \quad \overset{\text{def}}{=} \quad \{o_1 \succsim o_2 \mid o_1 \in O_1 \wedge o_2 \in O_2\} \tag{12}$$

$$O_1 \wr C \quad \overset{\text{def}}{=} \quad \{o_1 \wr C \mid o_1 \in O_1\} \tag{13}$$

We also define an operator for inner union of sets of interaction obligations:

$$O_1 \uplus O_2 \quad \overset{\text{def}}{=} \quad \{(p_1 \cup p_2, n_1 \cup n_2) \mid (p_1, n_1) \in O_1 \wedge (p_2, n_2) \in O_2\} \tag{14}$$

3.4   Semantics of Sequence Diagrams

The semantics of sequence diagrams is defined by a function

$$[\![\,\_\,]\!] \in D \to \mathbb{P}(O)$$

that for any sequence diagram d yields a set $[\![\, d \,]\!]$ of interaction obligations.

An event is represented by infinitely many unary positive traces – one for each possible assignment of timestamp to its timestamp tag:

$$[\![\,(k, m, t)\,]\!] \quad \overset{\text{def}}{=} \quad \{(\{\langle(k, m, t \mapsto r)\rangle \mid r \in \mathbb{R}\}, \varnothing)\} \quad \text{if } (k, m, t) \in E \quad (15)$$

The neg construct defines negative traces:

$$[\![\,\text{neg } d\,]\!] \quad \overset{\text{def}}{=} \quad \{(\{\langle\rangle\}, p \cup n) \mid (p, n) \in [\![\,d\,]\!]\} \quad (16)$$

Notice that a negative trace cannot be made positive by reapplying neg. Negative traces remain negative. Negation is an operation that characterizes traces absolutely and not relatively. The intuition is that the focus of the neg construct is on characterizing the positive traces in the operand as negative. Negative traces will always propagate as negative to the outermost level. The neg construct defines the empty trace as positive. This facilitates the embedding of negs in sequence diagrams also specifying positive behavior.

The assert construct makes all inconclusive traces negative. Except for that the sets of positive and negative traces are left unchanged:

$$[\![\,\text{assert } d\,]\!] \quad \overset{\text{def}}{=} \quad \{(p, n \cup (H \setminus p)) \mid (p, n) \in [\![\,d\,]\!]\} \quad (17)$$

Note that contradictory obligation pairs remain contradictory.

The alt construct defines potential traces. The semantics is the union of the trace sets for both positive and negative:

$$[\![\,d_1 \text{ alt } d_2\,]\!] \quad \overset{\text{def}}{=} \quad [\![\,d_1\,]\!] \uplus [\![\,d_2\,]\!] \quad (18)$$

The xalt construct defines mandatory choices. All implementations must be able to handle every interaction obligation:

$$[\![\,d_1 \text{ xalt } d_2\,]\!] \quad \overset{\text{def}}{=} \quad [\![\,d_1\,]\!] \cup [\![\,d_2\,]\!] \quad (19)$$

Notice that the sets of negative traces are not combined as is the case with the alt. This is due to the fact that we want to allow behaviors that are positive in one interaction obligation to be negative in another interaction obligation. The intuition behind this is as follows: All positive behaviors in an interaction obligation serve the same overall purpose, e.g. different ways of making beef. Alternative ways of making beef can be introduced by the alt operator. Hence, a behavior cannot be present in both the positive and negative trace sets of an interaction obligation as this would lead to a contradictory specification. However, behaviors specified by different interaction obligations are meant to serve different purposes, e.g. make beef dish and make vegetarian dish. There is nothing wrong about stating that a behavior which is positive in one interaction obligation is negative in another. E.g. steak beef would definitely be positive in a beef context and negative in a vegetarian context. By insisting on separate negative sets of interaction obligations we achieve this wanted property.

The par construct represents a parallel merge. Any trace involving a negative trace will remain negative in the resulting interaction obligation:

$$[\![\, d_1 \text{ par } d_2 \,]\!] \quad \overset{\text{def}}{=} \quad [\![\, d_1 \,]\!] \parallel [\![\, d_2 \,]\!] \tag{20}$$

The seq construct defines weak sequencing which is the implicit composition mechanism combining constructs of a sequence diagram. For explicit composition, the combined fragments are used:

$$[\![\, d_1 \text{ seq } d_2 \,]\!] \quad \overset{\text{def}}{=} \quad [\![\, d_1 \,]\!] \succsim [\![\, d_2 \,]\!] \tag{21}$$

The tc construct defines the effect of a time constraint. The positive traces of the operand that do not fulfill the constraint become negative in the result. The negative traces of the operand remain negative regardless of whether they fulfill the constraint:

$$[\![\, d \text{ tc } C \,]\!] \quad \overset{\text{def}}{=} \quad [\![\, d \,]\!] \wr C \tag{22}$$

4   Two Abstractions

An example to illustrate the importance of distinguishing between the message reception and the message consumption event when dealing with timed specifications goes as follows: A restaurant chain specifies in a sequence diagram (see Figure 3) that it should never take more than 10 minutes to prepare a beef dish. The specification is handed over to the local restaurant owner who takes these requirements as an input to the design process of her/his local restaurant. When testing the time it takes to prepare a beef the restaurant finds that it is in accordance with the timing requirements. However, when the restaurant chain inspector comes to verify that the timing policies of the chain are obeyed in the operational restaurant he finds that it takes much longer time than 10 minutes to prepare the beef. Thus, the inspector claims that the restaurant is not working according to the timing requirements while the restaurant owner claims they are working according to the requirements. Who is right? According to UML both are right as there is no notion of buffering of communication in UML. Whether the message arrival of "main dish please" to the kitchen shall be regarded as message reception or consumption is not defined in the semantics of UML, and hence, it is up to the users of the diagrams to interpret the meaning.

In this section we define two abstractions over the triple event semantics that match the two different views in the example above, namely the standard interpretation and the black-box interpretation.

4.1   Standard Interpretation

The standard interpretation is meant to represent the traditional way of interpreting graphical sequence diagrams, namely that the input event of a message

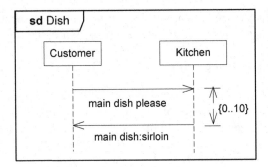

Fig. 3. Restaurant specification with time constraint

at a lifeline represents a consumption. We then only take send (!) and consume (?) events into consideration. Thus, we abstract away the fact that a message will arrive and be stored before it is consumed by the object. The standard interpretation sees graphical sequence diagrams like the diagram in Figure 3 as "standard diagrams".

The semantics of standard diagrams is defined in exactly the same manner as for general sequence diagrams in Section 3, except that the semantics of events is redefined as follows:

$$[\![(k, m, t)]\!] \stackrel{\text{def}}{=} \{(\{h' \frown \langle (k, m, t \mapsto r) \rangle \frown h'' \in H \mid \qquad (23)$$

$$h', h'' \in E(l, \sim)^{\omega} \wedge \#h' < \infty \wedge r \in \mathbb{R}\},$$

$$\varnothing)\}$$

where $l = tr.e$ if $k.e = !$ and $l = re.e$ if $k.e = ?$.

This definition says essentially that in a standard diagram, reception events may happen anywhere on the relevant lifeline (as long as the well-formedness conditions (2) and (3) are obeyed) since they are considered irrelevant in this setting.

If we apply the standard interpretation to the diagram in Figure 3, every positive trace h is such that

$$\{e \in [\![E]\!] \mid k.e \neq \sim\} \circledS h =$$
$$\langle (!, m, t_1 \mapsto r_1), (?, m, t_3 \mapsto r_3), (!, n, t_4 \mapsto r_4), (?, n, t_6 \mapsto r_6) \rangle$$

where $r_4 \leq r_3 + 10$, m stands for "main dish please" and n stands for "main dish:sirloin". The implicit reception of m can happen at any point between the corresponding transmission and consumption events, and similarly for n (and any other message).

4.2   Black-Box Interpretation

The black-box interpretation represents the view where the input event of a message at a lifeline represents a reception event. The black-box interpretation sees graphical sequence diagrams like the diagram in Figure 3 as "black-box diagrams".

As with standard diagrams, the semantics of black-box diagrams is defined in exactly the same manner as for general sequence diagrams in section 3 except that the semantics of events is redefined as follows:

$$[\![(k, m, t)]\!] \quad \overset{\text{def}}{=} \quad \{ (\{ h' \frown \langle (k, m, t \mapsto r) \rangle \frown h'' \in H \mid \tag{24}$$

$$h', h'' \in E(l, ?)^\omega \wedge \#h' < \infty \wedge r \in \mathbb{R} \},$$

$$\varnothing) \}$$

where $l = tr.e$ if $k.e = !$ and $l = re.e$ if $k.e = \sim$.

If we apply the black-box interpretation to the diagram in Figure 3, every positive trace h is such that

$$\{ e \in [\![E]\!] \mid k.e \neq ? \} \circledS h =$$
$$\langle (!, m, t_1 \mapsto r_1), (\sim, m, t_2 \mapsto r_2), (!, n, t_4 \mapsto r_4), (\sim, n, t_5 \mapsto r_5) \rangle$$

where $r_4 \leq r_2 + 10$. Note that we do not impose any constraint on the implicit consumption events, except that the consumption cannot take place before its reception (if it takes place at all).

5   The General Case

We have shown that input events are most naturally (standard) interpreted as consumption when they appear on lifelines that represent atomic processes and their concrete implementations should be derived from the lifelines. We have also shown that there are reasons, e.g. timing constraints, that sometimes make it necessary to consider the input event as representing the reception. Moreover, we have seen that timing constraints may also make good sense when applied to consumption events.

In fact we believe that notation for both reception and consumption events are necessary, but that most often for any given message a two-event notation will suffice. Sometimes the message will end in the reception and sometimes in the consumption, but seldom there is a need to make both the reception and the consumption explicit. There are, however, exceptions where all three events must be present to convey the exact meaning of the scenario. Hence, we will in the following introduce graphical notation in order to be able to explicitly state whether a message input event at a lifeline shall be interpreted as a reception event or a consumption event. That is, whether standard or black-box interpretation shall be applied.

Figure 4 shows the graphical notation to specify that a message input event at a lifeline shall be interpreted as a consumption event. Syntactically this notation is equal to the one applied for ordinary two-event sequence diagrams.

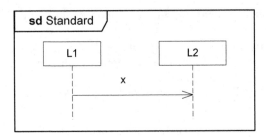

Fig. 4. Graphical syntax for specifying standard interpretation

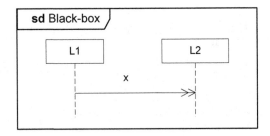

Fig. 5. Graphical syntax for specifying black-box interpretation

We express that a message input event at a lifeline shall be interpreted as a reception event and thus be given black-box interpretation by the double arrowhead as shown in Figure 5. We will in the following give some examples of the full approach describing reception events as well as consumption events explicitly.

Let us return to the dinner example where we may assume that the cook is not really one single person, but actually a chef and his apprentice. We may decompose the cook lifeline into new sequence diagrams where the chef and apprentice constitute the internal lifelines. We have shown this in Figure 6 for the preparation of beef shown originally in Figure 2. Let us assume that the apprentice wants to go and get the meat before heating the stove. His priorities may be so because heating the stove is more of a burden, or because the refrigerator is closer at hand. For our purposes we would like to describe a scenario that highlights that the apprentice fetches the meat before heating the stove even though he received the order to turn on the heat first.

In Figure 6 we have shown some explicit reception events, but we have chosen not to show explicitly the corresponding consumptions. This is because our needs were to describe the relationship between the receptions and the actions (outputs) of the apprentice.

The consumptions were considered less important. The disadvantage of this is that we cannot from Figure 6 deduce whether the apprentice actually fetched the meat because he received the order "go fetch meat" or the order "go turn on heat". The reader should appreciate that the "fetch_meat" message crosses the other messages only due to the need to graphically let the formal gates match the

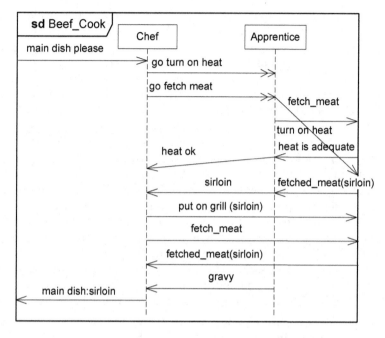

Fig. 6. Prioritizing to fetch the meat

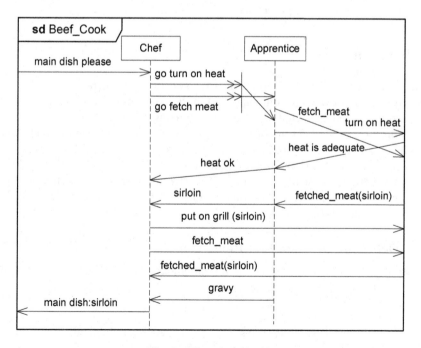

Fig. 7. The whole truth

events on the decomposed Cook lifeline shown in Figure 2. Semantically there is no ordering between gates. For a formal treatment of gates, see [HHRS04].

If we want to give an even more detailed account of the apprentice's options, we may introduce both reception and consumption events. We have done so in Figure 7.

In Figure 7 we see that the chef instructs the apprentice to go turn on heat and to go and fetch meat. The apprentice makes independent decisions for the order of consumption. Here he has decided to consume the order to go fetch meat before consuming go turn on heat. Now we can easily see that the apprentice reacts adequately to the consumptions. It is of course rather risky for the apprentice not to react immediately to the chef's order to turn on the heat, but we may remedy this by timetagging the message receptions of "go turn on heat" and "go fetch meat". Then we specify that the scenario is only valid if these receptions are sufficiently close together in time by a formula including these time tags.

As the examples in this section demonstrate, we have cases where we need to explicitly describe both reception and consumption events in the same diagram, but seldom for the same message. This means that general diagrams may contain standard, black-box as well as three-event arrows. The semantics of such diagrams is fixed by the definitions in Section 3 with two exceptions:

- The semantics of a consumption event of a standard arrow should be as for consumption events in the standard case (see Section 4.1).
- The semantics of a receive event of a black-box arrow should be as for receive events in the black-box case (see Section 4.2).

6   Refinement

Refinement means to add information to a specification such that the specification becomes closer to an implementation. The set of potential traces will be narrowed and situations that we have not yet considered will be supplemented. We define formally two forms of refinement - glass-box refinement which takes the full semantics of the diagram into account, and black-box refinement which only considers changes that are externally visible.

Negative traces must always remain negative in a refinement, while positive traces may remain positive or become negative if the trace has been cancelled out. Inconclusive traces may go anywhere.

6.1   Definition of Glass-Box Refinement

An interaction obligation (p_2, n_2) is a refinement of an interaction obligation (p_1, n_1), written $(p_1, n_1) \leadsto_r (p_2, n_2)$, iff

$$n_1 \subseteq n_2 \quad \wedge \quad p_1 \subseteq p_2 \cup n_2 \tag{25}$$

A set of interaction obligations O_1' is a glass-box refinement of a set O_1, written $O_1 \leadsto_g O_1'$, iff

$$\forall o \in O_1 : \exists o' \in O_1' : o \leadsto_r o' \tag{26}$$

A sequence diagram d' is then a glass-box refinement of a sequence diagram d, written $d \leadsto_g d'$, iff

$$[\![\, d \,]\!] \leadsto_g [\![\, d' \,]\!] \tag{27}$$

The refinement semantics supports the classical notion of compositional refinement providing a firm foundation for compositional analysis, verification and testing. In [HHRS04] we prove that refinement as defined above is transitive. We also prove that it is monotonic with respect to the operators presented in Section 3.4, except from assert. For assert, we have monotonicity in the special case of narrowing defined below.

6.2   Supplementing and Narrowing

Supplementing and narrowing are special cases of the general notion of refinement. Supplementing categorizes inconclusive behavior as either positive or negative. An interaction obligation (p_2, n_2) supplements an interaction obligation (p_1, n_1), written $(p_1, n_1) \leadsto_s (p_2, n_2)$, iff

$$(n_1 \subset n_2 \quad \wedge \quad p_1 \subseteq p_2) \qquad \vee \qquad (n_1 \subseteq n_2 \quad \wedge \quad p_1 \subset p_2) \tag{28}$$

Narrowing reduces the allowed behavior to match the problem better. An interaction obligation (p_2, n_2) narrows an interaction obligation (p_1, n_1), written $(p_1, n_1) \leadsto_n (p_2, n_2)$, iff

$$p_2 \subset p_1 \quad \wedge \quad n_2 = n_1 \cup (p_1 \setminus p_2) \tag{29}$$

6.3   Example of Glass-Box Refinement

We want to refine the Beef_Cook diagram presented in Figure 7. In a glass-box refinement we are interested in the complete traces described by the diagram, and a selection and/or a supplement of these traces.

Figure 8 is a glass-box refinement of Figure 7. In this diagram we state that we no longer want gravy, but Beárnaise sauce instead. Defining gravy as negative is a narrowing, as it means to reduce the set of positive traces of the original specification. The traces with Beárnaise sauce was earlier considered inconclusive (i.e. neither positive nor negative), but are now defined as positive. This is an example of supplementing. In addition, the diagram in Figure 8 permits using no sauce at all. This is because the neg fragment also introduces the empty trace ($\langle \rangle$) as positive. We summarize these changes in Figure 9.

6.4   Definition of Black-Box Refinement

Black-box refinement may be understood as refinement restricted to the externally visible behavior. We define the function

$$ext \in H \times \mathbb{P}(L) \to H$$

to yield the trace obtained from the trace given as first argument by filtering away those events that are internal with respect to the set of lifelines given as second argument, i.e.:

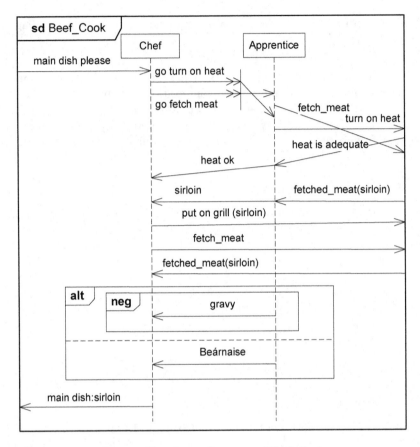

Fig. 8. Glass-box refinement of Beef_Cook

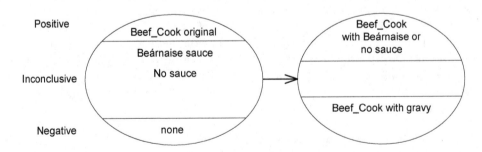

Fig. 9. Summary glass-box refinement

$$ext(h, l) \stackrel{\text{def}}{=} \{e \in [\![E]\!] \mid (tr.e \notin l \lor re.e \notin l) \land k.e \neq ?\} \circledS h \qquad (30)$$

The *ext* operator is overloaded to sets of traces, to pairs of sets of traces, and sets of pairs of sets of traces in the standard pointwise manner, e.g.:

$$ext(s, l) \stackrel{\text{def}}{=} \{ext(h, l) \mid h \in s\} \tag{31}$$

A sequence diagram d' is a black-box refinement of a sequence diagram d, written $d \leadsto_b d'$, iff

$$\forall o \in [\![\ d\ ]\!] : \exists o' \in [\![\ d'\ ]\!] : ext(o, ll(d)) \leadsto_r ext(o', ll(d')) \tag{32}$$

Notice that the *ext* operator also filters away all consumption events regardless of lifeline, as was the case with black-box interpretation of sequence diagrams. Thus, black-box refinement is mainly relevant in the context of black-box interpretation (even though it may also be applied to standard diagrams).

6.5   Example of Black-Box Refinement

It is obvious from the definition of black-box refinement that any glass-box refinement is also a black-box refinement. What would be a black-box refinement in our Beef_Cook context, but not a glass-box refinement? If we in a refinement of the specification in Figure 7 had just replaced the gravy with Bearnaise, this change would not affect the externally visible behavior of Beef_Cook as it is defined, and would therefore be a legal black-box refinement. However, it would not be a glass-box refinement since the traces involving gravy have been lost (they are now inconclusive), and this violates the definition.

6.6   Detailing

When we increase the granularity of sequence diagrams we call this a detailing of the specification. The granularity can be altered in two different ways: either by decomposing the lifelines such that their inner parts and their internal behavior are displayed in the diagram or by changing the data-structure of messages such that they convey more detailed information.

Black-box refinement is sufficiently general to formalize lifeline decompositions that are not externally visible. However, many lifeline decompositions are externally visible. As an example of a lifeline decomposition that is externally visible, consider the decomposition of Beef_Cook in Figure 6. The messages that originally (in Figure 2) had the Cook as sender/receiver, now have the chef or the apprentice as sender/receiver.

To allow for this, we extend the definition of black-box refinement with the notion of a lifeline substitution. The resulting refinement relation is called lifeline decomposition. A lifeline substitution is a partial function of type $L \to L$. LS denotes the set of all such substitutions. We define the function

$$subst \in D \times LS \to D$$

such that $subst(d, ls)$ yields the sequence diagram obtained from d by substituting every lifeline l in d for which ls is defined with the lifeline $ls(l)$.

We then define that a sequence diagram d' is a lifeline decomposition of a sequence diagram d with respect to a lifeline substitution ls, written $d \leadsto_l^{ls} d'$, iff

$$d \leadsto_b subst(d', ls)$$

Changing the data-structure of messages may be understood as black-box refinement modulo a translation of the externally visible behavior. This translation is specified by a sequence diagram t, and we refer to this as an interface refinement.

We define that a sequence diagram d' is an interface refinement of a sequence diagram d with respect to a sequence diagram t, written $d \rightsquigarrow_i^t d'$, iff

$$d \rightsquigarrow_b (t \text{ seq } d')$$

Detailing may then be understood as the transitive and reflexive closure of lifeline decomposition and interface refinement.

6.7   Refinement Through Time Constraints

Having given examples of refinement in terms of pure event manipulation and trace selection, we go on to present an example where time constraints represent the refinement constructs.

We will now introduce two time refinements as indicated in Figures 10 and 11. First we would like to make sure that beefs are neither burned nor raw when fetched from the stove. To make sure that this constraint holds we will put the time constraint on the consumption event of the "put on grill" message. This is because it is the time that the beef is actually present on the stove that matters with respect to how much it is grilled, not the time the beef lies on a plate beside the stove waiting for free space on the stove. All behaviors that do not meet this time constraint are considered negative according to definition (22) of time constraint semantics. Traces that originally were positive are because of the new time constraint now defined as negative. Thus, this step constitutes a glass-box refinement according to definition (27). In fact, it is a narrowing as defined by definition (29). Since the consumption events and transmit events locally define the object behavior, it is only the behavior of the stove that is affected by this refinement step, and not the environment. Using double arrowhead on the "put on grill" message we would not be able to express the intended refinement because it is necessary to talk about message consumption. On the other hand, comparing Figure 10 with the original diagram in Figure 2, we have replaced a standard arrow with a three-event arrow. This is a valid refinement, as it means to make explicit one of the implicit reception events that are already present in the semantics of Figure 2.

Next we would like to limit the overall time it takes to prepare a beef. This represents a customer requirement on the kitchen as illustrated in Figure 11. However, the customer does not care about the details of beef preparation, just that it is prepared in time. As seen from Figure 11 this can be interpreted as a time constraint on the reception event. In the same manner as with the glass-box refinement above, the introduction of the time constraint is a narrowing that "moves" traces from the set of positive traces to the set of negative traces. We are not concerned about where the beef spends its time in the kitchen during the preparation process, just that it is prepared in time.

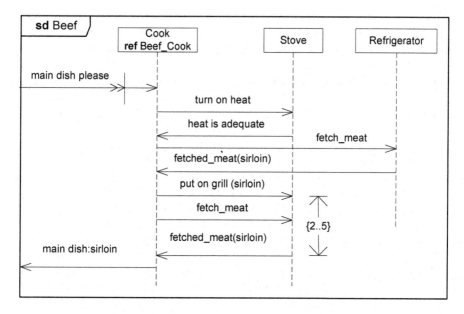

Fig. 10. Imposing constraints on timing

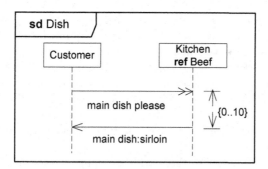

Fig. 11. Customer requirement on the beef preparation time

7   Conclusions and Related Work

We have presented Timed STAIRS, a formal approach to the step-wise, incremental development of timed sequence diagrams. It is based on trace semantics. Traces are sequences of events. Events are representations of sending, receiving and consuming messages.

Three event semantics of sequence diagrams has been considered before. In [EMR97] the event ordering imposed by the MSCs is used to determine the physical architecture needed for implementing the specified behavior such as a FIFO buffer between each of the processes. In Timed Stairs we implicitly assume that every object has one associated input buffer unless something else is explicitly specified in the diagrams. Thus, we do not deduce the communication architecture from the sequence diagrams but instead make it an option for the designer to explicitly specify the wanted architecture in the diagrams. The main rationale for introducing the three event semantics in Timed STAIRS is to be able to distinguish between reception and consumption of messages in order to specify time-constraints on black-box behavior as well as message consumption. Hence, the purpose of the three event semantics is quite different from [EMR97] where time and black-box behavior is not considered.

To consider not only positive traces, but also negative ones, has been suggested before. In [Hau95] the proposed methodology stated that specifying negative scenarios could be even more practical and powerful than only specifying the possible or mandatory ones. It was made clear that the MSC-92 standard [ITU93] was not sufficient to express the intention behind the scenarios and that the MSC documents had to be supplemented with informal statements about the intended interpretation of the set of traces expressed by the different MSCs.

The algebraic semantics of MSC-92 [ITU94] gave rise to a canonical logical expression restricted to the strict sequencing operator and a choice operator. When the MSC standard evolved with more advanced structuring mechanisms, the formal semantics as given in [ITU98] and [Ren98] was based on sets of traces, but it was still expressed in algebraic terms. The MSC approach to sequence diagram semantics is an interleaving semantics based on a fully compositional paradigm. The set of traces denoting the semantics of a message sequence chart can be calculated from its constituent parts based on definitions of the semantics of the structuring concepts as operators. This is very much the approach that we base our semantics on as we calculate our semantics of an interaction fragment from the semantics of its internal fragments. The notion of negative traces, and the explicit distinction between mandatory and potential behavior is beyond the MSC language and its semantics. The Eindhoven school of MSC researchers led by Sjouke Mauw concentrated mainly on establishing the formal properties of the logical systems used for defining the semantics, and also how this could be applied to make tools.

The need for describing also the intention behind the scenarios motivated the so-called "two-layer" approaches. In [CPRO95] they showed how MSC could be combined with languages for temporal logics such as CTL letting the scenarios constitute the atoms for the higher level of modal descriptions. With this one could describe that certain scenarios should appear or should never appear.

Damm and Harel brought this further through their augmented MSC language LSC (Live Sequence Charts) [DH99]. This may also be characterized as a two-layer approach as it takes the basic message sequence charts as starting point and add modal characteristics upon those. The modal expressiveness is strong in LSC since charts, locations, messages and conditions are orthogonally characterized as either mandatory or provisional. Since LSC also includes a notion of subchart, the combinatory complexity can be quite high. The "inline expressions" of MSC-96 (corresponding to combined fragments in UML 2.0) and MSC documents as in MSC-2000 [Hau01] (corresponds to classifier in UML 2.0) are, however, not included in LSC. Mandatory charts are called universal. Their interpretation is that provided their initial condition holds, these charts must happen. Mandatory as in LSC should not be confused with mandatory as in Timed STAIRS, since the latter only specifies traces that must be present in an implementation while the first specifies all allowed traces. Hence, mandatory as in Timed STAIRS does not distinguish between universal or existential interpretation, but rather gives a restriction on what behaviors that must be kept during a refinement. Provisional charts are called existential and they may happen if their initial condition holds. Through mandatory charts it is of course indirectly also possible to define scenarios that are forbidden or negative. Their semantics is said to be a conservative extension of the original MSC semantics, but their construction of the semantics is based on a two-stage procedure. The first stage defines a symbolic transition system from an LSC and from that a set of executions accepted by the LSC is produced. These executions represent traces where each basic element is a snapshot of a corresponding system.

The motivation behind LSC is explicitly to relate sequence diagrams to other system descriptions, typically defined with state machines. Harel has also been involved in the development of a tool-supported methodology that uses LSC as a way to prescribe systems as well as verifying the correspondence between manually described LSCs and State Machines [HM03].

Our approach is similar to LSC since it is basically interleaving. Timed STAIRS is essentially one-stage as the modal distinction between the positive and negative traces in principle is present in every fragment. The final modality results directly from the semantic compositions. With respect to language, we consider almost only what is UML 2.0, while LSC is a language extension of its own. LSC could in the future become a particular UML profile. Furthermore, our focus is on refinement of sequence diagrams as a means for system development and system validation. This means that in our approach the distinction between mandatory and provisional is captured through the interaction obligations.

The work by Krüger [Krü00] addresses similar concerns as the ones introduced in this article and covered by the LSC-approach of Harel. Just as with LSC MSCs can be given interpretations as existential or universal. The exact and negative interpretations are also introduced. Krüger also proposes notions of refinement for MSCs. Binding references, interface refinement, property refinement and structural refinement are refinement relations between MSCs at different level of abstraction. Narrowing as described in Timed STAIRS corresponds closely to property refinement in [Krü00] and detailing corresponds to interface refinement and structural refinement. However, Krüger does not distinguish between intended non-determinism and non-determinism as a result of under-specification in the refinement relation.

Although this paper presents Timed STAIRS in the setting of UML 2.0 sequence diagrams, the underlying principles apply just as well to MSC given that the MSC language is extended with an xalt construct similar to the one proposed above for UML 2.0. Timed STAIRS may also be adapted to support LSC. Timed STAIRS is complementary to software development processes based on use-cases, and classical object-oriented approaches such as the Unified Process [JBR99]. Timed STAIRS provides formal foundation for the basic incremental steps of such processes.

Acknowledgements

The research on which this paper reports has partly been carried out within the context of the IKT-2010 project SARDAS (15295/431) funded by the Research Council of Norway. We thank Mass Soldal Lund, Atle Refsdal, Ina Schieferdecker and Fredrik Seehusen for helpful feedback.

References

[BS01]   M. Broy and K. Stølen. *Specification and Development of Interactive Systems: Focus on Streams, Interfaces, and Refinement.* Springer, 2001.

[CPRO95]   P. Combes, S. Pickin, B. Renard, and F. Olsen. MSCs to express service requirements as properties on an SDL model: Application to service interaction detection. In *7th SDL Forum (SDL'95)*, pages 243–256. North-Holland, 1995.

[DH99]   W. Damm and D. Harel. LSCs: Breathing life into message sequence charts. In *Formal Methods for Open Object-Based Distributed Systems (FMOODS'99)*, pages 293–311. Kluwer, 1999.

[EMR97]   A. Engels, S. Mauw, and M.A. Reniers. A hierarchy of communication models for message sequence charts. In *Formal Description Tecniques and Protocol Specification, Testing and Verification*, pages 75–90. Chapman & Hall, 1997.

[Hau95]   Ø. Haugen. Using MSC-92 effectively. In *7th SDL Forum (SDL'95)*, pages 37–49. North-Holland, 1995.

[Hau01]   Ø. Haugen. MSC-2000 interaction diagrams for the new millennium. *Computer Networks*, 35:721–732, 2001.

[HHRS04]   Ø. Haugen, K. E. Husa, R. K. Runde, and K. Stølen. Why timed sequence diagrams require three-event semantics. Technical Report 309, Department of Informatics, University of Oslo, 2004.

[HM03]   D. Harel and R. Marelly. Specifying and executing behavioral requirements: The play-in/play-out approach. *Software and System Modeling*, 2:82–107, 2003.

[HS03]   Ø. Haugen and K. Stølen. STAIRS – Steps to analyze interactions with refinement semantics. In *Sixth International Conference on UML (UML'2003)*, number 2863 in Lecture Notes in Computer Science, pages 388–402. Springer, 2003.

[ITU93]   International Telecommunication Union. *Recommendation Z.120 — Message Sequence Chart (MSC)*, 1993.

[ITU94]   International Telecommunication Union. *Recommendation Z.120 Annex B: Algebraic Semantics of Message Sequence Charts*, 1994.

[ITU98]   International Telecommunication Union. *Recommendation Z.120 Annex B: Formal Semantics of Message Sequence Charts*, 1998.

[ITU99]   International Telecommunication Union. *Recommendation Z.120 — Message Sequence Chart (MSC)*, 1999.

[JBR99]   I. Jacobson, G. Booch, and J. Rumbaugh. *The Unified Software Development Process*. Addison-Wesley, 1999.

[Krü00]   I. Krüger. *Distributed System Design with Message Sequence Charts*. PhD thesis, Technische Universität München, 2000.

[OMG00]   Object Management Group. *Unified Modeling Language, Version 1.4*, 2000.

[OMG04]   Object Management Group. *UML 2.0 Superstructure Specification*, document: ptc/04-10-02 edition, 2004.

[Ren98]   M. A. Reniers. *Message Sequence Chart: Syntax and Semantics*. PhD thesis, Eindhoven University of Technology, 1998.

Some Methodological Observations Resulting from Experience Using LSCs and the Play-In/Play-Out Approach*

David Harel, Hillel Kugler, and Gera Weiss

Department of Computer Science and Applied Mathematics,
The Weizmann Institute of Science, Rehovot, Israel
{David.Harel, Hillel.Kugler, Gera.Weiss}@weizmann.ac.il

Abstract. The play-in/play-out approach is a method for specifying and developing complex reactive systems. It is built upon a scenario-based philosophy, and uses the language of live sequence charts (LSCs) and a support tool called the Play-Engine. We present some conclusions from the initial experience we have had using the approach on several projects, and discuss methodological aspects rising from this experience. The projects are from aviation, telecommunication and system manufacturing domains.

1   Introduction

Understanding system and software behavior by looking at various "stories" or scenarios seems a promising approach, and it has focused intensive research efforts in the last few years. One of the most widely used languages for specifying scenario-based requirements is that of message sequence charts (MSCs), adopted long ago by the ITU [Z1296], or its UML variant, sequence diagrams [UML]. Sequence charts (whether MSCs or their UML variant) possess a rather weak partial-order semantics that does not make it possible to capture many kinds of behavioral requirements of a system. To address this, while remaining within the general spirit of scenario-based visual formalisms, a broad extension of MSCs has been proposed, called live sequence charts (LSCs) [DH01]. LSCs distinguish between behaviors that may happen in the system (existential) from those that must happen (universal). A universal chart contains a *prechart*, which specifies the scenario which, if successfully executed, forces the system to satisfy the scenario given in the actual chart body. The distinction between mandatory (hot) and provisional (cold) applies also to other LSC constructs, e.g., conditions

---

* This research was supported in part by the John von Neumann Minerva Center for the Verification of Reactive Systems, by the European Commission projects OMEGA (IST-2001-33522) and AMETIST (IST-2001-35304) and by the Israel Science Foundation (grant No. 287/02-1).

and locations, thus creating a rich and powerful language, which among many other things can express forbidden behavior ('anti-scenarios').

In [HM03a, HM03b] a methodology for specifying and validating requirements, termed the "play-in/play-out approach" is described. According to this approach, requirements are captured by the user playing in scenarios using a graphical interface of the system to be developed or using an object model diagram. The user "plays" the GUI by clicking buttons, rotating knobs and sending messages (calling functions) to objects in an intuitive manner. By similarly playing the GUI, the user describes the desired reactions of the system and the conditions that may, must or may not hold. As this is being done, the supporting tool, called the Play-Engine, constructs a formal version of the requirements in the form of LSCs. Note that it is not always necessary to spend much time designing a fancy graphical interface. In many cases, it is enough to use a standard object model diagram. Our tool, the Play-Engine, support class diagrams and allows to work with, so called, internal objects that are not reflected in the GUI.

Play-Engine =   Scenarios DB + Input Mechanism + Execution Engine + Analysis Tools
                    (LSCs)   (Play-In)   (Play-Out)   (Smart Play-Out)

Fig. 1. Play-Engine Scheme

Play-out is a complementary idea to play-in, which, rather surprisingly, makes it possible to execute the requirements directly. In play-out, the user simply plays the GUI application as he/she would have done when executing a system model, or the final system implementation, but limiting him/herself to "end-user" and external environment actions only. While doing this, the Play-Engine keeps track of the actions and causes other actions and events to occur as dictated by the universal charts in the specification. Here too, the engine interacts with the GUI application and uses it to reflect the system state at any given moment. This process of the user operating the GUI application and the Play-Engine causing it to react according to the specification has the effect of working with an executable model, but with no intra-object model having to be built or synthesized.

The play-in/play-out approach is supported by a prototype tool called the Play-Engine, described in detail in [HM03a]. The approach appears to be useful in many stages in the development of reactive software, including requirements engineering, specification, testing and verification. In the long run it might also pave the way to systems that are constructed directly from their requirements, without the need for intra-object or intra-component modeling or coding.

Being a new approach that suggests a different way of developing systems, there are many aspects that are not yet fully understood when one attempts to apply the methodology and tools to real-world applications. In this paper we describe the initial experience we have had using the approach on several projects, and discuss methodological aspects arising from this experience. The projects are from aviation, telecommunication and system manufacturing domains. We should add that another important application of the play-in/play-out approach is in modeling biological applications [KHK+03], a domain that will not be described here but which has also significantly contributed to our methodological experience.

This paper is not intended as a technical introduction to LSCs. We instead, try to keep the discussion at a high level, trying to emphasize more general ideas. Although the focus is on working with LSCs, we believe that our observations are relevant to other formalisms and modeling methods.

2   Applications

In this section we briefly overview the applications in which the play-in/play-out approach and Play-Engine tools were applied. This provides an initial idea of what kinds of systems are well fitted to the approach. Later on in the paper, these applications will be used to demonstrate and discuss the methodological issues arising while using the play-in/play-out approach.

2.1   IAI - Sensor Voting and Monitoring

In this application, provided by the Israeli Aircraft Industry (IAI), a subsystem of a flight control computer in an unmanned air vehicle (UAV) is modeled using LSCs and the Play-Engine. The main role of a flight control computer is to implement control loops of servo actuators controlling the air vehicle surfaces. The computer computations are influenced by the actual values provided periodically by different sensors installed in the air vehicle. To achieve high reliability, a redundancy of sensors and flight control computers is used. A voting and monitoring procedure samples the redundant sensors determining that they are in a reasonable range, disqualifying sensors that are out of range for several consecutive rounds. The communication between the sensors and computers is via a central bus. Timing play a critical role in this application, and among the goals of our work is to prove the correctness of the voting and monitoring algorithm and to suggest optimized time delays that can still guarantee correctness.

2.2   NLR - MARS Application

The Medium Altitude Reconnaissance System (MARS) is deployed by the Royal Netherlands Air Force on the F16 aircraft. The system employs two cameras to capture high resolution images, and corrects the image degradation caused by the forward motion of the aircraft. The system is responsible for producing frame annotation, performing health monitoring and alarm processing functions. A high level description of system requirements of a subsystem of MARS dealing with data capturing and processing activities has been modeled using LSCs and the Play-Engine. Again, timing information plays a very important part in the requirements.

2.3   FTRD - Depannage

This application is a telecommunication service called Depannage, provided by France Telecom. The Depannage service allows a user to make a phone call and ask for the help of a doctor, fire brigade, car maintenance, etc. The service invocation software first asks for authentication of the calling user, and then searches for the calling location. Once the calling location is found, the software searches in a data base for numbers of potential service providers corresponding to the Depannage society members in the vicinity of the caller. Once various numbers are found, the service tries to connect the caller to one of the potential called numbers (in a sequential or parallel way). In any case the caller should be connected to a secretary or to a vocal box. In parallel a second logic will make periodic location requests to the Depannage society members in order to record their latest locations in the data base. The Depannage service is implemented as a layered application consisting of several components. Each layer or component is described by a group of scenarios; the connection between layers is very clean and precise. The objects in each layer communicate only among themselves and with the objects in the adjacent layers. This architecture enables applying methodological approaches to break down the complexity of the system as is described later on.

2.4   Cybernetix - Smart-Card Manufacturing

This application involves a smart-card personalization machine. For a more comprehensive description see [Alb02]. The personalization machine is a typical production line consisting of a belt that moves artifacts (smart cards) between production stations that handle different aspects of the manufacturing, until at the end of the belt final smart-card products are collected. CYBERNETIX manufactures machines for smart-card personalization. These machines take piles of blank smart-cards as raw material, program them with personalized data, print and test them. The machines have a throughput of thousands of cards per hour. It is required that the output of cards occurs in a predefined order. Unfortunately, some cards are defective and they have to be discarded, but without changing the output order of personalized cards. Decisions on how to reorganize the flow of cards must be taken within fractions of a second, if no production time is to be lost. The aim of this case study is to model the desired production requirements, the timing requirements of operations of the machine and on this basis synthesize the coordination of the tracking of defective cards. The goal is to maximize the throughput of the machine under certain error assumptions. Another design objective, specified by CYBERNETIX, is to shorten the machine, i.e., use less slots. This means that we would like to show that it is possible to handle all errors using the minimal number of belt slots.

3   Methodology

3.1   How to Build the GUI

A central idea in the play-in/play-out approach is that a graphic user interface (GUI) of the system is constructed and then used to specify the requirements in the play-in stage and to show the execution during play-out. How do we go about starting the job of building an appropriate GUI? How do we define the objects and corresponding attributes and methods, that will later be used in play-in/play-out?

These questions lead to the observation that there are certain applications for which a graphical representation is natural and straightforward. For these the play-in/play-out approach seems particularly effective. An example is the smart-card manufacturing system described in Section 2.4. The GUI used for this application appears in Fig. 2.

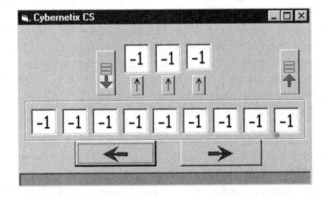

Fig. 2. Smart Card Manufacturing GUI - CYBERNETIX

Our experience showed that building the GUI is a task that should be done carefully, as much as possible considering in advance the scenarios and properties that we later plan to specify and analyze. In a case where several developers and domain experts are involved, early feedback from all participants is crucial. In the IAI application (Section 2.1) such feedback helped in building a model that was natural, useful and relevant to different members of the team. The GUI used for this application appears in Fig. 3. Building the GUI should be considered to be a full-fledged modeling activity, and the GUI should reflect interesting and important parts of the system but not the system in full detail.

An iterative approach for developing the GUI can be useful, starting with a simple GUI, playing scenarios in via it and then extending it after gaining better understanding of the application. When refining a GUI in such a manner, for a certain class of changes, e.g., adding new objects or adding a new attribute to an existing object, the tool allows performing the changes in the GUI without the need to re-play in the already existing scenarios. For more complex changes, such

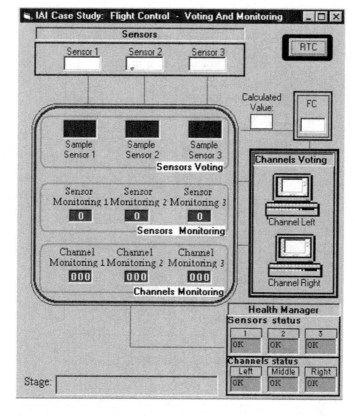

Fig. 3. Voting and monitoring GUI - IAI case study

as deleting objects and attributes, the existing scenarios must be re-played on the new GUI. Being a research prototype tool, emphasis was not put on supporting complex GUI refinements in an automatic fashion, but such directions may be explored in future versions of the tool.

3.2   GUI vs. Internal Objects

Internal objects, described in the form of an object model diagram [UML], can be used to describe objects that do not have a meaningful or convenient graphical representation. The Play-Engine supports describing some of the objects in the GUI and others as internal objects represented in an object model diagram. An example from the FTRD application appears in Fig. 4. In object model diagrams each object is depicted by a box, showing its attributes and methods. During play-out the values of attributes are updated in the diagram as they change, and arrows are drawn dynamically by the PlayEngine to reflect the message communication between objects. The play-in and play-out processes are fully supported in the Play-Engine for internal objects. This capability also provides an alternative to building a specially tailored GUI, thus saving valuable time.

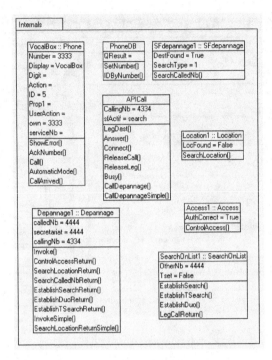

Fig. 4. Internal objects in the FTRD case study

In two of our applications, those of NLR (Section 2.2) and FTRD (Section 2.3), most of the system was described using internal objects, partly due to the fact that the systems were not graphical in nature, and also to allow quick progress to the scenario elucidation phase. This success causes us to believe that using variants of object model diagrams is a practical approach. We expect that better tool support for this, which would allow, for example, the use of multiple diagrams and the application of layout algorithms, would enhance the usage of internal objects. We indeed plan this as part of future versions of the engine.

Although using internal objects and object model diagrams proved practical, we still think that building a GUI is very worthwhile. The ability to work with an executable model reflected in a friendly GUI seems important during project meetings, makes it easier to get feedback and explain issues by the the various members of the team — not only the programmers.

3.3   GUI's for Ever-Growing Systems

When modeling real-world systems using the Play-Engine, maintaining the complexity of the graphical representation, either the GUI or internal object diagrams becomes quite a challenge. Using a GUI rather than only object diagrams allows a more succinct representation and so enables capturing larger systems. Still, even for GUI's there is a limitation on the amount of information that can be represented. Recently, the Play-Engine has been extended to support multiple GUI forms. The basic extension allows different objects to be displayed in different GUI forms, thus making it possible to decompose the application into subsystems, maintaining full support for the play-in and play-out activities.

A more advanced extension is presented in the recent work on InterPlay [BHM04]. InterPlay is a simulation engine coordinator that supports cooperation and interaction of multiple simulation and execution tools. It enables connecting several Play-Engines and also connecting a statechart-based executable model to the Play-Engine. GUI forms and internal object diagrams can thus be distributed between various Play-Engines, which makes it possible to handle larger systems. These new features have not yet been used in the applications described in this paper, but we hope to use them soon. Our experience in the applications showed that the internal object diagrams are very useful, and we plan to support multiple object diagrams within the same Play-Engine in the future. We believe that experience in other tools that handle large systems in diagrammatic forms is relevant here and in time will be integrated into the Play-Engine tool.

3.4   Large LSCs vs. Small Ones

One of the methodological questions raised while working on the case studies was whether we should describe scenarios using large LSCs that specify rich behavior or to break the behavior into several smaller LSCs that activate and interact with each other. Although there is no clear answer to this, our experience shows that a single LSC should not be too large and complex, and that understanding the relationship between many smaller LSCs can provide insight into the developed system. We thus suggest that, at least in the initial modeling stages, one should specify smaller LSCs that describe the basic scenarios. In later stages, more complex charts can be constructed either separately, or by composing the basic charts. Our experience also shows that from the perspective of efficient analysis, handling many small and simple charts that can be interleaved in numerous ways is harder, thus for the process of applying smart play-out pre-merging small charts into larger ones has an advantage.

At this stage it is still hard to define precisely what is small vs. large when it comes to LSCs, and this probably also depends on the context of the application. However, we believe that being aware of this tradeoff even without a precise definition is important for users of scenario-based approaches.

To illustrate the above discussion, we describe our experience with the smart card case study described above. In this case study, a manufacturing machine is modeled. The machine is composed of a belt and stations that put/take cards from belt slots and sometimes carry some manufacturing steps. To allow modularity, we assigned each station with its own scenarios. This defines reusable objects that can be combined in different ways in order to test various design options for the machine. To improve the performance of the analysis, we merged many small scenarios to one big LSC. This improved the speed of properties validation by several orders of magnitude. In principle, merging charts is a formal process that can be mechanized, e.g., using algorithms developed in [Gil03]. We used both models, interchangeably, depending on which aspect of the system we wanted to examine.

3.5   Refinement of LSCs

The counterexample guided abstraction refinement approach is a known method for model-checking multilayered systems [CGJ⁺00, CGLZ95, Kur95]. It consists of an iterative double phase process. The abstraction phase hides the internal logic of various objects, hence considering them as inputs. This type of abstraction may lead to traces that cannot be simulated on the complete model. The refinement phase consists of checking whether the counterexample is real or spurious. If the example turns out to be incompatible with parts of the model abstracted out, one can refine the abstraction based on the counterexample. The process is repeated until the abstraction is good enough to carry an analysis on the objects that are not abstracted.

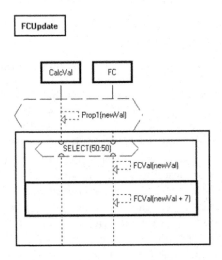

Fig. 5. Abstracting the behavior of the Flight Control Computer

This technique is particularly useful for layered models. Layers separation is conveniently facilitated by putting each layer in a different use-case. Occasionally, some interesting analysis involves only one layer so it can be carried out on that layer only. Other properties can be analyzed progressively by breaking them to separate properties of the layers.

The process of abstraction and refinement of LSCs goes as follows. The user chooses a part of the system to analyzed. Other parts of the system are removed from the execution configuration. The specification for objects that are interfacing with the part that is analyzed is only given in a coarse level or not given at all (over-approximation of the interface). Then, the part that is fully specified is analyzed in the usual way (by simulation or smart play-out [HKMP02] or both).

Clearly, such an analysis can lead to traces that are not compatible with the full system. To verify that a trace is not spurious, the designer can save it as an existential chart and see if the remaining components can satisfy this chart. If this is not the case, it is possible to refine the abstraction by adding more objects and charts to the analyzed part or by addition of more constraints to the specification of the abstracted part.

We found that it is useful to alter the "External" flag for some objects. As the name suggests, objects with an "External" flag turned on are considered part of the environment. Therefore, one way to abstract out the internal behavior of an object is to remove the charts that specify this behavior from the execution configuration and make the object external.

A simple example of abstracting behavior appears in the chart of Fig. 5. Instead of modeling the exact behavior of the flight control computer, which is quite complex, we can assume at the initial modeling stages that its values are correlated with those of the CalcVal object. When CalcVal is assigned a new value, the flight control is nondeterministically assigned either the same value or that value incremented by 7. In later modeling stages this behavior becomes more precise, until at the final stages we may model the flight control behavior in full detail.

3.6   Generic Scenarios

The Play-Engine allows generic scenarios in several ways. One is facilitated by the use of symbolic instances [MHK02]. This is extremely useful when big systems are modeled. Specifically, when there are classes of objects with common behavior, one would like to play-in the behavior using one sample instance but have the specification apply to all, or some of, the other objects in the class. This is done by adding annotations to the played-in chart. The annotations specify the range of objects of the class that the chart should apply to and information that tells the play-out mechanism how the messages in the chart generalize.

An example of specifying generic behavior in the smart-card application appears in the chart of Fig. 6. In part (a) an exact scenario of personalization of a card in personalization site 1 is described, and in part (b) it is turned into a generic scenario, which holds for any of the personalization sites.

Methodologically, generic charts allow better modularity but are more difficult to maintain. Once a behavior is well modeled by generic charts that use symbolic features, it can be used even if objects are added, deleted or moved. On the other hand, it is more difficult to carry out changes to generic charts because all possible instantiations need to be considered.

Our conclusion is that scenarios should be made generic only after some testing and verification has been done. First, some copies of concrete charts should be created and tested. Once the specification is stable to the satisfaction of the modeler, annotations can be added and redundant charts eliminated. Sometimes it is possible to model a small part of the system for testing and to extend the specification to other objects by symbolic annotations once the test is passed satisfactorily.

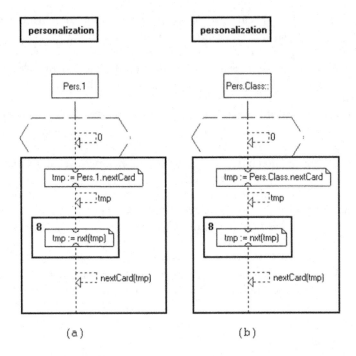

Fig. 6. Symbolic Instances - Smart-Cards

3.7   Applying Smart Play-Out

Formal modeling alone is useful, but the true power shows when advanced analysis tools are incorporated. Once you have a formal LSCs model of a system, you can use an analysis tool called Smart play-out [HKMP02, HM03a] to analyze and execute it. In particular, it is useful to compute a smart execution for the model.

Let us explain what a smart execution is: the standard execution called "naive play-out" does not involve backtracking. The naive play-out chooses one execution option arbitrarily, i.e., it makes decisions without thinking ahead. Surprisingly, this execution is very useful for many models. Nevertheless, there are systems for which such a naive execution is not relevant. For these systems, Smart play-out comes handy. After some analysis, if possible, the engine computes an execution that doesn't get stuck.

The smart play-out mechanism allows an LSCs designer to run advanced queries and get answers based on state-space exploration. Such queries are proved useful as guidance toward a refinement of a specification or a validation of properties. The queries come in the form of scenarios that the designer want to verify. The designer plays-in a scenario and asks the tool if this scenario can be executed without violating the model. For example, one can ask if some error can be fixed within a given time or resources limits.

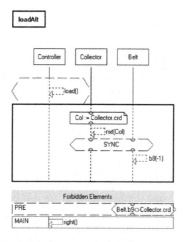

Fig. 7. Forbidden Conditions

Verification by state-space exploration, often referred to as *model checking*, is the technological basis for smart play-out, and is an effective method for analyzing concurrent reactive systems (e.g., communication protocols). Smart play-out performs an exploration of the model state space. This search recursively explores all successor states of all states encountered during the search, starting from the initial state, by executing all enabled transitions in each state. Of course, the number of visited states can be very large: this is the well-known state-explosion problem, which limits the applicability of state-space exploration techniques.

Since it is rarely possible to model-check industrial sized problems, we suggest a semi-automatic methodology for smart play-out. In various case studies, a manual refinement process supported by state space exploration proved fruitful. Methodologically, we found that it is better to invoke the smart play-out module only when the degrees of freedom of the model have been reduced. First, the designer performs a coarse strategy based on simulations with the naive play-out and intuition. When the strategy is formed such that only a few parameters are left unknown, smart play-out should be used. The tool is useful both for the verification of a strategy and for resolving unknowns. Even if a strategy is refuted, a counter example will be given. This counter example can guide the designer towards a better strategy.

Before applying smart play-out, the user should provide any available knowledge and understanding of the system in terms of invariants, preconditions and postconditions. More technically, in LSCs this is done using forbidden elements which are drawn at the bottom of the chart, as shown in Fig. 7, and have as their scope the chart, prechart or subchart (see Chapter 17 of [HM03a]). These impose necessary conditions for the execution of the entire chart or parts of it. If it clear that it is only relevant to execute a chart under a known condition, the designer can render the negation of this condition forbidden. Forbidden conditions reduce the explored state-space dramatically and allow smart play-out to handle much larger designs.

Another way to reduce the explored state space is to remove unnecessary nondeterminism. Occasionally, LSC models leave the order of messages unresolved. Such nondeterminism can arise when different time-lines on a chart are not synchronized. Adding synchronization may help facilitate the use of smart play-out. Also, when the model consists of many small scenarios, we often get numerous symmetric executions that model the same behavior. Thus, one way to allow better performance of the smart play-out is to merge charts.

3.8   Queries Supported by Smart Play-Out

As described in Section 3.7, smart play-out can be used to execute LSCs directly or answer queries. For direct LSC execution, naive play-out seems currently more useful than smart play-out due to its quick response time. The main use we have made of smart play-out in our applications is for answering queries. Given an existential chart and a set of universal charts (an execution configuration) smart play-out can be asked to try to satisfy the existential chart and all activated universal charts. If it manages to do so, the satisfying run is played out, providing full information on the execution and reflecting the behavior in the GUI.

An example of a simple existential chart to be satisfied appears in Fig. 8. This existential chart requires that eventually the `Collector` obtain the value 7, which can occur after six cards have been manufactured successfully. Thus applying smart play-out to this query finds and exhibits a strategy for manufacturing six cards.

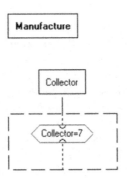

Fig. 8. Satisfying an existential chart - smart card manufacturing

Two modes of satisfying an existential chart are supported, the standard one tries to satisfy the existential chart from the current system configuration, i.e., starting from the current given attribute values of all objects. The second mode tries to satisfy the existential charts from any system configuration, allowing the system to nondeterministically guess the values of the object attributes.

Currently, in this mode, smart play-out can set the values of attributes that are designated as "externally changeable". Our experience shows that it may be useful to allow advanced users of smart play-out to designate more precisely which attributes should be set to initial values by smart play-out while satisfying an existential chart.

Work on the NLR case study raised several issues regarding spontaneous initiation of system events while satisfying an existential chart. This has led to a modification of smart play-out to support an additional mode of queries. According to the default mode, system events appearing in the existential chart to be satisfied can be taken in a spontaneous manner, even without the event appearing in the main chart of an activated universal chart. This mode is useful during initial stages of building the requirements model, to check whether a certain behavior is still possible and is not contradicted by the existing universal charts, or to make sure that a certain 'bad' behavior is explicitly ruled out. In later development stages, the new mode does not allow spontaneous system events to occur, thus a chart can be satisfied only if it can be satisfied by direct execution of the LSC specification, e.g., using a play-out mechanism were nondeterminism is resolved in a certain way. The user has full control over which mode is to be used by selecting the appropriate checkbox in the smart play-out menu.

4   Related Work

A large amount of work has been done on scenario-based specifications. Amyot and Eberlein [AE03] provide an extensive survey of scenario notations. Their paper also defines several comparison criteria and then uses them to compare the different notations. The idea of using sequence charts to discover design errors such as race conditions, time conflicts and pattern matching at early stages of development has been investigated in [AHP96, MPS98]. The language used in these papers is that of classical Message Sequence Charts, with the semantics being simply the partial order of events in a chart. In order to describe actual system behavior, such MSC's are composed into hierarchal message sequence charts (HMSC's) which are basically graphs whose nodes are MSC's. As has been observed in several papers, e.g. [AY99], allowing processes to progress along the HMSC with each chart being in a different node may introduce non-regular behavior and is the cause of undecidability of certain properties. Undecidability results and approaches to restrict HMSC's in order to avoid these problems appear in [HMKT00a, HMKT00b, GMP01]. In [MR96] a notion of refinement is defined for the Interworkings scenario-based graphical language. Refinements for message sequence charts are studied in [Krü00]. The enhanced expressive power of LSCs makes a definition and application of the refinement concepts more challenging.

The more expressive language of live sequence charts (LSCs) has been used for testing and verification of system models. Lettrai and Klose [LK01] present a methodology supported by a tool called TestConductor, which is integrated into Rhapsody [IL]. The tool is used for monitoring and testing a model using a restricted subset of LSCs. Damm and Klose [DK01, KW01] describe a verification environment in which LSCs are used to describe requirements that are verified against a Statemate model implementation.

We believe that one contribution of the present paper is summarizing the experience we have gained in applying LSCs and the play-in/play-out approach to several real-world applications. A significant amount of the actual work was carried by industrial partners, allowing us to get effective evaluation and feedback. We believe that this experience is interesting also for the general application of related scenario-based methods and tools.

Acknowledgements. We would like to thank our industrial collaborators, Guy Halman, Aviram Lahav and Meir Zenou from the Israeli Aircraft Industry (IAI), Yuri Yushtein from the Dutch Aerospace Laboratory (NLR), Pierre Combes and Benoit Parruaux from France Telecom Research and Development (FTRD) and Patrice Gauthier and Mathieu Agopian from Cybernetix. Special thanks also to the OMEGA and AMETIST partners for helpful discussions on the topics presented here.

References

[AE03]   D. Amyot and A. Eberlein. An Evaluation of Scenario Notations and Construction Approaches for Telecommunication Systems Development. *Telecommunications Systems Journal*, 24(1):61–94, 2003.

[AHP96]   R. Alur, G.J. Holzmann, and D. Peled. An analyzer for message sequence charts. *Software Concepts and Tools*, 17(2):70–77, 1996.

[Alb02]   S. Albert. Cybernetix case-study: Informal description. AMETIST web page http://ametist.cs.utwente.nl, 2002.

[AY99]   R. Alur and M. Yannakakis. Model checking of message sequence charts. In *10th International Conference on Concurrency Theory (CONCUR99)*, volume 1664 of *Lect. Notes in Comp. Sci.*, pages 114–129. Springer-Verlag, 1999.

[BHM04]   D. Barak, D. Harel, and R. Marelly. InterPlay: Horizontal Scale-Up and Transition to Design in Scenario-Based Programming. In *Lectures on Concurrency and Petri Nets*, volume 3098 of *Lect. Notes in Comp. Sci.*, pages 66–86. Springer-Verlag, 2004.

[CGJ+00]   E.M. Clarke, O. Grumberg, S. Jha, Y. Lu, and H. Veith. Counterexample-guided abstraction refinement. In *A. Emerson and P. S. Sistla, editors, Proc. 12th Intl. Conference on Computer Aided Verification (CAV'00)*, volume 1855 of *Lect. Notes in Comp. Sci., Springer-Verlag*, Lect. Notes in Comp. Sci., pages 154–169. Springer-Verlag, 2000.

[CGLZ95]   E.M. Clarke, O. Grumberg, D.E. Long, and X. Zhao. Efficient generation of counterexamples and witnesses in symbolic model checking. In *Proc. Design Automation Conference 95 (DAC95)*, 1995.

[DH01]   W. Damm and D. Harel. LSCs: Breathing life into message sequence charts. *Formal Methods in System Design*, 19(1):45–80, 2001. Preliminary version appeared in Proc. 3rd IFIP Int. Conf. on Formal Methods for Open Object-Based Distributed Systems (FMOODS'99).

[DK01]   W. Damm and J. Klose. Verification of a radio-based signalling system
             using the statemate verification environment. *Formal Methods in System
             Design*, 19(2):121–141, 2001.

[Gil03]   A. Gilboa. Finding All Super-Steps in LSC Specifications. Master's
             thesis, Weizmann Institute of Science, Israel, 2003.

[GMP01]   E. L. Gunter, A. Muscholl, and D. Peled. Compositional message se-
             quence charts. In *Proc. 7th Intl. Conference on Tools and Algorithms
             for the Construction and Analysis of Systems (TACAS'01), volume 2031
             of Lect. Notes in Comp. Sci., Springer-Verlag*, pages 496–511, 2001.

[HKMP02]   D. Harel, H. Kugler, R. Marelly, and A. Pnueli. Smart play-out of behav-
             ioral requirements. In *Proc. 4th Intl. Conference on Formal Methods in
             Computer-Aided Design (FMCAD'02), Portland, Oregon*, volume 2517
             of *Lect. Notes in Comp. Sci.*, pages 378–398, 2002. Also available as
             Tech. Report MCS02-08, The Weizmann Institute of Science.

[HM03a]   D. Harel and R. Marelly. *Come, Let's Play: Scenario-Based Program-
             ming Using LSCs and the Play-Engine*. Springer-Verlag, 2003.

[HM03b]   D. Harel and R. Marelly. Specifying and Executing Behavioral Require-
             ments: The Play In/Play-Out Approach. *Software and System Modeling
             (SoSyM)*, 2(2):82–107, 2003.

[HMKT00a]   J.G. Henriksen, M. Mukund, K.N. Kumar, and P.S. Thiagarajan. On
             message sequence graphs and finitely generated regular MSC languages.
             In J.D.P. Rolim U. Montanari and E. Welzl, editors, *Proc. 27th Int.
             Colloq. Aut. Lang. Prog.*, volume 1853 of *Lect. Notes in Comp. Sci.*,
             pages 675–686. Springer-Verlag, 2000.

[HMKT00b]   J.G. Henriksen, M. Mukund, K.N. Kumar, and P.S. Thiagarajan. Reg-
             ular collections of Message Sequence Charts. In *Proceedings of the 25th
             International Symposium on Mathematical Foundations of Computer
             Science(MFCS'2000)*, volume 1893 of *Lect. Notes in Comp. Sci.*, pages
             675–686. Springer-Verlag, 2000.

[IL]   Rhapsody.   I-Logix,   Inc.,   products   web   page.
             http://www.ilogix.com/products/.

[KHK+03]   N. Kam, D. Harel, H. Kugler, R. Marelly, A. Pnueli, E.J.A. Hubbard, and
             M.J. Stern. Formal Modeling of C. elegans Development: A Scenario-
             Based Approach. In Corrado Priami, editor, *Proc. Int. Workshop on
             Computational Methods in Systems Biology (CMSB 2003)*, pages 4–20.
             Springer-Verlag, 2003. Extended version appeared in Modeling in Molec-
             ular Biology, G.Ciobanu (Ed.), Natural Computing Series, Springer,
             2004.

[Krü00]   I. Krüger. *Distributed System Design with Message Sequence Charts*.
             PhD thesis, Department of Informatics, The Technical University of Mu-
             nich., 2000.

[Kur95]   R.P. Kurshan. *Computer Aided Verification of Coordinating Processes*.
             Princeton University Press, Princeton, New Jersey, 1995.

[KW01]   J. Klose and H. Wittke. An automata based interpretation of live se-
             quence chart. In *Proc. 7th Intl. Conference on Tools and Algorithms for
             the Construction and Analysis of Systems (TACAS'01), volume 2031 of
             Lect. Notes in Comp. Sci., Springer-Verlag*, 2001.

[LK01]   M. Lettrari and J. Klose. Scenario-based monitoring and testing of real-
             time UML models. In *4th Int. Conf. on the Unified Modeling Language,
             Toronto*, October 2001.

[MHK02]   R. Marelly, D. Harel, and H. Kugler. Multiple instances and symbolic variables in executable sequence charts. In *Proc. 17th Ann. ACM Conf. on Object-Oriented Programming, Systems, Languages and Applications (OOPSLA'02)*, pages 83–100, Seattle, WA, 2002.

[MPS98]   A. Muscholl, D. Peled, and Z. Su. Deciding properties for message sequence charts. In *Proceedings of the 1st International Conference on Foundations of Software Science and Computation Structures (FOSSACS '98)*, number 1378 in Lect. Notes in Comp. Sci., pages 226–242. Springer-Verlag, 1998.

[MR96]   S. Mauw and M. A. Reniers. Refinement in interworkings. In U. Montanari and V. Sassone, editors, *7th International Conference on Concurrency Theory (CONCUR96)*, volume 1119 of *Lect. Notes in Comp. Sci.*, pages 671–686. Springer-Verlag, 1996.

[UML]   UML. Documentation of the unified modeling language (UML). Available from the Object Management Group (OMG), http://www.omg.org.

[Z1296]   Z.120 ITU-TS Recommendation Z.120: Message Sequence Chart (MSC). ITU-TS, Geneva, 1996.

Deciding Properties of Message Sequence Charts

Anca Muscholl[1] and Doron Peled[2]

[1] LIAFA, Université Paris VII & CNRS,
2, pl. Jussieu, case 7014 75251 Paris cedex 05, France
[2] Department of Computer Science, University of Warwick,
Coventry, CV4 7AL, United Kingdom

Abstract. Message Sequence Charts (MSCs) is a notation used in practice by protocol designers and system engineers. It is defined within an international standard (ITU Z120), and is also included, in a slightly different form, in the popular UML standard (called there *sequence diagrams*). We present some of the main results related to this notation, in the context of specification and automatic verification of communication protocols. We look at issues related to specification and verification. In particular, we look at automatic verification (model checking) of MSCs. We study the expressiveness of MSCs, in particular the ability to express communication protocols, and appropriate formalisms for specifying properties of MSC systems.

1 Introduction

Specifying the behavior of software systems is of major importance for engineers. When concurrency is involved, the specification becomes even more challenging. Even before considering the actual notation to be used for specification, there is a large choice of models of execution. Different models vary in the detailed information they carry, the intuition they provide and the difficulty of checking properties of the modeled systems.

Perhaps the most successful model for describing concurrent systems is the interleaving model. An interleaved execution is simply an alternating sequence of actions and states, where each action is *enabled* in the preceding state, and after *executing* it, results in a new state. In this model, all the events are linearly ordered, and concurrently executed events are modeled by ordering them in an arbitrary way. Simple formalisms, such as linear temporal logic, are available for describing properties of interleaving sequences. In the finite case, there are simple decision procedures for checking properties of such models. The *partial order* model allows events to be unordered, if they can independently (concurrently) occur. After the selection of the model, we are still left with a wide choice of notation, affecting our level of abstraction and the complexity of deciding their properties.

Message sequence charts (MSCs) is a partial-order based standard formalism [15]. It has a visual notation, which clearly demonstrates the interaction between the involved concurrent processes. It is already used in practice by protocol designers, a fact which gives it an advantage over other formalisms in technology transfer. On the other hand,

S. Leue and T.J. Systä (Eds.): Scenarios, LNCS 3466, pp. 43–65, 2005.
© Springer-Verlag Berlin Heidelberg 2005

working with an existing standard, which was developed by a committee, initially without a full view of algorithms and complexity issues, can be challenging. In this survey we discuss several issues in specification and verification using message sequence charts.

2   Preliminaries

Each MSC describes a scenario where some processes communicate with one another. Such a scenario includes a description of the messages sent, messages received, the local events, and the ordering between them. In the visual description of MSCs, each process is represented as a vertical line with process name in a box at the top. We usually end a process line with a horizontal line at the bottom. A message is represented by a horizontal or slanted arrow from the sending process to the receiving one, as appears in the left part of Figure 1. The corresponding textual representation of that MSC appears in the right part of Figure 1.

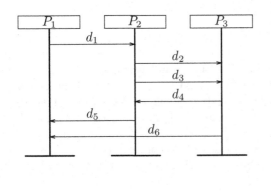

```
msc MSC;
inst P1: process Root,
P2: process Root,
P3: process Root;
instance P1;
out d1 to P2;
in d5 from P2;
in d6 from P3;
endinstance;
instance P2;
in d1 from P1;
out d2 to P3;
out d3 to P3;
in d4 from P3;
out d5 to P1;
endinstance;
instance P3;
in d2 from P2;
in d3 from P2;
out d4 to P2;
out d6 to P1;
endinstance;
endmsc;
```

Fig. 1. Visual and textual representation of an MSC

Definition 1. *[15] An MSC M is given as a tuple $\langle V, <, \mathcal{P}, \mathcal{N}, L, K, N, m \rangle$, where*

- *V is a finite and nonempty set of events,*
- *$< \subseteq V \times V$ is an acyclic relation (with further details below),*

- $\mathcal{P}$ is a set of processes,
- $\mathcal{N}$ is a set of message names,
- $L : V \rightarrow \mathcal{P}$ is a mapping that associates each event with a process,
- $K : V \rightarrow \{\mathsf{s}, \mathsf{r}, \mathsf{l}\}$ is a mapping that describes the kind of each event as send, receive or local, respectively,
- $N : V \rightarrow \mathcal{N}$ maps every event to a name,
- $m \subseteq V \times V$ is a nonempty relation called matching that pairs up send and receive events. Each send is paired up with exactly one receive. Events v_1 and v_2 can be paired up with each other, only if $N(v_1) = N(v_2)$, $K(v_1) = \mathsf{s}$ and $K(v_2) = \mathsf{r}$.

A type is a triple (i, j, C), including the indexes of the sending process $P_i \in \mathcal{P}$ and receiving process $P_j \in \mathcal{P}$, and a message name $C \in \mathcal{N}$. Each send or receive event has a type, according to the origin and destination of the message, and the label of the message. The type of a local event of process $P_i \in \mathcal{P}$ is (i, i). Matching events have the same type. A message consists of a pair of matched send and receive events. For two events v_1 and v_2, we have $v_1 < v_2$ if and only if one of the following holds:

- v_1 and v_2 are matching send and receive events, respectively.
- v_1 and v_2 belong to the same process, with v_1 appearing before v_2 on the process line.

We assume FIFO (first in first out) message passing, i.e., message arrows on the same channel do not cross each other:

$$(m(v_1, v_1') \wedge m(v_2, v_2') \wedge v_1 < v_2 \wedge$$
$$L(v_1) = L(v_2) \wedge L(v_1') = L(v_2')) \Rightarrow v_1' < v_2'$$

Denote by $u \longrightarrow v$ the fact that $u < v$ and either u and v are matching send and receive events, or u and v belong to the same process and there is no event between u and v on the same process line. We say in this case that u immediately precedes v.

Definition 2. The transitive closure $<^*$ of the relation $<$ is a partial order called the visual ordering of events. Clearly, the visual ordering can be defined equivalently as the transitive closure of the relation $\longrightarrow$. A chain of events $e_1 <^* e_2 \ldots <^* e_n$ is called a causal chain.

The MSC notation represents a partial order execution, where the fact that two events u, v are ordered according to the visual order means that u happens before v. A linearization of an MSC $M = \langle V, <, \mathcal{P}, \mathcal{N}, L, K, N, m \rangle$ is a total order on V, which extends the relation $(V, <)$.

Example 1. Consider the example MSC given in Figure 1. For each message d_i, $1 \leq i \leq 6$, denote by s_i the send event and by r_i the receive event. Then we have $V = \{s_1, \ldots, s_6, r_1, \ldots, r_6\}$, $\mathcal{P} = \{P_1, P_2, P_3\}$, $\mathcal{N} = \{d_1, \ldots, d_6\}$ and $N(s_i) = N(r_i) = d_i$ for each i. The events located on P_1 are $L^{-1}(P_1) = \{s_1, r_5, r_6\}$, with $K(s_1) = \mathsf{s}$, $K(r_5) = K(r_6) = \mathsf{r}$, and $s_1 < r_5 < r_6$. This ordering is the time ordering of events on P_1. We also have $m(s_i, r_i)$ and $s_i < r_i$ for each i (message ordering). In particular, $s_1 < r_1 < s_2 < r_2$.

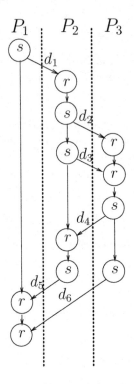

Fig. 2. The partial order between the events of the MSC in Figure 1

The partial order between the *send* and *receive* events of Figure 1 is shown in Figure 2. In this figure, only the 'immediately precedes' order $\longrightarrow$ is shown. Notice for example that the *send* events s_5 and s_6, of the two messages, d_5 and d_6, respectively, are unordered.

Definition 3. *The* concatenation $M_1 M_2$ *of two MSCs,*

$$M_k = \langle V_k, <_k, \mathcal{P}, \mathcal{N}_k, L_k, K_k, N_k, m_k \rangle, \text{ for } k = 1, 2.$$

over a common set of processes $\mathcal{P}$ and disjoint sets of events $V_1 \cap V_2 = \emptyset$ (we can always rename events so that the sets become disjoint) is defined as $\langle V_1 \cup V_2, <, \mathcal{P}, \mathcal{N}_1 \cup \mathcal{N}_2, L_1 \cup L_2, K_1 \cup K_2, N_1 \cup N_2, m_1 \cup m_2 \rangle$, where

$$< \; = \; <_1 \cup <_2 \cup \{(u, v) \in V_1 \times V_2 \mid L_1(u) = L_2(v)\}.$$

That is, the events of M_1 precede the events of M_2 for each process, respectively. If $M = M_1 M_2$, we say that M_1 is a *prefix* of M, and denote this by $M_1 \sqsubseteq M$. This also means containment between the different process events of the MSCs M_1 and M. Notice that no synchronization of the different processes is assumed in the definition of concatenation. Thus, $M_1 M_2$ does not necessarily describe a behavior that starts according to M_1 and after completing all the events from M_1 progresses to behave according to the events in M_2. In particular, it is possible in $M_1 M_2$ that one process is still involved in some actions of process P_i, while another process has advanced to events from another process P_j. Such a situation is demonstrated later in this section. The infinite concatenation of finite MSCs is defined in a similar way, and it allows defining infinite MSCs as well.

Definition 4. *Let M_1, M_2, ... be an infinite sequence of finite MSCs. Define a sequence M_1', M_2', ... as follows: Let $M_1' = M_1$, and for $i > 1$, $M_i' = M_{i-1}'M_i$. (Thus, for $i < j$, $M_i' \sqsubseteq M_j'$.)*

Let $M_i' = \langle V_i, <_i, \mathcal{P}, \mathcal{N}_i, L_i, K_i, N_i, m_i \rangle$. Then, $V_i \subseteq V_{i+1}$, $<_i \subseteq <_{i+1}$, $\mathcal{N}_i \subseteq \mathcal{N}_{i+1}$, $L_i \subseteq L_{i+1}$, $K_i \subseteq K_{i+1}$, $N_i \subseteq N_{i+1}$ and $m_i \subseteq m_{i+1}$. The infinite concatenation $M_1 M_2 \ldots$ is defined as the infinite MSC $M = \langle V, <, \mathcal{P}, \mathcal{N}, L, K, N, m \rangle$ where $V = \cup_{i \geq 1} V_i$, $\mathcal{N} = \cup_{i \geq 1} \mathcal{N}_i$, $L = \cup_{i \geq 1} L_i$, $N = \cup_{i \geq 1} N_i$, $K = \cup_{i \geq 1} K_i$, $N = \cup_{i \geq 1} N_i$, $m = \cup_{i \geq 1} m_i$ and $<= \cup_{i \geq 1} <_i$. Each component defining M is thus the limit of the partial unions for the same component in the finite prefixes M_i'.

Since a communication system usually involves multiple (or even infinitely many) MSC scenarios, a high-level description is needed for combining them. The standard description consists of a graph called HMSC (high-level MSC), where each node contains one finite MSC as in Figure 3. Each maximal path in this graph (i.e., a path that is either infinite or ends with a node without outgoing edges) that starts from a designated initial state corresponds to a single *execution* or *scenario*.

Definition 5. *[15] An HMSC is a 4-tuple $\langle \mathcal{S}, \mathcal{M}, c, \tau, \mathcal{S}_0 \rangle$ where $\mathcal{S}$ is a finite set of nodes, $\mathcal{M}$ is a set of finite MSCs with sets of events disjoint from one another. The mapping $c : \mathcal{S} \rightarrow \mathcal{M}$ associates a node $g \in \mathcal{S}$ with an MSC $c(g)$. By $\tau \subseteq \mathcal{S} \times \mathcal{S}$ we denote the edge relation. The initial nodes $\mathcal{S}_0$ are a subset of $\mathcal{S}$. An execution of the HMSC is a (finite or infinite) MSC $c(g_0) c(g_1) c(g_2) \cdots$ associated with a maximal[1] path $g_0, g_1, \ldots$ of the HMSC that starts with some initial node $g_0 \in \mathcal{S}_0$.*

The set of executions of an HMSC is also referred to as the set of MSC *generated* by that HMSC. Figure 3 shows an example of an HMSC. The node in the upper left corner, denoted M_1, is the starting node, hence it has an incoming edge that is connected to no other node. Initially, process P_1 sends a message to P_2, requesting a connection (e.g., to an internet service), according to node M_1. This can result in either an approval message from P_2, according to the node M_2, or a failure message, according to node M_3. In the latter case, a report message is also sent from P_2 to some supervisory process P_3. There are two progress choices, corresponding to the two arrows out of node M_3. We can decide to try and connect again, by choosing the arrow from M_3 to M_1, or to give up and send a service request (from process P_1 to process P_3), by choosing to progress according to the arrow from M_3 to M_4. Note how the HMSC description abstracts away from internal process computation, and presents only the communications. The executions of this system are either finite or infinite. Consider the path $M_1 M_3 M_4$. According to the HMSC semantics, process P_2 in Figure 3 does not necessarily have

---

[1] By maximality we mean that a path is either infinite, or terminates with a node that has no successor according to the relation τ.

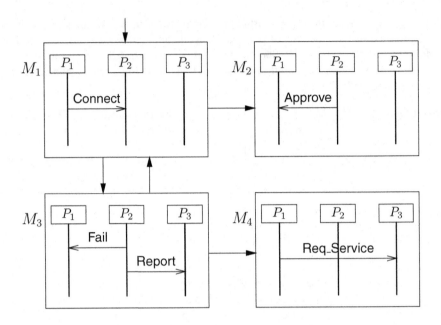

Fig. 3. An HMSC graph

to send its Report message in M_3 before the execution of process P_1 has progressed according to M_4 sent its Req_service message. However, process P_3 must receive the Report message before the Req_service message.

According to the ITU standard [15], an HMSC can be hierarchical, i.e., an HMSC node can be mapped into another (lower level) HMSC. We ignore this feature, which is orthogonal to the discussion in this survey and refer to [9] for algorithms on hierarchical HMSCs.

3 Expressiveness

Message sequence charts (MSCs) (including the extension to High level MSCs, i.e., HMSCs) is a formalism that is used in practice by protocol developers and software engineers. Unlike some other specification formalisms, it was not designed by researchers to fit into existing theory or tools. This calls for the study of its properties, in an attempt to adapt some formal methods techniques, or develop new ones.

There are several interesting aspects of the MSC notation that pose a challenge to the researchers and the developers of tools. For example, the HMSC notation does not necessarily represents *finite* state systems, as there is no bound on the size of message channels and due to concurrent processes. This fact has implications on the ability to automatically verify properties of HMSCs. Consider for example the HMSC in Figure 4. This is the simplest example of an HMSC with infinitely many global states. In order to formalize this observation, we define the notion of a *global state* of an MSC.

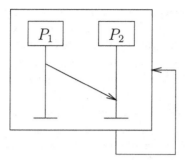

Fig. 4. Simple example with infinite state space

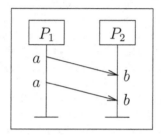

Fig. 5. An MSC with two messages

Definition 6. *Let* $M = \langle V, <, \mathcal{P}, \mathcal{N}, L, K, N, m \rangle$ *be a finite or infinite MSC (the latter case is obtained, e.g., by an infinite execution of an HMSC). A* global state *G is a finite subset of the events of V, such that if $f \in G$ and $e <^* f$, then $e \in G$. (We say that G is 'history closed'.)*

Now, it is easy to see that the states of the unique and infinite execution of the HMSC in Figure 4 consists of k *sends* and l *receives* for *any* natural numbers $k \geq l$. A global state of M is usually defined, in the context of software verification, as an assignment function from the program variables to their values. In the MSC context, the assignment can return the sequence of pending messages on each channel, together with the last event on each process.

It is interesting to know what is the expressive power of HMSCs. In order to remain within the domain of formal languages, we will look at the *linearizations* of MSC executions, i.e., their completions into total orders. We will label each event in an MSC node with a label from a finite alphabet Σ. We allow (but do not force) labeling of different events of the *same type and kind* by the same letter.

Consider the MSC in Figure 5. It has two messages, i.e., 4 events. We labeled the *sends* with a, and the *receives* with b. This MSC generates two linearizations (words): *abab* and *aabb*. These languages of linearizations are closed under certain permutation of adjacent occurrences of events. We have three *permutation rules*:

1. If b is a *receive* of a message from P_i to P_j, and a is a *send* from P_i to P_j, then we can permute $\sigma_1 ba\sigma_2$ ($\sigma_1, \sigma_2 \in \Sigma^*$) to obtain $\sigma_2 ab\sigma_2$. Note this rule does not necessarily permit us to permute in the reverse direction, i.e., from $\sigma_1 ab\sigma_2$ to $\sigma_1 ba\sigma_2$.

2. If a is a *send* from P_i to P_j, and b is a *receive* from P_i to P_j, we can permute a with b in $\sigma_1 ab\sigma_2$ provided that the following condition hold: $\#_a\sigma_1 > \#_b\sigma_1$, where $\#_c\sigma$ denotes the number of c's appearing in the word σ.

3. If a and b belong to different processes, and their types do not match as in the previous case, then we can permute a with b. (In fact, we can also permute b with a, from the symmetry of this condition.)

The reason that reverse permutation of the first rule is not necessarily allowed is that it may cause a *receive* to appear before the corresponding *send*. For example, given the linearization $abab$ of the MSC in Figure 5, we cannot permute the first a with the first b to obtain $baab$. The second rule specifies the condition under which the reverse permutation is allowed. Under this rule, the adjacent a and b, which can be permuted, are *not* a matching pair. Also note that for MSCs, it is not possible to use a fixed symmetric independence relation between events, as in *trace theory* [23].

We can define the *language of an HMSC* as follows. Let $\mathcal{L}(M)$ be the (finite) language of an HMSC node M. Let $\mathcal{K}$ be the language of the graph of the HMSC, where each node in the graph is assigned some unique letter (disjoint from the letters in Σ). According to Kleene's construction, the language $\mathcal{K}$ is a regular language. Substitute in $\mathcal{K}$ each letter corresponding to a node M by the language of $\mathcal{L}(M)$. This is still a regular language, denoted $\tilde{\mathcal{K}}$. Now close $\tilde{\mathcal{K}}$ under the permutation rules to obtain $[\tilde{\mathcal{K}}]$. Such permutations are achieved by using context sensitive grammar rules of the form $XabY \rightarrow XbaY$. Hence the language $[\tilde{\mathcal{K}}]$ of an HMSC is context sensitive. Note that the language of an HMSC H is the set of all linearizations of executions of H. Note also that we can only permute events according to the first and third permutation rules given above. This is sufficient due to the fact that we took *all* the linearizations of each separate MSC node. This is because a *send* event a from P_i to P_j in a node g and a *receive* event b, also from P_i to P_j of a later node h can never be commuted; the event a necessarily precedes the *send* event that matches with the *receive* b.

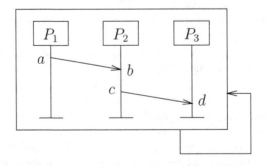

Fig. 6. An MSC with context-free behavior

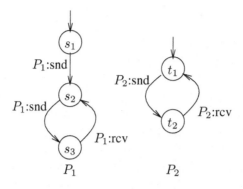

Fig. 7. A simple two process protocol

Thus, HMSC languages are obtainable from regular languages (ω-regular in the case of infinite executions) by closing under a given set of permutations. To show that the language of HMSCs is, in general, not regular or context free, consider the example in Figure 6. The global states of this example have l times a events, m times c events, and n times d events, where $l \geq m \geq n$ (also the number of b events is the same or greater than, by exactly one, than the number of c events). This can be easily shown not to be in the class of context-free (and not regular) languages.

On the other hand, we show that the HMSC notation does not allow representing all the possible communication skeletons of finite state communication protocols [11]. This makes HMSCs incomparable with regular languages.

As an example, consider the infinite MSC that is generated from the simple protocol in Figure 7. A finite prefix of the MSC description of the (unique and infinite) execution of this protocol appears in Figure 8. We show that this infinite MSC cannot be decomposed into a concatenation of finite MSCs. We start with the *send* event e_1 and *receive* event f_1. Obviously, because of the compulsory matching between corresponding *send* and *receive* events in HMSCs, they must belong to the same MSC node. We have the *send* event g_1 preceding f_1, on the same process line, while its corresponding *receive* event h_1 succeeds the *send* e_1. Thus, the events g_1 and h_1 cannot be in an MSC preceding the one containing the events e_1 and f_1, nor it can be in an MSC succeeding it. Consequently, these four events must be in the same HMSC node. For the same reason, we have that e_2 and f_2 must belong to the same node with g_1, and h_1, and so forth.

The problem lies within the restriction of the MSC nodes to contain matched messages. A different view of the expressiveness problem is that any global state that corresponds to a finite path in an HMSC (i.e., a global state that contains complete MSC nodes) has a matched set of *send* and *receive* events. In the partial order execution in Figure 8, there is no global state with this property. Hence, we cannot decompose this execution into finite MSCs (which will occur infinitely many times along some path of an HMSC).

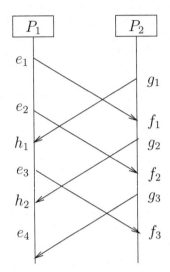

Fig. 8. A prefix of an MSC execution that cannot be decomposed

3.1   Compositional MSC

An extension of the HMSC notation is described in [11]. It allows MSC nodes with unmatched *send* and *receive* events. Thus, a *send* event in one node may be matched with a *receive* event in a later node.

In order to represent communication protocols, whose description could only be approximated using standard MSCs, we suggest an extension of the MSC standard. Intuitively, a *compositional MSC*, or *CMSC*, may include *send* events that are not matched by corresponding *receive* events and vice versa. An HCMSC is a graph whose nodes are CMSCs. An unmatched *send* event in one node in a path may be matched in future HCMSC nodes on that path. Similarly, an unmatched *receive* event may be matched in previous HCMSC nodes. The definition of a CMSC is hence similar to an MSC, except that unmatched *send* and *receive* messages are allowed.

Definition 7. *[11] A CMSC M is defined as in Definition 1, except for the following modification:*

> $m \subseteq V \times V$ *is a* partial *function called* matching *that pairs up send and receive events. Each send event is paired up with at most one receive event and vice versa. Events that are paired up are called* matched, *otherwise, they are* unmatched. *Matching events must have the same type.*

Unmatched *send* events are supposed to be matched by *receive* events belonging to subsequent nodes, whereas unmatched *receive* events are supposed to be matched by *send* events belonging to preceding nodes. The above definition allows unmatched *receive* events that do not correspond to any unmatched *send* event. (Allowing unmatched *send* events that do not correspond to a later *receive* is a lesser problem, as this can actually happen in communication protocols.)

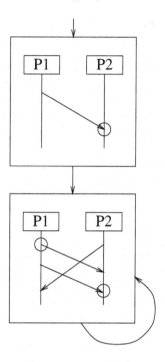

Fig. 9. A decomposition of the execution in Figure 8

We denote an unmatched *send* by a message arrow, where the *receive* end (the target of the arrow) appears within an empty circle. Similarly, an unmatched *receive* is denoted by an arrow where the *send* part (the source of the arrow) appears within a circle. CMSC arrows where both the *send* and the *receive* events are unmatched events are forbidden. In Figure 9, we can see an HCMSC that represents the execution that is approximated in Figure 8.

Definition 8. *A CMSC is called* left-closed, *if it does not contain unmatched receive events, or any unmatched send event that precedes another matched send of the same type (the latter condition excludes send events that could never be matched without violating the FIFO order).*

Definition 9. *Consider two CMSCs $M_1 = \langle V_1, <_1, \mathcal{P}, \mathcal{N}_1, L_1, K_1, N_1, m_1 \rangle$ and $M_2 = \langle V_2, <_2, \mathcal{P}, \mathcal{N}_2, L_2, K_2, N_2, m_2 \rangle$ over disjoint events sets. Define the matching function m' that pairs up unmatched send events of M_1 with unmatched receive events of M_2 according to their order on their process lines. That is, the ith unmatched send in M_1 is paired up with the ith unmatched receive event of the same type in M_2.*

The concatenation $M_1 M_2$ *is then defined as* $\langle V_1 \cup V_2, <, \mathcal{P}, \mathcal{N}_1 \cup \mathcal{N}_2, L_1 \cup L_2, K_1 \cup K_2, N_1 \cup N_2, m_1 \cup m_2 \cup m' \rangle$, *where*

$$< \; = \; <_1 \cup <_2 \cup$$
$$\{(v_1, v_2) \in V_1 \times V_2 \mid L_1(v_1) = L_2(v_2)\} \cup m'$$

provided that $M_1 M_2$ is a CMSC satisfying the FIFO property when restricting the events to the matched pairs of events.

Clearly, the concatenation of CMSCs is not associative anymore. Hence, when we write $M_1 \cdots M_k$ we mean the concatenation $(\cdots (M_1 M_2) M_3) \cdots M_k)$. Again, we can define the prefix relation $M_1 \sqsubseteq M$ if there exists M_2 such that $M_1 M_2 = M$. The definition of an infinite concatenation for CMSCs follows the lines of Definition 4. Note that in an infinite concatenation, there can be infinitely many unmatched messages sent from one process to another.

The formal definition of HCMSCs is the same as Definition 5. Similarly, an HCMSC *execution* is the CMSC $c(g_0)c(g_1)\ldots$ associated with a path $g_0, g_1, \ldots$ in the HCMSC graph, starting with some initial node g_0, as in Definition 5.

3.2 Safe HCMSC

The definition of HCMSCs allows obtaining some "unreasonable" paths in HCMSCs, e.g. in which at some points there are more *receive* events than the corresponding *send* events for some ordered pair of processes. It is not clear how to treat such paths. One way, is to disregard such paths as executions of the HCMSC system. Another approach, which will be taken in this section, is to forbid HCMSCs with such paths.

Remark 1. [15] An HCMSC is *safe*[2] if the execution of every finite path starting with the initial state is a left-closed CMSC.

Note that we explicitly allow executions with unmatched *send* events. The HCMSC of Figure 9 is such that every finite execution is a left-closed CMSC with unmatched *send* events. However, the unique maximal execution corresponds to an infinite MSC, where all the events are pairwise matched. Definition 8 of left-closedness guarantees that no unmatched *send* can prevent the system to satisfy the FIFO condition by matching it later.

We will show how to test whether an HCMSC is safe. From the definition of safe HCMSCs, we can focus on messages sent from each P_i to another process P_j separately. There are three situations that violate the safety of a HCMSC on a given prefix of a path:

1. There are more unmatched *receive* events than *send*s.
2. Reaching a matched *send-receive* pair, the kth unmatched *send* is before the matched pair, but the kth unmatched *receive* comes after that matched pair. This will generate a non-FIFO behavior.
3. The kth unmatched *send* has a message name C, while the kth unmatched *receive* has a message name D, where $D \neq C$.

To check whether an HCMSC is safe [11], we construct a nondeterministic pushdown automaton $\mathcal{S}_{i,j}$ for each ordered pair of processes P_i, P_j that exchange messages in the HCMSC. A pushdown automaton is a quadruple, $\mathcal{S} = \langle Q, \Gamma, \Sigma, \Delta \rangle$, such that

---

[2] Such HCMSCs are called realizable in [11]. This name usually refers to the realizability/implementability problem, so we prefer to recast it into "safe".

- Q is a finite set of control states,
- Γ is a finite stack alphabet which in our case will be $\Gamma = \{\bot, 1\}$, where $\bot$ is the 'stack bottom' symbol,
- Σ is the input alphabet, which includes *unmatched-send C*, *unmatched-receive C*, or *matched-C*, such that C is a message name from $\mathcal{N}$, and $\Delta \subseteq (Q \times \Sigma \times \Gamma) \times (Q \times \{pop, push, skip\})$ is the set of transition rules. Depending on the current state and symbol at the top position at the stack and the current input symbol, a pushdown automaton has a choice of
  - the next state and
  - whether to *pop* the current top element from the stack, *push* another symbol on top of it, or *skip*, i.e., keep its current contents. The stack contents in our case always belongs to $\bot 1^*$.

The stack is used as a counter, where the counter value is the number of '1' symbols on the stack, and a zero is represented by a stack containing only '$\bot$'. We can partition the transitions according to their effect on the number of '1' symbols in the stack: incrementing, decrementing, or testing whether the contents of the stack is zero.

For every pair of processes P_i, P_j we define the pushdown automaton $\mathcal{S}_{i,j}$ by replacing each node in the HCMSC by a linearization (total ordering) of the matched and unmatched *send* and *receive* events. We allow only linearizations in which unmatched *receive* events of some type precede all the unmatched *send* events of the same type. It follows easily from the definitions that such a linearization always exists. The automaton $\mathcal{S}_{i,j}$ will follow such events in a node, and then will continue according to the events of a successor of the current node and so forth (nondeterministically, as there can be more than one HCMSC successor). The pushdown automaton will reach an *accept* state exactly when it discovers that the HCMSC is not safe due to communications from P_i to P_j.

We describe now the automaton $\mathcal{S}_{i,j}$ informally. It contains two phases. In the first phase, it increments each time an unmatched *send* event occurs, and decrements each time an unmatched *receive* occurs. It moves to an *accept* state when either the stack is empty (containing only $\bot$), and an unmatched *receive* occurs, or when a matched *send-receive* event occurs and the stack is not empty. This takes care of the cases 1 and 2 above. To take care of case 3, upon the occurrence of an unmatched *send*, the automaton can nondeterministically 'guess' that the corresponding *receive* has a different name. It saves the message name C in its finite control and ignores all subsequent events, except for unmatched *receive* events, where it decrements one '1' from the stack. Upon reaching an empty stack, it compares the last *receive* name D with the name stored C. If $C \neq D$, it transfers to an *accept* state, and otherwise, it just ignores the rest of the events. Reaching an *accept* state means that the HCMSC is *not* safe.

The motivation behind the definition of compositional MSCs was to capture finite state communication protocols, like the one of Figure 8:

Theorem 1. *[11] Every finite state communication protocol can be transformed into an equivalent safe HCMSC (in polynomial size).*

Clearly, the converse of the theorem above does not hold. This happens for the same reasons as for HMSCs, as demonstrated in Figure 6.

4   Undecidable Versions of Model Checking for HMSCs

Once we characterize HMSC languages as context sensitive languages, it is not too surprising that certain decision problems become undecidable. The state based model checking (see e.g. [14, 19, 30, 7]) prescribes using a finite state model for representing the execution sequences of a system and another finite state automaton (over finite or infinite words) for representing the specification. The specification describes the *bad* executions, i.e., the ones we do not want the system to have. We take the intersection of the languages of the system automaton and the specification automaton to find whether there are bad sequences allowed by the system. We can try, along these lines, to specify the bad or unwanted executions of a system using the HMSC formalism. If the intersection of the linearizations of two HMSCs is nonempty, we can easily take one and generate back an MSC.

Alternatively, we can use a specification of the *good* sequences, i.e., the executions we allow. However, in this case we need to perform a test for language inclusion, which is often of higher complexity when using HMSCs. The reason is that contrary to logical specifications, that can be negated without any blow-up, HMSCs cannot be always complemented. As an example, consider the trivial HMSC with one node labeled by the empty MSC over the process set $\mathcal{P}$. This HMSC generates the empty set and its complement (i.e., the set of all MSCs over $\mathcal{P}$) cannot be generated by an HMSC (neither by a safe CHMSC).

The corresponding HMSC model checking problem is to intersect two HMSCs, one corresponding to the system description, and another representing the 'bad' MSC executions. It is known that the emptiness of the intersection of two context sensitive languages is undecidable. We still have to prove that for HMSC languages, as they form a subset of the context sensitive languages:

Theorem 2. *[27] The problems of intersection of two HMSCs is undecidable.*

Proof. By reduction from Post Correspondence Problem (PCP). The input for PCP is a finite sequence of pairs of words

$$(w_1, v_1), (w_2, v_2), \ldots, (w_n, v_n)$$

The problem is to decide whether there is a finite sequence of indexes $i_1, i_2, \ldots, i_m$ such that $w_{i_1} w_{i_2} \ldots w_{i_m} = v_{i_1} v_{i_2} \ldots v_{i_m}$.

We construct two HMSCs. One for concatenating words that appear in the left components of the above pairs, and one for concatenating words that appear in the right components. Consider the HMSC for the left components. We have 4 processes $P_1, \ldots P_4$. For each word w_j, we construct an MSC node M_j with messages from P_1 to P_2 labeled by the letters of w_j. We also have a node R_j, with one message, from P_3 to P_4, labeled by the index j. We also have an initial node E, with a message from P_1 to P_4, and a node F, with a message from P_4 to P_1. The structure of the automaton can be represented by the regular expression $E(\sum_{j=1..n} M_j R_j)^+ F$, which is also demonstrated in Figure 10. That is, we need to start with the initial node E, then repeatedly make a nondeterministic choice of $M_j R_j$ for $1 \leq j \leq n$, and finally end with node F.

The automaton for concatenating the right components is constructed similarly. Now notice that the events in the M_j components can commute with the events in the R_j

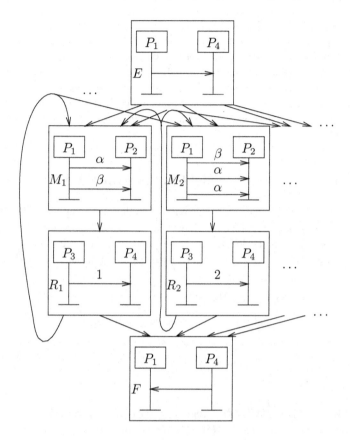

Fig. 10. An HMSC graph for the PCP reduction

components, since they involve disjoint processes. Therefore, any word in the intersection has the same characters according to the sequence of M_js, and the same indexes according to the sequence of R_js.   ∎

Another attempt for providing model checking is to write the specification (or the negation of the specification, describing the bad executions) using an automaton over finite or infinite words, or using linear temporal logic (LTL). Unfortunately, the intersection of HMSC languages with regular languages, or the language of words satisfying linear temporal logic formulas, is undecidable as well.

To see this, replace in the previous proof the HMSC for the right components (the 'specification automaton') by an LTL formula (or regular expression, or a finite state automaton over infinite words) that represents some of the linearizations of the HMSC as follows: for an MSC node M, let $\text{lin}(M)$ be the single linearization of M that includes matching *send* and *receive* events appearing adjacent. (Note that this kind of linearization is not always possible for an MSC, but is possible in our case because of the particular construction of the nodes in the reduction.) Thus the linearization of M_j, representing the word $w_j = \alpha\beta\beta\alpha$ will be $s_\alpha r_\alpha s_\beta r_\beta s_\beta r_\beta s_\alpha r_\alpha$, where s_ρ represents a *send* of a message labeled by ρ, and r_ρ represents a *receive* of that message. The LTL formula will represent the language $\text{lin}(E)(\bigcup_{j=1..n} \text{lin}(M_j)\text{lin}(R_j))^+\text{lin}(F)$ (this is a counter-free language, and thus can be represented using LTL).

The intersection of the (language of the) HMSC, representing the left words in the PCP problem, and the language of the LTL formula above, representing the right words, would include exactly the words that are solutions to the PCP problem. That is, we have the same concatenation of words, with the same sequence of indexes. Hence, LTL model checking of HMSCs is undecidable.

5   Decidable Versions of Model Checking for HMSCs

There are several positive solutions for providing model checking algorithms for HM-SCs. One possibility is to consider restricted classes of HMSCs. The most restrictive approach considers regular HMSCs, that correspond to finite state systems for which the usual model checking approaches can be used. Other solutions are listed below.

5.1   Regular and Cooperative HMSCs

A constraint for HMSCs ensuring regularity is the following [5, 26].

Definition 10. *The communication graph $CG^M = \langle P, \rightarrow \rangle$ of an MSC M contains the processes $P \in \mathcal{P}$ of M that occur in M, and with edges $P_i \rightarrow P_j \in E$ if there is a message from P_i to P_j in M.*

Definition 11. *[5, 26] An HMSC H is regular, if for each loop σ in the graph of H, the communication graph CG^M of the MSC M labeling σ is strongly connected.*

The definition of regular HMSCs is syntactic, and be checked in co-NP [26, 5]. Model checking becomes decidable for regular HMSCs [26, 5], since their languages are regular. More precisely:

Theorem 3. *[17, 18] A set of MSCs is generated by a regular HMSC if and only if it has a regular set of linearizations and is generated by a finite set of MSCs.*

An *HMSC state* is a global state associated with an execution M of the HMSC H. We will show that the number of pending messages (i.e., messages that are sent but not yet received) in any HMSC state of a regular HMSC is finite. Note however that a bound on pending messages does not suffice for representing HMSC linearizations using a finite state automaton. As an example, consider a (non-regular) HMSC over processes P_1, P_2, P_3, P_4 consisting of two nodes g_0, g_1. The initial node g_0 has a self-loop and a transition to the sink node g_1. Node g_0 is labeled by the following MSC with 4 messages: there is a message from P_1 to P_2, and back, and a message from P_3 to P_4, and back. Node g_1 is labeled by the empty MSC. Now, the number of pending messages is at most 2, but the set of linearizations is not regular.

Theorem 4. *For any regular HMSC there is a bound on the number of pending messages in any HMSC state.*

Proof. It is sufficient to show that for each pair of processes P and Q, there is a bound on the number of occurrences of a regular HMSC node g that can contribute to the pending messages.

Let $n = |\mathcal{P}|$, i.e., the number of processes. An upper limit on the number of graphs with n nodes, and also on the number of simple paths in such a graph is $k = 2^{n^2}$. Consider a global state G generated for a maximal path (i.e., a finite MSC) σ. Consider the occurrences of unreceived *send* events from process P to process Q on σ in G. Let g be a node of the HMSC that includes such an event. Assume for the contradiction that there are $l = nk + 3$ such occurrences g_0, g_1, ..., g_{nk+2}, of g that contribute to the global state G.

There are nk cycles, g_i to g_{i+1} for $1 \leq i \leq nk + 1$, *after* the first occurrence g_0 of g and *before* the last occurrence g_{nk+2}. Each such cycle σ_i is a subpath of σ. By the choice of l, considering the communication graphs corresponding to the cycles σ_i, at least one such graph repeats n times. Let μ be a simple path in such a communication graph from the node corresponding to process Q to the node corresponding to process P. Hence μ consists of at most $n - 1$ edges.

Distinguish s and r as a *send–receive* pair of g_0, from process P to process Q, where s is in G but r is not. Similarly, let s' and r' be a similar pair of g_{nk+2}. We can now construct a causal (according to $<^*$) chain of events in the subpath of σ as follows: from the σ_i cycle we select a *send–receive* pair according to the ith edge of μ. (We may not assume that a chain of events appears according to the order in μ in one cycle σ_i, hence we need to form the chain by collecting events from different cycles.) This forms a causal chain of events, as each *receive* selected precedes the following *send* on the same process line. The first *send* on this chain appears later than the event r. It appears in g_1 and both belong to process Q. The last *receive* precedes the event s'. Both events belong to process P. According to our assumptions, r is not included in G while s' is included. Thus by our construction, $r <^* s'$. This is a contradiction, since a global state must be history closed.   ∎

This result is also related to the star problem in trace languages [28]. The restriction to regular HMSCs is quite strong, for instance the simple protocol in Figure 4 is not regular. However, this HMSC is *globally-cooperative*, and belongs to a large subclass of HMSCs with a decidable model-checking problem.

Definition 12. *[13] An HMSC H is* globally-cooperative, *if for each loop σ in the graph of H, the communication graph CG^M of the MSC M labeling ρ is weakly connected.*

It is interesting to note that regular HMSCs are precisely globally-cooperative HMSCs that use only bounded channels.

Model-checking globally-cooperative HMSCs is decidable, and has the same complexity as for regular HMSC [13]. Instead of having a regular set of linearizations, globally-cooperative HMSCs have a regular set of *representative* linearizations, which suffice for doing model-checking operations.

Theorem 5. *[13] Checking intersection of two globally-cooperative (regular, resp.) HMSCs is PSPACE-complete. Checking inclusion of two globally-cooperative (regular, resp.) HMSCs is EXPSPACE-complete.*

Allowing 'gaps' in the semantics of the specification HMSC gives another decidable case for model checking. A *specification* HMSC representing the bad executions is interpreted in a different way than the HMSC representing the system. The former represents only part of the events. In particular, two adjacent events a and b on the same process line of the specification HMSC may match some nonadjacent events of the same type in the system HMSC. The (scattered) pattern matching problem between these two HMSCs is decidable, and is in NP-hard, in the size of the HMSCs [27].

5.2   The Logic TLC$^-$

Using a partial order based specification formalism can also regain decidability of model checking. Consider a specification that has a language $\mathcal{L}$ that is regular and is already closed under the permutation rules. The emptiness of the intersection of such a specification with an HMSC language can be decided. The reason is that an HMSC language $[P]$ is generated from a regular language P by closing it under permutations. If $\mathcal{L} = [\mathcal{L}]$, then $\mathcal{L} \cap P \neq \emptyset$ iff $\mathcal{L} \cap [P] \neq \emptyset$. Thus, it is sufficient to check the emptiness of the intersection of $\mathcal{L}$ with the regular generator P of the HMSC language. Similarly, for the inclusion problem we have $P \subseteq \mathcal{L}$ iff $[P] \subseteq \mathcal{L}$ and this can be decided, provided that the specification $\mathcal{L}$ is complementable[3].

A solution that involves partial order based formalisms is the use of a subset of the logic TLC [4], as applied on HMSCs in [29]. According to this solution, we use temporal modalities to reason over the events of the MSC system. We use the same modalities symbols as in LTL, but give them a different interpretation; over paths of events, generated by the $<$ relation, rather than over linearizations of the partial order.

The logic TLC$^-$ is a subset of the logic TLC [4]. A model of the logic is a finite or infinite partial order $\zeta = (V, <, \longrightarrow)$, where $< \subset V \times V$ is a partial order relation, and $\longrightarrow \subset <$ is the 'immediately precedes' relation. The set of formulas $\mathcal{L}$ of TLC$^-$ over a set of atomic formulas AP is as follows: *true, false* $\in \mathcal{L}$, if $p \in AP$, then $p \in \mathcal{L}$, and if φ, ψ are in $\mathcal{L}$ then $\varphi \wedge \psi, \varphi \vee \psi, \neg\varphi, \exists \bigcirc \varphi, \forall \bigcirc \varphi, \varphi U \psi, \varphi R \psi \in \mathcal{L}$.

An *interpretation function* $I : V \mapsto 2^{AP}$ assigns to each event of V a set of propositions from AP. Each proposition in AP represents some property (e.g., of an event, or the local state before or after the event, when the events are taken from some system execution). Then, $I(v)$ returns the set of atomic propositions that hold for v. The semantics of the logic is defined as follows.

$(\zeta, v) \models$ *true*.
$(\zeta, v) \models p$ if $p \in I(v)$
$(\zeta, v) \models \varphi \wedge \psi$ if $(\zeta, v) \models \varphi$ and $(\zeta, v) \models \psi$.
$(\zeta, v) \models \neg\varphi$ if it is not the case that $(\zeta, v) \models \varphi$.
$(\zeta, v) \models \exists \bigcirc \varphi$ if for some w such that $v \longrightarrow w$, it holds that $(\zeta, w) \models \varphi$.
$(\zeta, v) \models \varphi U \psi$ if there is a path $v = v_0 \longrightarrow v_1 \longrightarrow \ldots \longrightarrow v_n$, such that $(\zeta, v_n) \models \psi$,
    and for $0 \leq i < n, (\zeta, v_i) \models \varphi$.

---

[3] As in the case of logics, as described next. Note however that HMSCs cannot be complemented.

We define *false* $\equiv \neg true$, $\varphi \vee \psi \equiv \neg(\neg\varphi \wedge \neg\psi)$, $\varphi R \psi \equiv \neg(\neg\varphi U \neg\psi)$, $\forall \bigcirc \varphi \equiv \neg \exists \bigcirc \neg\varphi$. Two additional modalities, $\Diamond$ and $\Box$, can be defined in terms of the previous ones: $\Diamond\varphi \equiv true U \varphi$, and $\Box\varphi \equiv false R \varphi$. For TLC⁻ we have selected an *existential until* 'U' operator, hence its dual *release* 'R' operator is universal. The full logic TLC contains also a universal *until*, an existential *release*, and a *concurrent with* operator '$||$'. The modalities U and R satisfy the following equations: $\varphi U \psi \equiv \psi \vee (\varphi \wedge \exists \bigcirc \varphi U \psi)$, $\varphi R \psi \equiv \psi \wedge (\varphi \vee \forall \bigcirc \varphi R \psi)$. A TLC⁻ formula φ can then be interpreted over an HMSC execution M, treated as a partially ordered set of events. We can denote $M \models \varphi$ when M satisfies φ. Like in the case of LTL, where satisfaction is extended from a single execution to the collection of executions of a system [25], we can extend TLC⁻ satisfiability and define $H \models \varphi$ for an HMSC H when $M \models \varphi$ for each execution M of H.

Thus, the assertion $\bigcirc\varphi$ holds for events that have an immediate successor under the relation $<$ for which φ holds. $\Diamond\varphi$ holds for events e from which there is a path according to $<$, leading to some event f for which φ holds (thus, $e <^* f$). Similarly, for $\psi U \varphi$ to hold for e, we require, that ψ holds for each event along such a path from e to some event f where φ holds. Finally, in order to satisfy the usual duality $\Box\varphi = \neg\Diamond\neg\varphi$, we interpret $\Box\varphi$ as follows: it holds for events e that satisfy that for every event f such that $e <^* f$, φ holds for f.

Some examples for TLC⁻ specification are as follows:

$\Box(req \rightarrow \Diamond ack)$ Every request is causally followed by an acknowledgement.

$\Box(recA \rightarrow \exists \bigcirc sendB)$ A message B is sent immediately after receiving a message A.

$\neg\Diamond(tranA \wedge \Diamond(tranB \wedge \Diamond tranA))$ Transaction B cannot interfere with the events of transaction A.

$\Box(beginA \rightarrow \exists \bigcirc (tranA\, U\, finishA))$ The execution of transaction A is not interrupted by any other event.

One intuition behind the decidability (and model checking algorithm) of TLC⁻ over HMSC is that although HMSC linearizations are not regular languages, they are 'almost regular', up to some commutations, as shown in Section 3. The TLC⁻ logic does not distinguish between linearizations that are equivalent up to such commutations. A TLC⁻ formula can thus be equally be interpreted over a regular subset of *representatives* linearizations. More precisely, for the permutation rules the situation is actually a little bit subtler than in Section 3. The reason is that from a TLC⁻ formula we cannot get the set of *all* linearizations of its MSC models, since this would involve counting of pending messages. We can compute instead the set of all linearizations where is the number of pending messages is bounded. The bound can be provided by the HMSC that is model-checked. Another decidable model checking solution with the same flavor is based on using second order monadic logic over partial orders [22].

6   Other Decision Problems

A natural problem that arises with MSCs is whether the MSCs contain *race conditions*. A race condition can result from the fact that we have only a limited control on the

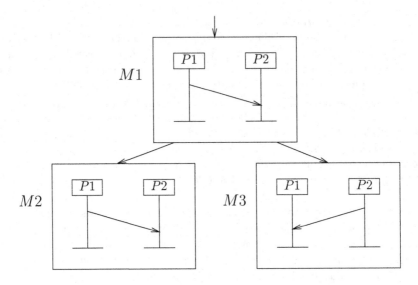

Fig. 11. A non-local choice

order between pairs of events that include at least one receive event (except for two receives corresponding to messages sent from the same process, according to the FIFO semantics). For example, the MSC in Figure 1 contains two receive events of process P_1 (of messages d_5 and d_6). Since each process line is one dimensional, the MSC notation forces choosing one of the receive events to appear above the other. However, these two messages were sent from different processes, P_2 and P_3, and it might happen that d_6 arrives quicker than d_5. Thus, there is no reason to trust that these messages will arrive in the particular order depicted using the MSC.

Formally, we can define a race condition for pairs of MSC *receive* events $p, q \in V$ for messages sent from different processes such that $L(p) = L(q)$, i.e., p and q appear on the same process line. A race occurs if $p < q$, i.e., p appears above q on the process line, and it is *not* the case that $p <^* q$, i.e., there is no path from p to q according to the relation $<$. Detecting races in an MSC is thus simple. All we need is to calculate the transitive closure $<^*$ and compare it against relation $<$.

It is shown in [3] that the calculation of the transitive closure $<^*$ of $<$ is quadratic in the number of events, and not cubic as is the general case for transitive closure. This stem from the fact that the number of *immediate* successors of each event p under $<$ (i.e., events q such that $p < q$, and there is no r such that $p < r < q$) if limited to 2.

We can define the race conditions for HMSCs. This turns out to be an undecidable problem [27]. We regain decidability by limiting the structure of the HMSCs, as described in Section 5.

Another problem related to HMSC specification is that of *non-local branching choice* [6, 26]. A problem potentially arises when different processes behave according to different choices in the HMSC graph, resulting in a behavior that is not following any of the branching choices.

Consider the example in Figure 11. After Process P_1 sends a message to Process P_2 in M_1 it may proceed according to M_2 and send another message to P_2. However, the HMSC allows also the possibility that after receiving the message in M_1, P_2 would send some acknowledge message, according to the node M_3. If P_1 proceeds according to M_2 and P_2 proceeds according to M_3, we obtain a behavior that is not consistent with any path of the HMSC.

The definition of non-local branching choice is difficult because it is not clear what would constitute a problematic behavior. In the above example, it is possible that P_1 initially decides on the choice, and lets P_2 know about it through the message that is sends in M_1. On the other hand, it could be argued that in that case, we should have split M_1 into two nodes, according to the branch into M_2 and M_3. One solution is to try and detect whether some non-local choice occurs, while another is to restrict the HMSCs so that they would not allow such a choice [6, 26]. In the first case consider *local-choice* HMSCs, i.e., HMSCs that do not have any non-local branching choice. Such specifications are very interesting, since they can be implemented without deadlock by CFMs [13] with additional control data. Although local-choice is a syntactic property, it can be decided whether an HMSC is equivalent to a local-choice HMSC [10].

The problem of implementing HMSCs by CFM has deserved a lot of attention in past years, since it represents an important validation step when using HMSC specifications. The implementation notion used in [1] assumes that the CFM does not use additional data or messages compared to the HMSC. Unfortunately, this notion is not decidable in general, even for regular HMSCs [2], or very expensive if we ask for deadlock-free implementations [21]. The paper [16] shows that local-choice HMSCs cannot be implemented without deadlock if no control (message) data is allowed. For regular HMSCs [24] and globally-cooperative HMSCs [13] implementations with additional (bounded) control data have been proposed.

Acknowledgement

We would like to thank our collaborators in studying message sequence charts: Rajeev Alur, Blaise Genest, Elsa Gunter, Gerard Holzmann, Markus Lohrey and Zhendong Su for many fruitful and pleasant collaborations. We would also like to thank the two anonymous reviewers of this paper for their insightful remarks, which helped to improve the presentation.

References

1. R. Alur, K. Etessami, and M. Yannakakis. Inference of message sequence charts. In *Proc. of the 22nd Int. Conf. on Software Engineering*, 304–313, ACM, 2000.
2. R. Alur, K. Etessami, and M. Yannakakis. Realizability and verification of MSC graphs. In *Proc. of (ICALP'01)*, Lecture Notes in Computer Science 2076, Springer-Verlag, 797–808, 2001.
3. R. Alur, G. H. Holzmann, and D. A. Peled. An analyzer for message sequence charts. *Software Concepts and Tools*, 17(2):70–77, 1996.

4. R. Alur and D. Peled and W. Penczek. Model Checking of Causality Properties. In *Proc. of Logic in Computer Science (LICS'95)*, 90-100, 1995.

5. R. Alur and M. Yannakakis. Model checking of message sequence charts. In *Proc. of CONCUR'99*, Lecture Notes in Computer Science 1664, Springer-Verlag, 114–129, 1999.

6. H. Ben-Abdulla, S. Leue. Symbolic Detection of Process Divergence and Non-local Choice in Message Sequence Charts. In *Proc. of Tools and Algorithms for the Construction and Analysis of Systems (TACAS'97)*, Lecture Notes in Computer Science 1217, Springer-Verlag, 259–274, 1997.

7. E. M. Clarke, O. Grumberg, D. Peled, *Model Checking*, MIT Press, 1999.

8. J. Esparza, D. Hansel, P. Rossmanith, S. Schwoon. Efficient algorithms for model checking pushdown systems, *Proc. of CAV'00*, Chicago, IL, Lecture Notes in Computer Science 1855, Springer-Verlag, 232-247, 2000.

9. B. Genest and A. Muscholl. Pattern matching and membership for Hierarchical Message Sequence Charts. In *Proc. of LATIN 2002*, Lecture Notes in Computer Science 2286, Springer-Verlag, 326–340, 2002.

10. B. Genest. Compositional Message Sequence Charts (CMSCs) are better to Implement than MSCs. In *Proc. of Tools and Algorithms for the Construction and Analysis of Systems (TACAS'05)*, to appear 2005.

11. E. Gunter, A. Muscholl, D. Peled, Compositional Message Sequence Charts. In *Proc. of Tools and Algorithms for the Construction and Analysis of Systems (TACAS'01)*, Lecture Notes in Computer Science 2031, Springer-Verlag, 496–511. Journal version in *International Journal on Software Tools for Technology Transfer (STTT)* 5(1): 78-89 (2003).

12. B. Genest, A. Muscholl, and D. Peled. Message sequence charts, *Lectures on Concurrency and Petri Nets*, Lecture Notes in Computer Science 3098, Springer-Verlag, 537–558, 2003.

13. B. Genest, A. Muscholl, H. Seidl, and M. Zeitoun. Infinite-state High-level MSCs: Model-checking and realizability. In *Proc. of ICALP'02*, Lecture Notes in Computer Science 2380, Springer-Verlag, 657–668, 2002. Journal version to appear in *JCSS* 2005.

14. G. Holzmann, *Design and Validation of Computer Protocols*, Prentice-Hall, 1992.

15. *ITU-T Recommendation Z.120, Message Sequence Chart (MSC)*, 1996.

16. L. Hélouët and C. Jard. Conditions for synthesis of communicating automata from HMSCs. In *5th International Workshop on Formal Methods for Industrial Critical Systems*, Berlin, 2000.

17. J. G. Henriksen, M. Mukund, K. Narayan Kumar, and P.S. Thiagarajan. On Message Sequence Graphs and finitely generated regular MSC languages. In *Proc. of ICALP'00*, Lecture Notes in Computer Science 1853, Springer-Verlag, 675–686, 2000.

18. J. G. Henriksen, M. Mukund, K. Narayan Kumar, and P.S. Thiagarajan. Regular collections of message sequence charts. *Proc. of MFCS'00*, Lecture Notes in Computer Science 1893, Springer-Verlag, 405–414, 2000.

19. R. P. Kurshan. *Computer-Aided Verification of Coordinating Processes: The Automata-Theoretic Approach*. Princeton University Press, 1994.

20. D. Kuske. Regular sets of infinite message sequence charts. *Information and Computation*, (187):80–109, 2003.

21. M. Lohrey. Safe realizability of high-level message sequence charts. In *Proc. of CONCUR'02*, Lecture Notes in Computer Science 2421, Springer-Verlag, 177–192, 2002.

22. P. Madhusudan. Reasoning about sequential and branching behaviours of message sequence graphs. In *Proc. of ICALP'01*, Lecture Notes in Computer Science 2076, Springer-Verlag, 809–820, 2001.

23. A. Mazurkiewicz, Basic notions of trace theory, REX workshop 1988, Lecture Notes in Computer Science 354, Springer-Verlag, 285–363, 1988.

24. M. Mukund, K. Narayan Kumar, and M. Sohoni. Synthesizing distributed finite-state systems from MSCs. In *Proc. of CONCUR'00*, Lecture Notes in Computer Science 1877, Springer-Verlag, 521–535, 2000.

25. Z. Manna, A. Pnueli, *The Temporal Logic of Reactive and Concurrent Systems: Specification*, Springer-Verlag, 1991.

26. A. Muscholl and D. Peled. Message sequence graphs and decision problems on Mazurkiewicz traces. In *Proc. of MFCS'99*, Lecture Notes in Computer Science 1672, springer-Verlag, Szklarska Poreba, Poland, 1999, 81–91.

27. A. Muscholl, D. Peled, and Z. Su. Deciding properties of message sequence charts. In *Proc. of FoSSaCS'98*, Lecture Notes in Computer Science 1378, Springer-Verlag, 226–242, 1998.

28. E. Ochmanski. Recognizable trace languages. In *The Book of Traces*, V. Diekert, G. Rozenberg, (eds.), World Scientific, 1995, 167–204.

29. D. Peled. Specification and verification of message sequence charts. *FORTE/PSTV 2000*, Kluwer, Pisa, Italy, 2000, 139–154.

30. M. Y. Vardi, P. Wolper. An automata-theoretic approach to automatic program verification. In *Proc. of Logic in Computer Science (LICS'86)*, pp. 332–344, 1986.

Operational Semantics of Security Protocols

Cas Cremers and Sjouke Mauw

Eindhoven University of Technology,
Department of Mathematics and Computer Science,
P.O. Box 513, NL-5600 MB Eindhoven, The Netherlands

Abstract. Based on a concise domain analysis we develop a formal semantics of security protocols. Its main virtue is that it is a generic model, in the sense that it is parameterized over e.g. the intruder model. Further characteristics of the model are a straightforward handling of parallel execution of multiple protocols, locality of security claims, the binding of local constants to role instances, and explicitly defined initial intruder knowledge. We validate our framework by analysing the Needham-Schroeder-Lowe protocol.

1 Introduction

Security protocols are often expressed in the form of a diagram displaying the interactions between the principals, such as a Message Sequence Chart. The MSC in Figure 1 describes perhaps the most well-known example of a flawed security protocol. We will explain the details in Section 4. The protocol was developed in 1978 by Roger Needham and Michael Schroeder [1] and proven correct with BAN logic [2] in 1989. In 1995 Gavin Lowe found an attack on the protocol [3], because he assumed a more powerful intruder model, allowing agents to conspire with the intruder. This so-called man-in-the-middle attack is displayed in Figure 2. Currently, this situation is explained by pointing at a shift of the assumptions on the environment of the system: from a trusted local network that should be protected against external threats to a network with internal attackers.

This example clearly shows that a theory of security protocols should be flexible enough to vary over the parameters that determine the problem, such as the intruder model. Looking at Figure 1 it is clear that this informal protocol specification states nothing about the precise intruder model assumed. In fact, more information is lacking. Information which is needed to precisely understand the meaning of this diagram. How does an agent check, for instance, if an incoming message satisfies the expected message format? If we assume that he will not check the types of the messages, yet another attack will become viable, which is called a type-flaw attack.

It is our goal to give an unambiguous and generic description of the interpretation of such security protocols and what it means for a protocol to ensure some security property. Although the security protocol takes the shape of a Message Sequence Chart, there is so much additional structure in the problem that

S. Leue and T.J. Systä (Eds.): Scenarios, LNCS 3466, pp. 66–89, 2005.

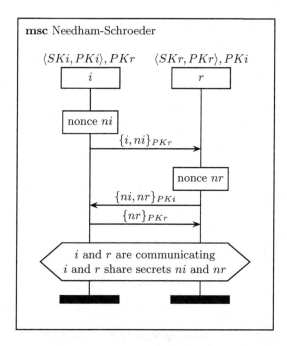

Fig. 1. The Needham-Schroeder public key authentication protocol. (The full notation will be explained in Section 4)

we cannot rely on the MSC semantics to provide an answer. Therefore, we will define a formal semantics of security protocols.

Our first step to come to a formal semantics is to conduct a concise domain analysis (loosely following [4]). The purpose of this step is to informally sketch the issues that make up the problem space and its boundaries. We will identify the points of variation and decide whether these are considered as parameters of the problem or that design decisions have to be made. In this process we are guided by the following starting points. First of all, the formal model must be generic (e.g. over the intruder model). Second, the formal model should offer a framework to verify security protocols, both manually and with computer support. Third, the formal model should be easily extendable with additional features (such as forward secrecy) to make it applicable to a wide range of problems. Finally, the formal model should enable the development of meta-theory (e.g. compositionality properties of security protocols). We have chosen to define an operational semantics based on state transitions.

The rest of this paper is structured as follows. In Section 2 we will conduct a short domain analysis and introduce the basic concepts. Section 3 describes an operational semantics of security protocols, based on the domain analysis. We will validate our semantical approach by formally analysing the Needham-Schroeder protocol in Section 4. In Section 5 we discuss the relation between our approach and other published models and in Section 6 we will summarise our results and provide an outlook on future research.

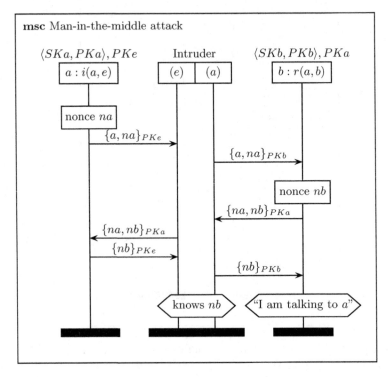

Fig. 2. Man-in-the-middle attack on the Needham-Schroeder protocol

2   Security Protocols: A Domain Analysis

Rather than starting right away with the development of a formal semantics we first conduct a concise domain analysis. The purpose of this analysis is to make some of the design decisions explicit and to decompose the problem into smaller parts.

We start with the following informal description of involved concepts. A security protocol describes a number of behaviours. Each such behaviour we will call a role. We have, for instance, the *initiator* role and the *responder* role in a protocol. A system consists of a number of communicating agents. Each agent performs one or more roles (possibly from several security protocols). A role performed by an agent is called a run. For instance, agent a can perform two initiator runs and one responder run in parallel. The agents execute their runs to achieve some security goal (e.g. the confidential exchange of a message). While agents pursue their goals, an intruder may try to oppose them. The *capabilities* of the intruder determine its strength in attacking a protocol run. However, threats do not only come from the outside. Agents partaking in a protocol run may also conspire with the intruder and try to invalidate the security goals. In order to resist attacks, an agent can make use of *cryptographic primitives* when constructing messages.

Given this global description, we can identify the following components of the security protocol model.

Protocol specification
Protocol specification
Agent model
Communication model
Threat model
Cryptographic primitives
Security requirements

We will discuss each of these sub-models, list their points of variation and make appropriate design decisions. Of course, every subdivision of the problem is artificial, but we found that this approach helped in adding structure and restricting the problem space. The sub models mentioned are not independent entities. For instance, the protocol specification makes use of the provided cryptographic primitives and the communication model is connected to the intruder model if the intruder has complete control over the network.

Protocol Specification. The protocol specification describes the behaviour of each of the roles in the protocol. We consider this as a parameter of our semantics. We define an (abstract) syntax to specify a security protocol. Most often, a role in a security protocol is specified as a sequential list of events. In practise, a security enhanced communication protocol requires a more expressive specification language, but for an abstract description of e.g. an authentication protocol a sequential list will suffice. The set of events usually contains send and read events. Furthermore, we will consider security claims as special events. Timers (and all time related information) are not included in our model. A protocol specification is not complete without a specification of the initial knowledge required to execute a role and the declaration of functions, constants and variables occurring in the protocol specification. The protocol specification is expressed in a formal language for which we will define an abstract syntax and static requirements.

Agent Model. Agents execute the roles of the protocol. The agent model is based on a *closed world assumption.* By this we mean that honest agents show no behaviour other than the behaviour described in the protocol specification. Thus, unless specified explicitly in the protocol, an honest agent will never leak classified information. The closed world assumption does not imply that an agent will only execute one run of the protocol. We assume that an agent may execute any number of runs in parallel (in an interleaved manner). Although restrictions on the number (and type) of runs may be of interest in practical applications, we will not parameterise over this property. The agent model also describes how an agent interprets a role description. An agent executes its role description sequentially, waiting at read events until an expected input message becomes available. This implies that an agent ignores unanticipated messages. More specifically, an incoming message will be matched against the expected message format as described in the protocol specification. Our semantics will be parameterized over this matching function, e.g. to allow for detection of type-flaw attacks.

Communication Model. The communication model describes how the messages between the agents are exchanged. We have chosen the model of asynchronous communication. This model is more general than the synchronous communication model. Thus, if a security protocol is proven correct in the asynchronous model it will also be correct in the synchronous model. Assuming asynchronous communication, the next step is to select the type of buffering. Again, we will choose the most general model: one single multiset buffer for all agents.

Threat Model. In 1983 Dolev and Yao led the basis for a network threat model that is currently the most widely used model [5]. In the Dolev-Yao model the intruder has complete control over the communication network. The intruder can intercept any message and insert any message, as long as he is able to construct its contents from his knowledge. Conspiring agents are modeled by including their initial knowledge in the knowledge of the intruder. Intruder models that are weaker than the Dolev-Yao model are also of interest, for instance when studying protocol stacks or special communication media. Wireless communication, for instance, implies that an intruder has the choice of jamming or eavesdropping, but not both for the same message. Therefore, we will consider the intruder model as a parameter of our semantics.

Cryptographic Primitives. Cryptographic primitives are (idealized) mathematical constructs such as encryption. In our treatment of cryptographic primitives we use the so-called *black box approach*. This means that we do not exactly know which mathematical objects are used to implement such constructs, but that we only know their relevant properties. We will only consider symmetric and asymmetric encryption and discard other primitives, such as signing. The *perfect cryptography assumption* roughly states that nothing can be learned of a plain text from its encrypted version, without knowing the decryption key.

Security Requirements. Security requirements state the purpose of a security protocol. They are mostly expressed as safety properties (i.e. something bad will never happen). In our semantics we will only study secrecy and two forms of authentication. However, the semantics is set up in such a way that other trace-based security properties are evenly expressible.

In the next section, we will make the above models precise.

3   Formal Semantics

In this section we will use the domain analysis as a starting point for the development of an operational semantics. First, in Section 3.1, we define the security protocol level which specifies the roles of a protocol. The cryptographic primitives are also treated here. Next, in Section 3.2, the abstract syntax is provided with a static semantics. The roles only define behaviour schemes, which are instantiated into runs in Section 3.3. This section also contains the agent model by describing the operational rules which define the behaviour of a network of agents. The threat model is described in Sections 3.4 and 3.5. The latter contain some examples of intruder capabilities. Finally, in Section 3.6, we define secrecy and synchronisation, which is a strong authentication property.

3.1   Security Protocol Specification

A protocol specification defines the exchange of message terms between agents. We start by explaining a number of basic elements of these terms, such as constants, roles and variables. Next, we add constructors for pairing and tupling to construct the set *RoleTerm*, that will be used in role descriptions.

Basic Sets. We start off with the following sets: $\mathcal{V}$ (denoting variables), $\mathcal{C}$ (denoting constants which are local to each instantiation of a role), $\mathcal{R}$ (denoting roles), and $\mathcal{F}$ (denoting function names). Functions from the set $\mathcal{F}$ are considered to be global, and have an arity which must be respected in all terms. If global constants occur in a protocol, we model them as functions of arity zero. In Table 1 we show some typical elements of these sets, as used throughout this paper.

Terms. We introduce constructors for pairing and encryption, and we assume that pairing is associative.

$$RoleTerm ::= \mathcal{V} \mid \mathcal{R} \mid \mathcal{F}(RoleTerm^*) \mid \mathcal{C} \mid$$
$$(RoleTerm, RoleTerm) \mid \{RoleTerm\}_{RoleTerm}$$

Table 1. Basic sets and some typical elements

Description	Set	Typical elements
Variables	$\mathcal{V}$	V, W, X, Y, Z
Constants	$\mathcal{C}$	$ni, nr, sessionkey$
Roles	$\mathcal{R}$	i, r, s
Functions	$\mathcal{F}$	$sk, pk, k,$ hash
Trusted agents	$\mathcal{A}_T$	a, b, c
Untrusted agents	$\mathcal{A}_U$	e

Terms that have been encrypted with a term, can only be decrypted by either the same term (for symmetric encryption) or the inverse key (for asymmetric encryption). To determine which term needs to be known to decrypt a term, we introduce a function that yields the inverse for any role term.

$$\_^{-1} : RoleTerm \rightarrow RoleTerm$$

We require that $\_^{-1}$ is its own inverse, i.e. $(t^{-1})^{-1} = t$. Terms are reduced according to $\{\{s\}_t\}_{t^{-1}} = s$.

Throughout this article we will assume that pk and sk are functions of arity 1, that map to asymmetric keys, such that $\forall_{r \in \mathcal{R}} pk(r)^{-1} = sk(r)$ and vice versa. All other terms t are considered to be symmetric keys, for which we have $t^{-1} = t$.

Role Knowledge. Besides terms to be sent and received, a role specification describes the initial knowledge needed to execute the role We define a role knowledge set as $RoleKnow = \mathcal{P}(RoleTerm)$.

Role Specification. We define a role specification as a set of initial knowledge, and a list of events. We define the set of events $\mathcal{E}$ using two new sets: labels $\mathcal{L}$ and security claims *Claim*, which we explain below.

$$\mathcal{E} = \{ send_\ell(r, r', t), read_\ell(r', r, t), claim_\ell(r, c\,[,t]) \mid$$
$$\ell \in \mathcal{L}, r, r' \in \mathcal{R}, t \in RoleTerm, c \in Claim \}$$

Event $send_\ell(r, r', t)$ denotes the sending of message t by r, apparently to r'. Likewise, $read_\ell(r', r, t)$ denotes the reception of message t by r', apparently sent by r. Event $claim_\ell(r, c\,[,t])$ expresses that r upon execution of this event expects security goal c to hold with optional parameter t. A claim event denotes a *local claim*, which means that it only concerns role r and does not express any expectations at other roles.

The labels ℓ extending the events are needed to disambiguate similar occurrences of the same event in a protocol specification. A second use of these labels will be to express the relation between corresponding send and read events, as we will see in Section 3.6.

Now we can specify a role. A role specification consists of a list of events, and some initial knowledge: $RoleSpec = RoleKnow \times \mathcal{E}^*$.

Protocol Specification. A protocol specifies the behaviour for a number of roles by means of a partial function from the set $ProtSpec = \mathcal{R} \to RoleSpec$.

We will use $MR^p(r)$ as a shorthand for the initial knowledge of role r in a protocol specification p. In many cases we omit the parameter p if the intented protocol is clear from the context.

Example. The following role description models the initiator role of the Needham-Schroeder protocol, without any security requirements.

$$ns(i) = (\{i, r, ni, sk(i), pk(i), pk(r)\},$$
$$send_1(i, r, \{i, ni\}_{pk(r)}) \cdot$$
$$read_2(r, i, \{ni, V\}_{pk(i)}) \cdot$$
$$send_3(i, r, \{V\}_{pk(r)}))$$

This role description follows from Figure 1 by selecting the left-most axis and its associated events. Notice that we have to clarify which constructs in the terms are variables (because they receive their value at reception of a message) and which are constants (because they are determined by the role itself). Therefore, we define $i, r \in \mathcal{R}$, $ni \in \mathcal{C}$, $sk, pk \in \mathcal{F}$, $pk(i)^{-1} = sk(i)$, $pk(r)^{-1} = sk(r)$, $1, 2, 3 \in \mathcal{L}$, and $V \in \mathcal{V}$.

3.2   Static Requirements

In the previous section we have explained the context-free abstract syntax for a protocol specification. A proper protocol specification will also have to satisfy a number of well-formedness rules.

Well-Formed Roles. For each role, we require that it meets certain criteria. These range from the fairly obvious, e.g. each event in a role definition has the same actor, to more subtle requirements regarding the messages. For the messages we require that the messages that are sent can actually be constructed by the sender. This is satisfied if the message is in the knowledge of the sending role. For variables we require that they first occur in a read event, where they are instantiated, before they can occur in a send event.

For read events the situation is a bit more complex. As can be seen in the example above, which describes the initiator role of the Needham-Schroeder protocol, a read event may impose some structure upon the incoming messages. A receiver can only match a message against such an expected pattern if his knowledge satisfies certain requirements.

We introduce a predicate *WF* (Well Formed) to express that a role definition meets these consistency requirements, using an auxiliary predicate *Readable* and a knowledge inference operator $\_ \vdash \_ : RoleKnow \times RoleTerm$.

Agents can compose and decompose pair terms. A term can be encrypted if the agent knows the encryption key, and an encrypted term can be decrypted if the agent knows the corresponding decryption key. This is expressed by the knowledge inference operator, which is defined inductively as follows.

$$t \in M \implies M \vdash t$$
$$M \vdash t_1 \land M \vdash t_2 \iff M \vdash (t_1, t_2)$$
$$M \vdash t \land M \vdash k \implies M \vdash \{t\}_k$$
$$M \vdash \{t\}_k \land M \vdash k^{-1} \implies M \vdash t$$

Composing terms t_1, t_2 into a term t by encryption or tupling implies that t has t, t_1 and t_2 as subterms. The subterm operator $\sqsubseteq$ is inductively defined as follows.

$$t \sqsubseteq t \qquad t_1 \sqsubseteq (t_1, t_2) \qquad t_1, \ldots, t_n \sqsubseteq f(t_1, \ldots, t_n)$$
$$t \sqsubseteq \{t\}_k \qquad t_2 \sqsubseteq (t_1, t_2)$$

The predicate *Readable* : $RoleKnow \times RoleTerm$ expresses which role terms can be used as a message pattern for a read event of an agent with a specific knowledge set. A variable can always occur in a read pattern. Any other term can only occur in a read pattern, if it can be inferred from the knowledge of the agent. Only then can it be compared to the incoming messages.

In order to be able to read a pair, we must be able to read each constituent, while extending the knowledge with what can be inferred from the other component. An encrypted message can be read if it can be inferred from the knowledge or if it can be inferred after decryption, which requires that the decryption key is in the knowledge.

$Readable(M, t) =$

$$
\begin{cases}
\text{True} & \text{if } t \in \mathcal{V} \\
M \vdash t & \text{if } t \in \mathcal{C} \cup \mathcal{R} \cup \mathcal{F}(RoleTerm^*) \\
Readable(M \cup \{t_2\}, t_1) \wedge Readable(M \cup \{t_1\}, t_2) & \text{if } t \equiv (t_1, t_2) \\
(M \vdash \{t_1\}_{t_2}) \vee (M \vdash t_2^{-1} \wedge Readable(M, t_1)) & \text{if } t \equiv \{t_1\}_{t_2}
\end{cases}
$$

We can now construct the predicate $WF : \mathcal{R} \times RoleSpec$, that expresses that a role is well formed. The first argument of this predicate is used to express that the active role in an event should match the role which behaviour is being defined. Terms occurring in a send or claim event must be inferable from the knowledge, while terms occurring in a read event must be readable according to the definition above.

$WF(r, (M, s)) =$

$$
\begin{cases}
\text{True} & \text{if } s \equiv \varepsilon \\
M \vdash (r', r) \wedge Readable(M, t) \wedge WF(r, (M \cup \{t\}, s')) & \text{if } s \equiv read_\ell(r', r, t) \cdot s' \\
M \vdash (r, r', t) \wedge WF(r, (M, s')) & \text{if } s \equiv send_\ell(r, r', t) \cdot s' \\
M \vdash (r\,[, t]) \wedge WF(r, (M, s')) & \text{if } s \equiv claim_\ell(r, c\,[, t]) \cdot s' \\
\text{False} & \text{otherwise}
\end{cases}
$$

For a protocol specification p we require that all roles are well formed with respect to their initial knowledge, which is expressed by: $\forall_{r \in dom(p)} WF(r, p(r))$.

Examples. The next two examples are incorrect role descriptions:

$wrong1(i) = (\{i, r, k\},$
$\qquad send_1(i, r, \{i, r, V\}_k)\cdot$
$\qquad read_2(r, i, \{V, r\}_k) \,)$

$wrong2(i) = (\{i, r, k\},$
$\qquad read_1(r, i, \{i, r, \{V\}_{k2}\}_k)\cdot$
$\qquad send_2(i, r, \{V\}_{k2}) \,)$

Role description *wrong1* is not well formed because it sends variable V before it is read. The read event in *wrong2* contains a subterm $\{V\}_{k2}$. The intention is that V is initialised through this read. However, since $k2$ is a symmetric key, and $k2$ is not in the knowledge of the role, the value of V cannot be determined through this read. Therefore, this role description is not well formed. The correct role description would be the following:

$wrong2corrected(i) = (\{i, r, k\},$
$\qquad read_1(r, i, \{i, r, W\}_k)\cdot$
$\qquad send_2(i, r, W) \,)$

3.3   Runs

The protocol specification describes a set of roles. These roles serve as a blueprint for what the actual agents in a system should do. A run is defined as an instantiated role. In order to instantiate a role we have to bind the role names to the names of actual agents and we have to make the local constants unique for each instantiation. Furthermore, we have to take into account that the bindings of values to the variables are local to a run too. Thus, the set of terms occurring in a run differs from the set of terms used in role descriptions.

Run Terms. We assume existence of a set *Runid* to denote run identifiers and a set $\mathcal{A}$ to denote agents. The set $\mathcal{A}$ is partitioned into sets $\mathcal{A}_T$ (denoting the *trusted agents*) and $\mathcal{A}_U$ (denoting the *untrusted agents*). Run terms are defined similarly to role terms. The difference is that abstract roles are replaced by concrete agents, that local constants are made unique by extending them with a run identifier, and that variables are instantiated by concrete values. The run term set also includes the set $\mathcal{C}^I$ of terms constructed by an intruder. This set will only be used from Section 3.4 onwards, and it will be explained there. As for role terms, we have associativity of pairing.

$$RunTerm ::= \mathcal{A} \mid \mathcal{F}(RunTerm^*) \mid \mathcal{C}\sharp Runid \mid \mathcal{C}^I \mid$$
$$(RunTerm, RunTerm) \mid \{RunTerm\}_{RunTerm}$$

Instantiation. A role term is transformed into a run term by applying an instantiation.

$$Inst = Runid \times (\mathcal{R} \to \mathcal{A}) \times (\mathcal{V} \to RunTerm)$$

The first component of an instantiation determines with which run identifier the constants are extended. The second component determines the instantiation of roles by agents. The third determines the valuation of the variables.

We extend the inverse function to *RunTerm*. The functions $roles : RoleTerm \to \mathcal{P}(\mathcal{R})$ and $vars : RoleTerm \to \mathcal{P}(\mathcal{V})$ determine the roles and variables occurring in a term. We extend these functions to the domain of *RoleSpec* in the obvious way.

For instantiation $(rid, \rho, \sigma) \in Inst$, $f \in \mathcal{F}$ and terms $t, t_1, \ldots, t_n \in RoleTerm$ such that $roles(t) \subseteq dom(\rho)$ and $vars(t) \subseteq dom(\sigma)$, we define instantiation by:

$$(rid, \rho, \sigma)(t) = \begin{cases} \rho(r) & \text{if } t \equiv r \in \mathcal{R} \\ f((rid, \rho, \sigma)(t_1), \ldots, (rid, \rho, \sigma)(t_n)) & \text{if } t \equiv f(t_1, \ldots, t_n) \\ c\sharp rid & \text{if } t \equiv c \in \mathcal{C} \\ \sigma(v) & \text{if } t \equiv v \in \mathcal{V} \\ ((rid, \rho, \sigma)(t_1), (rid, \rho, \sigma)(t_2)) & \text{if } t \equiv (t_1, t_2) \\ \{(rid, \rho, \sigma)(t_1)\}_{(rid, \rho, \sigma)(t_2)} & \text{if } t \equiv \{t_1\}_{t_2} \end{cases}$$

Example. We give two examples of instantiations that might occur in the execution of a protocol:

$$\left(1, \{i \mapsto a, r \mapsto b\}, \emptyset\right) \left(\{i, ni\}_{pk(r)}\right) = \{a, ni\sharp 1\}_{pk(b)}$$
$$\left(2, \{i \mapsto c, r \mapsto d\}, \{W \mapsto ni\sharp 1\}\right) \left(\{W, nr, r\}_{pk(i)}\right) = \{ni\sharp 1, nr\sharp 2, d\}_{pk(c)}$$

Runs. A run is an instantiated role specification. As the knowledge of a role is already statically defined by the role description, we can omit it from the run specification and define $Run = Inst \times \mathcal{E}^*$. As we will see later on, each run in the system will have a unique run identifier by construction.

State. The system that we consider consists of a number of runs executed by some agents. Communication between the runs is asynchronous (buffered). In order to conveniently model the intruder behaviour, we will route communication through two buffers: one output buffer from the sending run and one input buffer from the receiving run (for a discussion on the expressive power of such construction, see [6]). The intruder capabilities will determine how the messages are transferred from the output buffer to the input buffer.

Both the output buffer and the input buffer store sent messages. Messages contain a sender, a recipient, and a run term: $MSG = \mathcal{A} \times \mathcal{A} \times RunTerm$. Notice that, if we identify set product with pairing, we obtain $MSG \subset RunTerm$. A buffer is a multiset of such messages: $Buffer = \mathcal{M}(MSG)$.

Since the knowledge of the intruder is dynamic, we will consider this a component in the state of the system, too. It consists of instantiated terms as they occur in the runs, and is represented by $RunKnow = \mathcal{P}(RunTerm)$.

The state of a network of agents executing roles in a security protocol is defined by

$$State = RunKnow \times Buffer \times Buffer \times \mathcal{P}(Run),$$

and thus contains the intruder knowledge, the contents of the output buffer, the contents of the input buffer, and the (remainders of the) runs that still have to be executed.

Match. Messages from the buffer are accepted by agents if they match a certain pattern, specified in the read event. We introduce a predicate *Match* that expresses that a message matches the pattern for some instantiation of the variables. The definition of this predicate is a parameter of our system, but we will give an example of a straightforward typed match.

For each variable, we define a set of run terms which are allowed values. We introduce an auxiliary function $type : \mathcal{V} \to \mathcal{P}(RunTerm)$, that defines the set of run terms that are valid values for a variable. Then we define the predicate *Welltyped* on $(\mathcal{V} \to \mathcal{P}(RunTerm))$, that expresses that a substitution is well-typed: $Welltyped(\sigma) = \forall_{v \in dom(\sigma)} (\sigma(v) \in type(v))$.

Using this predicate, we define the typed matching predicate $Match : Inst \times RoleTerm \times RunTerm \times Inst$. The purpose of this predicate is to match an incoming message (the third argument) to a pattern specified by a role term (the second argument). This pattern is already instantiated (the first argument), but may still contain free variables. The idea is to assign values to the free variables such that the incoming message equals the instantiated role term. The old instantiation extended with these new assignments provides the resulting instantiation (the fourth argument).

$$Match(inst, pt, m, inst') \iff inst = (rid, \rho, \sigma) \land inst' = (rid, \rho, \sigma') \land$$
$$\sigma \subseteq \sigma' \land dom(\sigma') = dom(\sigma) \cup vars(pt) \land$$
$$Welltyped(\sigma') \land (rid, \rho, \sigma')(pt) = m$$

Assume $\rho = \{i \mapsto a, r \mapsto b\}$. Then, some examples for which the predicate is true are:

inst	pt	m	inst'		
$Match(\ (1,\rho,\emptyset),$	$X,$	$nr\sharp 2,$	$(1, \rho, \{X \mapsto nr\sharp 2\})\ )$	$\iff$	$True$
$Match(\ (1,\rho,\emptyset),$	$\{r, ni\}_{pk(i)},$	$\{b, ni\sharp 1\}_{pk(a)},$	$(1, \rho, \emptyset)$ $)$	$\iff$	$True$

Some examples where the predicate does not hold, if we assume matching is typed, and the type of X is the set $\mathcal{A} \cup \mathcal{C} \sharp Runid \cup \mathcal{C}^I$

inst	pt	m	inst'		
$Match(\ (1, \rho, \emptyset),$	$nr,$	$nr\sharp 2,$	$-\ )$	$\iff$	$False$
$Match(\ (1, \rho, \emptyset),$	$X,$	$(nr\sharp 2, ni\sharp 1),$	$-\ )$	$\iff$	$False$
$Match(\ (1, \rho, \emptyset),$	$\{i, ni\}_{pk(i)},$	$\{b, ni\sharp 1\}_{pk(a)},$	$-\ )$	$\iff$	$False$

· By varying over the function *type* we can express whether the protocol is vulnerable to type flaw attacks or not. This also allows for expressing that only basic type flaws can be detected by the agents.

Derivation Rules. The behaviour of the system is defined as a transition relation (see [7]) between system states. A transition is labeled with an element of the set *Transitionlabel* ::= $(Inst, \mathcal{E})$ | $create(Run)$ | $Networkrules(MSG)$. The set of network/intruder rules *Networkrules* is a parameter of the system, and we will discuss some of the possibilities in Section 3.5.

A protocol description allows for the creation of runs. The runs that can be created are defined by the function $runsof : ProtSpec \to \mathcal{P}(Run)$:

$$runsof(p) =$$
$$\left\{ ((rid, \rho, \emptyset), p(r)) \ \middle|\ r \in dom(p) \land rid \in Runid \land \rho \in roles(p(r)) \times \mathcal{A} \right\}$$

For $F \in \mathcal{P}(Run)$ we use $F[r'/r]$ to denote the substitution of r by r' in F. We define the set of active run identifiers as

$$runids(F) = \left\{ rid \ \middle|\ ((rid, \rho, \sigma), ev) \in F \right\}$$

Let $p \in ProtSpec$. Then the basic derivation rules for the system are given in Table 2. The *create* rule expresses that a new run can only be created if its run identifier has not been used yet. The *send* rule states that if a run executes a send event, the sent message is added to the output buffer and the executing run proceeds to the next event. The *read* rule determines when an input event can be executed. It requires that the (partially) instantiated pattern specified in the read event should match any of the messages from the input buffer. Upon

Table 2. SOS rules

$$[create] \frac{run = ((rid, \rho, \sigma), s) \in runsof(p), rid \notin runids(F)}{\langle M, BS, BR, F \rangle \xrightarrow{create(run)} \langle M, BS, BR, F \cup \{run\}\rangle}$$

$$[send] \frac{run = (inst, send_\ell(m) \cdot s) \in F}{\langle M, BS, BR, F \rangle \xrightarrow{(inst, send_\ell(m))} \langle M, BS \cup \{inst(m)\}, BR, F[(inst, s)/run]\rangle}$$

$$[read] \frac{run = (inst, read_\ell(pt) \cdot s) \in F, m \in BR, Match(inst, pt, m, inst')}{\langle M, BS, BR, F \rangle \xrightarrow{(inst', read_\ell(pt))} \langle M, BS, BR \setminus \{m\}, F[(inst', s)/run]\rangle}$$

$$[claim] \frac{run = (inst, claim_\ell(r, c\,[,t]) \cdot s) \in F}{\langle M, BS, BR, F \rangle \xrightarrow{(inst, claim_\ell(r, c\,[,t]))} \langle M, BS, BR, F[(inst, s)/run]\rangle}$$

---

execution of the read event, this message is removed from the input buffer and the executing run advances to the next event. The *claim* rule expresses that an enabled claim event can always be executed. Notice that in all these cases the intruder knowledge is not affected. The dynamical behaviour of the intruder knowledge will be defined by the network/intruder rules in Section 3.5.

A state transition is the conclusion of finitely many applications of these rules. In this way, starting from the initial state, we can derive all possible behaviours of a system executing security protocol p. This is what we consider the operational semantics of p.

Initial State. In the initial state of the system both buffers are empty, and no runs have been created yet. Thus the initial state of the system is given by

$$s_0 = \langle M_0, \emptyset, \emptyset, \emptyset \rangle$$

where M_0 refers to the intruder knowledge, which we define in the next section.

3.4   Initial Intruder Knowledge

We assume the intruder can create a possibly infinite number of constants, defined as the set $\mathcal{C}^I$. The initial knowledge of the intruder includes this set. We model untrusted agents by including their initial knowledge in the initial intruder knowledge.

We could choose to define the initial knowledge of the intruder as the static knowledge of all the roles, for all untrusted agents. However, for some protocols we require that the untrusted agents cannot play certain roles. It is e.g. undesirable that an untrusted agent plays the role of the certificate server that knows the secret keys of all the agents. We define these roles as the set of trusted roles $\mathcal{R}_T$. All other roles are called the untrusted roles $\mathcal{R}_U$. Unless stated otherwise, we assume $\mathcal{R}_T = \emptyset$, and thus $\mathcal{R}_U = \mathcal{R}$.

The intruder learns all initial knowledge of a role before it is instantiated in a specific run. Thus, This excludes any local constants, as well variable names (because they are not instantiated yet). The initial intruder knowledge will consist of e.g. the names and public keys of all agents, and the secret keys of the intruder. The following table shows some examples for the knowledge of a role $i \in \mathcal{R}$.

$$\{i\} \subseteq MR(i) \Rightarrow \mathcal{A}_U \subseteq M_0$$
$$\{r\} \subseteq MR(i) \Rightarrow \mathcal{A} \subseteq M_0$$
$$\{pk(r), sk(i)\} \subseteq MR(i) \Rightarrow \{pk(a), sk(e) \mid a \in \mathcal{A} \wedge e \in \mathcal{A}_U\} \subseteq M_0$$

If the i role knowledge contains e.g. $sk(i), pk(r)$, we see that the intruder knowledge contains $sk(e)$ for each untrusted agent e acting in this role. Untrusted agents are however able to communicate with trusted agents, and thus $pk(a)$ is in the initial intruder knowledge for each agent a.

To instantiate the role knowledge, we only need to know how the role names are mapped to agent names: information about a run or instantiation of the variables is not needed. For a protocol p, an untrusted agent e in an untrusted role r, the knowledge that is passed to the intruder is defined as

$$\bigcup_{\substack{\rho \in \mathcal{R} \to \mathcal{A} \\ \rho(r)=e}} \{(\_, \rho, \_)t \mid t \in MR(r) \wedge \forall_{t' \sqsubseteq t}(t' \notin \mathcal{V} \cup \mathcal{C})\}$$

For a protocol p, we define the initial intruder knowledge as the union of this knowledge of all untrusted agents and roles:

$$M_0 = \mathcal{C}^I \cup \bigcup_{\substack{\rho \in \mathcal{R} \to \mathcal{A} \\ r \in \mathcal{R}_U \\ \rho(r) \in \mathcal{A}_U}} \{(\_, \rho, \_)t \mid t \in MR(r) \wedge \forall_{t' \sqsubseteq t}(t' \notin \mathcal{V} \cup \mathcal{C})\}$$

For example, for the Needham-Schroeder protocol, the initial intruder knowledge would simply consist of the set $\mathcal{C}^I$, the names and public keys of all agents, and the secret keys of the untrusted agents.

3.5   Network/Intruder Rules

In the context of security protocol verification the Dolev-Yao intruder model is commonplace. In this model, the intruder has complete control over the network. Messages can be learnt, deflected, and created by such an intruder. However, often this intruder model is too powerful, for example when an intruder can

Table 3. Network/intruder rules

$$[transmit] \frac{m \in BS}{\langle M, BS, BR, F \rangle \xrightarrow{transmit(m)} \langle M, BS \setminus \{m\}, BR \cup \{m\}, F \rangle}$$

$$[deflect] \frac{m \in BS}{\langle M, BS, BR, F \rangle \xrightarrow{deflect(m)} \langle M \cup \{m\}, BS \setminus \{m\}, BR, F \rangle}$$

$$[inject] \frac{M \vdash m}{\langle M, BS, BR, F \rangle \xrightarrow{inject(m)} \langle M, BS, BR \cup \{m\}, F \rangle}$$

$$[eavesdrop] \frac{m \in BS}{\langle M, BS, BR, F \rangle \xrightarrow{eavesdrop(m)} \langle M \cup \{m\}, BS \setminus \{m\}, BR \cup \{m\}, F \rangle}$$

$$[jam] \frac{m \in BS}{\langle M, BS, BR, F \rangle \xrightarrow{jam(m)} \langle M, BS \setminus \{m\}, BR, F \rangle}$$

---

only eavesdrop on the network, or in wireless communications. In such cases, it might be desirable to develop more lightweight protocols that are correct for this weaker intruder model. Therefore, we parameterise over the intruder model, which is defined as a set of capabilities. Each intruder rule defines a capability by explaining the effect of the intruder action on the output buffer, the input buffer and the intruder knowledge. In Table 3 we give some examples of intruder rules. The *transmit* rule describes transmission of a message from the output buffer to the input buffer without interference from the intruder. If the intruder has eavesdropping capabilities, as stated in the *eavesdrop* rule he can learn the message during transmission. The *deflect* rule states that an intruder with deflection capabilities can delete any message from the output buffer. The difference witht the *jam* rule is that the intruder can read the deflected message and add it to its knowledge. The *inject* rule describes the injection of any message inferable from the intruder knowledge into the input buffer.

Next, we define some interesting intruders. In a network without an intruder we only have the *transmit* rule, so *NoIntruder* = {*transmit*}. In the Dolev-Yao model the intruder has full control over the network. Every message is read and analysed, and anything that can be constructed can be inserted into the network, so *DolevYao* = {*deflect, inject*}. A wireless communication network is weaker than Dolev-Yao, because it does not allow learning from a message and blocking it at the same time. Thus we define *Wireless* = {*eavesdrop, jam, inject*}. If the intruder can only eavesdrop, we have *ReadOnly* = {*eavesdrop*}.

It is possible to construct more intruder rules, for intruder capabilities such as rerouting of messages or the modification of messages.

3.6   Security Properties

Traces. We will discuss some trace based security properties, therefore, we define the traces generated by the above derivation rules. For $\alpha = \alpha_0 \ldots \alpha_{n-1} \in$ *Transitionlabel** we use $s_0 \xrightarrow{\alpha} s_n$ to denote $\exists_{s_1,\ldots s_{n-1}} s_0 \xrightarrow{\alpha_0} s_1 \ldots s_{n-1} \xrightarrow{\alpha_{n-1}} s_n$. We use $s \xrightarrow{\alpha}$ to denote $\exists_{s'} s \xrightarrow{\alpha} s'$. The length of a sequence of labels α is denoted by $|\alpha|$.

The set of traces $Tr : ProtSpec \to \mathcal{P}(Transitionlabel^*)$ is defined as $\{a \in Transitionlabel^* \mid s_0 \xrightarrow{a}\}$, where s_0 is the initial state of the protocol. For trace α, we use α_i to denote the ith action label from α.

We reconstruct state information from a trace as follows. If α_i is an action from trace α, then M_i^{α} (or simply M_i) is the intruder knowledge right before the execution of α_i.

Secrecy. For $t \in RoleTerm$, we introduce the claim $claim_\ell(r, secret, t)$.

A protocol p is correct with respect to secrecy if the following holds for all traces $\alpha \in Tr(p)$ and $i \in N$.

$$\alpha_i = ((rid, \rho, \sigma), claim_\ell(r, secret, t)) \wedge rng(\rho) \subseteq \mathcal{A}_T \Rightarrow$$
$$\forall_{i \leq j \leq |\alpha|}(rid, \rho, \sigma)(t) \notin M_j^{\alpha}$$

Synchronisation. We define a strong authentication requirement called synchronisation. A thorough description of this form of authentication can be found in [8]. A synchronisation claim boils down to the requirement that the corresponding sends and reads of two communicating runs exactly match each other. This property resembles the notion of intensional specifications [9] and is stronger than the well-known agreement property, which can also be described in our framework.

Synchronisation is defined with help of some auxiliary functions and predicates. The first predicate expresses that for label ℓ two runs agree on the occurrences of the $send_\ell$ event and the $read_\ell$ event. We use the function $sendrole(\ell)$ to denote the role in which the event $send_\ell$ occurs. The function $readrole(\ell)$ is defined likewise.

We define the projection function $runidof : Inst \to Runid$ by $runidof(rid, \rho, \sigma) = rid$. For all traces α, $k \in N$, labels ℓ and run identifiers rid_1, rid_2, the single-label synchronisation predicate *1L-SYNCH* is given by

$$1L\text{-}SYNCH(\alpha, k, \ell, rid_1, rid_2) \iff$$
$$\exists_{i,j \in N, inst_1, inst_2 \in Inst, m_1, m_2 \in MSG}$$
$$i < j < k \wedge$$
$$\alpha_i = (inst_1, send_\ell(m_1)) \wedge runidof(inst_1) = rid_1 \wedge$$
$$\alpha_j = (inst_2, read_\ell(m_2)) \wedge runidof(inst_2) = rid_2 \wedge$$
$$inst_1(m_1) = inst_2(m_2)$$

This predicate is generalised to sets of labels in the following way. For all traces α, $k \in N$, label set L, and $cast : \mathcal{R} \rightarrow Runid$, the multi-label synchronisation predicate $ML\text{-}SYNCH$ is given by

$$ML\text{-}SYNCH(\alpha, k, L, cast) \iff$$
$$\forall_{\ell \in L} \; 1L\text{-}SYNCH(\alpha, k, \ell, cast(sendrole(\ell)), cast(readrole(\ell)))$$

If $ML\text{-}SYNCH(\alpha, k, L, cast)$ holds, we say that the set of labels L has correctly occurred in a trace α before position k with respect to the instantiation $cast$.

In order to determine the relevant set of labels which should be checked if a synchronisation claim occurs, we define the set $prec(p, cl)$. This set contains the causally preceding communications of a claim role event labeled with cl, for a security protocol p and is given by

$$prec(p, cl) = \{\ell \mid read_\ell(\_, \_, \_) \prec claim_{cl}(\_, \_)\}$$

We introduce the claim $nisynch \in Claim$. A protocol p is correct with respect to $NI\text{-}SYNCH$ if the following holds for all traces $\alpha \in Tr(p)$.

$$\alpha_i = (rid, \rho, \sigma, claim_\ell(r, nisynch)) \wedge rng(\rho) \subseteq \mathcal{A}_T$$
$$\Rightarrow \exists_{cast:\mathcal{R} \rightarrow Runid} \; (cast(r) = rid \wedge ML\text{-}SYNCH(\alpha, i, prec(p, \ell), cast))$$

4   The Needham-Schroeder(-Lowe) Protocol

In this section we will take a closer look at the Needham-Schroeder protocol from Figure 1 and illustrate our definitions. The protocol goal is to ensure mutual authentication and as a side effect secrecy of the involved nonces. Starting point of the protocol is a public key infrastructure. This is depicted by the initial knowledge above each of the roles in the protocol. The initiator starts the protocol by sending an encrypted initialisation request to the responder. The nonce is used to prevent play-back attacks. Only the responder is able to unpack this message and replies by sending the initiator's nonce together with his own fresh nonce. Then the initiator proves his identity by replying the responder's nonce.

The man-in-the-middle attack in Figure 2 only requires two runs. One of trusted agent a performing the initiator role in a session with untrusted agent m and one of trusted agent b performing the responder role in a session with agent a. The intruder impersonates both m and a and in this way uses a as an oracle to unpack message from b. At the end he has fooled b into thinking that he is talking to a, while he is talking to the intruder.

Knowing this attack, it is straightforward to reconstruct it formally with our semantics. Our experience shows that when trying to prove a flawed protocol correct, the way in which the proof fails often indicates the attack. Rather than showing the details here, we will prove correctness of the fixed Needham-Schroeder protocol, which is called the Needham-Schroeder-Lowe protocol. The protocol is hardened by extending message 2 with the responder name. It is specified as follows.

$$nsl(i) = (\{i, r, ni, pk(r), pk(i), sk(i)\}, \qquad nsl(r) = (\{i, r, nr, pk(i), pk(r), sk(r)\},$$

$$\begin{aligned}
&send_1(i, r, \{i, ni\}_{pk(r)}) \cdot && read_1(i, r, \{i, W\}_{pk(r)}) \cdot \\
&read_2(r, i, \{ni, V, r\}_{pk(i)}) \cdot && send_2(r, i, \{W, nr, r\}_{pk(i)}) \cdot \\
&send_3(i, r, \{V\}_{pk(r)})) \cdot && read_3(i, r, \{nr\}_{pk(r)})) \cdot \\
&claim_4(i, secret, ni) \cdot && claim_7(r, secret, nr) \cdot \\
&claim_5(i, secret, V) \cdot && claim_8(r, secret, W) \cdot \\
&claim_6(i, nisynch)) && claim_9(r, nisynch))
\end{aligned}$$

We assume that there are no trusted roles. For this protocol, the initial intruder knowledge (cf. Section 3.4) is given by

$$M_0 = \mathcal{C}^I \cup \bigcup_{a \in \mathcal{A}} \{a, pk(a)\} \cup \bigcup_{e \in \mathcal{A}_U} \{sk(e)\}$$

First we introduce some notation and present results which support verification. We define $msgs(p)$ as the set of all role messages sent in the protocol. The first lemma helps to infer that secret information which is never transmitted, remains secret forever.

Lemma 1. *Let p be a protocol, i an instantiation and t a basic term. If t is not a subterm of any message that is ever sent, and $i(t)$ is not a subterm of the initial intruder knowledge, then $i(t)$ will never be known by the intruder. Formally:*

$$\forall_{t' \in msgs(p)} t \not\sqsubseteq t' \;\wedge\; \forall_{m:M_0 \vdash m} i(t) \not\sqsubseteq m \;\Rightarrow\; \forall_{\alpha \in Tr(p), 0 \leq j \leq |\alpha|} M_j^\alpha \not\vdash i(t)$$

The correctness of this lemma follows from the SOS-rules.

The next lemma expresses that roles are executed from the beginning to the end. The predicate $e \prec_r e'$ means that event e precedes event e' in the specification of role r.

Lemma 2. *Let α be a trace of a protocol, let (rid, ρ, σ) be an instantiation and e', e events, such that $e' \prec_r e$ for some role r. If for some i $(0 \leq i < | \alpha |)$ $\alpha_i = (rid, \rho, \sigma, e)$ then there exists j $(0 \leq j < i)$ and $\sigma' \subseteq \sigma$ such that $\alpha_j = (rid, \rho, \sigma', e')$.*

The correctness of this lemma follows from Table 2 by observing that every run is "pealed off" from the beginning, while taking into account that the *Match* predicate is defined such that it only extends the valuation of the variables.

The next lemma is used to infer from an encrypted message reception that the message must have been sent by an agent if it contains a component which is not known to the intruder. In most applications of this lemma we can infer l' by inspection of the role specification and we have $(rid, \rho, \sigma)(\{m\}_k) = (rid', \rho', \sigma')(m')$, rather than a subterm relation.

Lemma 3. *Let α be a trace and let i be an index of α. If $\alpha_i = ((rid, \rho, \sigma), read_\ell(x, y, \{m\}_k))$ and $M_0 \not\vdash (rid, \rho, \sigma)(\{m\}_k)$, and $M_i^\alpha \not\vdash (rid, \rho, \sigma)(m)$, then there exists index $j < i$ such that $\alpha_j = (rid', \rho', \sigma', send_{\ell'}(x', y', m'))$ and $(rid, \rho, \sigma)(\{m\}_k) \sqsubseteq (rid', \rho', \sigma')(m')$.*

The correctness of this lemma follows from the fact that if the intruder does not know m when the message containing $\{m\}_k$ is read, he could not have constructed the encryption. Thus, it must have been sent as a subterm earlier.

The final lemma is characteristic for our model. It expresses that when two instantiations of a constant (such as a nonce or session key) are equal, they were created in the same run.

Lemma 4. *Let (rid, ρ, σ) and (rid', ρ', σ') be instantiations, and let $n \in \mathcal{C}$. If $(rid, \rho, \sigma)(n) = (rid', \rho', \sigma')(n)$ we have $rid = rid'$.*

Theorem 1. *The Needham-Schroeder-Lowe protocol is correct in the Dolev-Yao intruder model with conspiring agents and without type flaws.*

Proof. We will sketch the proofs for $claim_7$ and $claim_9$. The other claims are proven analogously.

First observe that the intruder will never learn secret keys of trusted agents. This follows directly from Lemma 1, since none of the messages contain an encryption key in the message text. Since the set of keys known to the intruder is constant, it must be the case that if the intruder learns a basic term he learns it from unpacking an intercepted message which was encrypted with the key of an untrusted agent.

Proof Outline. We construct proofs for the Needham-Schroeder-Lowe protocol. The proof construction would fail for the Needham-Schroeder protocol, and we will use a marker † to indicate where the difference occurs. After the proof of $claim_7$, we briefly discuss this difference.

Both proofs will roughly follow the same structure. We examine the occurrence of a claim event in a trace of the system. Based on the rules of the semantics, we gradually derive more information about the trace, until we can conclude that the required property holds.

Proof of $claim_7$. In order to prove $claim_7$ we assume that α is a trace with index $r7$, such that $\alpha_{r7} = ((rid_{r7}, \rho_{r7}, \sigma_{r7}), claim_7(r, secret, nr))$ and $rng(\rho_{r7}) \subseteq \mathcal{A}_T$. Now we assume that the intruder learns nr and we will derive a contradiction. Let k be the smallest index such that $(rid_{r7}, \rho_{r7}, \sigma_{r7})(nr) \in M_{k+1}$, and thus $(rid_{r7}, \rho_{r7}, \sigma_{r7})(nr) \notin M_k$. Inspection of the derivation rules learns that this increase in knowledge is due to an application of the send rule, followed by an application of the deflect rule. Therefore, there must be a smallest index $p < k$ such that $\alpha_p = ((rid', \rho', \sigma'), send_\ell(m))$ and $(rid_{r7}, \rho_{r7}, \sigma_{r7})(nr) \sqsubseteq (rid', \rho', \sigma')(m)$. Since we have three possible send events in the NSL protocol, we have three cases: $\ell = 1, 2$, or 3.

$[\ell = 1]$ In the first case we have $\alpha_p = ((rid', \rho', \sigma'), send_1(i, r, \{i, ni\}_{pk(r)}))$. Since constants i and ni both differ from nr, the intruder cannot learn $(rid_{r7}, \rho_{r7}, \sigma_{r7})(nr)$ from $(rid', \rho', \sigma')(i, r, \{i, ni\}_{pk(r)})$, which yields a contradiction.

$[\ell = 2]$ In the second case $\alpha_p = ((rid', \rho', \sigma'), send_2(r, i, \{W, nr, r\}_{pk(i)}))$. The intruder can learn nr because $\rho'(i)$ is an untrusted agent and either

$(rid_{r7}, \rho_{r7}, \sigma_{r7})(nr) = (rid', \rho', \sigma')(W)$ or $(rid_{r7}, \rho_{r7}, \sigma_{r7})(nr) = (rid', \rho', \sigma')(nr)$. We discuss both options separately.

(i) For the former equality we derive that $(rid', \rho', \sigma')(W) \notin M_p$, so we can apply Lemmas 2 and 3 to find $i1$ with $\alpha_{i1} = ((rid_{i1}, \rho_{i1}, \sigma_{i1}), send_1(i, r, \{i, ni\}_{pk(r)}))$. This gives $(rid_{i1}, \rho_{i1}, \sigma_{i1})(ni) = (rid', \rho', \sigma')(W) = (rid_{r7}, \rho_{r7}, \sigma_{r7})(nr)$, which cannot be the case since ni and nr are distinct constants.

(ii) That the latter equality yields a contradiction is easy to show. Using Lemma 4 we derive $rid_{r7} = rid'$ and since run identifiers are unique, we have $\rho_{r7} = \rho'$. So $\rho_{r7}(i) = \rho'(i)$, which contradicts the assumption that $\rho_{r7}(i)$ is a trusted agent.

$[\ell = 3]$ In the third case we have $\alpha_p = ((rid', \rho', \sigma'), send_3(i, r, \{V\}_{pk(r)}))$. In order to learn $(rid_{r7}, \rho_{r7}, \sigma_{r7})(nr)$ from $(rid', \rho', \sigma')(i, r, \{V\}_{pk(r)})$ we must have that
$(rid', \rho', \sigma')(V) = (rid_{r7}, \rho_{r7}, \sigma_{r7})(nr)$ and that $\rho'(r)$ is an untrusted agent. Using Lemma 2 we find index $i2$ such that $\alpha_{i2} = ((rid', \rho', \sigma'), read_2(r, i, \{ni, V, r\}_{pk(i)}))$. Because $(rid', \rho', \sigma')(V) \notin M_p$ we can apply Lemma 3 to find index $r2$ with $\alpha_{r2} = ((rid_{r2}, \rho_{r2}, \sigma_{r2}), send_2(r, i, \{W, nr, r\}_{pk(i)}))$.
This gives $\rho'(r) = \rho_{r2}(r)$. (†)

Next, we derive $(rid_{r2}, \rho_{r2}, \sigma_{r2})(nr) = (rid', \rho', \sigma')(V) = (rid_{r7}, \rho_{r7}, \sigma_{r7})(nr)$. Applying Lemma 4 yields $rid_{r2} = rid_{r7}$ and thus $\rho_{r2} = \rho_{r7}$, so $\rho'(r) = \rho_{r2}(r) = \rho_{r7}(r)$. Because $\rho'(r)$ is an untrusted agent while $\rho_{r7}(r)$ is trusted, we obtain a contradiction. This finishes the proof of $claim_7$.

Note †: Please notice that the step in the proof marked with † fails for the Needham-Schroeder protocol, which gives an indication of why the hardening of the second message exchange is required.

Proof of claim$_9$. Let $\alpha \in Tr(nsl)$ be a trace of the system. Suppose that for some $r9$ and $(rid_r, \rho_r, \sigma_{r9}) \in Inst$, with $rng(\rho_r) \subseteq A_T$, we have $\alpha_{r9} = ((rid_r, \rho_r, \sigma_{r9}), claim_9(r, nisynch))$. In order to prove this synchronisation claim correct, we must find a run executing the initiator role which synchronises on the events labeled 1, 2, and 3, since $prec(nsl, 9) = \{1, 2, 3\}$. By applying Lemma 2, we find $r1, r2, r3$ $(0 \leq r1 < r2 < r3 < r9)$ and $\sigma_{r1} \subseteq \sigma_{r2} \subseteq \sigma_{r3} \subseteq \sigma_{r9}$, such that

$$\alpha_{r1} = ((rid_r, \rho_r, \sigma_{r1}), read_1(i, r, \{i, W\}_{pk(r)}))$$
$$\alpha_{r2} = ((rid_r, \rho_r, \sigma_{r2}), send_2(r, i, \{W, nr, r\}_{pk(i)}))$$
$$\alpha_{r3} = ((rid_r, \rho_r, \sigma_{r3}), read_3(i, r, \{nr\}_{pk(r)})).$$

We have already proved that nr remains secret, so we can apply Lemma 3 and find index $i3$ and $(rid_i, \rho_i, \sigma_{i3})$ such that $i3 < r3$ and
$\alpha_{i3} = ((rid_i, \rho_i, \sigma_{i3}), send_3(i, r, \{V\}_{pk(r)})) \wedge (rid_r, \rho_r, \sigma_{r3})(nr) = (rid_i, \rho_i, \sigma_{i3}(V)$.
By applying Lemma 2 we obtain $i1 < i2 < i3$ such that

$$\alpha_{i1} = ((rid_i, \rho_i, \sigma_{i1}), send_1(i, r, \{i, ni\}_{pk(r)}))$$
$$\alpha_{i2} = ((rid_i, \rho_i, \sigma_{i2}), read_2(r, i, \{ni, V, r\}_{pk(i)}))$$
$$\alpha_{i3} = ((rid_i, \rho_i, \sigma_{i3}), send_3(i, r, \{V\}_{pk(r)})).$$

Now that we have found out that run rid_i is a candidate, we only have to prove that it synchronises with run rid_r. Therefore, we have to establish $r2 < i2$, $i1 < r1$ and that the corresponding send and read events match each other.

First, we observe α_{i2}. Since $(rid_r, \rho_r, \sigma_{r3})(nr)$ is secret, $(rid_i, \rho_i, \sigma_{i2})(V)$ is secret too and we can apply Lemma 3, obtaining index $r2' < i2$ such that $\alpha_{r2'} = ((rid_{r'}, \rho_{r'}, \sigma_{r2'}), send_2(r, i, \{W, nr, r\}_{pk(i)}))$ such that we have $(rid_i, \rho_i, \sigma_{i2})(\{ni, V, r\}_{pk(i)}) = (rid_{r'}, \rho_{r'}, \sigma_{r2'})(\{W, nr, r\}_{pk(i)})$. This implies that we have $(rid_r, \rho_r, \sigma_{r3})(nr) = (rid_i, \rho_i, \sigma_{i3}(V) = (rid_{r'}, \rho_{r'}, \sigma_{r2'})(nr)$, so from Lemma 4 we have $rid_r = rid_{r'}$, and thus $r2 = r2'$. This establishes synchronisation of events α_{i2} and α_{r2}.

Next, we look at α_{r1}. Because $(rid_r, \rho_r, \sigma_{r1})(W)$ is secret (cf. claim 8), we can apply Lemma 3, which gives index $i1' < r1$ such that $\alpha_{i1'} = ((rid_{i'}, \rho_{i'}, \sigma_{i1'}), send_1(i, r, \{i, ni\}_{pk(r)}))$ and $(rid_r, \rho_r, \sigma_{r1})(\{i, W\}_{pk(r)})) = (rid_{i'}, \rho_{i'}, \sigma_{i1'})(\{i, ni\}_{pk(r)})$. Correspondence of α_{i2} and α_{r2} gives $(rid_i, \rho_i, \sigma_{i2})(ni) = (rid_r, \rho_r, \sigma_{r2})(W) = (rid_r, \rho_r, \sigma_{r1})(W) = (rid_{i'}, \rho_{i'}, \sigma_{i1'})(ni)$. By lemma 4 rid_i and $rid_{i'}$ are equal, which establishes synchronisation of events α_{r1} and α_{i1}. This finishes the synchronisation proof of $claim_9$.

5   Related Work

There is a wealth of different approaches for the modeling of security protocols. Very often the focus is on verification tools, yielding a model which is only informally or implicitly defined.

We will briefly compare our approach to the three prominent approaches: BAN logic (because of its historic interest), Casper/FDR (because it has powerful tool support), and Strand spaces (because this approach has much in common with ours). We conclude with short remarks on the spi calculus and modeling security protocols as open systems.

In 1989 Burrows, Abadi and Needham published their ground breaking work on a logic for the verification of authentication properties [2]. In this so-called BAN-logic, predicates have the form "P believes X". Such predicates are derived from a set of assumptions, using derivation rules like "If P believes that P and Q share key K, and if P sees message $\{X\}_K$ then P believes that Q once said X". Note that this rule implies a peculiarity of the agent model, which is not required in most other approaches, viz. an agent can detect (and ignore) his own messages. The BAN-logic has a fixed intruder model, which does not consider conspiring agents. The Needham-Schroeder protocol (see Figure 1) was proven correct in BAN-logic because the man-in-the-middle attack from Figure 2 could not be modeled. Another major difference with our approach is that the BAN-logic uses a rather weak notion of authentication. The authentication properties verified for most protocols have the form "A believes that A and B share key K" (or "...share secret X"), and "A believes that B believes that A and B share key K". This weak form of agreement is sometimes even further reduced to *recent aliveness*. Furthermore, type-flaw attacks cannot be detected using BAN-logic. An interesting feature is that BAN logic treats time stamps at an appropriate abstract level, while an extension of our semantics with time stamps is not obvious. Due to the above mentioned restrictions interest in BAN logic has decreased. Recent research concerns its extension and the development of models for the logic.

Developed originally by Gavin Lowe, the Casper/FDR tool set as described in [10] is not a formal security protocol semantics, but a model checking tool. However, as the input is translated into a CSP process algebraic model, there is an implicit semantics. The reason we mention it here, is that Casper/FDR is a mature tool set, and none of the other semantics we mention has such a tool set available. In the research for Casper/FDR many interesting security properties have been formulated in terms of CSP models (see e.g. [11]) and some of these have been consequently adapted in other models. An advantage of using process algebra for modeling security protocols is that the model is easily extended. However, for Casper/FDR there is no explicit formal semantics of the protocol language and properties except in terms of CSP. Because of this, it is difficult to get results about properties besides using the tools.

The Strand space approach [12] is closely related to the use of Message Sequence Charts which we advocate for the description of protocols and protocol runs. Roughly, the difference is that we provide a totally ordered semantics, whereas Strand spaces describe a partial order on the events. The notion of a strand is similar to our notion of run, and a strand space is the set of all possible combinations of strands, reflecting our semantical model of interleaved runs. Strand spaces seem to be very tightly linked to the Dolev-Yao intruder model and although the intruder is modeled as a collection of strands, just like normal agents, it is not easy to vary over the intruder network model. With respect to the security properties, we mention that both secrecy and agreement are expressible in the Strand spaces model. Additional research must indicate whether synchronisation can be expressed. Finally, we mention that our focus on security claims which are local to the agent's run is not reflected in Strand spaces.

As an example of a process calculus approach, we have the spi calculus developed by Abadi and Gordon in [13]. It is an extension of the pi calculus in [14]. Although this has advantages, it also inherits properties of the pi calculus that do not immediately seem useful for security protocol analysis. As an example, expressing that a run is synchronising with another run over multiple messages is non-trivial, because it can be hard to tell two runs of the same role (with identical parameters) apart. To always be able to distinguish two runs, additional constructs are needed as in [15]. Having an explicit run identifier in the semantics makes it easier to express such properties.

Recently, Martinelli has proposed to analyse security protocols as open systems in [16]. A process calculus for security protocols is proposed, where the intruder process is left unspecified. This allows for protocol properties to be checked with respect to any intruder, which (for safety properties) amounts to the Dolev-Yao intruder model. Properties can also be checked or with respect to a specific intruder, which is similar to having different intruder rules in our semantics. Two main drawbacks are that the analysis assumes a finite number of agents and runs, and that it cannot be used to find type flaw attacks.

In the methods mentioned here, the construction of the initial intruder knowledge is left implicit.

6   Conclusions and Future Research

We have developed a generic canonical model for fundamental analysis of security protocols. Some characteristics of this model are that we give explicit static requirements for valid protocols, and that the model is parametric with respect to the matching function and intruder network capabilities. Multi-protocol analysis, by which we mean the analysis of running several different protocols or protocol roles concurrently, is handled in an intuitive way by simply adding more role descriptions to the model. In line with this, security properties are defined as local claims. Furthermore, local constants are bound to runs, which can assist in the construction of proofs.

As future work, we will be formulating metaresults. For instance, we are interested in results about the composition of protocols, and the decomposition of problems into simpler components. Related to this are transformations of protocols in a given intruder model such that the same security properties are met.

Results in composition of protocols can lead to security by construction. Given a set of security properties and an intruder model, we would like to construct a correct protocol.

We have already developed a tool for model checking secrecy based on this model [17]. Future work will be to develop this into a mature toolset. Parallel to this we are investigating state space reduction techniques for certain settings in our model, such as only eavesdropping, and specific properties.

Acknowledgements. Thanks are due to Erik de Vink for his comments on our work and the stimulating discussions on security protocol semantics. Furthermore, we would like to thank Niek Palm for his study on the application of our semantics to the verification of a collection of security protocols.

References

1. Needham, R.M., Schroeder, M.D.: Using encryption for authentication in large networks of computers. Commun. ACM **21** (1978) 993–999
2. Burrows, M., Abadi, M., Needham, R.: A logic of authentication. ACM Transactions on Computer Systems **8** (1990) 18–36
3. Lowe, G.: Breaking and fixing the Needham-Schroeder public-key protocol using FDR. In: Proceedings of TACAS. Volume 1055., Springer Verlag (1996) 147–166
4. Mauw, S., Wiersma, W., Willemse, T.: Language-driven system design. International Journal of Software Engineering and Knowledge Engineering (2004) To appear.

5. Dolev, D., Yao, A.: On the security of public key protocols. IEEE Transactions on Information Theory **IT-29** (1983) 198–208
6. Engels, A.G., Mauw, S., Reniers, M.: A hierarchy of communication models for Message Sequence Charts. Science of Computer Programming **44** (2002) 253–292
7. Plotkin, G.: A structural approach to operational semantics. Technical Report DIAMI FN-19, Computer Science Department, Aarhus University (1981)
8. Cremers, C., Mauw, S., de Vink, E.: Defining authentication in a trace model. In Dimitrakos, T., Martinelli, F., eds.: FAST 2003. Proceedings of the first international Workshop on Formal Aspects in Security and Trust, Pisa, IITT-CNR technical report (2003) 131–145
9. Roscoe, A.W.: Intensional Specifications of Security Protocols. In: Proc. 9th Computer Security Foundations Workshop, IEEE (1996) 28–38
10. Lowe, G.: Casper: A compiler for the analysis of security protocols. In: Proc. 10th Computer Security Foundations Workshop, IEEE (1997) 18–30
11. Lowe, G.: A hierarchy of authentication specifications. In: Proc. 10th Computer Security Foundations Workshop, IEEE (1997) 31–44
12. Thayer Fábrega, F., Herzog, J., Guttman, J.: Strand spaces: Why is a security protocol correct? In: Proc. 1998 IEEE Symposium on Security and Privacy, Oakland, California (1998) 66–77
13. Abadi, M., Gordon, A.: A calculus for cryptographic protocols: The spi calculus. Inf. Comput. **148** (1999) 1–70
14. Milner, R., Parrow, J., Walker, D.: A calculus of mobile processes, i. Inf. Comput. **100** (1992) 1–40
15. Bodei, C., Degano, P., Focardi, R., Priami, C.: Primitives for authentication in process algebras. Theor. Comput. Sci. **283** (2002) 271–304
16. Martinelli, F.: Analysis of security protocols as open systems. Theor. Comput. Sci. **290** (2003) 1057–1106
17. Cremers, C., Mauw, S.: Checking secrecy by means of partial order reduction. In Amyot, D., Williams, A., eds.: SAM 2004: Security Analysis and Modelling. Volume LNCS 3319 of Proceedings of the fourth SDL and MSC Workshop., Ottawa, Canada, Springer-Verlag, Berlin (2004) 177–194

Autonomous Shuttle System Case Study*

Holger Giese and Florian Klein**

Software Engineering Group, University of Paderborn,
Warburger Str. 100, D-33098 Paderborn, Germany
{hg, fklein}@upb.de

1   Introduction

At the University of Paderborn, the Railcab project is developing an intelligent rail-based transportation system. Its vision is to combine flexible, on-demand scheduling with cost and resource effectiveness, thus offering the advantages of both individual and public transportation. Fleets of intelligent shuttles capable of transporting a small number of passengers or a single freight container autonomously navigate a passive track system and make independent and decentralized operational decisions.

At the Dagstuhl Seminar *Scenarios: Models, Transformations and Tools*, a case study focussing on the logistic aspects of this system was used in an extra design session. As it is consequently referenced by several papers in these proceedings, we provide a short description of the case study in the following sections. After a short overview in Section 2, we describe the architecture of the provided simulator in Section 3 and finally outline the possible interaction scenarios in Section 4. For further information and a detailed interface specification, please consult the case study web site.[1]

2   System Overview

The case study is based on a very simple system model. Shuttle agents move around on a topology consisting of railway stations interconnected by track sections. Orders for transportation tasks that consist of moving a certain number of passengers from one station to another while respecting a certain deadline are published and auctioned off among the shuttles. The lowest bidder is awarded the task and paid upon successful completion, but risks a contractual penalty in case of tardiness. Shuttles need to pay for track usage and maintenance.

The Network. The railway network is modelled as a directed graph. Nodes may be stations or either converging or diverging switches. Stations can simultaneously accom-

---

* This work was developed in the course of the Special Research Initiative 614 - Self-optimizing Concepts and Structures in Mechanical Engineering - University of Paderborn, and was published on its behalf and funded by the Deutsche Forschungsgemeinschaft.
** Supported by the International Graduate School of Dynamic Intelligent Systems.

[1] http://www.upb.de/cs/ag-schaefer/CaseStudies/ShuttleSystem/. There, you may also download a more detailed case study description and a simulation environment implementing the specification, which can serve as a testbed for shuttle designs.

S. Leue and T.J. Systä (Eds.): Scenarios, LNCS 3466, pp. 90–94, 2005.
© Springer-Verlag Berlin Heidelberg 2005

modate an unlimited number of shuttles. Maintenance is carried out at stations, but only if explicitly initiated by the shuttle.

The directed edges represent tracks that may only be traversed in the specified direction. Paths on the graph correspond to track sections. A track section that directly connects two stations is called a connection and needs to be unique. Connections may share common track sections, but it is currently not possible to deviate from a connection once the traversal has been started. They may be temporarily disrupted, which does not affect the shuttles currently travelling on it, but only keep new shuttles from entering it. All shuttles are duly informed about disruptions and may opt for an alternate route.

Orders. Orders are published and auctioned by a broker. They specify a starting point, a destination, the number of passengers, and the contractual penalty. Besides, they are stamped with their publication time, the time the auction ends and the deadline for the completion of the order. The deadline is computed by adding the predetermined processing time to the time when the order is accorded to the lowest-bidding shuttle at the end of the auction. Any shuttle may place bids for any order. In case of a tie, the shuttle that first made the offer is awarded the order.

Shuttles. Shuttles are responsible for processing and executing the orders. They have a fixed maximum capacity for transporting passengers. They may transport any number of orders at a time within the limits of their available capacity. There is no limitation on the number and total capacity of the orders a shuttle may bid for and obtain simultaneously. Shuttles complete orders by travelling to the starting point, explicitly picking up the passengers, proceeding to the destination and unloading. Passengers may not be unloaded anywhere but at their destination.

Income and Expenses. At initialization time, shuttles receive a fixed seed capital. A shuttle with a negative balance is bankrupt. It is retired at the next train station.During the run of the simulation, orders are a shuttle's only source of income. Upon successful completion of an order, the shuttle needs to claim the payment. An order may specify one of two possible modes of payment: credit card payments are transfered immediately upon receipt of the claim, while invoiced payments may be deferred. A shuttle may need to send up to two reminders, each preceded by a waiting period of no less than 2500 simulation periods, before it is paid. All invoices are paid eventually. Premature reminders are ignored, however. Shuttles incur three different kinds of expenses:

- Toll: a fee for the utilization of connections is levied upon arrival at the destination. The amount is fixed and determined by the topology.
- Maintenance: maintenance takes place at train stations and consumes both time and money. It is automatically triggered once the distance travelled since the last maintenance exceeds a certain limit, but may also be scheduled at any earlier time by the shuttle. It can not be interrupted, however. Payment is immediate.
- Contractual penalties: if a shuttle does not complete an order before the associated deadline, it needs to pay the specified contractual penalty. It is still compelled to complete the order, but will receive no payment. If the shuttle has not even loaded the order before the deadline, it needs to pay the amount of its bid in addition to the penalty and loses the order.

3   Architecture

All interactions between the different agents in the system are realized using messages. The key aspect of the system's architecture is therefore the approach to message passing. The control logic of each of the system's agents, most notably of each shuttle, is run in a dedicated thread in order to ensure a fairer distribution of resources and keep individual agents from blocking one another. While Java method calls are by nature synchronous, a mechanism was devised to enable the simulation of asynchronous message passing by means of a message handler. It accepts message objects, relinquishes control of the sending thread immediately afterwards and then delivers the message at the appropriate time. As it is responsible for queuing, routing and delivering all internal and external messages, the message handler is the central entity of the system (see Figure 1).

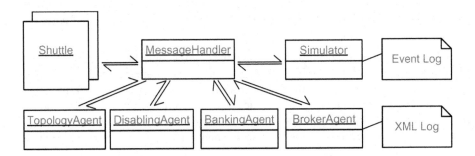

Fig. 1. Kernel components

All components of the system are derived from the Agent type. It provides the basic interfaces and data structures for interfacing with the communication framework. The kernel consists of five agents.

- The *Topology Agent* stores and publishes the network's topology
- The *Broker Agent* loads or generates a sequence of orders, publishes them, and manages the auctioning process. The generated sequences of orders are logged to an XML file that may be used to reuse an identical scenario for testing and controlled experimentation.
- The *Banking Agent* is in charge of transferring money from and to the shuttles, and the invoicing process
- The *Disabling Agent* randomly disables connections between stations
- The *Simulator* simulates the physical part of the system. Running inside the Simulator, there is a shuttle process representing the hardware component of each shuttle. Shuttles may communicate with their shuttle process using a special set of messages defined below. The Simulator keeps a debug log that can be used for the analysis of a simulation run.
- The *Shuttle Agents* control the shuttles' operation. They must be derived from the ShuttleAgent type and, for performance reasons, may not create additional threads nor read from or write to files.

4   Interaction Scenarios

A set of interaction scenarios between shuttles, their physical sensors and actuators and the agents of the system kernel exists. Shuttles can issue commands, e.g. to move to a station, or request information about the environment, e.g. whether a particular connection is currently interrupted.

Though central to the architecture, the message handler is just repeating received messages and does not add anything to the interaction semantics from the application perspective. In order to increase their clarity, we will therefore omit the message handler from the descriptions and treat all exchanges like direct interactions. Nonetheless, a delay occurs whenever messages are passed to the message handler, which has to be considered when requesting wake-up calls or calculating internal deadlines.

As most exchanges are fairly basic, we only provide a diagram to illustrate a more complex example in order to keep this document compact. As the message handler simulates asynchronous communication, the diagram uses the arrow shape expressing asynchronicity.

Shuttle Commands. All shuttle command messages follow a basic command and reply schema. The shuttle agent expresses its desire to perform a certain action, then the shuttle process gives the appropriate response. Commands include moving to a destination, loading and unloading tasks, initiating maintenance, etc. The shuttle process checks the associated requirements, e.g. in case of a move command whether source and destination are valid, no maintenance is due, and there is sufficient money to pay the toll. The shuttle process then replies with a message indicating whether a request was valid or invalid, and a second message once the command has been executed completely in the former case.

Broker Agent Interaction. The Broker Agent publishes Orders with the *OrderAvailable* message. Shuttles may then calculate their price and reply with a *MakeOffer* message. The broker then evaluates the offers and sends an *AssignOrder* message to the winner. The losing bidders are not informed about the result of the auction.

Topology Agent Interaction. The topology represents one of the most important features of the shuttles' environment. During initialization, shuttles request this information from the Topology Agent, which returns a collection of *TopologyDataObjects*. Additionally, the agent sends a *GameConstantsMessage* containing the simulation's parameters.

Banking Agent Interaction. The Banking Agent is in charge of all financial transactions. It is the recipient of claims and reminders, and checks their validity and timeliness. It transfers payments to the shuttles' accounts, but is also responsible for deducing tolls, penalties, and maintenance cost.

Auxiliary Messages. There are four classes of auxiliary messages. The first type allows the shuttle to enquire about the state of the environment, e.g. the current simulation time, its own position and account balance, or disabled track sections. Secondly, a shuttle may send messages to the visualization component, usually containing some implementation-specific details to display. Then, there is the possibility to request a wake-up call from the simulator at a certain time or when a certain event occurs, and send the shuttle thread to sleep in order to save processing resources. A shuttle will equally be activated whenever any other message is sent to it.

Exemplary Interaction. The diagram below (see Figure 2) shows a typical sequence of interactions between a shuttle and various kernel agents. A shuttle bids for, obtains and successfully completes an order.

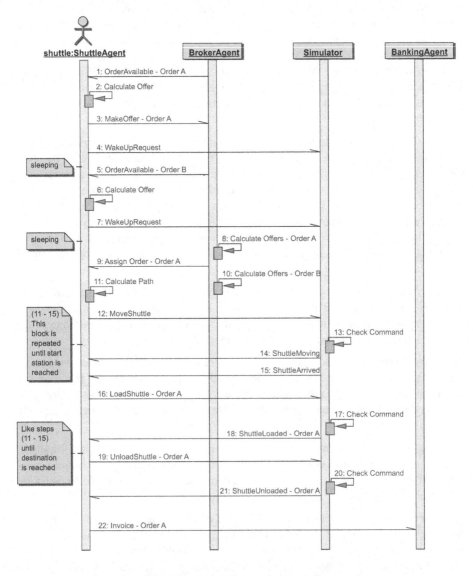

Fig. 2. Exemplary interaction scenario

Genetic Design: Amplifying Our Ability to Deal With Requirements Complexity

R. Geoff Dromey

Software Quality Institute, Griffith University,
Nathan, Brisbane, Qld., 4111, Australia
g.dromey@griffith.edu.au

Abstract. Individual functional requirements represent fragments of behavior, while a design that satisfies a set of functional requirements represents integrated behavior. This perspective admits the prospect of constructing a design out of its requirements. A formal representation for individual functional requirements, called behavior trees makes this possible. Behavior trees, derived by rigorous translation from individual functional requirements stated in natural language, may be composed, one at a time, to create an integrated design behavior tree (DBT). We can then transition from this problem domain representation directly and systematically to a solution domain representation of the component architecture of the system and the behavior designs of the individual components that make up the system – both are emergent properties of a DBT. The Early Warning System case study is used to illustrate this genetic design method, and show its potential for defect detection and control of complexity compared with the Statechart design method.

1 Introduction

The Early Warning System is typical of many problems that are relatively easy to state informally and loosely in natural language. Such problem statements often have two significant characteristics: they imply a lot more than they state and they contain defects that can significantly impact subsequent design efforts. Confronted with these challenges, existing methods for requirements analysis [2], representation and then design usually opt for producing multiple partial views of a system. Our position is that the multiple partial views approaches, which include Statecharts, usually make it difficult to see many types of defects, particularly those that involve interactions between requirements [1][6][8]. A more practical way forward, we suggest, is to use a single integrated view. The challenges we must confront in his endeavour are:

- how to get on top of requirements complexity,
- how to preserve, and where necessary, clarify the intention of stakeholders, and
- how to systematically, repeatably, detect requirements defects early as possible.

We suggest there is a way to deliver these benefits and consistently make real progress with the requirements problem. It demands that we use the requirements of a system in a very different way to existing software development methods. Traditionally the goal of systems development is to build a system that will *satisfy* the agreed

S. Leue and T.J. Systä (Eds.): Scenarios, LNCS 3466, pp. 95 – 108, 2005.

requirements. We suggest this task is too hard, particularly if there is a large and complex set of requirements for a system. *A much simpler and easier task is to seek to build a system* **out of** *its requirements.* If we opt to do this it implies two things:

- we have a representation that will formally represent the behavior in individual requirements
- we have a way of combining/integrating individual requirements to create a system that will satisfy all requirements.

Behavior Trees handle both of these needs.

2 Behavior Trees

The Behavior Tree Notation captures in a simple tree-like form of composed component-states what usually needs to be expressed in a mix of other notations. Behavior is expressed primarily in terms of components realizing [State], ??Event??, ?Decision?, <Data_Out>, >Data_In< component attribute assignment ":=", and reversion "^" to an equivalent component-state mentioned higher up in the tree. This notation is augmented by the logic and graphic forms of conventions found in programming languages to support composition.

The vital question that needs to be settled, if we are to build a system out of its requirements, is can the same formal representation of behavior be used for requirements and for a design? Behavior trees make this possible, and as a consequence, clarify the requirements-design relationship. Behavior trees provide a direct and clearly traceable relationship between what is expressed in the natural language representation and its formal specification. Translation is carried out on a sentence-by-sentence, word-by-word basis, e.g.., the sentence "the bell sounds when the button is pressed" is translated to the behavior tree below:

3 Genetic Design

Conventional software engineering applies the underlying design strategy of constructing a design that will satisfy its set of functional requirements. In contrast to this, a clear advantage of the behavior tree notation is that it allows us to construct a design out of its set of functional requirements, by integrating the behavior trees for individual requirements behavior trees (RBTs), one-at-a-time, into an evolving DBT [3]. This very significantly reduces the complexity of the design process and any subsequent change process. What we are suggesting is that a set of functional requirements, represented as behavior trees, in principal at least (when they form a complete and consistent set), contains enough information to allow their composition. This property is the exact same property that a set of pieces for a jigsaw puzzle and a set of genes possess [12]. The obvious question that follows is: "what information is possessed by a set of functional requirements that might allow their composition or integration?" The answer follows from the observation that the behavior expressed in functional requirements does not "just happen". There is always a precondition that must be satisfied in order for the behavior encapsulated in a functional requirement to be accessible or applicable or executable. We call this requirement of genetic design, the precondition axiom.

Precondition Axiom

Every constructive, implementable individual functional requirement of a system, expressed as a behavior tree, has associated with it a precondition that needs to be satisfied in order for the behavior encapsulated in the functional requirement to be applicable.

A second building block is needed to facilitate the composition of functional requirements expressed as behavior trees. Jigsaw puzzles, together with the precondition axiom, give us the clues as to what additional information is needed to achieve integration. With a jigsaw puzzle, what is key, is not the order in which we put the pieces together, but rather the *position* where we put each piece. If we are to integrate behavior trees in any order, one at a time, an analogous requirement is needed. We have already said that a functional requirement's precondition needs to be satisfied in order for its behavior to be applicable. It follows that some *other* requirement, as part of its behavior tree, must establish the precondition. This requirement for integrating functional requirements expressed as behavior trees is expressed as follows.

Interaction Axiom

For each individual functional requirement of a system, expressed as a behavior tree, the precondition it needs to have satisfied in order to exhibit its encapsulated behavior, must be established by the behavior tree of at least one other functional requirement that belongs to the set of functional requirements of the system. The behavior tree that forms the root of the integrated tree is excused from this requirement.

The precondition axiom and the interaction axiom play a central role in defining the relationship between a set of functional requirements for a system and the corresponding design. What they tell us is that in the first stage of the design process, in the problem domain, we can proceed by first translating each individual natural language representation of a functional requirement into one or more behavior trees. We may then proceed to integrate those behavior trees just as we would with a set of jigsaw puzzle pieces. What we find when we pursue this whole approach to software design is that the process can be reduced to the following four overarching steps:

- Requirements translation – (problem domain)
- Requirements integration – (problem domain)

- Component architecture transformation (solution domain)
- Component behavior projection (solution domain)

Each overarching step needs to be augmented with a verification and refinement step designed specifically to isolate and correct each class of defects that show up in the different work products generated by the process. Because of space limitations here we only have room to show the results of translating then integrating the originally stated functional requirements for the Early Warning System (see each sentence in Table 1). We will also provide brief commentary on the main steps. Elsewhere each of the steps in the process is described in more detail [3]

Table 1. Early Warning System Functional Requirements

The EWS receives a signal from an external sensor. When the sensor is connected, the EWS processes the signal and checks if the resulting value is within a specified range. If the value of the processed signal is out of range, the system issues a warning message on the operator display and posts an alarm. If the operator does not respond to this warning within a given time interval, the system prints a fault message on a printing facility and stops monitoring the signal. The range limits are set by the operator. The system becomes ready to start monitoring the signal only after the range limits are set. The limits can be redefined after an out-of-range situation has been detected or after the operator has deliberately stopped the monitoring.

D.Harel, M.Politi, "Modeling Reactive Systems with Statecharts", McGraw-Hill, N.Y (1998).

3.1 Requirements Translation

Requirements translation is the first formal step in the Genetic Design process. Its purpose is to translate each natural language functional requirement, one at a time, into one or more behavior trees. Translation identifies the components (including actors and users), the states they realise (including attribute assignments), the events and decisions/constraints that they are associated with, the data components exchange, and the causal, logical and temporal dependencies associated with component interactions. Nouns in the text that have associated behavior are identified as components.

When requirements translation has been completed each individual functional requirement is translated to one or more corresponding RBTs. In Figure 1 we show the "raw" translations for sentences S1, S5 and S6 from the original statement of requirements in Table 1. As originally stated each of the three requirements is missing implied precondition information that would allow their direct integration. Implied preconditions (colour-coded yellow, and marked with a "+" where colour is not available) have been added to allow the requirements to be directly integrated by finding where the root of one RBT occurs in another RBT. With S1 we have dropped the adjective "external" and acknowledged that something must be "sent" <... > in order to be "received" > ... <. From the context the behavior in S1 can only happen if the

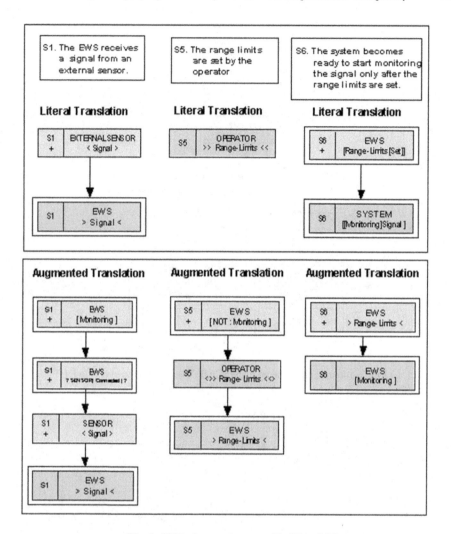

Fig. 1. RBTs for requirements S1, S5 and S6

EWS is monitoring and the sensor is connected. In S5 the screen input ">> ... <<" must be sent somewhere (to the EWS). This all happens when the EWS is not monitoring. In S6 "system" is an alias for "EWS".

3.2 Requirements Integration

Once we have carried out all the requirements translations we can systematically and incrementally construct a design behavior tree that will satisfy all its requirements *by integrating the individual requirements' behavior trees* one at a time. Integrating two behavior trees turns out to be a relatively simple process that is guided by the precondition and interaction axioms referred to above. In practice, it most often involves locating where, (if at all) the component-state root node of one behavior tree occurs in

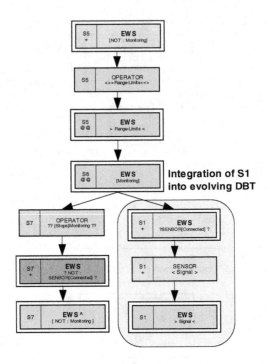

Fig. 2. Integration of the augmented RBT for S1 into the evolving DBT

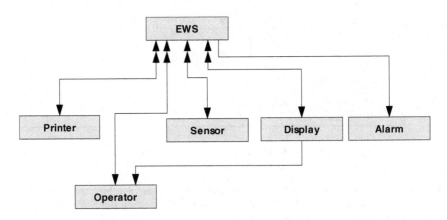

Fig. 3. CIN derived from EWS DBT in Figures 5 and 6

another tree and grafting the two trees together at that point. This process generalises when we need to integrate N behavior trees. We only ever attempt to integrate two behavior trees at a time. In some cases, because the precondition for executing the behavior in an RBT has not been included, or important behavior has been left out of a requirement, it is not clear where a requirement integrates into the design. This immediately points to a problem with the requirements. In other cases, there may be requirements/behavior missing from the set which prevents integration of a requirement. Attempts at integration uncover such problems with requirements at the earliest possible time. At the same time, such problems preclude automating requirements integration. Consider the case of integrating S1, S5, S6 and S7. It is not possible to integrate the initial literal translations for this set of requirements because they all have missing precondition information and a number of other problems. Each needs to be augmented as we have done above to make direct integration possible. The result of integrating the augmented requirements is shown in Figure 2.

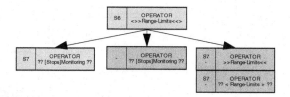

Fig. 4. Operator Component Behavior Projected from Figures 5 and 6 and augmented

Take the case of integrating S1 "the EWS receives a signal from an external sensor" with the other requirements. The literal translation of this requirement gives no direct clue how to integrate it. Examining the requirement the first thing we notice is that it implies that the sensor must "send" the signal in order for it to be subsequently "received". For this to happen the sensor needs to be connected. Including this behavior still does not give us an RBT that can be directly integrated. To push the analysis further we must ask the question "what state must the EWS be in to receive a signal – the answer is, it must be in a "monitoring" state. When this precondition is added the augmented RBT for requirement S1 can be integrated with requirement S6 as shown in Figure 2. Similarly S7 integrates with S6. So what we see from the case of integrating S1 is that the process reveals problems with individual requirements that prevent direct integration. It also constructively provides clues about what preconditions are needed. Clearly, in this case the EWS is only in a position to receive a signal if it is monitoring and the sensor is connected. In some cases knowledge from a domain expert is necessary to resolve an integration problem. In other cases, temporal or causal information, and/or the states other components need to be in for integration to take place guide the decision.

In Figures 5 and 6 (following the paper) we show the DBT that results from integrating the RBTs that were produced by requirements translation of the sentences in Table 1, and then either direct integration or augmentation where needed to enable integration followed by integration. It is easy to see because of the tags, S1, S2, etc, where each functional requirement occurs in the integrated DBT. "@@" mark integration points. As well as finding integration problems, the translation and integration steps help us find and confront ambiguities and the use of aliases in the original statement of requirements.

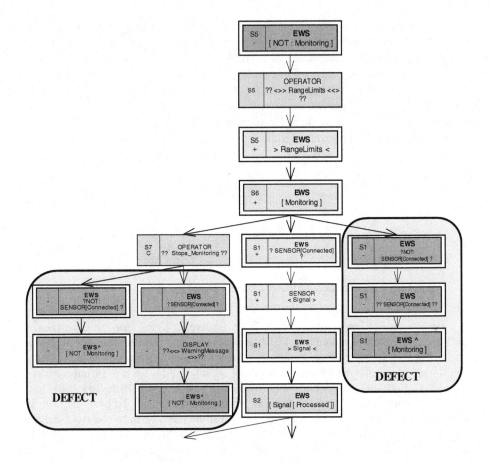

Fig. 5. Top Half of the Integrated DBT for the EWS

3.3   Inspection of the Integrated Design Behavior Tree

The design behavior tree turns out to be a very effective representation for revealing a range of incompleteness and inconsistency defects that are common in original statements of requirements. The Early Warning System case study has its share of incompleteness defects.

With the DBT there is the opportunity to do a manual visual formal inspection. Behavior Trees have been given a formal semantics [11] which has enabled us to build and use tools to do automated formal analyses as well. In combination, these tools provide a powerful armament for defect finding. With simple examples like the EWS it is very easy to do just a visual inspection and identify a number of defects. For larger systems, with large numbers of states and complex control structures the automated tools are essential for systematic, logically based, repeatable defect finding.

The tool [9] we have built allows us to graphically enter behavior trees and store them using XML. From the XML we generate a CSP (Communicating Sequential

Processes) representation. There are several translation strategies that we can use to map behavior trees into CSP. Details of one strategy for translating behavior trees into CSP are given in [11]. One simple strategy involves defining sub-processes in which state transitions for a component are treated as events. The CSP generated by the tool is then fed directly into the FDR model-checker. This allows us to check the DBT for deadlocks, live-locks and also to formulate and check some safety requirements [11]. We are currently extending the tool to do a number of consistency checks on a DBT. One important check that we are able to do is a reversion "^"check where control reverts back to an earlier established state. What this check allows us to do is see whether all components are in the *same* state at the reversion point as the original state realization point (e.g., with the EWS we can check EWS[Monitoring] and EWS^[Monitoring] for consistency of all the component-states that define these two system state realizations). Such a consistency check reveals that the alarm is in the "Posted" state when reversion "^" takes place, whereas it is in the "Off" state when the EWS has just realized the "Monitoring" state. This identifies an inconsistency which we have corrected in the DBT by including ALARM[Off] in requirement S3.

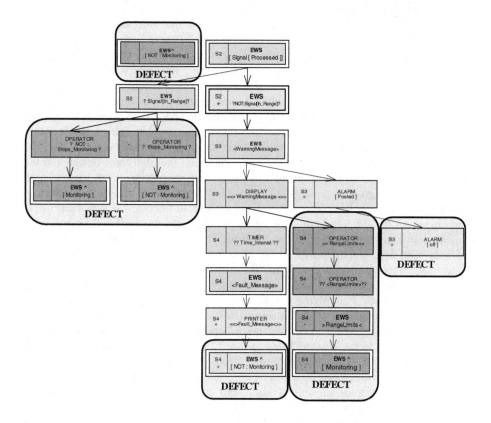

Fig. 6. Bottom half of the integrated DBT for the EWS

Table 2. Missing Behavior found by Inspection of the DBT

1. The requirements do not say what to do if the sensor is not connected - presume must wait for connection event then start monitoring.
2. Does not say what to do if signal is "in range" - presume just goes back to monitoring.
3. Does not say what response operator needs to make if signal is not in range - presumed input new range limits.
4. Does not say what to do after printing fault message - here have presumed it goes back to a "not monitoring" state.

As we mentioned earlier for systems like the EWS it is relatively easy to do a visual inspection to identify incompleteness defects. Table 2 lists four incompleteness defects identified by inspection of the DBT for missing alternative cases.

What is interesting when a comparison is made with the Statechart design (see figs. B2, B3, and B4, ref [6]) for this system is that none of these issues are seen as "defects" and yet the original requirements are silent in each of the cases. Perhaps some of these "defects" can be resolved as "commonsense". However when all "gaps" are filled in this way it raises the chances of factoring in new requirements and new behavior that was not intended in the original requirements. What genetic design allows us to do is separate out what was actually stated and intended from other behavior that needs to be added in to make the behavior of a system complete. This latter behavior should be clearly delineated until it has been authorised by the stakeholders.

There is also another significant difference between the Statechart design and the design that results from requirements translation and integration. What we find with the Statechart design is that things get "added in" to the design that do not appear in the original statement of requirements. For example, in the original statement of requirements for the EWS there is no mention of the power going off and on and yet it appears in the design (see figs. B2 and B4, ref [6]) without any comment. We have no issue with need for the power to be off and on. However when these sort of design/requirements decisions are done "on the fly" then traceability to original requirements is lost. Also the chances of introducing something that was not intended are greatly increased. In applying genetic design to industry applications and comparing the design documents produced using UML and other representations, time and time again we have observed discrepancies between originally stated requirements and what ends up in the design. Things get left out and things get added in with no acknowledgement of what has happened or why it has happened. Genetic design with behavior trees provides a practical way of controlling and avoiding such problems.

The processes of translation, integration, and inspection of the DBT have revealed a number of defects and where they occurred. The incompleteness problems are identified in Table 2 and in Figures 5 and 6. The method has constructively guided us in the resolution of the missing requirements. To give some indication of the constructive "pull" of genetic design, only approximately two-thirds of the behavior in the DBT came from the original requirements. The other third of the behavior was either missing "-" or implied "+" in the original set of statements we have used to guide the design. We have been able to systematically transition from a loose natural language, high-level statement of requirements to a complete and consistent integrated formal set of requirements that preserve the intent of the original requirements.

Once the missing behaviors and other problems with the DBT have been rectified it is then possible to transition to the *solution domain*. A design behavior-tree is the *problem domain* view of the "shell of a design" that shows all the states and all the flows of control (and data), modelled as interactions without any of the functionality needed to realize the various states that individual components may assume. *It has the genetic property of embodying within its form two key emergent properties of a design: (1) the component-architecture of a system and, (2) the behaviors of each of the components in the system.*

3.4 Architecture Transformation

The component architecture, which is an emergent property of the DBT is described elsewhere [5]. We will use the Early Warning System DBT given in Figures 5 and 6 to illustrate how this transformation is done and how the architecture is derived. In the DBT, a given component may appear in different parts of the tree in different states (e.g., the EWS component may appear in the Monitoring-state in one part of the tree and in the NOT : Monitoring-state in another part of the tree). To implement the architecture transformation we need to convert a design behavior-tree to a component-based design in which each distinct component is represented only <u>once</u>.

This amounts to shifting from a representation where functional requirements are integrated to a representation, which is part of the **solution domain**, where the components mentioned in the functional requirements are themselves integrated. A simple algorithmic process may be employed to accomplish this transformation from a tree into a network [3,5]. *Informally, the process starts at the root of the design behavior tree (here EWS[NOT : Monitoring]) and moves systematically down the tree towards the leaf nodes including each component (e.g. OPERATOR is included next after EWS) and each component interaction (e.g. arrow) that is not already present.* When this is done systematically the tree is transformed into a component-based design (in general a network) in which each distinct component is represented only <u>once</u>. When this algorithm is applied to the EWS DBT we get the Component Interaction Network (CIN) representation (Figure 3), which is simply a component dependency network for all the components in the requirements. Notice in the DBT that DISPLAY receives input from the EWS and produces outputs to OPERATOR and the EWS. These relationships (arrows) are retained in CIN below. The "double-headed arrow in the EWS – OPERATOR case indicates that control flows first to the OPERATOR (singled-headed arrow) then subsequently from the OPERATOR back to the EWS (double-headed arrow). Clearly the CIN shows that the EWS (in this case acting as the system component in the design) is the principal controlling and integrating agent for the behavior of the system.

This CIN represents a "first-cut" at the architecture. We can often simplify the component interfaces. Space does not permit this process to be discussed here (see [3,5] for more details.

3.5 Component Behavior Projection

In the design behavior tree, the behavior of individual components tends to be dispersed throughout the tree (for example, see the OPERATOR component-states in the EWS system DBT). To implement components that can be embedded in, and operate within, the derived component interaction network, it is necessary to "concentrate" each component's behavior. We can achieve this by systematically *projecting* each component's behavior tree (CBT) from the design behavior tree. We do this by essentially ignoring the component-states of all components other than the one we are currently projecting. In addition we must preserve branching information at the time of projection. The resulting connected "skeleton" behavior tree for a particular component defines the behavior of the component that we will need to implement and encapsulate in the final component-based implementation. To illustrate the effect and significance of component behavior projection we show the projection of the OPERATOR component from the DBT for the EWS in Figures 5 and 6.

   Component behavior projection is a key design step in the solution domain that needs to be done for each component in the design behavior tree. As part of the process it is necessary to check the projected leaf nodes to see that they properly revert "^". Here we need to add reversions "^" that requires that the operator will need to input new range limits after stopping monitoring. From this we see that projection helps to clearly identify and remove another class of defects from components.

4   Comparison with Statecharts and Other Methods

As Jackson wisely observed, new notations and new design methods are generally not enthusiastically received [7]. Such proposals are seen as just muddying the waters and tinkering around the edges. What we have tried to show in this treatment and the accompanying case study is that there are some significant differences and potential advantages of Behavior Trees/genetic design over the leading, and most mature state-based design method - Statecharts[6]. Time, more widespread use, and independent validation of the method is needed to confirm these advantages.

   We summarize some of the major differences and advantages we claim for genetic design:

- The most significant advantage of genetic design over Statecharts, UML and other methods is that it allows designers to focus on the complexity/detail of each individual requirement one at a time, while not having to worry about the detail in other requirements. That requirements can be dealt with one at a time (both for translation and integration) significantly reduces the complexity of creating a design. This, in turn, very significantly reduces the short-term memory overload problem that has plagued software development for so long. In fact, this approach to design actually amplifies our ability to deal with complexity.

- Another important advantage of genetic design over Statecharts and other methods is that the component architecture and the component behavior designs of all individual components in a system are both *emergent properties* of the design behavior tree that is constructed by integrating all the functional requirements of the system.

- We have also shown using the case study, and elsewhere [4] that integration of functional requirements is a powerful constructive force for finding *behavior gaps* and other incompleteness and inconsistency defects with a set of functional requirements. Because the use of Statecharts does not have the same focus on defect detection it is unlikely to consistently deliver a comparable detection rate.
- Statecharts and other development methods, also run a much greater risk of not preserving original intention because they do not employ a rigorous translation process to transition from an informal statement of requirements to a formal representation. Evidence of this is seen in figs. B2, B3 and B4 of ref. [6]. We find a number of new terms (e.g., "setting up", "idle"," halt", and so on) appear in the design figures that are not in the original statement of requirements (see Table 1) while others like alarm "posted" disappear. This change in terminology contrasts with the focus in genetic design on direct translation of individual functional requirements which maximizes the chances of preserving and clarifying original intent and guaranteeing traceability to original statements of requirements. Because the focus is on translation the genetic design approaches repeatability in transitioning from and informal to a formal representation. Genetic design also provides a single integrated view of the requirements compared with the multiple views, (statecharts, activity charts and module charts) of the Statechart method. The integrated view, we claim, makes it easier to see and find defects either manually or using automated tools. It also makes it easier to see that original intent has been preserved in a design. For example, take the fourth sentence in Table 1. "If the operator does not respond to this warning in a given time interval, the system prints a fault message on a printing facility and stops monitoring the signal". In the DBT (figs. 5 and 6) this requirement is directly traceable as the behavior fragment S4. In addition, the alternative case (not included in Table 1), when the operator responds is also accommodated. In contrast, with the statechart (fig. B4, ref. [6]) we claim it is much less obvious that this original intent has been completely and accurately captured.
- We have not emphasised it here but genetic design provides a formal, automatable method for mapping changes of requirements to changes in the architecture, the component interfaces, and the behaviors of the individual components affected by the change [10]. This follows because the architecture and individual component designs are emergent properties of the DBT that is modified by the change in functional requirements of the system.
- Genetic design also uses *structure trees*, *composition trees* and *user-interface behavior trees* to provide equally useful <u>integrated views</u> of all the data requirements, the formal structural requirements and the interaction requirements that we almost always encounter when designing large-scale systems.
- Behavior trees provide strong support for requirements elicitation and requirements analysis. They can be used equally well with broad user requirements, or a detailed SRS, or to formally model an individual scenario. The method does not however depend on requirements being nicely structured.

5 Conclusion

Amplification of our ability to deal with complexity is the single most important problem to overcome in order to advance the practice of software engineering. Genetic design has the potential to make an important contribution to solving this problem because it allows us to consider, translate, and integrate only one requirement at a time. Application of the method to the Early Warning System Case Study has demonstrated the constructive power of requirements integration as a means for complexity control and the early detection and resolution of significant problems with original high-level statements of requirements. The case study will allow others to benchmark genetic design against Statecharts, the leading state-based design method.

Genetic design has been successfully applied to a diverse range of real (often large) industrial applications. In all cases the method has proved very effective at defect detection and in the control of complexity (in larger systems there can be layers of behavior – the method easily accommodates this). We expect the utility of the method will increase as we enhance the tool we are building to support the method.

References

1. Booch, G., Rumbaugh, J., Jacobson, I.: *The Unified Modelling Language User Guide*, Addison-Wesley, Reading, Mass. (1999)
2. Davis, A.: A Comparison of Techniques for the Specification of External System Behavior, *Comm. ACM*, vol. 31, No. 9, (1988), pp. 1098-1115
3. Dromey, R.G.: From Requirements to Design: Formalizing the Key Steps, SEFM 2003, IEEE International Conference on Software Engineering and Formal Methods, (Invited Keynote Address), Brisbane, September, (2003),pp.2-11.
4. Dromey, R.G.: Using Behavior Trees to Model the Autonomous Shuttle System, ICSE-2004, 3rd International Workshop on Scenarios and State Machines: Models, Algorithms and Tools, (SCESM'04), Edinburgh, May, (2004)
5. Dromey, R.G:, Architecture as an Emergent Property of Requirements Integration, ICSE-2003, Software Requirements to Architecture Workshop – STRAW' 03, Portland, USA, May (2003).
6. Harel, D., Politi, M., *Modeling Reactive Systems with Statecharts*, McGraw-Hill, N.Y. (1998).
7. Jackson, D.: Alloy: A Lightweight Object Modelling Notation, MIT Lab. for Comp. Sci. Report (1999)
8. Shlaer, S., Mellor, S.J.: *Object Lifecycles*, Yourdon Press, New Jersey (1992).
9. Smith, C., Winter, K., Hayes, I., Dromey, R.G., Lindsay, P., Carrington, D.: An Environment for Building a System Out of Its Requirements, Tools Track, 19th IEEE International Conference on Automated Software Engineering, Linz, Austria, Sept. (2004).
10. Wen, L., Dromey, R.G: From Requirements Change to Design Change: A Formal Path, SEFM 2004, IEEE International Conference on Software Engineering and Formal Methods, Eds., J.R. Cuellar, Z. Liu, Beijing, September, (2004), pp. 104-113.
11. Winter, K.: Formalising Behavior Trees with CSP, International Conference on Integrated Formal Methods, IFM'04, LNCS vol. 2999, (2004), pp. 148 – 167.
12. Woolfson, A: *Life Without Genes*, Flamingo, London (2000)

Applying Story Driven Modeling to the Paderborn Shuttle System Case Study

Ira Diethelm, Leif Geiger, and Albert Zündorf

University of Kassel, Software Engineering Research Group,
Department of Computer Science and Electrical Engineering,
Wilhelmshöher Allee 73, 34121 Kassel, Germany
{ira.diethelm, leif.geiger, albert.zuendorf}@uni-kassel.de
http://www.se.eecs.uni-kassel.de/se/

Abstract. Story Driven Modeling (SDM) is a technical software development process employing UML-based modeling in all project phases, including implementation and test. SDM may be considered as a simple version of Model Driven Software Development as proposed by the OMG. SDM uses scenarios in analysis and test phases and provides practical guidelines for the synthesis of statecharts and method behavior specifications. SDM proposes object games for refining textual use case scenarios into so called story boards, i.e. sequences of UML interaction diagrams. From these story boards the modeler derives class diagrams, UML-based, operational behavior specifications and UML-based JUnit tests. The code generators of the Fujaba CASE tool turn this automatically in a Java implementation and run the JUnit tests. This paper is a case study applying SDM to the Paderborn shuttle system. This case study exemplifies how applications that deal with complex object structures may be modeled using SDM.

1   Introduction

This paper describes how Story Driven Modeling can be applied to the Paderborn shuttle system case study, cf. [SEUPB04]. It is a major extension of [DGZ04]. While [DGZ04] focuses on the derivation of behavior specifications only, this paper has room to cover the whole SDM process for the case study. *Story Driven Modeling* (SDM) aims to provide a simple process for the development of object-oriented software where practical guidance for the actual modeling activities of each development step is provided, cf. [KNNZ00, Zü01, DGMZ02, DGZ02].

SDM proposes an agile software development process where each iteration is organized in the following steps:

1. requirements elicitation employing textual use case scenarios
2. requirements analysis using object games
3. requirements elaboration using story boards
4. derivation of class diagrams
5. derivation of automatic JUnit tests
6. design of method behavior using story diagrams

7. generation of implementation using Fujaba
8. automatic scenario validation

In the following sections we describe these activities step by step. Then we discuss related work and sum up.

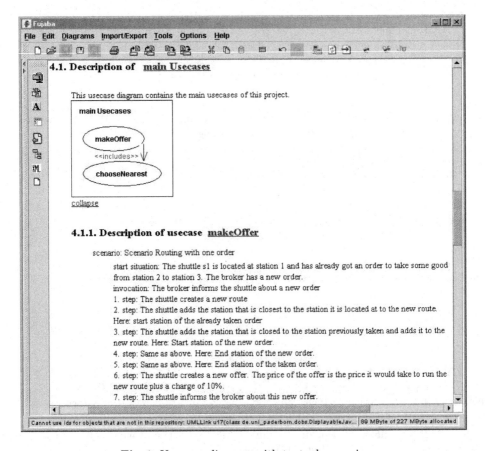

Fig. 1. Use case diagram with textual scenario

2   Requirements Elicitation

The Paderborn shuttle system case study [SEUPB04] provides a pretty good textual requirements description highlighting certain execution steps of the desired system, e.g. in section 2 of [SEUPB04] you find:

2.2. Orders
Orders are made known to all shuttles by a broker. An order defines start and destination stations as well as the allowed time for completion.

The deadline is derived from the time of acceptance of an order and the predefined processing time, which begins at the time of acceptance. Additionally, an order has a certain size, namely the number of people wishing to travel. Orders will be paid for by the passengers either by credit card or invoice. . . .

This kind of requirements description is pretty common. However, in our approach (as in many others) scenarios play a central role. Thus SDM proposes to turn requirements as given above into textual use case scenario descriptions. Such textual use case scenario descriptions should focus on typical collaborations of system constituents in response to use case invocations. As usual, such an use case scenario consists of a description of the start situation, an invocation, an elicitation of all executed steps and a description of the resulting situation, cf. Figure 1.

According to our experiences, developers agree on such textual scenario descriptions very easily. However, textual descriptions remain very vague and even if all stakeholders are happy with some scenario description, later refinement and formalization of the scenario will most likely reveal severe misunderstandings and disagreement. Thus, textual requirements descriptions are just not enough for a sufficient modeling of requirement scenarios.

3   Requirements Analysis with Object Games

To elaborate the use case scenarios, the developers may perform a so-called object game. In the object game the steps of the textual use case scenario are considered one by one and each is modeled using an object or collaboration diagram. This may be done in a team session. The developers may use a white board. The steps of the scenario are protocolled as sequences of object diagrams, e.g. using a digital camera or a digital smart board.

Figure 2 shows one snapshot from such an object game for our case study. It focuses on the problem of re-scheduling orders in case of a new order. In the upper half, the track system is outlined. In the lower part there are already two orders $o1$ and $o2$, scheduled in that order. Now a third order $o3$ arrives. Order $o3$ starts at station B which is just the station next to the shuttles current position A. Thus it seems efficient to pick up order $o3$ first and to re-schedule orders $o2$ and $o1$ in that order. The load (l) and unload (u) links in the route lists at the bottom show the visiting order and tasks for the old and the new route.

In addition to the depicted situation, we considered scenarios with overlapping orders, orders in large distances, and routes with side trips e.g. resulting if order $o3$ targets station E instead of D. After all, this object game gave us a very good idea of the object structures and algorithms we wanted to employ in our system.

In SDM, the role of the object games is to change the perspective from "I am executing this scenario step" to the perspective "The computer executes this scenario step". This change of perspective requires to model how the information required for a certain step is stored / organized in the computer and how the

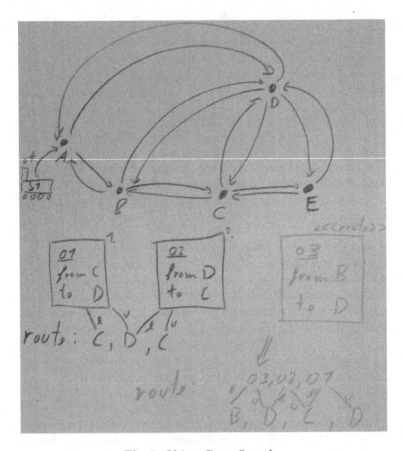

Fig. 2. Object Game Snapshot

desired program may work on this data. In addition, this change of perspective and the use of semi-formal UML diagrams implies a more precise description of data and computation steps than textual scenarios. According to our experience, this more precise, semi-formal scenario description already reveals a lot of severe misunderstandings between different stakeholders. This may result in heated discussions within the development team. However, it is very positive if such misunderstandings are resolved in such an early stage of the project.

The object game may also involve domain experts and customers that may have little skills in object-oriented modeling, UML, or programming. To help such people to participate in the discussion, on the white board objects may be depicted using icons or symbols from the application domain. For example in Figure 2 we used a small locomotive to depict a shuttle. Stations are depicted as dots on some kind of map. Similarly, we could have used a document icon to represent orders. According to our experiences, such little adaptions enable non-experts to participate in object games and to communicate with the development team about their domain knowledge.

We use such object games with great success with highschool students in their first programming course and we have very encouraging experiences from several research and some industrial projects. In one industrial project dealing with the configuration of the electrical elements of a car, our partners were two electrical engineers with a lot of domain knowledge but little programming and no UML skills. After some days of collaboration, the electrical engineers were able to participate in our discussions and after a week they came up with their own object diagrams in order to explain certain design aspects to us. In this project, object games have been a tremendous help for the transfer of domain knowledge.

SDM usually employs object or collaboration diagrams for the object games. This emphasizes the modeling of data. In case of simple or fairly static object structures, sequence diagrams may be used, similarly.

4 Story Boarding - Refining Use Cases

The object game results should now be entered into the Fujaba CASE tool as so-called *story boards*. A story board is a sequence of UML collaboration diagrams that show the changes of the object structure in this scenario comic strip alike. Turning object game snapshots into story boards results in a clean, printable, digital representation of the scenarios and it enables consistency checks and tool support for subsequent steps. Usually, during this step many details are added to the scenarios as e.g. object types, link names, attribute names, etc. In addition, the elaboration of story boards frequently reveals missing intermediate objects or functions or attributes or links that enable or facilitate the modeling of the desired behavior. Figure 12 shows a story board for re-scheduling a route for two offers.

The first activity of the story board in Figure 12 describes the start situation of the corresponding scenario: The *Shuttle s1* is located *at Station st1*. The shuttle currently travels route *r1* which visits the stations *st1*, *st2*, and *st3* in that order. Note, we visualize the order of the *visits* link by "next edges" between adjacent links. The shuttle has a pending order *o1* from Station *st2* to station *st3*. The broker *b1* has a new order *o2*.

Note, Fujaba allows to use icons as graphical stereotypes within object diagrams. As in object games this is especially important for domain experts and customers that participate in this phase. In order to save some space this paper employs such graphical stereotypes only in the first activity of Figure 10.

To allow a mapping of story board activities to the textual use case scenario steps, each story board activity contains the step number and the full step description as a comment at the top of the activity, cf. Figure 12. (Using Fujaba, changes to these texts are automatically propagated to the textual use case description.)

The second activity, i.e. the invocation step should always model the invocation of the scenario. In our approach this is usually a collaboration message / method call. Here, the method *makeOffer(o2)* is called on shuttle *s1*. Note, the second activity shows only a small cutout of the object structure of the previous step. This is just a change in perspective and not a deletion of the omitted objects. In story boards, modifications of elements is explicitly shown using ≪create≫ and ≪destroy≫ stereotypes or attribute assignments, cf. step 1 and 2 of Figure 12. In case of large object structures each step may focus on a different cutout of the scenario. Uninteresting objects from previous steps may just be omitted, not yet considered objects may be included. Objects taken over from a previous step are represented giving their name only. Objects that have not yet been shown but that appear the first time in this step are represented giving their name and their type. In Figure 12 the latter notation is used in the start situation, only.

In the first scenario execution step, i.e. in the third activity of Figure 12, a new *Route r2* is created. Note, that creation and deletion of objects / links is modeled in Fujaba using the stereotypes ≪create≫ and ≪destroy≫. Object *r2* is used to calculate a new route that includes the new order. A comparison of the costs of this new route with the previous route serves as basis for the calculation of an offer. Station *st1* is marked as first visit, as the shuttle is currently located at this station. All other start stations are marked as possible next stations via *possibleStations* links.

In this first analysis, we use a simple shortest-travel-first strategy for our routing. Therefore, in step 2, we call method *chooseNearest()* on the new *Route r2*. This shall select the possible station that is nearest to our position at this point of the tour. That station is removed from the list of possible next stations and appended to the list of visits, cf. the corresponding ≪destroy≫ and ≪create≫ markers in step 2. At station *st2* we plan to load offer *o1*. Then we will have to travel to the target station of *o1*. Therefore station *st3* is added to the list of possible next stations. In addition we update the *cost* of route *r2* to *10* (the distance to be travelled, not shown in the figure) times the *costPerMile*.

Step 3 is very similar to step 2. In step 4 station *st5* is chosen, where offer *o2* is delivered. Here, we do not need to add a new station to the route. After the new route has been calculated, step 6 creates the offer for the broker. We have chosen to calculate the price from the difference between the new and the old route plus 10% gain plus some fixed price. Note, that we do not yet take shuttle capacities into account.

In the last step of this scenario, the broker is notified about the offer. It is now the brokers turn to decide which offer it accepts.

The story board for use case make offer employs method *chooseNearest* to determine the next station to be visited. Due to the complexity of this method, we decide to create a sub use case for it and to analyze it with another scenario and story board, cf. Figure 13.

The start situation of Figure 13 focuses on a number of *possibleStations* for route *r2*. Note, compared to the previous story board we have added some other station *st6* to create a more interesting scenario. We assume, that each pair of stations is connected by a direct track. If this is not the case in the original topology, virtual tracks may be added as short-hands for sequences of physical tracks, easily. Thus, for each possible station method *chooseNearest* visits the track connecting it to the last visited station *st1*. If the *current* station is closer than all previous candidates, it is marked by a *nearest* link and the *minDistance* is updated. This is illustrated by steps 1 through 3. Step 4 appends the nearest possible station to the route and removes it from the set of possible stations.

In this paper we show only one story board or scenario for each use case. Generally, there may be multiple scenarios for each use case covering different cases for the use case behavior. As story boards are based on activity diagrams, they could also be used to model branches or loops. However, we made the experience that concentrating on one example run is much easier and is very helpful especially for beginners. This is an important property e.g. for customers and newcomers to the project. So, our approach suggests to use a set of simple alternative scenarios instead of a small number of complex activity diagrams.

In SDM, each use case is mapped to exactly one method that is invoked in order to trigger its execution. This method has to realize the use case functionality. However, a use case may include user interaction or it may utilize other use cases. In our approach, one use case uses or includes another use case, if its story board calls the method that realizes the other. This information may be derived from the story boards belonging to a use case and it may be depicted in the use case diagram as ≪includes≫ relation, cf. Figure 1. Similarly, use case methods might be subscribed as listeners to some other use cases and these listeners might be invoked at certain extension points. Such a mechanism could be shown as a ≪extends≫ relation between use case. So far, SDM uses use case relationships via method invocations in story boards, only. Explicit use case relations in the use case diagram are future work. The ≪includes≫ relation in Figure 1 is only a fake showing our future vision.

Object games and story boarding are quite similar activities. However, object games are more informal and better suited for team discussions while story boarding is usually done with the Fujaba tool that requires a more formal use of object diagrams. Especially, Fujaba asks for types for all elements of a story board. The corresponding Fujaba dialogs show a list of already introduced class diagram elements. The developer may either re-use an existing type or add a new one on-the-fly. This actually creates a first version of a conceptual class diagram for the desired system. How this first class diagram is completed and refined is discussed in section 5.

In our projects, we develop the first object games and story boards in team sessions. After that, all team members have a detailed common understanding of the design and implementation concepts of the desired system and of the role of the different class diagram constituents. Now, the team members may work on different use case concurrently in an iterated, agile development process. Fujaba multi user support may be used to synchronize concurrent changes to the different project parts and especially to merge changes in the common class diagram. Used in this way, the common class diagram builds a team wide vocabulary of shared types.

SDM derives automatic JUnit tests from the story boards, cf. section 6. This supports a test-first principle as utilized in most agile processes. As for other agile processes, this approach creates the question of completeness for scenarios.

Do the scenarios and tests cover all important cases or are there still test cases missing? We will comment on this problem at the end of section 7.

To sum up, according to our experiences object games and story boards are excellent means for the refinement of textual requirements and for design discussions. Starting from textual use case scenarios enables this phase to focus on one scenario step at a time. Using icons from the application domain facilitates to involve domain experts and customers in this phase. In our projects, this worked great even with customers having no or little programming and modelling skills (if they are smart and have certain technical understanding). The effort for creating the story boards pays by the derivation of automatic JUnit tests that drive the agile development process. At the beginning or when non-IT persons are involved, one might develop pretty detailed story boards as e.g. the one for selecting the nearest station in Figure 13. More experienced developers tend to use more coarse grained story boards and they focus on the more complex scenarios. Such developers might have skipped the story board for selecting the nearest station or they might have combined several of its steps into a single one since the intermediate steps are clear for them. However, also for experienced developers, object games and story boards are a extremely valuable means for design discussions. In our group, we use them every day.

5   Derivation of the Class Diagram

After having understood the problem during the object games and having protocolled and elaborated it using story boards, the next phase is the systematic derivation of class diagrams and of behavior specifications. According to our experiences, usually most of the important design decisions are already made during object game and story boarding. In addition, our story boards already employ typed object diagrams and in Fujaba, the class diagram elements are introduced on-the-fly during story boarding. Thus, the derivation of a first class diagram is usually very straight forward, cf. Figure 3.

Of course, a class diagram derived by this approach still needs refinement. For example the on-the-fly derivation of class diagram elements does not create any kind of inheritance hierarchy for the employed classes. Thus, usually the user will have to refactor the derived class diagram e.g. by moving common properties of multiple classes into some super class. Design patterns like the Composite pattern or Observer pattern or State pattern may be introduced here, too. However, many of these patterns become evident already at the object diagram level. For example, if we use a delegation mechanism or a proxy object in our design, we introduce and discuss this already in the story boards and refactor the class diagram, accordingly. Note, during the analysis phase one may develop story boards on a more platform independent level. In later phases platform specific refinements as proxies or facades may be added to the design. This may be done in the class diagram as well as in the story boards.

One may worry about the quality of class diagrams derived on-the-fly. Actually, we discuss a lot of design issues during story boarding and during story

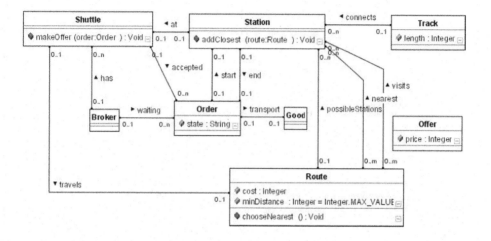

Fig. 3. Derived class diagram

board refinement. Once a design decision is made, the way one edits the class diagram does not matter that much. It probably depends on the problem, whether it is more appropriate to discuss a design issue using an object diagram or a class diagrams. For scenario related issues, object diagrams may work, for structural issues like the introduction of design patterns, the class diagram may be better. Sometimes you may need both views. However, from our teaching experiences, we observed that the quality of the class diagrams has been increased dramatically in our student courses, when we have introduced story boarding in the development process.

6   Derivation of Automatic JUnit Tests

When a scenario has been modeled by a story board, Fujaba provides a command to turn it automatically into a simple JUnit test for this scenario, cf. [GZ03]. Basically, the generated test consists of three major parts. The first part is derived from the modeled start situation of the story board. The generated test operation just creates a similar object structure at runtime. The second part is the invocation of the operation to be tested. The third part is derived from the last activity of the story board that is supposed to model the object structure that results from the scenario execution. We turn this into an operation that compares the object structure resulting from the test execution with the object structure modeled as the result of the scenario.

Using this test generator for the story board of Figure 13 results in a new test class. This test class contains the *setUp()* method shown in Figure 4. This method creates the object structure as modeled by the first step of the scenario (cf. Figure 13). For technical reasons every object of the start object structure is linked to the test object as well.

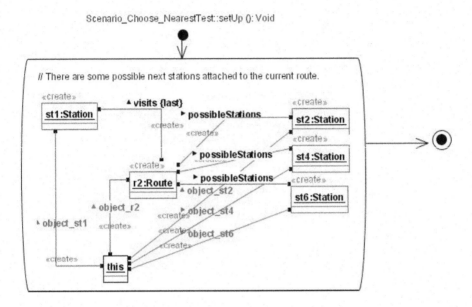

Fig. 4. Setting up the test object structure

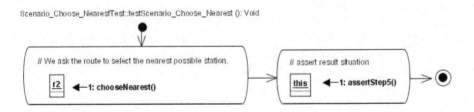

Fig. 5. The test method

The *setUp()* method is called by the JUnit framework every time before a test is executed. A test method then just has to perform the invocation and to assert that the result situation is reached. Because of the similar notations of scenario and behavior specifications, we just have to copy the invocation step from the story board to the story diagram of the test method as done in Figure 5.

If a test fails, we want to enable the developer to find out easily which step of the scenario has been executed and which one has not. Therefore, we generate *assertStepXY()* checks for every step of the scenario.

In this example, the check whether or not the result situation has been reached is thus encapsulated in method *assertStep5()*. Accordingly, the generated JUnit test method contains an *assertStep5()* call in its second activity, cf. Figure 5.

The *assertStep5()* method contains a copy of the result situation in the story board, as shown in Figure 6. In Fujaba, this object diagram is considered as a pattern to be matched against the actual object structure. This matching

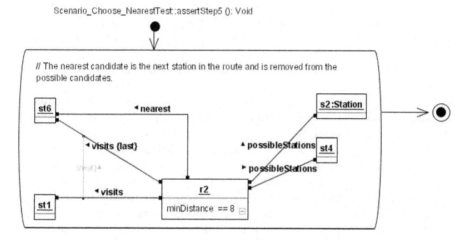

Fig. 6. Testing result situation

performs the wanted check. We use a special code generation flag to enable JUnit compliant checks in those methods. This way the developer can easily identify errors within the JUnit environment.

We have also added tool support for mapping JUnit error messages back to design level, see [Gei04]. So, if a test fails, it is visualized which part of the result situation is not recognized correctly.

7   Derivation of Method Behavior Using Story Diagrams

SDM uses the following guidelines for the derivation of method bodies from story boards:

1. identify all usages of a method in the story boards
2. for each usage:
   (a) identify all effects of this method call. These are changes to the object structure or subordinate method invocations. These effects may be shown in the current activity and in following activities. In case of subordinate method invocations, exclude effects caused by these methods.
   (b) identify the minimal context required for this method call to be able to execute the identified effects.
   (c) copy the minimal contexts to the state or activity diagram modeling the behavior of the considered method.
   (d) identify "similar" activities within the method body and try to merge them.
   (e) Resolve conflicts in the resulting control flow by adding appropriate branching conditions.
3. add loops and branches to cover the general case.

The result of this approach will be a UML interaction diagram, a so-called *story diagram*, that specifies the behavior of this method. The Fujaba CASE tool then generates executable Java code out of the class diagram and out of these method body specifications, cf. [Fu02, FNT98].

Using our approach for method *chooseNearest()*, we first have a look at the scenario from Figure 12. The first usage of the method *chooseNearest()* appears in the 2. step of the story board. In that step station *st2* is appended to the visits list and the end station of the corresponding order is added to the set of *possibleStations*. We decide that these modifications have to be executed by method *chooseNearest*. We now copy the minimal context needed for this modifications to the method body of method *chooseNearest()*. These are obviously the routing object and the effected order and stations and the connecting links, cf. the left activity of Figure 7. Note, that we have renamed the objects to indicate that we are now no longer dealing with an example scenario but with the general case.

The call of method *chooseNearest* in the 3. step is very similar to the one discussed above, so we do not deal with it here. But in the 4. step the derived story diagram does differ because we are now dealing with a station which is an end station of an offer and thus we do not need to add a new station to the set of *possibleStations*. Copying the minimal context of this method execution results in the right activity of Figure 7.

Note, now the activity diagram for method *chooseNearest* contains a conflict: The start activity has two outgoing transitions without conditions. Such conflicts arise, if the same method invocation shows different effects in different story boards or story board steps. Now the developer has to decide whether

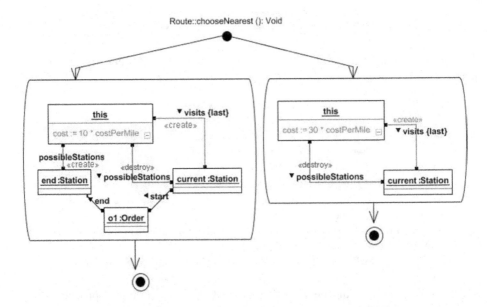

Fig. 7. Derived method body of method *chooseNearest()*

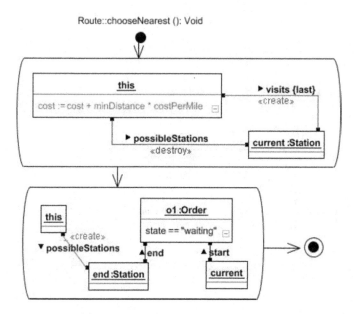

Fig. 8. Derived method body of method *chooseNearest()*

the two story board steps use the method inconsistently. In this case the story boards would need to be corrected. Otherwise, the method is called in two different situations and these differences need different handling in the method implementation. In this case, the developer has to specify branch conditions that choose the correct behavior.

In our example, the right activity of Figure 7 is somehow a sub-pattern of the left activity. The effects of the right activity are always needed. And if the selected station is the start station of an order, the additional effects of the left activity are required. The resulting reorganization of the method body is shown in Figure 8.

The so derived method body does not yet model the desired behavior. The problem is that any of the possible next stations might be chosen to be the nearest one. At this point, the developer should recognize, that the story board in Figure 12 does not model how the nearest station can be found. Now the developer has to go back to the story boarding phase and to add a story board that closes this gap. The story board in Figure 13 is such a refined story board.

Using the same guidelines as above, we derive the story diagram shown in Figure 9. Here the developer has to recognize, that we loop through the set of candidates. In story diagrams, we use for-each activities (with two stacked borders) to specify loops, cf. the first activity of Figure 9. Such a for-each activity is executed for every possible match of the contained object pattern.

Next the developer has to recognize that in the loop the visited station is handled in two different ways: Either it is ignored or if the visited station is closer than the current minDistance, it is marked by a nearest link and the

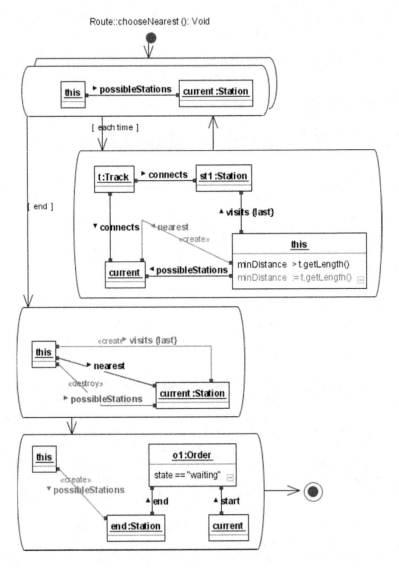

Fig. 9. Final version of method *chooseNearest()*

minDistance is updated. This condition and the desired effects are modeled by the second activity of Figure 9.

The last step of the story board in Figure 13 can be merged with the first activity from Figure 8. Figure 9 shows the resulting method specification. This specification finally has the desired behavior. From such a story diagram Fujaba generates executable Java code.

We may now consider the *makeOffer* operation called at the beginning of the story board of Figure 12. The 1. step of Figure 12 creates a new route and adds some *possibleStations* to it. While this step looks simple, it is actually pretty complicated to determine the set of *possibleStations*. The example adds station *st2* as the start station of a pending order and station *st4* as start station of the new order. These two cases are covered by the first and second activity of Figure 10. Note, for the second activity we directly identified that there might be multiple pending orders and that we should use a for-each activity to loop through all of them. Then we went on with the other steps of the story board. After finishing a first version of the method we applied a simple check list to it containing items like:

- normal activity: does it always match and if not is a failure handling modeled?
- branch activity: are all cases considered?
- for-each activity: does it iterate through all desired matches?
- for-each activity: does it apply to undesired matches?

In this example, the last check item uncovered that there might be an order that has already been loaded and that is pending just because it still needs to be delivered. In that case, we must not add the start station of the corresponding order but its end station. Thus, we had to split the second activity of Figure 10 and we added the third activity handling already loaded orders. Note, due to our experience, reviewing story boards and graphical method specifications is much easier than reviewing plain textual use case scenarios and plain source code. Generally, good readability is a major strength of our notation which is of high value for all kind of maintenance activities.

The derivation of the remaining elements of Figure 10 is left as an exercise for the reader.

We admit that the derivation of method body specifications is already close to programming. However, we claim, that it is done on a higher level of abstraction. In addition, the closeness of story boards and method specifications and the good readability of our notation facilitates this step, considerably. We do not yet have clean statistical evidence, but due to our experience we estimate that in the area of complex object structures the realization with story diagrams is about five times faster than conventional programming. This speed up is mainly achieved by the readability of our specifications that facilitates maintenance and peer cooperation.

We also have some experience with an industrial project done in C#. Since Fujaba currently generates Java, only, this project used Visio to create story boards and then the methods were derived in C# directly. In that project, the participants credited that story boards were extremely helpful for them. In addition, the story boards turned out as a very good basis for direct implementation of the employed methods in a conventional OO programming language, too. Thus, our approach may be used independent from the Fujaba CASE tool, too.

Note, story boards are no general testing method. They drive the behavior specification according to the test-first-principle of agile processes but they do not claim to achieve full test coverage. Actually, we observe that experienced

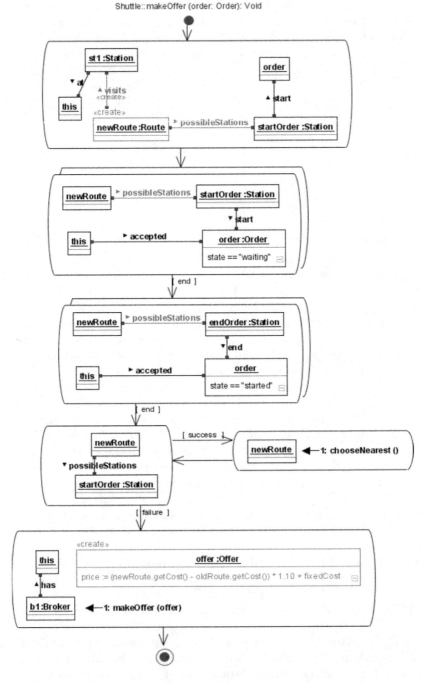

Fig. 10. Derived method body of method *makeOffer()*

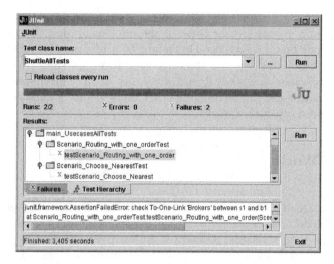

Fig. 11. JUnit test run directly after story boarding

developers tend to produce fewer story boards with fewer steps. However, these smaller story boards then contain much more interesting cases. For example, a really experienced story boarder would probably have included an end station in the step 1 of the story board for method chooseNearest, directly. Thereby, the method specification would have addressed this case directly, without a review and without testing.

8   Generation of Implementation Using Fujaba

At this point, we are already able to generate code for the whole system, cf. [Fu02, KNNZ00]. Note, Fujaba generates not only code from class diagrams but also from behavior specifications and from the JUnit test specifications. Since all methods have been specified by story diagrams, no manual coding in some programming language is required.

Note, measured in code size Fujaba generates about 5 to 10 pages Java code from about 1 page story diagram. While hand-written code would probably be somewhat shorter, we still claim that this indicates that story diagrams are on a somewhat higher level of abstraction compared to usual code. However, much more important is our experience, that one page story diagrams are much easier to read and to understand than several pages of Java code.

9   Automatic Scenario Validation

Directly after story boarding, JUnit tests may be derived and run. The result of such a run is shown in Figure 11. In that situation the JUnit test *should* fail since the implementation has not yet been done. Now the test may be used as a driving force for method derivation.

Note, the JUnit tests may be combined with a code coverage analysis. This coverage analysis may reveal certain parts of the implementation that are not required for the story board scenarios. This might be a hint on additional cases that have already been considered in the implementation but that are not yet documented by corresponding story board scenarios. Such a mechanism may provide us with some notion of completeness for story board documentations. This topic is a part of our future work.

10   Related Work

Our object game is comparable with CRC card approaches, see e.g. [Bo91]. However, the outcome of a CRC card session is some kind of class diagram. The outcome of our object games are sequences of object diagram snapshots that then are turned into story boards. Actually, CRC card approaches go through scenarios, too. However, they do not protocol the sequence of executed steps or the object structure evolution but CRC cards record only the employed classes, relations, and methods. Thus in CRC card approaches, the most valuable information get lost.

Several other approaches provide sophisticated support for turning sequence diagrams or MSCs into statecharts, cf. e.g. [WS00, WKS03, KMS01, KGSB99]. These approaches use sequence diagrams to describe scenarios. From these sequence diagrams statecharts are derived. While these approaches provide a much better automating, they do not deal with complex object structures that evolve dynamically. In the example of this paper, the actual topology plays an important role for the routing algorithm. For us, story boards and story diagrams are more appropriate in order to represent this topology and to reason about it. In general, above approaches and our approach complement each other and one may use the one which fits the problem best.

The Catalysis approach uses object diagrams as pre and post conditions for the characterization of use cases and of methods, too, cf. [DW99]. Actually, many ideas and even many notions are close to certain notions of our approach. However, Catalysis uses object diagrams as pre and post conditions more in the traditional sense of algebraic specifications which corresponds to the idea of design-by-contract proposed e.g. in Eiffel. The contracts set up the framework for method implementation. However, the developer gets no practical guidance for method implementation. Intermediate steps and algorithmic aspects are not addressed by definition. We felt, that support for the actual method derivation was desperately missing and thus story boarding deals with intermediate steps and algorithmic aspects more explicitly. This allows to provide more input for the derivation of methods behaviors. For large systems, both approaches might actually be combined. First, more generic use cases are considered and graphical contracts are derived. Second, the algorithmic aspects may be studied by refining the graphical contracts into story boards.

There are several other approaches which deal with scenario-based testing. The Rational Quality Architect [RQA02] for example uses sequence diagrams to define scenarios. From these sequence diagrams they generate test cases and test drivers. At test runtime, the signal flow is traced and protocolled using a sequence diagram which is then compared to the scenario sequence diagram. Again, the use of sequence diagrams make sense when dealing with complex signal flow, like e.g. in protocols. We think that for modeling applications with complex object structures, story boards are better suited. Another benefit of story boards is, that the developer may model complex post conditions using an object diagram, see e.g. the result situation of Figure 13. This is hardly done with sequence diagrams. More likely, one would use OCL expressions for this purpose. Here, we claim, that our graphical notation is easier to read than OCL post conditions.

The SCENT approach [RG00] derives statecharts from natural language scenarios. Test case generation is then done using path traversal within these statecharts. Again this approach lacks of support for complex object structures. In SDM, a scenario is in most cases just a sequence of activities. When deriving the behavioral specifications all these sequences are merged together into a "system statechart". So, path analysis techniques might be useful in SDM to identify paths in the implementation not yet covered by scenarios to achieve completeness. This is future work.

The TOTEM approach [BL01] uses again sequence diagrams for specification of scenarios. The test generation also takes inter-scenario relationships modeled in use case diagrams into account. As mentioned in section 4, SDM models inter-scenario relationships implicitly in the story boards by calling the methods of other scenarios. Unfortunately, this relationships are not yet considered at test generation.

Fujaba's graph transformations as used in the story diagrams are inspired by the ones used in PROGRES [Progres]. Actually, PROGRES is a predecessor of the Fujaba system and many graph transformation concepts have been carried over to Fujaba. However, the PROGRES process [SWZ95] (co-developed by one of the authors) does not have an explicit scenario analysis phase like our object game and story boarding activities. In this sense, SDM is a further development of the PROGRES process.

11   Summary

This paper introduces Story Driven Modeling (SDM) as systematic software development approach. Instead of CRC cards, SDM employs so-called object games. The steps of the object games are protocolled as so-called story boards. From these story boards, the developer derives the class diagram. Then behavioral specifications are derived by analysis and comparison of all story boards. Finally, our CASE tool generates executable code out of the derived class diagram and the behavioral specifications. In addition, story boards are turned into automatic JUnit tests. These JUnit tests ensure that the derived behavior specifications actually realize the provided use case scenarios. For all these steps, SDM tries to provide practical guidance for the actual software development work.

SDM has been used with great success in two projects with Gauss Highschool Braunschweig and in two courses at University of Kassel with 40 and 60 students, respectively. In addition, we have done a first project with an industrial partner and we use it in a research project for car industry these days. The results of these experiences are very promising. Especially, the object games and the story boards turn out to be an ideal way for requirements analysis and early design considerations. One of our industrial partners has been using CRC cards before. After the first project using object games and story boards instead, they instantly decided to make these the new standard for their work, cf. [Czok04].

At University of Kassel, we use SDM for the development of Fujaba itself. At our group we deal with about one million lines of the Fujaba implementation. We also deal with a lot of third-party tools, libraries and code. Even for this fairly large system, we use object games and story boards with great success for the analysis of new or changed functionality and how it might be blended with the rest of the tool. To be honest, method specification with story diagrams is not always possible, since the reverse engineering capabilities of Fujaba do not yet fully address method bodies. Thus, old methods are modified at code level.

As next steps, we try to provide more sophisticated tool support for our approach within the Fujaba CASE tool. Fujaba supports our story board and story diagram notation and code generation for the latter. We plan to extend this by an analysis component that looks for method calls within story boards that have not yet contributed to the derivation of method bodies. Similarly this analysis component shall point to not yet included invocations of a currently considered method within different story board(activitie)s. In addition the copying of minimal contexts should be supported as well as the identification and merging of equivalent states. In the reverse direction, one may start with a story diagram or one may modify a story diagram and Fujaba should either support the derivation of meaningful story boards or support the adaption of story diagram changes within existing story boards.

References

[BL01]   L. Briand, Y. Labiche: A UML-Based Approach to System Testing; Proc. 4th International Conference on the Unified Modeling Language (UML), pp. 194-208, Toronto, Canada, 2001.

[Bo91]   G. Booch: Object Oriented Design with Applications, Benjamin/Cummings Publishing Company, Inc, 1991.

[Czok04]   M. Czok: Evaluation of Story Driven Modeling on the development of a radio-based telegram protocoll (in German), Diploma Thesis, University of Kassel, 2004.

[DGMZ02]   I. Diethelm, L. Geiger, T. Maier, A. Zündorf: Turning Collaboration Diagram Strips into Storycharts, Workshop on Scenarios and state machines: models, algorithms, and tools; ICSE 2002, Orlando, Florida, USA, 2002.

[DGZ02]   I. Diethelm, L. Geiger, A. Zündorf: UML im Unterricht: Systematische objektorientierte Problemlösung mit Hilfe von Szenarien am Beispiel der Türme von Hanoi, in Forschungsbeiträge zur "Didaktik der Informatik" - Theorie, Praxis und Evaluation (in german); GI-Lecture Notes, pp. 33-42, 2002.

[DGZ04]   I. Diethelm, L. Geiger, A. Zündorf: Systematic Story Driven Modeling, Workshop on Scenarios and State Machines: models, algorithms, and tools; workshop at ICSE 2004, Edinburgh, 2004.

[DW99]   D. F. D'Souza, A. C. Wills: Objects, Components, and Frameworks with UML, The Catalysis Approach; Addison-Wesley, ISBN 0-201-31012-0, 1999.

[FNT98]   T. Fischer, J. Niere, L. Torunski: Konzeption und Realisierung einer integrierten Entwicklungsumgebung für UML, Java und Stroy-Driven-Modeling (in german), Diploma Thesis, University of Paderborn, 1998.

[Fu02]   Fujaba Homepage, University of Paderborn, http://www.fujaba.de/.

[Gei04]   L. Geiger: Automatische JUnit Testgenerierung aus UML-Szenarien mit Fujaba (in German), Diploma Thesis, Technical University of Braun-schweig, 2004.

[GZ03]   L. Geiger, A. Zündorf: Transforming Graph Based Scenarios into Graph Transformation Based JUnit Tests, Applications of Graph Transformations with Industrial Relevance (AGTIVE), Charlottesville, Virginia, USA, 2003.

[JBR99]   I. Jacobson, G. Booch, J. Rumbaugh: The Unified Software Development Process; Addison-Wesley, ISBN 0-201-57169-2, 1999.

[KGSB99]   I. Krüger, R. Grosu, P. Scholz, M. Broy: From MSCs to Statecharts; Franz J. Rammig (ed.): Distributed and Parallel Embedded Systems, Kluwer Academic Publishers, 1999.

[KMS01]   J. Koskinen, E. Mäkinen, T. Systä: Minimally Adequate Synthesizer Tolerates Inaccurate Information during Behavioral Modeing, SCASE 2001, Enschede, Netherlands, 2001.

[KNNZ00]   H. Köhler, U. Nickel, J. Niere, A. Zündorf: Integrating UML Diagrams for Production Control Systems; in Proc. of ICSE 2000 - The 22nd International Conference on Software Engineering, June 4-11th, Limerick, Ireland, acm press, pp. 241-251, 2000.

[Progres]   http://www-i3.informatik.rwth-aachen.de/research/projects/progres/

[RG00]   J. Ryser, M. Glinz: Using Dependency Charts to Improve Scenario-Based Testing; in Proceedings of the 17th International Conference on Testing Computer Software (TCS2000), Washington D.C., USA, 2000.

[RQA02]   Rational Software Corporation: Rational Quality Architect Realtime Edition User's Guide, http://publibfp.boulder.ibm.com/epubs/pdf/12656660.pdf, 2002.

[SEUPB04]   Software Engineering Group University of Paderborn: Shuttle System Case Study, Version 1.0, 10.1.2004, University of Paderborn, http://wwwcs.upb.de/cs/ag-schaefer/CaseStudies/ShuttleSystem/, 2004.

[SWZ95]   Schürr A., Winter A, Zündorf A.: Graph Grammar Engineering with PROGRES, in: Schäfer W. (ed.): Software Engineering - ESEC '95, LNCS 989, pp 219-234, Springer, 1995

[WKS03]   J. Whittle, R. Kwan, J. Saboo: From Scenarios to Code: An Air Traffic Control Case Study, ICSE2003, Portland, USA, 2003.

[WS00]   J. Whittle, J. Schumann: Generating Statechart Designs From Scenarios, ICSE2000, Limerick, Ireland, 2000.

[Zü01]   A. Zündorf: Rigorous Object Oriented Software Development, Habilitation Thesis, University of Paderborn, 2001.

A   Story Boards

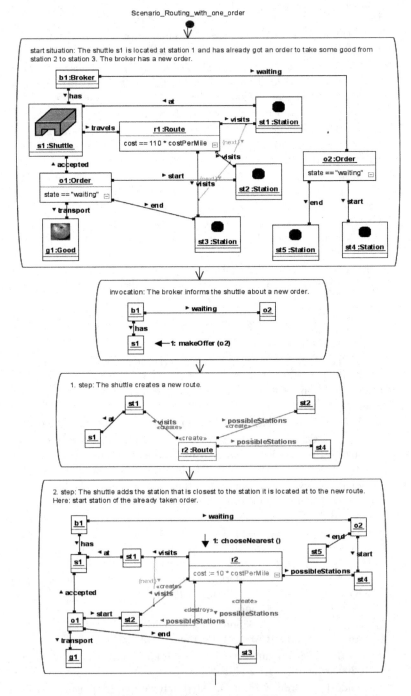

Fig. 12. Story board for the makeOffer scenario

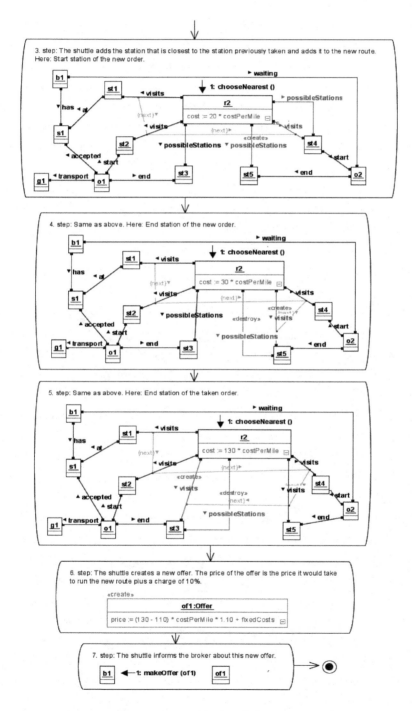

Fig. 12. (continued)

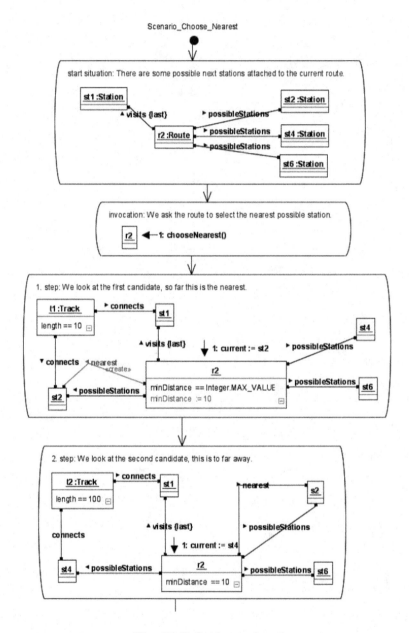

Fig. 13. Refined story board

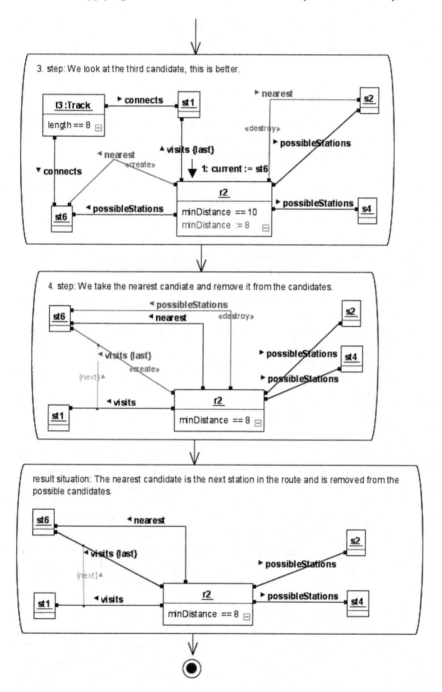

Fig. 13. (continued)

Traceability and Evaluation in Scenario Analysis by Use Case Maps

Dorin B. Petriu[1], Daniel Amyot[2], Murray Woodside[1], and Bo Jiang[2]

[1] Department of Systems and Computer Engineering,
Carleton University, Ottawa, Ontario, Canada, K1S 5B6
{dorin, cmw}@sce.carleton.ca
[2] SITE, University of Ottawa,
800 King Edward, Ottawa, Ontario, Canada, K1N 6N5
{damyot, bojiang}@site.uottawa.ca

Abstract. The Use Case Map (UCM) scenario notation has some strong features related to rapid capture and evaluation of requirements models. In this paper, we explain how a UCM model was developed from a requirements oracle case study: the Autonomous Shuttle Transport System. We further consider establishing links between scenario elements and other types of requirements. These links, which can be supported by requirements management tools, are useful to maintain both the scenarios and requirements during their evolution. We also demonstrate how simple performance models generated from UCMs may impact high-level requirements and architectures.

1 Introduction

Requirements, which are expressions of ideas to be embodied in the system or application under development and the conditions under which it will operate, are often collected in unconstrained forms including text, diagrams, tables, and equations or logical formulae. Requirements analysis then uses various techniques to investigate the consistency, completeness, feasibility, and consequences of the requirements. Nuseibeh and Easterbrook discuss integrated requirements engineering, combining a variety of techniques with automated tool support for effective requirements management [17]. They identify the need to move from contextual enquiry to elicit requirements, to more formal representations for analysis.

One form of requirements may be *scenarios*, which describe sequences of operations to be carried out in response to given events, requests, or interactions. Scenarios may be used to drive the elicitation and development of requirements, to refine requirements stated in other ways, and to connect other requirements whose relations would be otherwise unapparent. Lamsweerde gives a thorough discussion on the relationships between goals and scenarios, between informal and formal methods, and between scenarios and other requirements models [14]. Like many others, he noted that scenario specifications are incomplete and cannot be used as a substitute for all types of requirements. Various non-functional requirements, goals, quality attributes, and informal annotations are found in most requirements documents.

In order for scenarios to be used in cooperation with general requirements, they must be connected to external requirements in a way that supports traceability, navigation, and analysis. This paper presents an approach where Use Case Map (UCM) scenarios are constructed from an informal collection of requirements. UCM scenario elements are then imported into a popular *requirements management system* (RMS), namely Telelogic DOORS [21], and linked to other types of requirements. UCMs are abstract scenarios that are close to the requirements abstraction level, and they contain many types of elements that are potentially traceable to other types of requirements.

Scenario management and *scenario evolution*, which are discussed in their largest context by Jarke *et al.* [13], face the issue of maintaining traceability of scenarios that relate to each other and that evolve over time. To avoid an explosion in the number of individual scenarios describing a complex system, several approaches have been developed to capture common parts (often called episodes) and describe interdependencies through relationships such as precedence, alternatives, inclusion, extension, usage, etc., while at the same time improving consistency and maintainability. Breitman and Leite provided an extensive case study on scenario evolution based on such relationships, and they identified the need to develop suitable management systems that would take into consideration scenario relationships [8]. Interestingly, Use Case Maps contain many such relationships as first-class language constructs. Unfortunately, few substantial results are available for either the management of graphical scenarios like UCMs, or their integration to general requirements, with the noticeable exception of the work of Alexander [1] and a recent DOORS add-on called Analyst [22], which will both be discussed in section 6.

This paper introduces a scenario-oriented requirements engineering framework and focuses on three complementary contributions. First, sections 2 and 3 illustrate several steps used in the construction of a UCM model from informal requirements. The case study selected here is the Autonomous Shuttle Transport System (ASTS), presented as a requirements oracle at the *Scenarios: Models, Algorithms and Tools* Dagstuhl seminar [7]. ASTS is a rail-based transport system under development intended to enable individual traffic of people and goods, which today is mainly conducted by cars and trucks, by autonomously acting shuttles on rail [20]. The second contribution is a novel approach to the integration of UCM scenarios in a RMS. Section 4 presents how UCMs can be imported into DOORS, how they can be connected to external requirements, and how these links can be exploited for evolving scenarios, requirements, and designs. We demonstrate the feasibility of such an approach with a new UCMNAV export filter, which generates documents that can be imported into a commercial requirements management system. A particular attention was paid to the unavoidable evolution of scenario models and other requirements. The third contribution (section 5) builds on previous work to show that simple analysis and evaluation of performance models generated from UCMs can influence several requirements and architectural decisions early in the development process. Finally, our conclusions are discussed in section 6.

2   Requirements Capture Using UCM

2.1   Basics of Use Case Maps

The Use Case Map notation was developed to capture scenario descriptions as causal flows of responsibilities for object-oriented design of real-time systems [9, 12]. In a requirements engineering context, UCMs also proved to have several benefits over many other scenario notations: they abstract from message exchanges, they support scenario integration and interaction detection, and they visually connect behaviour and architecture in a map view [3].

As shown in Fig. 1, the UCM notation uses filled circles for *start points* (triggering events and preconditions), bars for *end points* (resulting event and postconditions), crosses for *responsibilities* (abstract actions and activities), and rectangles for *components* (e.g., software module, hardware, actors). Components can contain responsibilities and sub-components. With *paths*, responsibilities can be causally linked in sequence, as alternatives, or in parallel. Maps can also be decomposed hierarchically with *stubs* (shown as diamonds on a path, see Fig. 2) and *plug-ins* (sub-maps bound to stubs). UCMs are currently being standardized

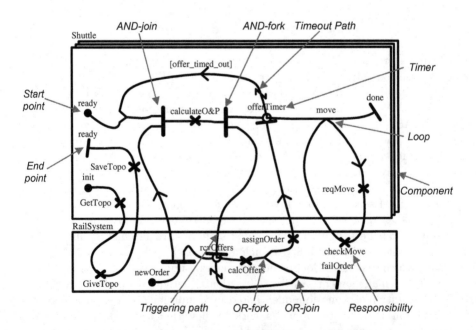

Fig. 1. Initial ASTS Use Case Map (version 1)

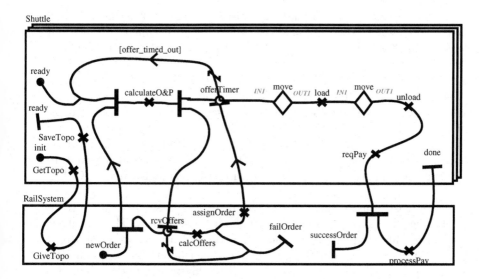

Fig. 2. ASTS UCM with move stubs (version 3)

by the International Telecommunications Union as part of the User Requirements Notation (URN) [2, 11].

The UCM Navigator (UCMNAV) is a multi-platform tool that supports the editing and analysis of UCM models [24], which can also be exported to various formats such as EPS (used for the figures in this paper), MIF, CGM, and SVG.

UCMs have been used as a basis for various kinds of model transformations. UCMNAV can extract individual scenarios from complex UCM models and export them as XML files, which can further be transformed and refined (e.g., with the UCMEXPORTER companion tool [4]) into Message Sequence Charts (MSC), UML 1.4 sequence diagrams, and TTCN-3 test case skeletons. We will take advantage of such transformations in section 4.3. UCM models have also proved to be a good basis for describing and synthesizing system component behaviour in LOTOS [5], SDL [10], and communicating state machines [6].

UCMs can be annotated with performance-oriented information, which enable UCMNAV to export performance models in the form of Layered Queueing Networks (LQN) [18]. Enabling scenario-based performance analysis early in the design process and as close to the requirements specification phase as possible may influence several major decisions regarding the system architecture. This topic will be explored further in section 5, again using ASTS as an example.

2.2   Capturing ASTS Scenarios Using UCM

The requirements for the ASTS were given to the workshop participants as handouts along with instructions to focus on the shuttle control [20]. One of the handouts provided a high-level overview of the system and described the railway network, the way in which customers place orders, the rail shuttles, and the way in which shuttle income and expenses are assessed. Another handout provided a more detailed description of the simulation environment in which the shuttle control software is evaluated as well as descriptions of typical Use Cases involving the shuttles.

UCMs capture the emerging behaviour of a system. This is done by tracing the behaviour and overlaying it on the system structure. The behaviour traces are called paths and the system structure is represented with components. Along the paths, responsibilities are identified and allocated to suitable components.

In this case, the first step towards creating a UCM for the ASTS involved identifying the system components. Initially the only components identified were the RailSystem and multiple Shuttles, as shown by the rectangles in the UCM in Fig. 1.

The second step was to identify the two main Use Cases from a shuttle's viewpoint which are initialization and serving customer orders. The initialization Use Case deals with the Shuttle acquiring the rail network topology from the RailSystem upon activation. The serving customer orders Use Case has the Shuttle waiting for a new order to arrive from the RailSystem and calculating and submitting an offer. If the offer is accepted, then the Shuttle proceeds to move and serve the customer.

The initialization Use Case is shown in Fig. 1 as the UCM path that begins at the init start point inside the Shuttle component. The path is based on the Receiving Topology sequence diagram from [20], which simply describes a request from the Shuttle and the answer provided by the RailSystem (referred to as Kernel in the original document). The Shuttle requests the network topology by executing the GetTopo responsibility. The RailSystem records the topology as represented by the GiveTopo responsibility. Finally the Shuttle receives the topology and saves it as part of the SaveTopo responsibility. The Shuttle is now ready to serve customers.

The serving customers Use Case is synthesized from various sequence diagrams from the initial requirements [20]. The path begins with the Shuttle being ready and awaiting the arrival of a newOrder from the RailSystem. The RailSystem sets a timer for waiting on offers from different Shuttles, shown in Fig. 1 as the rcvOffers timer. In the UCM notation, timers are shown with a clock symbol and they are set when reached on a path. When the connected end point from a different scenario path (i.e., the triggering path) is reached in time, the timer is reset and the scenario can progress on the original path, otherwise the time-out path (shown with a zigzag symbol) is taken. When a new order arrives, the Shuttle calculates an offer and a path through the rail network (the calculateO&P responsibility) and sends it to the RailSystem while also setting an offerTimer to wait for a notification that it has been awarded the order. The RailSystem evaluates all the offers and chooses the best one (the calcOffers responsibility). It then notifies the winning Shuttle (the assignOrder responsibility).

The successful Shuttle receives the order assignment and proceeds to serve it. The move loop shows how the Shuttle traverses a track segment by first requesting permission to move onto a new segment (reqMove). The RailSystem checks whether the Shuttle can move safely to the new segment and then notifies it. Any Shuttle that does not get the order times out on the offerTimer timer and resumes waiting for another newOrder.

If the RailSystem does not receive any offers for a given order during the bidding period (rcvOffers times out) or none of the offers are acceptable (calcOffers does not have a winning bid) then it aborts the processing of that order. An order failure handling mechanism was not specified in the ASTS handouts, but such a mechanism can be added later.

This first UCM model shown in Fig. 1 was created in a little over an hour by a single person interpreting the ASTS documents and entering the UCM in the UCMNav tool. The advantage of UCMNav is that it provides a platform for quick editing of UCMs with facilities for exporting and importing models.

3   Scenario Evolution Using UCM

The ASTS scenario was rapidly created and improved during the Dagstuhl seminar, which illustrates one of the strengths of the approach. During a group discussion of about an hour, the initial UCM shown in Fig. 1 was evolved through six steps. After specific feedback following a presentation to the other participants, version 7 (shown in Fig. 4) was created.

Scenarios evolve by the addition of functionality, steps to correct the logic of the path, encapsulation of detail, and restructuring of a set of scenarios (as described in [8]). For example, the first change was by addition, to extend the successful order completion path to incorporate payment to shuttles and to name the successOrder and failOrder end points in the RailSystem. The second change added a second optional shuttle movement in the scenario to get the shuttle to the pickup station. To simplify the map, it also encapsulated the shuttle movement behaviour into a plug-in map within the stub move. This gave version 3 as shown in Fig. 2 and 3. The move stub is used twice (shown as the diamond shapes labelled move), and in both cases, the plug-in map is bound to the stub according to this relationship: $\{<IN1 \rightarrow \text{leave}>, <\text{arrive} \rightarrow OUT1>\}$, which ensures the continuation of the path accross connected maps.

The next steps are not shown by diagrams, but version 4 introduced an additional optional move of a shuttle for repositioning (as part of a global strategy to provide shuttles in all regions of the system), before a new order is received. Version 5 moved two responsibilities into two new components, a TopoAgent to create and maintain the system view of network topology, and a BankAgent to process payments. Initially these components were nested inside the RailSystem component, where the responsibilities were initially defined, but in version 6 they were made separate (as indicated in Fig. 4). Version 6 also introduced a CommunicationEnv component containing all the other components and representing the simulation communication environment. This was done in order to align the UCM with the deployment diagram provided in the informal requirements [20]. Version 6 was presented to the other participants in the requirements oracle session.

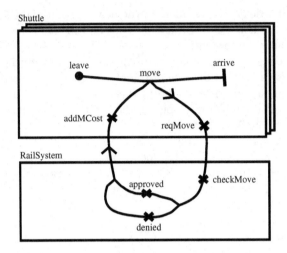

Fig. 3. Plug-in for the move stub in the ASTS UCM (versions 3 to 7)

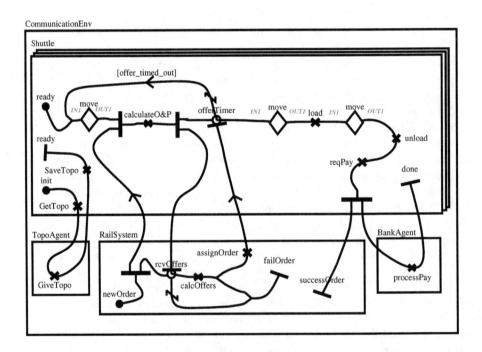

Fig. 4. ASTS UCM with additional move stub and three new components (version 7)

Fig. 4 shows the final version (version 7) created in response to feedback received from other participants after the presentation. The only major change was made to the move plug-in where we added approved and denied alternatives to the RailSystem response when a Shuttle requests to move to a new track segment, as well as an addMCost responsibility to account for each track segment that a Shuttle travels on. These were not in the original loop of Fig. 1, nor in the original plug-in map.

4   Managing UCM Evolution in DOORS

The creation and evolution of scenarios and other requirements can be intertwined in many ways. Typically, scenarios will be used to discover requirements or to provide an operational view of existing requirements for understanding and validation. In turn, requirements can also trigger the discovery or evolution of scenarios. Such iterative process can be supported by requirements management systems (RMS), for example Telelogic DOORS [21]. Most RMS focus on structured textual requirements, with support for traceability, access control, and version control. Adding scenarios brings in a complementary view that can be beneficial to many stakeholders.

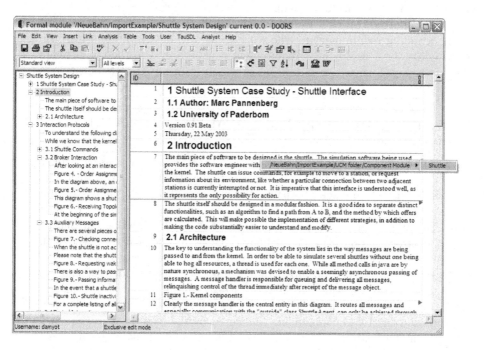

Fig. 5. Original ASTS description imported into DOORS, with links to/from UCMs

Many RMS can import requirements from various sources, including word processors. For instance, we can import the original ASTS informal requirements into DOORS, leading to an initial database of requirements objects, as shown by the document in Fig. 5. The nature of these requirements objects can vary from operational requirements to non-functional requirements and quality attributes. They can also be more or less structured, depending on the quality of the source document.

4.1   Combining UCMs with External Requirements

To combine scenario descriptions with other requirements, they should be linked using the facilities of the RMS. Links of this kind between scenarios and informal requirements were discussed also by Leite *et al.* [16], using an experimental RMS.

To use an RMS, the scenario elements must be imported into its data space. When this is done, the intrinsic links within the scenario can also be created as RMS links. These include predecessor/successor sequence links, linking responsibilities to the entity for the scenario, and linking components to scenarios and responsibilities. We have implemented this importation in DOORS using scripts native to the tool, and including facilities for incremental update from a modified scenario.

The process begins by representing the external requirements in the RMS. Fig. 5 shows the textual ASTS requirements in the DOORS tool. Then the scenario is imported, and its elements are linked to other requirements. For example, a timing requirement for the scenario as a whole can be linked to the scenario entity, or a deployment requirement can be linked to the components it references. Fig. 5 shows an indication of a link from an ASTS requirements object to a UCM.

4.2   Exploiting Traceability Links: UCM Elements and Other Requirements

The links are used in reasoning about requirements and about changes to requirements. Objects have categories and links are typed. Links are also directional ("A depends on B"), and may be navigated in either direction (that is from a requirement object to those that depend on it, or to those it depends on). Fig. 6 shows a DOORS display of ASTS UCM components and a link from Shuttle to its responsibilities (above) and a display of UCM responsibilities linked with their components (below). Link direction is indicated by an arrowhead.

A "big picture" of relationships through links can help to identify clusters of dependencies, and missing information. Fig. 7 shows a traceability matrix indicating links between entities in the text document (represented by the bars at the top) and the UCM components (indicated by the bars below). The black spots in the matrix indicate the existence of links. If a UCM requirement object is not directly or indirectly linked to external requirements, then this might indicate that a link is missing or that this UCM element is not required. If a requirements change is resolved by a scenario change, the scenario can be updated in the UCM end and re-imported. As mentioned above, links to entities which have not changed are maintained when the map is re-imported.

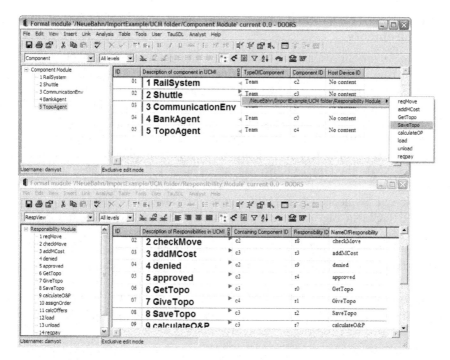

Fig. 6. UCM components and responsibilities in DOORS, with attributes and links

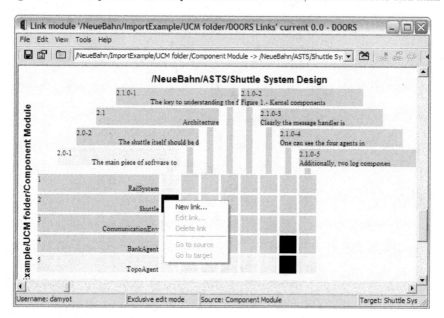

Fig. 7. Traceability matrix between UCM components and external requirements

4.3 Exploiting Traceability Links: UCM Scenarios and Other Requirements

A UCM scenario specification may imply many different paths, depending on the conditions that govern choices made during the execution. These choices can be specified as path preconditions, which are Boolean variables defining guarding conditions on OR-fork branches, timers, and dynamic stubs. The resulting scenario definition implies a corresponding sequential path or partial order. A UCM traversal mechanism [12], implemented in UCMNAV, is used to extract the specific scenario (partial order) corresponding to a given definition, and stores the result in a XML file. Our DOORS import capability includes these specific scenario definitions. The XML file can also be converted to various forms [4], such as a Message Sequence Chart (MSC) or a UML sequence diagram.

The ASTS UCM in Fig. 4 was supplemented with such variables and conditions. One scenario was defined to describe what happens when a new order fails because the shuttle's offer is not acceptable. UCMNAV can highlight the UCM paths traversed by this specific scenario. The resulting scenario was also converted to an MSC by UCMEXPORTER, hence enabling a better visualization of the complete, end-to-end scenario (Fig. 8). Note that the move loop was not traversed in this scenario in order to keep the trace short. In general,

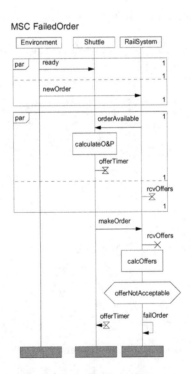

Fig. 8. Result of the *FailedOrder* scenario definition, converted to an MSC

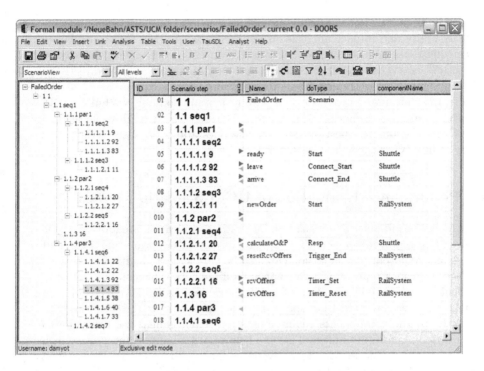

Fig. 9. *FailedOrder* scenario imported into DOORS & linked to other requirements

UCM start/end points are converted to MSC messages and responsibilities to actions. MSCs were preferred to UML 1.x sequence diagrams here because they support explicit parallel inline statements as well as timers (as in UML 2.0). Additional messages are synthesized during the transformation to insure that inter-component causality is preserved. These synthetic messages have been re-named with more meaningful names here (e.g., orderAvailable and makeOrder).

The same *FailedOrder* scenario was imported into DOORS, as shown in Fig. 9. This scenario view provides the means to connect UCM elements and external requirements in a way that would be difficult otherwise. Instead of manually linking each pair of relevant external requirements directly (there would be too many pairs, and many might be missed by requirements engineers), the traceability can be done more efficiently via UCM scenarios. For instance, the informal descriptions of shuttle and agents (respectively section 2 paragraph 1 and section 2.1.0 paragraph 4 of the informal document), discussed in the previous examples, can be linked in the following way:

- UCM element Shuttle to section 2 paragraph 1 (manual, but obvious)
- UCM element BankAgent to section 2.1.0 paragraph 4 (manual, but obvious)
- UCM scenario SuccessfulOrder (not shown here) to UCM element Shuttle and to UCM element BankAgent (not obvious, but automatic with scenario import)

Such links created automatically provide very helpful support when performing traceability and impact analysis on requirements. A RMS tool could hence answer questions such as "What is connected to this requirement, directly or indirectly?" or "What scenarios and external requirements would be directly or indirectly affected if we removed this responsibility or this component?". Additionally, this automated process would prevent missing non-obvious links, would be easier to use in a scenario/requirement evolution context, and would lead to clearer explanations to questions such as the ones above because of the availability of link types (providing rationales).

5   Performance Evaluation of UCM Scenario Models

Performance requirements represent an interesting application area for the types of links discussed in this paper. UCM scenarios can easily capture functional and operational requirements, but they can also be supplemented with annotations to describe various aspects of performance requirements. This combined view is sufficient to enable the generation of performance models [18]. Analysis of such models can be used to detect hot spots and trace them back to the scenarios and, indirectly, to the components requirements and environment requirements to which these scenarios are linked. This can help prioritize important issues which may lead to the evaluation of alternative requirements for (COTS) components, execution environments, and performance requirements altogether. A strategy where requirements are linked to scenarios analysed outside the RMS is likely to be more profitable and agile than a total integration strategy (scenario tool within the RMS) because the analysis complexity remains outside of the RMS environment. We are currently exploring this strategy.

UCMNAV incorporates a built-in export filter that generates Layered Queueing Network (LQN) performance models [15]. The path traversal and transformation algorithm for the generation of LQNs is explained in detail in [19]. Several path detail changes were made to version 7 of the ASTS UCM (Fig. 4) in order to comply with the usage rules for creating UCMs that are well-formed for the purpose of performance model generation, as described in [18].

Fig. 10 shows the LQN model generated from the ASTS UCM. The trapezoids in the diagram represent *tasks* and the arrows represent calling relationships between them – full arrow heads denote *synchronous calls* while half arrow heads denote *asynchronous calls*. LQN tasks are subdivided into *entries* which represent services that the task provides, as well as optional *activities* that represent the detailed breakdown of the workload for a given entry. For visual clarity, entry and activity details for the ASTS are left out of the LQN figures presented here. Instead, dashed lines are used to provide a graphical shorthand for the entry and activity sequencing inside tasks.

The documents provided at the requirements oracle session did not provide the workload parameters required to do a complete performance analysis of the ASTS. The LQN model was therefore generated with default parameter values as explained in [19]. Even with the use of these default parameters, running

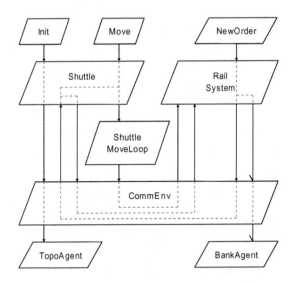

Fig. 10. ASTS LQN showing the calling relationships between tasks

the ASTS LQN model through the LQNS analytical solver does provide some interesting non-quantitative insights into the system architecture.

The LQNS solver tool can be configured to automatically detect call cycles in a model [15]. In the case of the ASTS LQN, it detected a cyclical calling pattern between the Shuttle and RailSystem tasks. These cycles can be seen in Fig. 10 and are representative of a breakdown in the layering of a system. Further inspection of the LQN reveals that these cycles are due to the bundling of the track segment management and the order management functions in the RailSystem task. This bundling is due to a lack of detail in the ASTS requirements. Since the documents were focused on explaining the shuttle behaviour requirements, there was no detailed description of the RailSystem itself. Thus the two functions are not actually required to be bundled together and can be separated.

Fig. 11 shows a repartitioned LQN for the ASTS. The RailSystem has been divided into an OrderMgr task to handle new orders and assign them to shuttles, and a TrackMgr task to deal with permissions for shuttles to use individual track segments. This repartitioning gives the system a well-layered architecture. In addition it also separates two functions that may have different performance requirements. The track permission functionality is safety-critical and should definitely have hard real-time constraints in term of response times and deadlines. The order management functionality is related to the overall usability of the system and only needs to perform within soft real-time constraints.

This evaluation could hence lead to modifications to the ASTS UCM (not shown here), such as the definition of two sub-components for RailSystem, with partitioning of the paths and responsibilities. This new version of the UCM, together with new versions of the resulting scenario files, could then be imported again into DOORS, where the requirements objects and links would be updated.

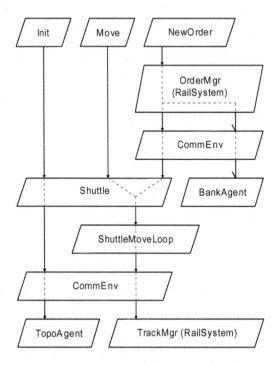

Fig. 11. Repartitioned ASTS LQN without cyclical calls

Specific and appropriate performance requirements could then be created for the new sub-components.

6   Conclusions

This paper has presented a framework for rapidly creating UCM scenario models from requirements documents, for rapidly refining those UCMs using the UCMNAV editor while maintaining traceability links between versions and to the original requirements through the use of a requirements management system, and for analysing the software architecture of the system based on an evaluation of the LQN performance model generated from the UCMs. The framework was illustrated using the ASTS as an example. Section 2 explained how the requirements documents were interpreted in order to create the initial ASTS UCM. Section 3 described the steps used in rapidly prototyping the resulting UCM so as to capture as much of the system behaviour as possible (at a high level of abstraction) and to incorporate additional details and thinking about the system resulting from discussions among requirements oracle participants.

Section 4 introduced a new, tool-supported iterative process for combining UCM scenarios with other types of requirements in the DOORS RMS. The UCM notation provides an appropriate means of capturing the important scenarios for a given system, of integrating them in a single model, and of linking them to external requirements and documentation. Such traceability to a scenario view can help assess the validity and the completeness of requirements. Since both scenarios and external requirements evolve over time, our tool also maintains the existing links whenever this is possible.

The novelty of the approach is also partly due to the open and flexible import interface with the RMS. Others have shown similar interests in combining graphical scenario models with an RMS. With *ScenarioPlus*, Alexander has extended DOORS to support various notations including UML 1.x Use Case diagrams and class diagrams [1]. However, the diagrams must be drawn directly within the RMS, causing substantial usability and performance problems. Earlier this year, a DOORS plug-in called *Analyst* became available [22], which supports most UML 2.0 diagrams. Analyst also uses a separate model editor and then synchronizes the updated models with the DOORS database, where links to other requirements objects are created. The number of supported modelling languages and the integration with the RMS are impressive, but this tool uses a rigid synchronization model and proprietary interfaces. The approach presented here is more open in the sense that one can freely adapt the RMS library or the UCMNAV export mechanism to import exactly the information that is needed. However, we see a lot of potential in combining our tools with the Analyst as this would provide a way to connect requirements and UCM scenarios with more detailed design aspects, in UML 2.0.

Finally, Section 5 builds on previous work to show that simple analysis and evaluation of performance models generated from UCMs can influence several requirements and architectural decisions early in the development process. The detection of cyclical calling dependencies between ASTS tasks and the resulting repartitioning of the system in order to remove those cycles illustrates the value of early performance analysis even on incomplete models, as well as the value of being able to automatically generate the performance models from tools such as UCMNAV.

This work has demonstrated the feasibility of the approach and has led to several additions to existing tools, especially to handle interoperability. Future work will involve the strengthening of the current prototypes in terms of coverage of UCMs, robustness, usability, and interoperability with performance tools and with UML 2.0 tools. We also plan further validation of the approach through industrial case studies.

Acknowledgments

This research was supported by the Natural Sciences and Engineering Research Council of Canada, through its programs of Strategic Grants and Collaborative Research and Development Grants. We are grateful to Telelogic for making their tools available via the ASERT lab.

References

1. Alexander, I.: ScenarioPlus - Tools for Requirements Engineering. http://www.scenarioplus.org.uk
2. Amyot, D.: Introduction to the User Requirements Notation: Learning by Example. Computer Networks, 42(3), 285–301, 21 June 2003.
3. Amyot, D. and Eberlein, A.: An Evaluation of Scenario Notations and Construction Approaches for Telecommunication Systems Development. Telecommunications Systems Journal, 24(1), 61–94, September 2003.
4. Amyot, D., Echihabi, A., He, Y.: UCMEXPORTER: Supporting Scenario Transformations from Use Case Maps. NOuvelles TEchnnologies de la RÉpartition (NOTERE'04), Saïdia, Morocco, June 2004.
   http://ucmexporter.sourceforge.net
5. Amyot, D. and Logrippo, L.: Use Case Maps and LOTOS for the Prototyping and Validation of a Mobile Group Call System. Computer Communication, 23(12), 1135–1157, 2001.
6. Bordeleau, F. and Buhr, R.J.A.: UCM-ROOM Modeling: From Use Case Maps to Communicating State Machines. Proc. of IEEE Engineering of Computer-Based Systems (ECBS'97), 169–179, Monterey, California, March 1997.
7. Bordeleau, F., Leue, S., and Systä, T.: Dagstuhl Seminar 03371 – Scenarios: Models, Transformations and Tools. Wadern, Germany, September 2003.
   http://www.dagstuhl.de/03371/
8. Breitman, K. and Leite, J.C.S.P.: Scenario Evolution: A Closer View on Relationships. Proc. of the Fourth Intl Conf. on Requirements Engineering (ICRE 2000), 95–105, Schaumburg, USA, 2000.
9. Buhr, R.J.A. and Casselman, R.S.: Use Case Maps for Object-Oriented Systems, Prentice Hall, 1996.
10. He, Y., Amyot, D., and Williams, A.W.: Synthesizing SDL from Use Case Maps: An Experiment. Reed, R., Reed, J. (Eds) 11th SDL Forum (SDL'01), Stuttgart, Germany, July 2003. Volume 2708 of Lecture Notes in Computer Science, 117–136.
11. ITU-T: Recommendation Z.150 (02/03), User Requirements Notation (URN) – Language Requirements and Framework. International Telecommunication Union, Geneva.
12. ITU-T, URN Focus Group: Draft Rec. Z.152 – UCM: Use Case Map Notation (UCM). Geneva, Switzerland, Sept. 2003. http://www.UseCaseMaps.org/urn/
13. Jarke M., Bui X.T., and Carroll J.M.: Scenario Management: An Interdisciplinary Approach. Requirements Engineering, 3(3/4), 155–173, 1998.
14. Lamsweerde A.v.: Requirements Engineering in the Year 00: A Research Perspective. Proc. of 22nd Intl Conf. on Software Engineering (ICSE), Limerick, Ireland, ACM Press, 5–19, 2000.
15. Layered Queueing Resource Page. http://www.layeredqueues.org/
16. Leite, J.C.S.P., Rossi, G., Maiorana V., Balaguer, F., Kaplan, G., Hadad, G., and Oliveros, A.: Enhancing a Requirements Baseline with Scenarios. Requirements Engineering, 2(4), 184–198, 1997.
17. Nuseibeh B. and Easterbrook S.: Requirements Engineering: A Roadmap. A. Finkelstein (Ed) The Future of Software Engineering, ICSE 2000, ACM Press, 35–46, 2000.
18. Petriu, D.B., Amyot, D., and Woodside, M.: Scenario-Based Performance Engineering with UCMNAV. Reed, R., Reed, J. (Eds) 11th SDL Forum (SDL'01), Stuttgart, Germany, July 2003. Volume 2708 of Lecture Notes in Computer Science, 18–35.

19. Petriu, D.B. and Woodside, M.: Software Performance Models from System Scenarios in Use Case Maps. Proc. 12 Intl Conf. on Modelling Tools and Techniques for Computer and Communication System Performance Evaluation (Performance TOOLS 2002), 141–158, London, April 2002.
20. Software Engineering Group: Autonomous Shuttle Transport System Case Study. University of Paderborn, Germany, January 2003. http://tele.informatik.uni-freiburg.de/dagstuhl03371/CaseStudy.html, http://www.cs.tut.fi/~systa/Dagstuhl03371/SWTPRA-case-study-v04b.pdf
21. Telelogic AB: DOORS/ERS. http://www.telelogic.com/products/doorsers/
22. Telelogic AB: DOORS/Analyst. http://www.telelogic.com/products/doorsers/analyst/index.cfm
23. Telelogic AB: DXL Reference Manual, 2001.
24. UCM User Group: Use Case Maps Navigator 2 (UCMNav). http://www.usecasemaps.org/tools/ucmnav/index.shtml

Scenario-Based Statistical Testing of Quality of Service Requirements

Matthias Beyer and Winfried Dulz

Institute for Computer Science, University of Erlangen-Nuremberg,
Martensstrasse 3, D-91058 Erlangen, Germany
Tel.: +49 9131 852 7929   Fax: +49 9131 852 7409
{msbeyer, dulz}@informatik.uni-erlangen.de

Abstract. In this paper a general framework is presented for testing time-critical systems and software. The main focus is to derive a state-oriented statistical usage model from a set of usage scenarios in order to automatically generate test cases. We describe a methodology that was developed within the European IST project MaTeLo to ease testing by combining the advantages of formal description techniques, namely MSC, UML and TTCN-3. In the first step of our approach, a MCUM (Markov Chain Usage Model) is constructed. This model represents the formal basis for deriving TTCN-3 test case descriptions to perform executable specification-based tests for the system under test (SUT). In order to be independent of the chosen specification technique, i.e. MSC or UML sequence diagrams, we have defined an XML-based representation format for the MCUM, called MCML (Markov Chain Markup Language). This format represents a common interface between various tools of the MaTeLo approach. All steps in our methodology do also support the testing of QoS (Quality of Service) requirements that are annotated in a UML profile standard notation.

Keywords: Software Testing, Automatic Test Generation, Markov Chain Usage Model, UML Sequence Diagram, MSC, TTCN-3, QoS.

1 Introduction

Model-based software development techniques are getting more and more attractive in order to master the inherent complexity of real-world applications. Different models are used for all kind of purposes during the software development cycle and handle static and dynamic aspects of the software system.

Specific functional and non-functional requirements can be verified and validated by models, which focus on semantic properties that are described in a formal notation. Examples are the assurance of deadlock freeness or to guarantee the correct time behavior for real-time software.

Nevertheless, in practice it is impossible to develop error-free software due to the system's complexity and testing is necessary to

S. Leue and T.J. Systä (Eds.): Scenarios, LNCS 3466, pp. 152–173, 2005.
© Springer-Verlag Berlin Heidelberg 2005

- detect programming faults,
- evaluate the code reliability or its performance and
- ensure that a critical function of a system meets given requirements.

Testing techniques can be classified and compared with respect to several criteria, e.g. the adequacy of the chosen set of test cases because exhaustive testing is not possible even for a small SUT. It is also possible to ask, whether the SUT is executed or not and if dynamic, respectively static tests have to be designed and to be developed. If implementation details and the internal structure of the SUT are of interest structural or white-box testing approaches are adequate, otherwise specification-based or black-box test techniques could be used.

Instead of focusing only on functional system properties, non-functional requirements are becoming more and more important [12]. The reason for this is that in many application domains, such as mobile communications, avionic or automotive QoS-oriented quantities like real-time behavior, performance and reliability issues represent essential non-functional requirements of the SUT.

The European IST project *MaTeLo* (Markov Test Logic)[1] started from recent research results in the field of statistical usage testing ([1,3,4,5]) and developed a dynamic specification-based testing technique. The main goal was to automate the test suite generation from use case scenarios, having "statistical usage testing" as its main test objective. This means to assure the software reliability from the user's point of view and to guarantee that this result will correspond to a statistical confidence interval.

At the start of the software development cycle, a formal description of the expected usage of the system has to be specified using either the UML 1.3 Sequence Diagram [17] or MSC-96 (Message Sequence Chart) [19] notation. From that specification a MCUM is generated automatically, which is the base for the automatic generating of TTCN-3 (Testing and Test Control Notation version 3) [18] test case descriptions.

In the next section we will first discuss testing techniques in more detail that have influenced our method, i.e. black-box testing with TTCN-3 and the statistical usage testing approach. In section 3 the QED framework (QoS Enhanced Development) for automated test generation, reflecting non-functional QoS requirements is described in more detail. Section 4 explains how to derive test cases step by step using the MaTeLo tool chain. Finally, we discuss specific implementation aspects and will close with summary and final remarks.

2 Testing Concepts and Techniques

2.1 Black-Box Testing with TTCN-3

TTCN-3 is the newest version of the well established test notation language TTCN, standardized by the ETSI [18]. It is a universal language for test specification, valid for any application domain e.g. protocol, service or module testing and suitable for different kinds of testing approaches, e.g. conformance, robustness, interoperability, regression, system or integration tests.

---

[1] IST-2001-32402, http://www.alitec.net/matelo/

The complete TTCN-3 test suite is written in an abstract way. The main building blocks are modules, consisting of a definitions part and an optional control part. Inside the definitions part, the test architecture, test behavior, test data and the data types have to be specified. The control part contains a description of the sequential execution of the test cases with subsequent test verdicts and corresponds to the "main"-method of programming languages. The executable or interpretable test suite is the TE (TTCN-3 Executable), which is shown in Fig. 1.

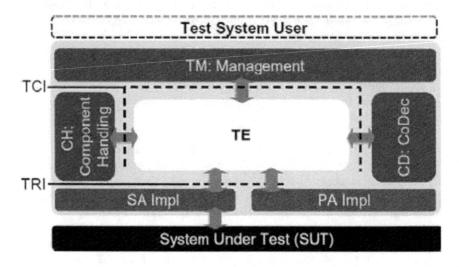

Fig. 1. General Structure of a TTCN-3 test system

In addition, other entities that are necessary to make the abstract concepts concrete are depicted. Via the TTCN-3 Control Interface (TCI) the test execution can be influenced with respect to test management and test logging (TM), test component handling for distributed testing (CH) and encoder/decoder functions for different representations of TTCN-3 data types (CD).

The TTCN-3 Runtime Interface (TRI) was defined to enable the interactions between the SUT and the test system by means of a standardized interface. Fig. 1 shows two parts of the TRI. The description of the communication system is specified in the SUT Adapter (SA). The Platform Adapter (PA) implements timers and external functions based on the underlying operating system.

Because the testing of non-functional requirements was not a primary issue for the TTCN-3 standardization group several extension proposals were made, e.g. PerfTTCN [9] and TimedTTCN-3 [10]. While PerfTTCN is designed for TTCN-2, the predecessor of TTCN-3, TimedTTCN-3 is lacking of describing traffic models, which are necessary to test the SUT for specific workload situations. We therefore decided to use our own QTTCN3 (QoS-TTCN-3) notation that is part of the QED framework.

A small TTCN-3 example is given below that corresponds to the UML sequence diagram in Fig. 6. It shows a simple test case for a mobile phone setup procedure.

```
testcase tc_init_MS() runs on MyTestComponent
system MyTestSystemType
{
  map(self:Port1, system:COM2);
  label Init;
  Port1.send("ATZ");
  alt{
  [] Port1.receive("OK") {
          setverdict(pass);}
  [] Port1.receive {
          setverdict(fail);}
  }
  Port1.send("ATE0");
  alt{
  [] Port1.receive("OK") {
          setverdict(pass);}
  [] Port1.receive {
          setverdict(fail);}
  }
  label Idle;
  unmap(self:Port1, system:COM2);
}
```

Fig. 2. TTCN-3 code example

2.2 Statistical Usage Testing

In statistical testing of software, testing is treated as an engineering problem that has to be solved by statistical methods. Because exhaustive testing is impossible for most real-world software systems, only a representative test sample can be chosen to represent the most probable usage behavior of the software.

A *usage model* as shown in Fig. 3 is a characterization of all possible scenarios of the software use at a given level of abstraction. Usage models can be constructed before code is written and are finite representations of infinite usage scenarios of a given system. A test case is any traversal of the usage model. A *random test case* is any traversal of the usage model based on state transitions that are randomly selected from a usage probability distribution. *Certification* of the software means attaining reliability and confidence goals for an environment of use and to define stopping criteria.

The basic principle behind statistical usage testing is that the tests are based on the anticipated operational usage of the system and test cases are generated from the user's external point of view. The general approach consists of a number of consecutive steps [1]:

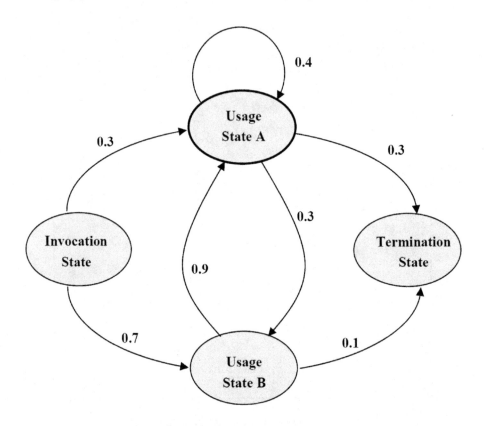

Fig. 3. Example for a Markov Chain Usage Model

1. Get a system specification of the SUT in any formal or informal description technique.
2. Derive the structure of a *MCUM* of the SUT, i.e. a graph consisting of state nodes and arcs between states (see section 3.3 for more details)Assign transition probabilities to the MCUM by using requirement definitions, simulation or monitored field data of a running similar / predecessor system, or simply by transferring annotated probabilities from the system specification. Because the system could work within different environments several sets of probabilities for a single MCUM structure are allowed.

3. Analyze and verify the MCUM by means of standard *Markov techniques*, such as the long-run occupancy, occurrence probability, occurrence frequency or first occurrence of certain states and the expected sequence length of a random run of the system. The outcome of the analysis may also lead to restructuring the MCUM or to reassign another set of transition probabilities to the arcs. In any case, steps 2 to 4 have to be repeated until the MCUM is stable and will represent the SUT in its typical behavior.

4. Create non-random test cases, possible types are e.g. model coverage tests, regression tests or importance tests

5. Planning of performing statistical tests means

   i. *Estimation* and generation of the number of random test cases that have to be run by using the expected test case length derived during model analysis. Each test case is a random walk through the MCUM, from its invocation state up to the termination state.

   ii. Definition of the *best-case* scenario, i.e. under the assumption that no failures will occur in random testing determine the values of product quality and process sufficiency that can be achieved by running the number of test cases generated in Step i.

   iii. Definition of the *worst-case* scenario, i.e. assume some profile of failures and construct a failure log based on the profile.

   iv. Analysis of the *coverage* of all model states, arcs, and paths that will occur during the test.

   v. Analysis might show that testing as planned cannot fulfill the assumptions for model coverage or the required reliability. In this case one has either to revise the goals or the test plans.

6. Perform the randomly generated test cases of the former step. As they were generated with respect to probabilities representing a usage profile, the test result allow the estimation of reliability.

7. Perform the test *certification* process, which calculates the merits of additional ongoing testing. The decision to stop testing can be derived from

   • the confidence in a reliability estimate
   • the degree to which testing experience has converged to the expected usage of the system
   • model coverage criteria based on a degree of state, arc, or path coverage during random testing.

Very often, only subjective criteria are used to decide to stop test campaigns. Using a statistical approach allows however to assess software's reliability and to define stopping criteria that rely on a mathematical approach. This is the main advantage of statistical usage testing.

2.3 UML SPT-Profile

To enable testing of non-functional QoS requirements one has to include QoS declarations into the specification of the SUT. This issue is addressed in the UML SPT Profile (Profile for Schedulability, Performance and Time Specification, [15]) that was standardized by the OMG in order to annotate QoS requirements within a given UML model.

Essentially, there exist three basic concepts in the SPT Profile related to time. *Timing mechanisms,* i.e. clocks or timer, offer time services with various characteristics like drift, resolution, offset etc. *Timed Actions* are used to model actions that need some time (also delays) and *Timed Stimuli* represent any stimuli, i.e. a communication instance between a sender and receiver, with associated timestamps.

The performance aspects in the SPT Profile deal with characterizing the workload and the resources used while executing the modeled scenarios. All kind of attributes can be specified, e.g. the population or occurrence patterns of the workload, the execution time of a single step or the throughput of available resources.

The SPT Profile also contains concurrency related concepts: 1) new stereotypes and tagged values to specify how resource services are performed, 2) stimuli to generate actions that are called *message actions* and 3) *concurrent units* representing concurrently executed active units.

Last but not least three primary types of entities are needed to support schedulability modeling that is 1) *scheduling job,* i.e. the system workload, 2) *shareable resource,,* which is used by the scheduling jobs during execution and 3) *execution engine* that represents the computing power. Since a schedulability model is normally not in the focus to be tested for a given SUT, it is not relevant for our further discussions.

3   Specification-Driven Testing

3.1   Quality of Service Enhanced Development (QED – Framework)

In general, the QED framework describes how a UML specified object-system is tested with a black box approach that is also reflecting non-functional QoS requirements of the SUT. In case of any functional or non-functional failure, a monitoring process can be attached as a second step (see Fig. 4).

The system specification containing functional and non-functional requirements as well is the base for deriving the test specification (Fig. 4a) that consists of the test architecture, test behavior, test data and data types. To support this specific application area the expressiveness of the UML is extended by the *UML Testing Profile* [14]. By adopting the QoS annotations from the system specification a QoS test can be described. Because this Profile was developed in order to operate with existing methods for black box testing, for a working test execution environment the mapping to a TTCN-3 test suite is straight forward (Fig. 4b).

SPT Profile compatible QoS requirements specifications in the UML model give additional information for testing. Properties of given timing mechanism specify requirements for the concrete time measurement device that is used to assure different time requirements during test execution. The basic behavior of the built-in TTCN-3 timer is represented by a "snapshot semantic" that fails especially in a distributed testing environment because of its restricted scope unit of a test component and the test control part. Here, a clock device for getting the absolute time is needed, one possible syntax and semantic is described within the ITU standardization proposal document [13].

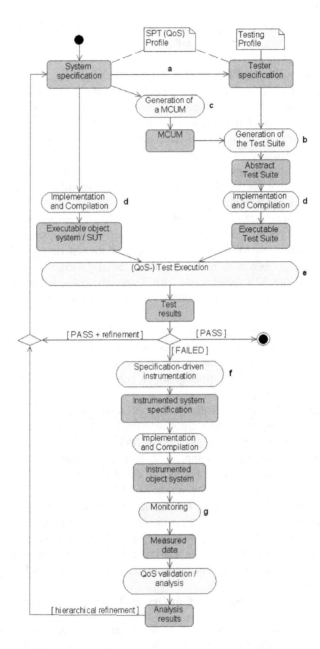

Fig. 4. QED framework for testing systems that contain QoS requirements

In order to test the system's performance, the specified workload has to be generated. During the test execution a time-stamped event trace is created that contains all monitored events for evaluating the performance requirements of the input demands.

This so-called foreground workload can be either generated by a hard-ware/software workload generator called by external functions, or by a dedicated TTCN-3 test component, respectively. In addition the tester needs information about the background workload of the SUT. Besides active triggering the system with artificially generated input stimuli, passive monitoring of the real data flow can be done. The first approach enables exact knowledge and control of the background load, the second one is closer related to the reality but (normally) lacks of extreme situations. To summarize, it is necessary to describe traffic models inside the TTCN-3 and to provide performance evaluation functions.

It is worth to note that concurrent stereotyped objects have separate threads of control. This means that their behavior is distributed over different test components, which are running concurrently within a TTCN-3 test suite.

Statistical usage testing, as described in section 2.2, for automatically deriving test cases is integrated in the framework (Fig. 4c). Based on the sequence diagrams of the system specification an MCUM is built and used to generate TTCN-3 test cases. These steps are described in more detail in the following sections.

The *SUT* and the *ETS* (Executable Test Suite) are compiled in step d of Fig. 4, which creates run able objects for testing, including different non-functional requirements (Fig. 4e).

Test verdicts are either used to enhance the system specification or to extend the tester specification, e.g. higher granularity, more test cases, and so on. If a FAILED verdict occurs with respect to a non-functional requirement, the black box test can be extended by attaching QoS monitoring, which is a specific white box test to discover the problematic code fragments.

To facilitate QoS monitoring, the system specification has to be instrumented, i.e. additional functionality to produce trace information is inserted into the SUT to output specific QoS information for a given PoI (Point of Interest) [2]. This can also be done automatically by using QoS annotated sequence diagrams of the system specification produced at the beginning of the QED development process. The result will be an instrumented system specification, as shown in Fig. 4f.

After compilation, the following execution-run can be monitored to derive a time stamped event trace (Fig. 4g) together with additional QoS data of the selected PoIs. After analyzing the SUT trace, supplementary information concerning QoS violations will be available. Depending on these analysis results proper changes to the system or the tester specification can be made, resulting in a new cycle within the QED approach.

3.2 Scenario-Based and Specification-Driven Test Case Generation

The MaTeLo tool-chain for *specification-driven test case generation* is shown in Fig. 5, realizing the upper part of QED i.e. steps 'a' to 'e' in Fig. 4. Rectangles in the diagram represent input and output data of the MaTeLo tools that are interconnected. Starting with sequence diagrams describing usage scenarios, there were different tools implemented for converting them to a MCUM, for editing and analyzing the model in a graphical environment, and for test case generation and execution.

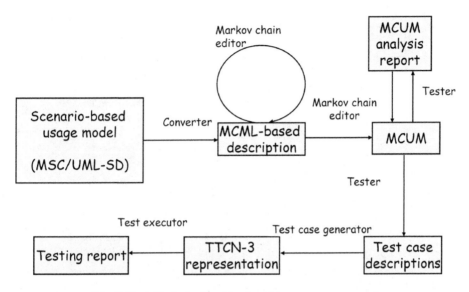

Fig. 5. Tool-Chain for Specification-driven test case generation

Core of the chain is the generation of a MCUM as a dedicated test model (explained in section 3.3). There exist several possibilities to derive the MCUM transition probabilities. The first one is the direct inclusion from probabilities that are given in annotated sequence diagrams. A second approach will calculate the transition probabilities from weighted sums to reach a successor state from its predecessor within the MCUM. If no further a-priori information is given all weights are equal and the transition probabilities in all successor states are the same, i.e. 1 divided by the number of successor states. A test-constraints based method is described in [21]. Another choice is to add probabilities manually within the graphical Markov chain editor of the MaTeLo tool chain. The internal MCUM representation for the editor is a particular XML-based description called MCML (Markov Chain Markup Language).

In the second step, QoS requirements can be added, by using a subset of the UML SPT Profile [15] with minor modifications. Only time and performance aspects were considered at the moment. Other aspects, such as internal concurrency are not testable by pure black-box techniques like TTCN-3 and will not be observable outside the SUT.

3.3 Generating the Structure of the Markov Chain Usage Model

Fig. 6 is an example sequence diagram from a usage specification, which contains all important scenarios of the future software usage given at a definite level of abstraction.

An algorithm is required to convert this set of UML sequence diagrams, respectively MSC specifications into a valid MCUM representation. During the conversion process, the following tasks will be executed:

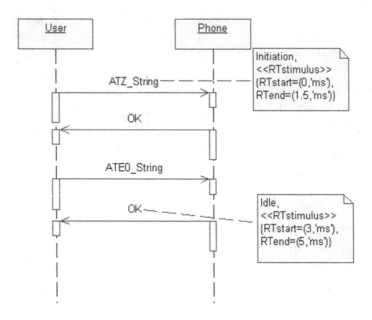

Fig. 6. UML-SD with user-defined state information for a mobile phone

- User-defined state information (UdI), attached to messages as comments, will be mapped to MCUM *states* (*Initiation* and *Idle* in Fig. 6 / Fig. 8),
- Identification of necessary *intermediate states*, i.e. automatically constructed states for the MCUM that occur as a result of message transmissions without given UdI annotations.

The algorithm for transforming scenarios into a MCUM representation consists of five consecutive steps:

1. Specification of the usage model via sequence diagrams, which also contain UdI annotations attached to messages. The meaning is as follows: a UdI attached to an input message is interpreted as the actual state before receiving that message, a UdI attached to an output message is the successor state after sending this message.
2. Selection of the *granularity* for the MCUM, i.e. what level of the system should be tested
   - complete system behavior, i.e. all objects within the usage scenarios
   - partial system behavior of a set of objects within the usage scenarios
   - individual behavior of exactly one object within the usage scenarios
3. Construction of the MCUM from the scenario descriptions.
   The main mapping algorithm is as follows: Let S and T be the set of *states*, respectively *transitions* in the final MCUM. A transition $t \in T$ is a 4-tupel (s1, i, o, s2), where s1, s2 $\in$ S and i and o are input, respectively output messages to and from the SUT. The interpretation of t is like this: if the MCUM is in state s1 and

a (possibly empty) input message i (the so-called *stimulus*) is send to the SUT, the SUT has to send the (possibly empty) output message o (the so-called *expected result*) and the MCUM is going into state s2. We forbid the case, where i and o are both empty within the same transition.

Fig. 7 shows the details of the MCUM construction algorithm as pseudo code:

i.   lines 2-3: some initialization work (e.g. set of states S and transitions T)
ii.   lines 4-28: loop for all available sequence diagrams
iii.   lines 5-11: get the first message and check, if it's an input message; if that is true, add the attached state information or - if missing - the new created artificial intermediate state to S
iv.   lines 12-27: loop for all following messages
v.   lines 15-18: get the user-defined/intermediate state information of the input message and check, if the predecessor was also an input message; if that is true, create a new transition t
vi.   lines 19-23: get the state information of the output message and check if the predecessor was an input message; create a new transition t according to its answer
vii.   lines 24-26: add the new state and transition to their set

```
01   MCUM_generation() {
02       S, T = { };                           // set of states and transitions
03       int i, k = 1;                          // indices
04       while(PENDING_SDs) {
05           m[i] = get_next_message();
06           if(m[i] != input) exit("not allowed, must be input");
07           else {
08               if((s[k] = m[i].get_attached_state) == empty) s[k] = create_interstate();
09               S = S ∪ s[k];
10               k++;
11           }
12           while(PENDING_MESSAGES) {
13               i++;
14               m[i] = get_next_message();
15               if(m[i] == input) {           // if input message
16                   if((s[k] = m[i].get_attached_state) == empty) s[k] = create_interstate();
17                   if(m[i-1] == input) t = create_transition(s[k-1], m[i-1],, s[k]);
18               }
19               else {                         // if output message
20                   if((s[k] = m[i].get_attached_state) == empty) s[k] = create_interstate();
21                   if(m[i-1] == input) t = create_transition(s[k-1], m[i-1], m[i], s[k]);
22                   else t = create_transition(s[k-1],, m[i], s[k]);
23               }
24               S = S ∪ s[k];
25               T = T ∪ t;
26               k++;
27           }
28       }
29   }
```

Fig. 7. MCUM construction algorithm

4. Minimization of the MCUM by *merging* superfluous states and *removing* redundant transitions. This action is done in parallel to step 3 above. A superfluous IS (intermediate state) occurs if outputs without UdI are directly followed by an input with UdI or an input without UdI directly follows an output with UdI. In these situations the IS is merged into the UdS (user-defined state derived from a corresponding UdI). Since one or more sequence diagrams may contain the same UdI, duplicate UdS are merged at the end to derive a MCUM that contains only unique state names. Two IS in a sequence are mapped to the first IS.

5. The final structure of the MCUM for testing a mobile phone is shown in Fig. 8, which was created from a set of five sequence diagrams. Because in more than one of the sequence diagrams the same UdI is used, i.e. Idle and Connected, the structure of the MCUM is not a linear chain but contains cycles between different states or loops into the same state.

6. Representation of the MCUM by means of an XML-based *MCML* (Markov Chain Markup Language) description. This allows transferring the MCUM conveniently between different parts of the MaTeLo tool set, i.e. MCML converter, graphical MCML editor and TTCN-3 test case generator. On the other hand it is wise to use existing XML tools as shown in the next section in order to reduce the costs for implementing the converter tool.

The MCML schema for constructing an MCUM model also contains definitions to apply the SPT Profile syntax for specifying non-functional QoS properties. Fig. 9 represents an excerpt of the MCML-file derived from Fig. 8 for testing the Phone object including the (highlighted) time attributes.

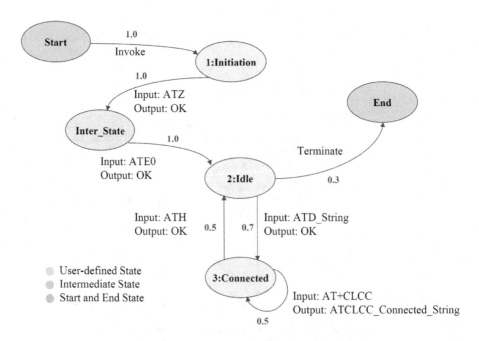

Fig. 8. MCUM for testing the behavior of a mobile phone

```xml
<?xml version="1.0" encoding="UTF-8"?>
<UML:MCMLS xmlns:UML="href://org.omg/UML/1.3" ID="0">
   <MCProp name="Phone" syntax="1.0" label="default"/>

   [...]

<dynamique>
   <invoke id="S9998" name="Invoke" x="" y="">
      <!-- The start point of the markov chain. -->
   </invoke>
   <terminate id="S9999" name="Terminate" x="" y="">
      <!-- The end point of the markov chain. -->
   </terminate>
   <states>
      <state name="Initiation" x="" y="" id="S10"/>
      <state name="Inter_State" x="" y="" id="S11"/>
      <state name="Idle" x="" y="" id="S12"/>
      [...]
   </states>

   [...]

   <event name="ATZ_String" id="T2" from="S10" to="S11">
      <proba profile="Profile1" value=""/>
      <proba profile="Profile2" value=""/>
      <input name="ATZ_String">
      <timing type="RTstimulus" RTstart="(0,'ms')"
RTend="(1.5,'ms')"
                        RTduration=""/>
         <dvalue/>
      </input>
      <expresultauto name="OK">
         <dvalue/>
      </expresultauto>
   </event>
   <event name="ATE0_String" id="T3" from="S11" to="S12">
      <proba profile="Profile1" value=""/>
      <proba profile="Profile2" value=""/>
      <input name="ATE0_String">
         <dvalue/>
      </input>
      <expresultauto name="OK">
      <timing type="RTstimulus" RTstart="(3,'ms')"
RTend="(5,'ms')"
                        RTduration=""/>
         <dvalue/>
      </expresultauto>
   </event>

   [...]

   </eve[...]nts>
</dynamique>
</UML:MCMLS>
```

Fig. 9. MCML code example

As mentioned before, we adopted the syntax and semantic as described within the UML SPT Profile [15] to handle stereotypes regarding time and performance aspects.

All real-time related stereotypes start with the prefix RT, performance stereotypes use the prefix PA. Stereotype *<<RTaction>>* specifies time aspects that are related to a message, the attributes describe start and end, respectively duration of the message. *<<RTstimulus>>* is used to express time requirements for which the user cannot specify the duration. *<<RTdelay>>* specifies the time duration that may happen before the occurrence of a given message. Stereotype *<<PAperformance>>* is used to specify required (*PAdemand*) and observed (*PArespTime*) time requirements of a given demand, utilization (*PAutilization*) and throughput (*PAthroughput*) specify performance properties of a resource within a given time duration.

Time related Stereotypes	
Stereotype	**Attribute**
RTaction	RTstart
	RTend
	RTduration
RTstimulus	RTstart
	RTend
RTdelay	RTduration

Performance related Stereotypes	
Stereotype	**Attribute**
PAperformance	PAdemand
	PArespTime
	PAutilization
	PAthroughput

4   Case Study: The Paderborn Shuttle System

At the University of Paderborn a new rail-based transport system is being developed [22]. This project was chosen as a case study for the Dagstuhl seminar on which the MaTeLo tool set was successfully applied. Fig. 10 shows the MSC for a correct delivery scenario of a single shuttle order.

Because the original document [22] only contains UML sequence diagrams with textual annotations to specify a looping behavior we first had to produce MSC diagrams. In the MSC standard additional inline expressions are standardized to handle alternatives, options, exceptions, loops or parallel behavior. For example, in Fig. 10 loops are used to express the movement of a shuttle from any point to the source and from source to destination after loading the shuttle. By the way, UML 2.0 interaction diagrams will also provide these features in the future.

In the previous algorithm for deriving the structure of the MCUM only linear behavior was reflected. Because inline expression structure the sequence of messages in a certain way - depending on the chosen construct - it is necessary to define the transformation into a MCUM for each of the inline expressions.

In Fig. 11 the loop inline expression and its corresponding MCUM structure is explained. In the MSC on the left side hexagons are used to represent conditions, which are very similar to the UdI state annotations we have introduced in our UML sequence diagrams. Thus, a loop construct is included between the user given conditions "initiation" and "idle". The meaning is that every state between "inline loop_begin" and "inline loop_end" is visited for each loop cycle. The "Loopback" transition in the MCUM has to assure that the number of cycles is within the allowed interval between 1 and 5 as defined in the MSC loop expression "loop <1,5>". This is done by a non-visible loop counter inside the transition

Fig. 12 shows a screenshot of the MaTeLo Markov chain Editor that contains the complete MCUM for the shuttle case study. Here, also a possible non-successful shuttle delivery and the resulting penalty are reflected. In the open Properties-Window of the selected transition several attributes, i.e. transition probabilities for two possible probability profiles, input message and expected result can be seen and edited.

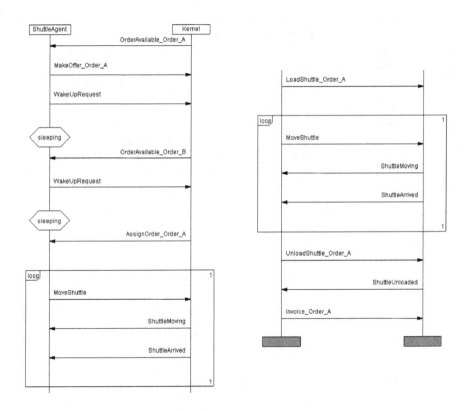

Fig. 10. MSC for a successful delivery

It is worth to mention that in our approach different probability sets, so-called profiles, can be handled. The reason is that under normal conditions the transition probabilities may be too small for reaching a certain set of states in the MCUM while

executing the test cases. For example, exception handling to handle correct error re-
covery will normally occur very seldom during normal operating phases of an SUT.
In order to cover this behavior during the test a different probability set can be
specified in a specific "exception profile". Important but little used transitions will
get a higher probability and are more thoroughly tested i.e. these transitions are
executed more often by random test cases. The resulting reliability calculation will
still reflect an unbiased value through application of the theory of importance sampling [23].

The diagram in Fig. 13 shows the Generation report window of the Markov chain
Tester. In the example a sample of 100 test cases was generated randomly using the
probabilities defined for Profile1. For each individual test case the length of the path
between the start and end state is reported. In the Mean TC length canvas the mean
length of the total set of 100 test cases based on the probabilities of Profile 1 is reported with 28.36. The coverage of states, transitions (events) and specific items from
an item list is also reported. Pressing the TTCN-3 button at the bottom generates several TTCN-3 files including all necessary test information like test behavior, test
components and templates for the test data.

After test execution the MaTeLo Report (Fig. 14) reveals all kinds of test results.
Failure rate (expected number of error states in a chain traversal), MTTF (expected
number of states to the first occurrence of an error state), reliability numbers based
on the different probability profiles and different calculation methods ([1,4]), lo-
calization of errors, uncovered elements and other supplementary information are
contained in the Report Generation window. Most parts are presented in a graph or
tabular oriented notation and thus represent in total a human friendly user interface.

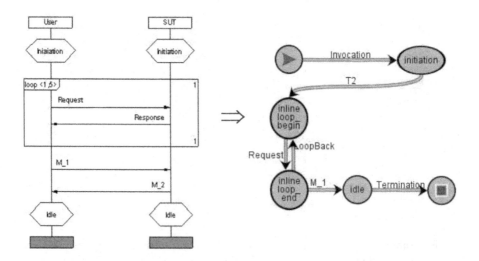

Fig. 11. MSC loop inline expression and corresponding MCUM

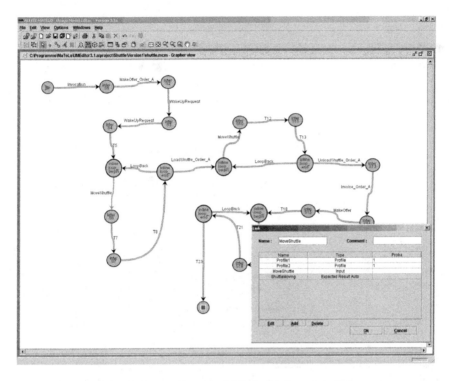

Fig. 12. Screenshot of the MaTeLo Markov chain Editor

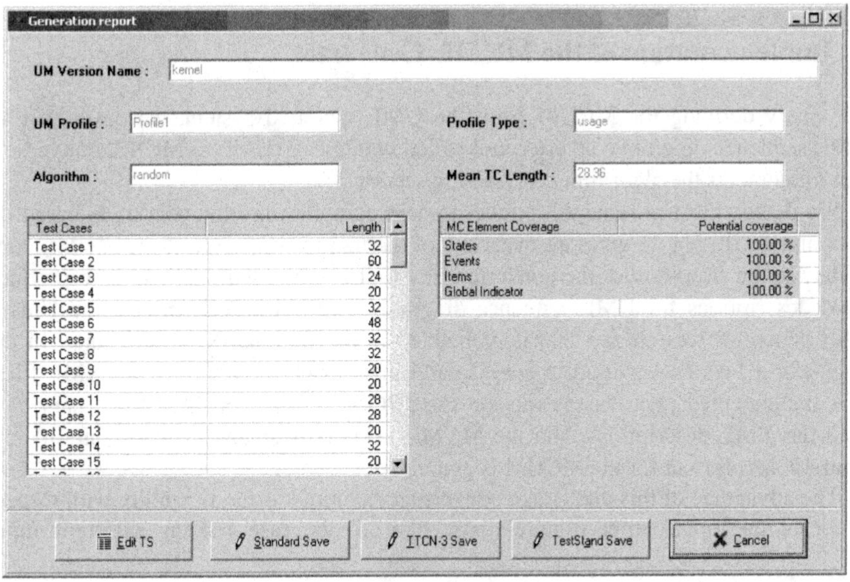

Fig. 13. Screenshot of the MaTeLo Tester

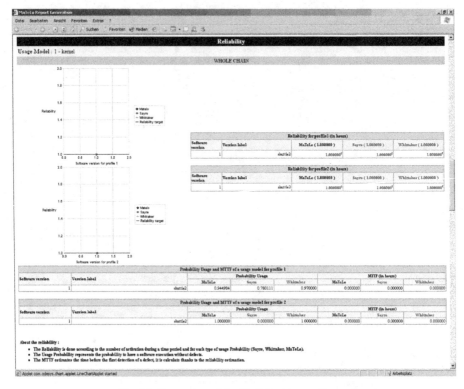

Fig. 14. Screenshot of the MaTeLo Report Generation

5   Implementation of the MCML Converter

For easily deriving the MCUM from the UML-specified system, we developed an
UML sequence diagram converter tool called *uml2mcml* (UML to MCML converter),
that implements the algorithm described in section 3.3.

We decided to use standard, public-domain compiler development tools based on
Java and XML. Fig. 15 gives an overview of the main parts inside of the MCML converter. In the *front-end* of the converter, any tool can be used that is able to produce
XMI descriptions for UML sequence diagrams. In the MaTeLo project the Unisys
XMI generator was chosen that is embedded in the Rational Rose tool suite. In the
back-end a Java tool is used to analyze and manipulate the intermediate XML files.
The implemented java classes rely on the JDOM API[2] and a SAX XML-parser[3] to
read the XML descriptions. Via the MCML DTD (Document Type Definition), the
final MCML format for the MCUM is generated.

The advantage of this dual-stage converting technique is the flexibility with respect
to changing input/output requirements, like in our case reading different input

---

[2] JDOM API Javadoc, http://www.jdom.org/docs/apidocs/
[3] SAX API Javadoc, http://www.saxproject.org/apidoc/

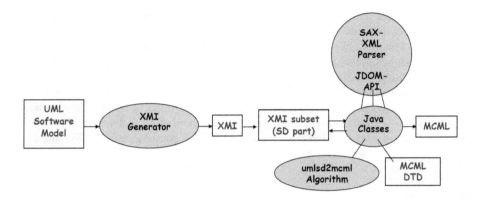

Fig. 15. Main components of the MCML converter

languages. To support a subset of the MSC-96 ITU standard [19], we used JavaCC[4] and JJTree[5] in order to implement the tool *msc2mcml* (MSC to MCML converter) [20]. In the back-end of this dual-stage converting process, we can easily derive different versions of the MCML, which contain for example different QoS annotations depending on the given MCML DTD.

6 Summary

To err is human". This statement remains correct even for better development processes and better specification, implementation or testing languages. From this point of view to let the test case selection, generation and execution further be a manual task without automatisms seems to be an anachronism. Therefore, an automated test case generation approach based on the TTCN-3 standard is a desired step towards a better quality assurance practice for real-time systems and software.

This paper presented the QED framework for testing UML specified systems, including QoS requirements specifications that are gaining more and more importance. In particular, we discussed the MaTeLo approach for automatic test case generation. Here, scenario-based statistical usage testing based on a MCUM is applied, which is not a common practice in the industrial world, because the lack of specific tools.

The key idea is to start from scenario specifications, i.e. UML sequence diagrams or MSCs in order to define a formal usage model. Next a MCUM is automatically built representing the test model enabling the validation of the SUT at a wanted level of confidence and reliability. In addition, Markov modeling techniques allow the application of innovative QoS analysis methods. Examples are the calculation of WCET (worst case execution time) when time constraints are given or performance evaluation of the SUT by using a rich theory that has been established in recent years.

---

[4] http://www.experimentalstuff.com/Technologies/JavaCC/
[5] Apache Software Foundation, http://ant.apache.org/manual/OptionalTasks/jjtree.html

Test case generation in the new TTCN-3 notation makes the test execution phase more efficient. Because TTCN-3 is no longer fixed to the conformance test of communication systems but offers modern component-oriented inter-communication facilities, it can be applied to the description and generation of executable test cases for many application domains.

There is a real need for metrics related to software and system reliability, performance or more general QoS characteristics. Important impacts on the development processes can therefore be expected: accurate predictions of software release time, better control of schedule and cost, increased quality, consumer satisfaction and last but not least safety within the resulting software products.

References

1. Kirk Sayre. Improved Techniques for Software Testing Based on Markov Chain Usage Models. PhD thesis, University of Tennessee, Knoxville, December 99.
2. Dauphin, P. and Dulz, W. and Lemmen, F. Specification-driven Performance Monitoring of SDL/MSC-specified Protocols. 8th Int. Workshop on Protocol Test Systems, Evry, Sept. 1995.
3. Jason M. Selvidge. Statistical usage testing: Expanding the ability of testing. 1999.
4. James A. Whittaker and J.H. Poore, and Carmen J. Trammel. Statistical testing of software based on a usage model. Software-practice and experience, 25 January 1995
5. Kai-Yuan Cai. Optimal software testing and adaptive software testing in the context of software cybernetics. Information and Software Technology, Vol. 44/11, p 841-855, Nov. 2002.
6. Schieferdecker, A. Rennoch and O. Mertens. Timed MSCs - an Extension to MSC´96. GI/ITG-Workshop on Formal Description Techniques for Distributed Systems, GMD-Studien Nr. 315, p. 165 - 174, Berlin 1997.
7. Lambert, L.. PMSC for Performance Evaluation. Workshop on Performance and Time in SDL and MSC, Erlangen, Germany, February 17.-19.1998.
8. J. Grabowski. Test Case Generation and Test Case Specification with Message Sequence Charts. Inauguraldissertation, Universität Bern, Feb. 1994.
9. Schieferdecker, B. Stepien and A. Rennoch. PerfTTCN, a TTCN language extension for performance testing. 10th Intern. Workshop on Testing of Communicating Systems IWTCS´97, Cheju Island, Korea, Sept. 1997.
10. Z. R. Dai, J. Grabowski, H. Neukirchen. TimedTTCN-3 – A Real-Time Extension For TTCN-3, March 2002
11. J. Grabowski, A. Wiles, C. Willcock and D. Hogrefe. On the design of the new testing language TTCN-3. Proceedings 13th IFIP International Workshop on Testing Communication Systems (TestCom 2000), Ottawa, August 2000.
12. F. Slomka, M. Dörfel, R. Münzenberger and R. Hofmann. Hardware/Software Codesign and Rapid-Prototyping of Embedded Systems. IEEE Design & Test of Computers, Special issue: Design Tools for Embedded Systems, Vol. 17, No. 2, April-June 2000.
13. M. Dörfel, W. Dulz, R. Hofmann, R. Münzenberger. Time Extensions and Non-Functional Requirements in SDL, Technical Report IMMD7-01-05, Department of Computer Science 7, Univ. of Erlangen/Nuremberg, August 2001.
14. Object Management Group. UML Testing Profile version 2.0, Final Adopted Specification, ptc/2004-04-02

15. Object Management Group. UML Profile for Schedulability, Performance and Time Specification, Version 1.0, September 2003, formal/03-09-01
16. Object Management Group. OMG XML Metadata Interchange (XMI) Specification Version 1.2, January 2002
17. Object Management Group. Unified Modeling Language Specification, Version 1.3a1, January 1999
18. ETSI. Methods for Testing and Specification (MTS); The Testing and Test Control Notation version 3; ES 201 873 V2.2.1, 2002
19. ITU. Message Sequence Chart. Standard Z.120, 1996
20. W. Dulz, F. Zhen. MaTeLo - Statistical Usage Testing by Annotated Sequence Diagrams, Markov Chains and TTCN-3. Third International Conference on Quality Software (QSIC 2003), Dallas, Texas , November 6-7 2003
21. G. H. Walton, J.H. Poore. Generating transition probabilities to support model-based software testing. Software – Practice and Experience 2000, 30, p. 1095-1106
22. W. Schaefer, Dept. of Computer Science, Software Engineering Group, Univ. of Paderborn, http://wwwcs.upb.de/cs/ag-schaefer/CaseStudies/ShuttleSystem/
23. Walter J. Gutjahr. Importance Sampling of Test Cases in Markovian Software Usage Models. Department of Statistics, Operations Research and Computer Science, University of Vienna, 1997

Lightweight Formal Methods for Scenario-Based Software Engineering

Yves Bontemps*, Patrick Heymans, and Pierre-Yves Schobbens

Institut d'Informatique, University of Namur,
rue Grandgagnage, 21,
B5000 - Namur (Belgium)
{ybo, phe, pys}@info.fundp.ac.be

Abstract. Two fundamental problems related to Scenario-based Software Engineering (SBSE) are presented: model checking and synthesis. The former is to verify that a design model is consistent with a scenario-based specification. The latter is to build a design model implementing correctly a specification. Model checking is computationally expensive and synthesis of distributed system is undecidable. Two lightweight techniques are thus presented that alleviate this intractability. These approaches sacrifice completeness for efficiency, but keep soundness.

1   Introduction

The difficulty to produce quality software requirements has long been identified [Jac92]. They all too often turn out to be unsuitable, incomplete, ambiguous, contradictory, redundant, continually changing, and so on. Researchers and practitioners have devoted much efforts trying to find solutions to capture better requirements. *Scenario*-oriented solutions are among the most successful attempts. They became increasingly popular over the past ten years, through the widespread adoption of UML [OMG03] and Use Cases [Jac92]. Remark that, although *Scenario-Based Software Engineering* (SBSE) actually covers a wider family of techniques expanding over elicitation, specification, verification, validation, inspection, prototyping, animation, negotiation,... [RG00, CM02, WPJH98], we are mostly interested in scenario-based specifications, their verification and their use for code generation.

Specification techniques range from the most informal ones to those having a precise, mathematically defined semantics. Our focus is on the latter, which are a necessary prerequisite to unambiguous specification and efficient automation. However, these problems are intractable. In this paper, we will present "lightweight" versions of algorithms solving these problems. We will sacrifice completeness but keep soundness of these algorithms.

Our contributions concern Live Sequence Charts (LSCs) [DH01], a notation introduced by David Harel and Werner Damm in order to overcome some limita-

---

* FNRS Research Fellow

S. Leue and T.J. Systä (Eds.): Scenarios, LNCS 3466, pp. 174–192, 2005.

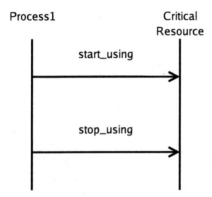

Fig. 1. Critical resource requirement specified with MSC

tions of Message Sequence Charts (MSCs) [ITU00], namely, the lack of *message abstraction* and the inability to specify the *modality* of a scenario. As an example, consider the following standard distributed system requirement: *"Whenever a process enters the critical section, it eventually exits it"*. Fig. 1 represents the corresponding MSC.

If this scenario is to be interpreted as recommended by the ITU standard, it means that *Start_using* is followed by *Stop_using*, without any other message being exchanged in the interval. This entails that the process may not send any requests to the critical resource when using it! Of course, the intended meaning of this scenario is different: the process starts using the critical section and after some time, during which no message *relevant to this requirement* is sent, it releases its lock on the critical resource.

The status or modality of the behaviour described by the MSC is also unclear: is it a simple example only used for illustrative purposes or is it a universal rule ("In given circumstances, the system shall always behave as specified")? Thus LSCs abstract away irrelevant messages and attach a modality to each scenario: universal, example (existential) or even counter-example (anti-scenario), as we will see in Section 3.2.

A typical SBSE process (see Fig. 2) is usually based on use cases. In such a process, one progressively moves from concrete, partial examples (or counter-examples) of behaviour to more general requirements statements. This way of doing fosters communication between software engineers and the other stakeholders [WPJH98]. Additionally, it facilitates the identification of test cases and the production of user-documentation. As this human-intensive bottom-up elicitation task progresses, the precision of the corresponding documentation should also evolve from informal, error-prone representations to more formal models. Hence, LSCs with their multiple modalities, intuitive MSC-like syntax and their formal semantics, seem worth considering to support the task.

But this is only the start of the process. What we devote our interest to in this paper are the subsequent steps. In his vision paper [Har01], David Harel essentially sees it as building a system model (made of two interrelated models,

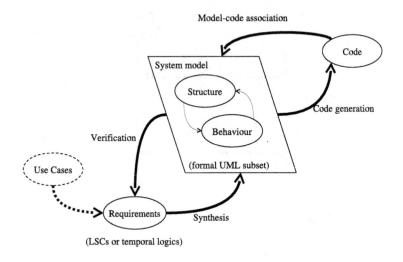

Fig. 2. Scenario-based Software Engineering (adapted from [Har01])

a structural model and a state-based behavioural model) and then producing code from it. He foresees a bright future in which the *synthesis* and *verification* will be formal and largely automated (see Fig. 2). The present paper is a first step in this direction.

A challenge that we face at this point is to transforming scenarios into a system model (and subsequently into code). This is a major *paradigm shift*. We start with a *scenario-based inter-component perspective* (scenarios typically describe component interactions vs internal actions) and we end with a *state-based intra-component perspective*. General techniques are thus computationally extremely expensive. We show here how to make them better. In counterpart, we have to abandon the idea to provide exhaustive algorithms, and just keep soundness. Still, we are convinced that our algorithms are effective in detecting specification problems and generating implementations.

2   Running Example

To illustrate our approach, we will use excerpts from a variation of the Center TRACON System (CTAS Case Study) from NASA [BHK03, WS02]. This system coordinates various air traffic related clients, in order to ensure that they all use the same weather information. We will focus on the part of the system in charge of updating the weather reports used by clients. The system is made of the following components:

Weather Control Panel (WCP): the User Interface through which operators manually trigger updates;

Communication Manager (CM): the central part of the system, in charge of synchronizing the various clients;

Client: distributed on the various sites, where accurate weather data is needed. We will assume that there are only two clients and that they are already connected to the system. In the original system, there is a part of the system in charge of connecting, disconnecting and initializing clients;

Database: from which the clients retrieve weather reports. We assume that there is only one database to which all clients direct their queries;

Terminal: computers on the distributed sites that make use of the weather reports downloaded by clients.

3 Models and Relationships

3.1 Structure

Fig. 3 gives the structural view of our example through a variant of object diagrams. Boxes represent agents. Associations (arrows) between agents are directed, denoting one-way communication channels. They are typed by the names of the messages/events they carry.

3.2 Inter-agent Specifications

Inter-agent specifications are partial "one story for all agents" [Har01][1] scenario-based descriptions constraining the overall system behaviour.

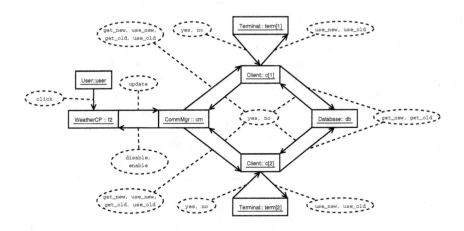

Fig. 3. Structure model

---

[1] [Har01] speaks in terms of objects rather than agents.

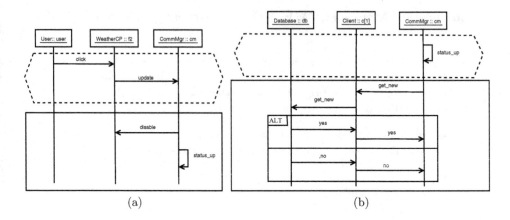

Fig. 4. Universal Live Sequence Charts (uLSCs)

An LSC resembles a Sequence Diagram [OMG03] or a bMSC [ITU00]. Fig. 4 presents two universal LSCs. An event (arrow) is instantaneous and can only appear between agent instances (vertical *lifelines*) which classes were declared to control or receive it, respectively, in the structure diagram. The points of a lifeline where events occur (i.e. the sources and targets of arrows) are called *locations*. On a given lifeline, locations are ordered chronologically from top to bottom. Events being instantaneous, senders and receivers synchronize on them.

Universal scenarios (uLSCs) embed a general trigger-response pattern as well as a frame axiom restricting which events can, must or cannot happen during the execution of a scenario. uLSCs consist of two concatenated *basic charts*: the *prechart* (i.e. the trigger) and the *main chart* (i.e. the response). The former is surrounded by a dashed hexagon. The latter comes below the prechart within a solid rectangle (see fig.4). The scenario in fig.4(a) asserts that, whenever the user **clicks** on the weather control panel **f2** and **f2** sends an **update** order to **cm**, **cm** must **disable f2** and set its own status to "updating" through **status_up**. Because all events appearing in the scenario are restricted, this scenario forbids the occurrence of **click** or **update** between **disable** and **status_up**.

The uLSC in fig 4(b) contains an ALT-box: only one of the two subboxes is chosen. ALT-boxes are treated in [Bon03], where all results are carried over.

Abstract Syntax In compliance with the semantics of MSCs [ITU00, CEMR98], a basic chart defines a *labeled partial order* on events [BS03]. First, the set of all events (arrow labels) is denoted by Σ. We assume that events contain information about their sender and receiver. Let Σ_a^s (resp. Σ_a^r) be the set of events sent (resp. received), by agent a. Locations are sources and targets of arrows. Two locations l and l' are directly ordered if they belong to the same lifeline and l is drawn higher up than l'. Since communication is instantaneous, the two locations of a same arrow shall be reached simultaneously; hence, they are order-equivalent. The transitive closure of this direct ordering defines a *preorder*.

All locations of an equivalence class must be labeled by the same event. This ensures that the quotient of the preorder defines a labeled partial order.

Definition 1 (Labeled partial order (LPO)). *A Σ-labeled partial order (LPO) is a tuple $\langle L, \leq, \lambda \rangle$, where*

- *L is a set of locations. If L is finite, the LPO is called finite.*
- *$\leq \subseteq L \times L$ is a partial order on L (a transitive, anti-symmetric and reflexive relation).*
- *$\lambda : L \to \Sigma$ is a labeling function associating events to locations.*

The LPO is deterministic *if furthermore $\forall l, l' \in L : \lambda(l) = \lambda(l') \implies l \leq l' \vee l' \leq l$. A* linearization *of a finite LPO is a word of $w_1 \ldots w_n \in \Sigma^*$ such that the LPO $\langle [n], \leq, \{(i, w_i) | i \in [n]\} \rangle$, where $[n]$ is a shortcut for the set $\{1, \ldots, n\}$, is isomorphic to some linear (total) order $\langle L, \leq', \lambda \rangle$ with $\leq \subseteq \leq'$. An* ideal *(or* cut*) in an LPO is a set $c \subseteq L$ such that $\forall l \in c : \forall l' \in L : l' \leq l \implies l' \in c$. By abuse of language, we call "ideal" the LPO resulting in the projection of an LPO on a given ideal.*

Using ideals, one can define a transition system.

Definition 2 (Ideals Transition System, $c \xrightarrow{e} c'$). *The states of ideals transition system are ideals in the considered LPO (see def. 1). Given two ideals c and c', there is a transition labeled by some event e (written $c \xrightarrow{e} c'$) iff there is an e-labeled location l which has all its predecessors in c, but is not in c and $c' = c \cup \{l\}$.*

This transition system has the property that $\emptyset \xrightarrow{w}{}^* c$ if, and only if, c is linearized by w.

Definition 3 (Universal LSC or uLSC).
A uLSC is a tuple $\langle L, \leq, \lambda, \Sigma_R, P \rangle$ such that

1. *$\langle L, \leq, \lambda \rangle$ is a deterministic Σ_R-LPO. Σ_R contains the restricted events[2] of the uLSC;*
2. *$P \subseteq L$ is the prechart. Every prechart location should occur before a main chart location: $P \times (L \setminus P) \subseteq \leq$.*

Semantics The semantics of a uLSC is, like linear temporal logics (LTL), given in terms of a *model relation*: for every possible infinite sequence of events $\gamma \in \Sigma^\omega$, we say that γ is a *model* of a uLSC $S = \langle L, \leq, \lambda, \Sigma_R, P \rangle$ (written $\gamma \models S$) iff, for every decomposition $uv\gamma'$ of γ ($u, v \in \Sigma^*$ and $\gamma' \in \Sigma^\omega$), if $v|_{\Sigma_R}$ linearizes P, then

$$\exists w \in \Sigma^* : \gamma' = w\gamma'' \wedge w|_{\Sigma_R} \text{ linearizes } M.$$

---

[2] That is, roughly, those events that must take place at the moments determined by the uLSC but cannot happen elsewhere while the scenario's main chart is "executing".

The language of a uLSC is its set of models. An LSC specification (say $\mathcal{S}$) is a set of uLSCs and its language ($\mathcal{L}(\mathcal{S})$) is the intersection of the languages of its component uLSCs.

We decompose the constraint expressed by a uLSC per event. Each participating agent will be responsible for the constraints linked to the events he sends. Consider a finite run $w \in \Sigma^*$ and an uLSC $S = \langle L, \leq, \lambda, \Sigma_R, P \rangle$. We say that this run *activates a location l in S* if there is some suffix v of w such that we can find an ideal c in S

1. in which l is maximal ($l \in c$ and $\forall l' > l : l' \notin c$),
2. which contains the prechart ($c \supseteq P$),
3. which does not contain all the locations ($c \subset L$),
4. which has $v|_{\Sigma_R}$ among its linearizations.

Definition 4 (required event, forbidden event). *If w activates some l such that $e \in \Sigma_R$ labels one of the direct successors of l, then we say that w requires e. Conversely, if w activates some l such that $e \in \Sigma_R$ does not label any of the direct successors of l, e is said to be forbidden by w.*

Definition 5 (e-safety, e-liveness). *A run $\gamma \in \Sigma^\omega$ is e-safe (resp. e-live) iff for every finite prefix $w \in \Sigma^*$ of γ, if w forbids (resp. requires) e, then $w \cdot e$ is not a prefix of γ (resp. $\exists v : w \cdot v \cdot e$ is a prefix of γ).*

The following theorem asserts that, by checking that forbidden events do not occur and required events eventually occur, we are sure that an LSC will be satisfied.

Theorem 1 (uLSC = Σ-liveness $\cap$ Σ-safety [BS03]). *For every $\gamma \in \Sigma^\omega$, $\gamma \models S$ iff γ is e-safe and e-live, for every $e \in \Sigma_R$.*

Our ultimate goal is to build an open reactive system. The structure diagram shows all the agents interacting in the application domain. Some of them are system agents, i.e. components of the system that we are in charge of building, while other are environment agents, whose behaviour is beyond our control.

Let $Sys \subset Ag$ be the set of "system" agents. Their controlled events are $\Sigma_{Sys} = \bigcup_{a \in Sys} \Sigma_a^s$. We define similarly $\Sigma_{Env} = \bigcup_{a \in Env} \Sigma_a^s$, the set of events controlled by the environment, as $Env = Ag \setminus Sys$).

As we already highlighted, a uLSC constrains how the various agents interact, by forcing them to behave as prescribed in the main chart, when they have been interacting as in the prechart. This constrains the system as well as its environment. Hence, when designing the system, we may safely assume that the environment will fulfill its safety and liveness obligations. This leads to the natural notion of "implementation correctness".

Definition 6 (Correct implementation). *Let Σ be partitioned into Σ_{Sys}, the set of system-controlled events, and Σ_{Env}, the set of environment-controlled events. A set of words $W \subseteq \Sigma^\omega$ is a* correct implementation *of a uLSC iff*

$$\forall \gamma \in W. \begin{cases} \gamma \text{ is } \Sigma_{Env}\text{-safe} \implies \gamma \text{ is } \Sigma_{Sys}\text{-safe} \\ \gamma \text{ is } \Sigma_{Env}\text{-live} \implies \gamma \text{ is } \Sigma_{Sys}\text{-live}. \end{cases}$$

So, we end up with a system that will guarantee the satisfaction of its specification, provided its environment behaves as assumed.

3.3   Intra-agent Specifications

We use a variant of the formalism of finite Input/Output Automata for specifying the behaviour of each agent separately. This formalism has been introduced in [LT89], originally without the restriction of being finite state. It is a conceptually simple model, which allows us to focus on proofs, abstracting from syntactic and semantic complexities. By its very nature, this formalism is adapted for describing distributed systems, when the focus is on interaction and synchronization. Indeed, the components specified are robust to scheduling; they may not make any assumptions on the relative speed of their environment. Furthermore, since we are interested in open systems, this formalism acknowledges the fact that no component can constrain its environment's behavior; this is guaranteed by the syntactic condition called "input-enabledness". Finally, to effectively support component-based software engineering, our model must make it possible to hierarchically build components from subcomponents, which shall themselves be open systems, while keeping refinement in mind [Bro03]. The framework of I/O automata has composition as a first-class citizen, which guarantees refinement.

Abstract Syntax

Definition 7 (I/O Automaton). *An input-output automaton is a tuple*

$$\langle \Sigma_i, \Sigma_o, Q, q_0, \Delta, \mathcal{P} \rangle,$$

- $\Sigma_i \subseteq \Sigma$ *is a set of input events;*
- $\Sigma_o \subseteq \Sigma$ *is a set of output events. Input and output events are disjoint;*
- Q *is a finite set of states;*
- q_0 *is an initial state;*
- $\Delta \subseteq Q \times (\Sigma_i \cup \Sigma_o) \times Q$ *is a transition relation. An I/O Automaton must be* input-enabled: *for every state q and input event $e \in \Sigma_i$, there must be a state q' such that $\Delta(q, e, q')$;*
- $\mathcal{P} \subseteq 2^{\Sigma_o}$ *is a fairness partition. It is a set of equivalence classes between output events that must be treated fairly (see def. below).*

Semantics A run of an I/O automaton is an alternating sequence of states and events, $r = s_0 e_0 s_1 e_1 \ldots$, starting at q_0 and following the transition relation: for every $i > 0$, $\Delta(s_{i-1}, e_{i-1}, s_i)$. The trace of r is the sequence of events observed on r ($e_0 e_1 \ldots$). An event e is said to be enabled at state q if there is a transition $\Delta(q, e, q')$. For a fairness class $E \in \mathcal{P}$, r is E-fair if, for every event $e \in E$,

1. there are infinitely many states s_i such that e is not enabled at s_i; or,
2. e occurs infinitely often in r.

A run is fair if it is E-fair, for every E in $\mathcal{P}$. The language of an I/O Automaton $\mathcal{A}$, denoted by $\mathcal{L}(\mathcal{A})$, is the set of words $\{\gamma \in \Sigma^\omega | \mathcal{A}$ has a fair run on $\gamma\}$.

Two I/O Automata can be composed, using a variation of the usual synchronous product of automata.

Definition 8 (Composition of I/O automata). *The composition of two automata* $\mathcal{A}^1$ *and* $\mathcal{A}^2$, *with* $\mathcal{A}^j = \langle Q^j, q_0^j, \Delta^j, \Sigma_i^j, \Sigma_o^j \rangle$, *for* $j = 1, 2$, *is defined if their output events are distinct* $(\Sigma_o^1 \cap \Sigma_o^2 = \emptyset)$. *In that case,* $\mathcal{A} = \mathcal{A}^1 \times \mathcal{A}^2$ *is*

1. $Q = Q^1 \times Q^2$;
2. $q_0 = (q_0^1, q_0^2)$;
3. $\Sigma_i = (\Sigma_i^1 \setminus \Sigma_o^2) \cup (\Sigma_i^2 \setminus \Sigma_o^1)$ *i.e. only input events controlled by neither agents are input events of the composition;*
4. $\Sigma_o = \Sigma_o^1 \cup \Sigma_o^2$: *we do not hide "local events", in order to ensure associativity;*
5. $\Delta((q^1, q^2), e, (s^1, s^2))$ *iff*
   - $e \in \Sigma^1 \cap \Sigma^2$ *and* $\Delta^i(q^i, e, s^i)$, *for* $i = 1, 2$;
   - *or,* $e \in \Sigma^1 \setminus \Sigma^2$, $q^2 = s^2$ *and* $\Delta^1(q^1, e, s^1)$ *or vice-versa.*
6. $\mathcal{P} = \mathcal{P}^1 \cup \mathcal{P}^2$, *i.e. we keep the original fairness conditions.*

The composition operation enjoys the following properties:

Lemma 1. *For every I/O Automata* $\mathcal{A}^1, \mathcal{A}^2, \mathcal{A}^3$, *provided composition is defined, we have*

Associativity: $\mathcal{A}^1 \times (\mathcal{A}^2 \times \mathcal{A}^3) = (\mathcal{A}^1 \times \mathcal{A}^2) \times \mathcal{A}^3$.
Commutativity: $\mathcal{A}^1 \times \mathcal{A}^2 = \mathcal{A}^2 \times \mathcal{A}^1$.
Refinement (Trace inclusion): $\mathcal{L}(\mathcal{A}^1 \times \mathcal{A}^2) \subseteq \mathcal{L}(\mathcal{A}^1)$

Proof. Associativity and commutativity are shown in [LT89]. The former relies on the fact that $\mathcal{A}^1$ output events caught by $\mathcal{A}^2$ are not hidden. Trace inclusion comes from the fact that $\mathcal{A}^2$ cannot block an $\mathcal{A}^1$ transition in the composition, by input-enabledness (see def.7) . Therefore, fairness is preserved.

3.4   Relationships Between Models

Usually, the meanings of inter- and intra-agent models overlap. Along the lines of [Har01], we take advantage of this redundancy by relating models in two ways:

Model checking: given a uLSC model $\mathcal{S}$ and a state-based model associating an I/O automaton to every *system* agent $(\mathcal{A}_1, \ldots, \mathcal{A}_n)$, we check that the composed system fulfills $\mathcal{S}$: $\mathcal{L}\left(\prod_{i=1}^n \mathcal{A}_i\right) \subseteq \mathcal{L}(\mathcal{S})$

Synthesis: given a uLSC model $\mathcal{S}$, we verify that it is possible to find one automaton per system agent such that their composition is a correct implementation of $\mathcal{S}$.

4   Previous Answers

There has already been much research for solving the two issues presented in section 3.4. However, the proposed solutions suffer performance problems.

4.1   Model Checking

LSCs can be translated to temporal logics [KHP$^+$01, Bon01] and fed into a model checker. LSCs can be translated to LTL, or CTL, or even ACTL [Eme90], or Büchi automata [KW01].

The formula obtained from a uLSC is

$$\Box \bigwedge_{w\in\ \text{lin}(P)} (\phi_w \implies \bigvee_{v\in\ \text{lin}(P)\cdot\text{lin}(M)} \phi_v),$$

where $\phi_\epsilon = \top$, $\phi_{a\cdot u} = (a \wedge \bigcirc(N\ \mathcal{U}\phi_u))$, and $N = \neg e_1 \wedge \ldots \wedge \neg e_n$, where $\Sigma_R = \{e_1, \ldots, e_n\}$.

However, these approaches face two obstacles:

1. The formula presented above is exponential in the size of the specification.
2. Computing the product of the numerous I/O Automata composing the system can lead to the state explosion problem.

4.2   Synthesis (Aka Realizability Checking)

We have implemented the exponential time algorithm presented in [BS03]. This program, called a *Realizability Checker* [Ros92], builds a correct implementation. This state machine is often exponential in size, and hardly readable by users.

We use the explanation power of animation [Hey01] to illustrate the flaws found by the realizability checker. If the specification is realizable, an implementation is built. Then, the analyst plays the role of the user, i.e. triggers environment events. The animator simulates the reaction of the system, according to the synthesized strategy. If the implementation is not behaving as expected, the model can be adjusted and synthesized again.

If the specification is *not* realizable, the algorithm builds a *sabotage plan* for the environment. Controlling environment events, it will lead *every* system implementation to failure. The roles are thus reversed during animation: the analyst plays the role of the future system whereas the animator plays an evil environment, following the sabotage plan. The analyst will always be driven to a state where he will have to violate some constraint. The animator announces conflicting constraints, such as "scenario X requires event e but this event is forbidden by scenario Y". The analyst can backtrack in the execution and try alternatives. Fig. 4.2 presents a screenshot of (part of) the animator.

The synthesis algorithm described above depends crucially on the *perfect information hypothesis*: every agent can sense every event. This ignores the interface description from the structural model, which explicitly defines which events are visible to each agent. It is more interesting to synthesize a distributed system in which every agent only listens to events specified in its interface. However, telling whether such an implementation exists is undecidable [Ros92].

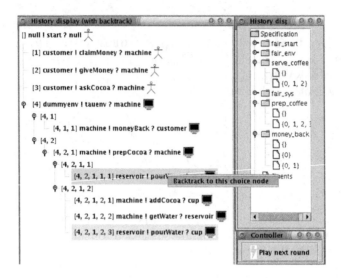

Fig. 5. Realizability checker/Animator screenshot

5   A Lightweight Approach

Since the problem is undecidable, we propose lose completeness but keep soundness: Every implementation produced is correct, but our algorithm may fail to find some implementations.

5.1   Model Checking

First, we suggest to use the techniques for minimizing the size of the formulae generated from uLSCs devised in [Bon01, KHP+01]. Typically, a uLSC can be split into several small formulae, in which we only need to check the proper ordering of *pairs* of events, and not all linearizations (as in sec. 4.1).

In order to address the state explosion problem, we suggest to ignore all components that do not participate in the verified uLSC. Suppose that only agents i through k participate in S. Hence, it is sufficient to check that the uLSC is correct, with respect to the subsystem composed of agents i through k only. Since we demonstrated that I/O automata composition is a refinement, proving that the uLSC is satisfied by this reduced system is enough to show that the global system is correct, too:

$$\mathcal{L}\left(\prod_{j=1}^{n} \mathcal{A}_j\right) \subseteq \mathcal{L}\left(\prod_{j=i}^{k} \mathcal{A}_j\right) \subseteq \mathcal{L}(S).$$

Furthermore, when the subsystem can satisfy the LSC on its own, it indicates that the design achieves low coupling: the fulfillment of the property does not depend on components which are not directly involved in it.

However, if model checking fails, it might be a false negative: the counter-example could have been avoided, had we included more agents in the system, which one can try.

5.2   Synthesis

Our lightweight algorithm is illustrated in fig. 6. Its steps are detailed in the rest of this section.

(1) Agent Selection As opposed to the previous algorithm, the lightweight algorithm focuses on a single agent at a time. It does not try to find a strategy for all participants in one run. For the rest of this section, let a be the selected agent.

(2) Sanity Check All scenarios in which a participates actively are checked to ensure that their causal order matches their visual order. Two locations are causally related if they are sending locations on the same lifeline or if they are the sending and receiving locations of the same event. This is done in polynomial time [AHP96]. Fig. 7 gives an example of a uLSC which does not fulfill this condition. Clearly, it is not simply distributable for agent obj3, because d may only be sent after c has occurred, which obj3 cannot see.

If this sanity check fails, the algorithm stops and explains why specification is not distributable.

(3) Scenario Projection All scenarios are projected onto the lifeline of agent a (e.g., the upper part of fig.6 illustrates an attempt to synthesize an implementation for c[1]). All uLSCs in which a is not required to perform any event are discarded. For instance, the scenario of fig 4(a) would be discarded because c[1] does not take part in it. In summary, Step 3 produces a set of non-empty uLSCs, reduced to the lifeline of a, one for each uLSC in which at least one event controlled by a is restricted.

(4) Construction of Most Representative SLI The I/O automaton built is input-enabled. It records in I all possible cuts of every scenario. The invariant of the automaton is: for every word w, if the automaton reads w and ends up in a state I then, for every ideal c, $c \in I$ iff some suffix of $w|_{\Sigma_R}$ linearizes c. For instance, in Fig. 6, the center state of the I/O automaton records the configuration where the last event was get_new (from cm to c[1]), as all its incoming transitions indicate. This means that the prechart of the projected scenario has been matched and get_new (from c[1] to db) is now required from agent c[1]. Since this event is not forbidden at that state, the *Standard Local Implementation (SLI)* rule (see below) allows it to be scheduled.

Definition 9 (Standard Local Implementation (SLI)). *Let the projected specification be composed of m non-empty uLSCs:* $\{S_1, \ldots, S_m\}$. *An I/O automaton fulfilling the following constraints is called a* Standard Local Implementation (SLI):

$$\langle \Sigma_a^r, \Sigma_a^s, Q, q_0, \Delta, \{\Sigma_a^r\}\rangle$$

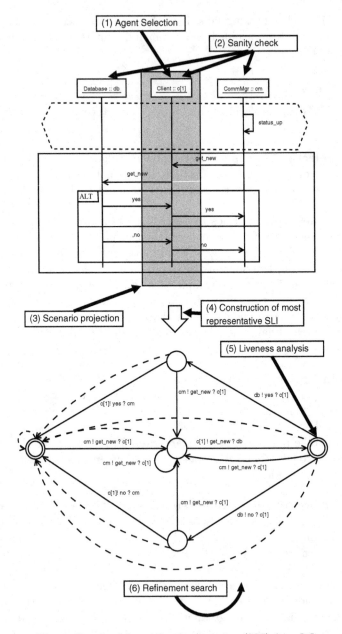

Fig. 6. Standard Local Implementation (SLI) for c[1]

where

- $Q = \prod_{i=1}^{m} 2^{2^{L_i x}}$, *i.e. every state keeps one configuration per uLSC, a configuration being a set of ideals.*

- $q_0 = (\{\emptyset\}, \dots, \{\emptyset\})$,
- $\Delta((I_1, \dots, I_m), e, (I'_1, \dots, I'_m))$ *implies both the following statements*
  1. Δ *follows the ideals transition system:*
     - *if* $e \notin \Sigma^i_R$, $I'_i = I_i$;
     - *if* $e \in \Sigma^i_R$, $I'_i = \{c' | \exists c \in I_i : c \overset{e}{\to} c'\} \cup \{\emptyset\}$. *The empty ideal is always added, because it is linearized by the empty word, which is a suffix of every word* $w \in \Sigma^*$, *thus preserving the invariant.*
  2. *If* $e \in \Sigma^s_a$, *there is some* i *such that* $c \in I_i$ *requires* e *and, for every* j, *there is no* $c \in I_j$ *forbidding* e.

Such an implementation is called "standard" because it follows the classical way of extracting state machines from MSCs (see sec.6). It is dubbed "local" because it only considers a single agent, restricting a scenario to the local view of that agent.

Note that there may exist many SLIs for a given specification, because the condition on Δ is only an implication. They differ only in the scheduling of Σ^s_a events. Thus, it is possible to order SLIs: an SLI $\mathcal{A}$ is *more general* than an SLI $\mathcal{A}'$ ($\mathcal{A}' \sqsubset \mathcal{A}$) iff, at every state q, if $\mathcal{A}'$ allows $e \in \Sigma^s_a$ event, then $\mathcal{A}$ allows e, too.

(5) Liveness Analysis The I/O automaton built according to the SLI rule is always safe, because the forbidden events may not be scheduled. To show this, we prove that the hypotheses made by a about the global state are valid:

Lemma 2 (SLIs are sound). *Let $\mathcal{A}$ be an SLI. Consider a finite run $w \in \Sigma^*$, decomposed in two parts $uv = w$ and a scenario L_j. If $v|_{\Sigma_R}$ linearizes some ideal c in L_j and $\mathcal{A}$ has a run on $v|_{\Sigma_a}$ leading to a state $(I_1, \dots, I_j, \dots, I_n)$, then I_j contains $c|_{\Sigma_a}$.*

Proof. By induction on w.

Lemma 3 (SLIs are safe). *All behaviours induced by an SLI are Σ^s_a-safe.*

Since SLIs guarantee Σ^s_a-safety, it suffices to ensure that the considered automaton is Σ^s_a-live to verify that it is a correct implementation.

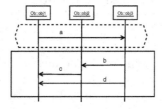

Fig. 7. Mismatch between causal order and visual order

Theorem 2. *Let A be an SLI. If all runs in A are Σ_a^s-live, then A is a correct implementation of a system consisting of agent a.*

Proof. By definition 6, if A is Σ_a^s-live (assumption) and Σ_a^s-safe (lem.3), it is a correct implementation.

In general, liveness is not true of all SLIs, because some required event might be postponed forever, since it is always unsafe. The liveness condition needs to be algorithmically checked; this is done in time quadratic in $|A|$: A is analyzed to check that, on all fair infinite paths, there are infinitely many occurrences of e or e is not required in infinitely many states, for every $e \in \Sigma_a^s$. In fig. 6, the states in which no event is required are drawn with a double line. This SLI example is live for agent c[1].

(6) Refinement Search If $A_\top$ is not a correct implementation, i.e. it is not live, we can try to find another SLI A such that $A \sqsubseteq A_\top$ and A is live. In order to do so, we consider refinement as a two-person game, between a "protagonist" and an "antagonist". The protagonist may remove some edges labeled by Σ_a^s events while the antagonist tries to prove that the resulting automaton is still unlive. If the protagonist has no winning strategy in this game, there is no live SLI for agent a. This game can be solved using classical algorithms, in time polynomial in the size of the graph [GTW02].

Remark 1 (Safety Assumptions). An SLI allows agents to make safety assumptions about their environment, which makes compositional reasoning feasible [AL92]. For instance, when synthesizing agent i, we can make use of the fact that we know *beforehand* that agents $1, \ldots, k$ will also be synthesized using the same method. In that case, when agent i receives an event from another "to-be-synthesized" agent j, he knows that some ideals of the configuration are not valid anymore. Indeed, if agent j sends this message, he must be required to do so. Now, if there is only one scenario which requires him to send j, the agent we are synthesizing can deduce the exact position in this scenario. For synthesizing the SLI of fig.6, our algorithm used this assumption.

Remark 2 (Efficiency). By construction, the I/O Automaton built here is *necessarily* smaller than the automaton constructed in [BS03]. This justifies our claim that this localized technique can sometimes be more efficient than the exact centralized one. However, in the worst case, the SLI is as big as the solution for the centralized case (and thus, exponential in the size of the specification [BS04]). Our running example is specified with 25 scenarios and contains 8 components. Our implementation of the centralized synthesis algorithm fails to analyze it, because of its size. However, the implementation of the lightweight algorithm successfully synthesizes an SLI for every component, but cm and db (see the next remark). cm cannot be synthesized because it participates in all scenarios; projecting the specification on it does not drastically reduce the size of the specification. The SLIs that we obtained had less than 20 states each and their synthesis took only a couple of seconds. This synthesis relied on the additional safety assumptions explained above.

Remark 3 (A Bad Case). The following specification cannot be implemented by any SLI. Assume that we have two scenarios for db, asserting that it must answer either db ! yes ? c[i] or db ! no ? c[i] to all queries of client c[i]. There is no SLI implementing this requirement for db, because the agent must remember the last request that it replied to. Otherwise, the system runs into starvation. Consider the following execution: c[1] and c[2] query db. This leads to some state q. In this state, db answers to c[1]. Immediately after, c[1] queries db again, going back to q. Since db has no means to remember that it replied to c[1] before, it replies to c[1] again. Thus, we enter a loop in which c[2] will never get a reply. Allowing db to use some fixed amount of additional memory, here one bit, could help in avoiding this situation.

6   Related Work

6.1   Play-Out

The play-out approach [HM03, HM01] is related to ours. The play-out algorithm works as follows. A state of the system is a set of ideals, called *live copies*. The user generates an environment event at a time. Assume that this event is e and the current state is $\{c_1, \ldots, c_n\}$. The following rules apply:

1. For every i $(1 \leq i \leq n)$, if $c_i \xrightarrow{e} c_i'$, then c_i is replaced by c_i'. Otherwise, if c_i is in the prechart, it is dropped.
2. If e labels a minimal location of some scenario S_j, a new live copy for S_j is spawn. Thus, $\{l\}$ is added to the next state, where l is the first location in S_j labeled by e.

If, in the next state, some system events are required but not forbidden, one of them is picked and performed. This updates the state, which, in turn, can trigger new events. We followed a similar scheme for designing the SLI rule: an agent will only schedule e if e is required and not forbidden. However, we use the global view of the behaviour to avoid being trapped in unsatisfiable states.

6.2   Synthesis from MSCs

Conceptually, the synthesis algorithms of [AEY00, Uch03, Krü00, LMR98] are very close to ours, except that they apply to MSCs. For every agent, a state machine is built, which tracks its current position on its lifeline. When it reaches a position in which the MSC dictates to send an event e, the machine proposes e. For MSCs, this procedure yields a distributed implementation encompassing all the behaviours specified by the MSCs. Nevertheless, it is possible that this distributed implementation is not correct. This happens when the implementation allows more behaviours than specified by the MSCs. These additional behaviours are called *implied scenarios*. Much work has been devoted to detecting and reporting on those implied scenarios [AEY00, UKM01, Uch03, BAL97].

The picture is slightly different in our case. Our SLIs do not necessarily encompass all the behaviours of the scenario-based specification. Indeed, in step 5 of our procedure, we detect liveness violations, that is *missing* scenarios.

The problem of component-based proofs from MSCs is investigated in [FK01], where causal MSCs are identified.

Algorithms synthesizing state machines from hMSC are able to deal with our running example. There are two main reasons for this difference in efficiency. First, synthesizing state machines from HMSCs is just a simple compilation problem. Our approach is more elaborate, because we have to *prove* that a specification is consistent. Second, using hMSCs, analysts have to combine scenarios to form a coherent whole behaviour, which facilitates the task of synthesis algorithms. In our case, a specification is made of many little scenarios that synthesis algorithms have to combine to form a correct implementation. This task is computationally expensive.

References

[AEY00]   Rajeev Alur, Kousha Etessami, and Mihalis Yannakakis. Inference of Message Sequence Charts. In *Proceedings of 22nd International Conference on Software Engineering*, pages 304–313, 2000.

[AHP96]   Rajeev Alur, Gerard J. Holzmann, and Doron Peled. An analyser for mesage sequence charts. In Tiziana Margaria and Bernhard Steffen, editors, *Tools and Algorithms for the Construction and Analysis of Systems*, volume 1055 of *Lect. Notes in Comp. Sci.*, pages 35–48. Springer-Verlag, 1996.

[AL92]   Martín Abadi and Leslie Lamport. Composing specifications. *ACM Transactions on Programming Languages and Systems*, 14(4):1–60, October 1992.

[BAL97]   Hanêne Ben-Abdallah and Stefan Leue.   Syntactic Detection of Process Divergence and Nonlocal Choice in Message Sequence Charrts. In E. Brinksma, editor, *Proceedings of the Tools and Algorithms for the Construction and Analysis of Systems, Third International Workshop, TACAS'97*, volume 1217 of *Lect. Notes in Comp. Sci.*, pages 259–274, Enschede, The Netherlands, 1997. Springer-Verlag.

[BHK03]   Yves Bontemps, Patrick Heymans, and Hillel Kugler. Applying LSCs to the specification of an air traffic control system. In Sebastian Uchitel and Francis Bordeleau, editors, *Proc. of the 2nd Int. Workshop on "Scenarios and State Machines: Models, Algorithms and Tools" (SCESM'03), at the 25th Int. Conf. on Soft. Eng. (ICSE'03)*, Portland, OR, USA, May 2003. IEEE.

[Bon01]   Yves Bontemps.   Automated Verification of State-based Specifications Against Scenarios (A Step towards Relating Inter-Object to Intra-Object Specifications). Master's thesis, University of Namur, June 2001.

[Bon03]   Yves Bontemps. Realizability of scenario-based specifications. Diplôme d'études approfondies, University of Namur, September 2003.

[Bro03]   Manfred Broy.   Unifying models and engineering theories of composed software systems. In Manfred Broy and Markus Pizka, editors, *Models, Algebras and Logics of Engineering Software*, volume 191 of *NATO Science Series, III: Computer and Systems Sciences*, pages 1–41. IOS Press, 2003.

[BS03]   Yves Bontemps and Pierre-Yves Schobbens. Synthesizing open reactive systems from scenario-based specifications. In Felice Balarin and Johan Lilius, editors, *Proc. of the 3rd Int. Conf. on Applications of Concurrency to System Design (ACSD'03)*, pages 41–50, Guimarães, Portugal, June 2003. IEEE Computer Science Press.

[BS04]   Yves Bontemps and Pierre-Yves Schobbens. The computational complexity of scenario-based agent verification and design. Technical Report 2004.35, CFV (Centre Fédéré en Vérification), October 2004. http://www.ulb.ac.be/di/ssd/cfv/publications.html.

[CEMR98]   J.M.H Cobben, A. Engels, Sjouke Mauw, and Michel Reniers, A. *Formal Semantics of Message Sequence Charts (ITU-T Recommendation Z.120 Annex B)*. International Telecommunication Union, Eindhoven, The Netherlands, April 1998. http://www.itu.int.

[CM02]   Benoit Caillaud and Anca Muscholl. VISS'02: Validation and Implementation of Scenario-based Specifications (ETAPS'02), April 2002. http://www.liafa.jussieu.fr/~anca/VISS02.html.

[DH01]   Werner Damm and David Harel. LSCs: Breathing life into message sequence charts. *Formal Methods in System Design*, 19(1):45–80, 2001.

[Eme90]   E. Allen Emerson. *Temporal and Modal Logic*, volume B, chapter 16, pages 997–1072. MIT Press and Elsevier Science Publishers, Cambridge, Massachusetts, 1990. ISBN 0-262-72015-9 (Second Printing, 1998).

[FK01]   Bernd Finkbeiner and Ingolf Heiko Krüger. Using message sequence charts for component-based formal verification. In *Proc. of OOPSLA 2001 Workshop on Specification and Verification of Component-Based Systems*, Tampa Bay, FL, USA, October 2001.

[GTW02]   Erich Grädel, Wolfgang Thomas, and Thomas Wilke, editors. *Automata Logics, and Infinite Games: A Guide to Current Research*, volume 2500 of *Lect. Notes in Comp. Sci.* Springer, November 2002. ISBN 3-540-00388-6.

[Har01]   David Harel. From play-in scenarios to code: An achievable dream. *IEEE Computer*, 34(1):53–60, January 2001.

[Hey01]   Patrick Heymans. *Animating Albert II Specifications*. PhD thesis, University of Namur, 2001.

[HM01]   David Harel and Rami Marelly. Capturing and Analyzing Behavioral Requirements: The Play-In/Play-Out Approach. Technical Report MCS01-15, The Weizmann Institute of Science, Faculty of Mathematics and Computer Science, Rehovot, Israel, September 2001.

[HM03]   David Harel and Rami Marelly. *Come, let's play! Scenario-based programming using LSCs and the Play-engine*. Springer, 2003. ISBN 3-540-00787-3.

[ITU00]   MSC-2000: ITU-T Recommendation Z.120 : Message Sequence Chart (MSC), 2000. http://www.itu.int/.

[Jac92]   Ivar Jacobson. *Object Oriented Software Engineering: a Use-Case Driven Approach*. ACM Press/Addison-Wesley, 1992.

[KHP+01]   Hillel Kugler, David Harel, Amir Pnueli, Lu Yuan, and Yves Bontemps. Temporal Logic for Live Sequence Charts. Unpublished draft, January 2001.

[Krü00]   Ingolf Heiko Krüger. *Distributed System Design with Message Sequence Charts*. PhD thesis, Technische Universität München, July 2000.

[KW01]   Jochen Klose and Hartmut Wittke. An Automata Based Interpretation of Live Sequence Charts. In T. Margaria and W. Yi, editors, *Proc. of TACAS (Tools and Algorithms for the Construction and Analysis of Systems) 2001*, volume 2031 of *Lect. Notes in Comp. Sci.*, page 512, Genova, Italy, April 2001. Springer-Verlag.

[LMR98]   Stefan Leue, L. Mehrmann, and M. Rezai. Synthesizing ROOM models from message sequence charts specifications. In *Proc. of 13th IEEE Conference on Automated Software Engineering*, Honolulu, Hawaii, October 1998.

[LT89]   N. A. Lynch and M. R. Tuttle. An introduction to input/output automata. *CWI Quarterly*, 2(3):219–246, 1989.

[OMG03]   Object Management Group (UML Revision Task Force). *OMG UML Specification (2.0)*, September 2003. http://www.omg.org/uml.

[RG00]   Johannes Ryser and Martin Glinz. SCENT: A Method Employing Scenarios to Systematically Derive Test Cases for System Test. Technical Report 2000/3, Institut für Informatik - Universität Zurich, Winterthurerstrasse 190, 8057 Zurich, Switzerland, 2000.

[Ros92]   Roni Rosner. *Modular Synthesis of Reactive Systems*. PhD thesis, The Weizmann Institute of Science, Rehovot, Israel, April 1992.

[Uch03]   Sebastian Uchitel. *Elaboration of Behaviour Models and Scenario-based Specifications using Implied Scenarios*. PhD thesis, Imperial College London, January 2003.

[UKM01]   Sebastian Uchitel, Jeff Kramer, and Jeff Magee. Detecting implied scenarios in message sequence chart specifications. In Volker Gruhn, editor, *Proceedings of the Joint 8th European Software Engeneering Conference and 9th ACM SIGSOFT Symposium on the Foundation of Software Engeneering (ESEC/FSE-01)*, volume 26, 5 of *SOFTWARE ENGINEERING NOTES*, pages 74–82, New York, September 10–14 2001. ACM Press.

[WPJH98] Klaus Weidenhaupt, Klaus Pohl, Matthias Jarke, and Peter Haumer. Scenario Usage in System Development: A Report on Current practice. *IEEE Software*, 15(2):34–45, March 1998.

[WS02]   Jon Whittle and Johan Schumann. Statechart Synthesis from Scenarios: an Air Traffic Control Case Study. In *Proc. of "Scenarios and State-Machines: models, algorithms and tools" workshop at the 24th Int. Conf. on Software Engineering (ICSE 2002)*, Orlando, FL, May, 20th 2002. ACM.

Pattern Synthesis from Multiple Scenarios for Parameterized Real-Time UML Models*

Holger Giese, Florian Klein,** and Sven Burmester**

Software Engineering Group, University of Paderborn,
Warburger Str. 100, D-33098 Paderborn, Germany
{hg, fklein, burmi}@upb.de

Abstract. The continuing trend towards more sophisticated technical applications results in an increasing demand for high quality software for complex, safety-critical systems. Designing and verifying the coordination between the components of such a system in order to ensure its overall correctness and safe operation are crucial and costly steps of the development process. In this paper, we extend our approach for the compositional formal verification of UML-RT models described by components and patterns [1], which addresses this challenge. We outline how scenario-based synthesis techniques can facilitate the design and verification steps by automatically deriving the required pattern behavior. Starting from a set of timed scenarios, the presented procedure generates a set of statecharts with additional real-time annotations that realize these scenarios. As parameterized timed scenarios are supported, different system configurations can be specified as required by adjusting the behavior using the specific timing constraints. The paper describes the proposed approach using a running example and presents first results obtained using a prototype implementation.

1 Introduction

The ever increasing complexity of technical systems and their software leads to a demand for automated support for the production of high quality real-time software in this domain. The design and verification of the system coordination is a costly step of the development of such systems, but crucial for the correctness and safe operation of the overall system. In this paper, we extend our approach for the compositional formal verification of UML-RT models described by components and patterns [1], which addresses this challenge. It uses real-time patterns as a means of structuring the necessary coordination mechanisms and enabling subsequent reuse.

During the early design phase, a number of scenarios are usually developed to identify and describe possible or required interaction behavior of the system components and embedded software. An operational model of the interaction, usually in the form of

---

* This work was developed in the course of the Special Research Initiative 614 - Self-optimizing Concepts and Structures in Mechanical Engineering - University of Paderborn, and was published on its behalf and funded by the Deutsche Forschungsgemeinschaft.
** Supported by the International Graduate School of Dynamic Intelligent Systems.

S. Leue and T.J. Systä (Eds.): Scenarios, LNCS 3466, pp. 193–211, 2005.
© Springer-Verlag Berlin Heidelberg 2005

some sort of state machines, is then constructed manually, which is a time-consuming, error-prone, but essential process.

In this paper, we propose to support and automate the design of the state-based real-time patterns using scenario-based synthesis. Several approaches exist which permit the use of the information provided by a given set of scenarios for the synthesis of the components' operational state-based behavior (cf. [2, 3, 4, 5]). In the real-time domain, however, the timing constraints within the scenario descriptions are an essential part of the specification and need to be transscribed to the synthesized state model.

Several proposals to check timed system models against scenario descriptions with time have been made (cf. [6]). For actively synthesizing such models from scenarios including timing constraints, in contrast, only very restricted proposals exist today. The approach proposed in [7] synthesizes only global solutions in form of a single automaton for non-parameterized scenarios, which assumes angelic non-determinism and does not support progress conditions. The approach of [8] results in a global non-parameterized timed automata which supports progress. It supports, however, only a very detailed scenario description in form of trees which is already half way between scenarios and the required operational behavior. In [9] the play-out of life sequence charts (LSC) with timers is presented. However, the play-out engine also constructs only a global behavior for non-parameterized LSCs.

In practice, it is difficult to specify all timing information such as worst-case execution times (wcet), deadlines, or timeouts in advance. The trade-offs between different alternative parameterizations need to be analyzed, which requires the ability to easily vary the constraints. With regard to reuse, the need for parameterized patterns is even more obvious. Our approach therefore supports parameterized timing constraints and their step-wise refinement.

Addressing the problem of scenario-based synthesis for parameterized real-time systems in its general form will probably result in scalability problems. For the synthesis problem for real-time patterns considered here, this is different as only the collaboration of a small number of roles by means of a managable number of scenarios has to be considered.

In this paper the ideas of an earlier proposal [10] are formalized and embedded into our overall approach for compositional design and model checking (cf. [1]) to enable the systematic development of the real-time coordination at the system level. We support UML 2.0 sequence diagrams with conditional behavior as input and can generate a real-time extension of statecharts (RTSC) [11] as its output. RTSC and real-time pattern are supported by the real-time version of the Fujaba CASE tool.[1] RTSC have a well-defined real-time semantics based on timed automata [12]. Code generation [11] as well as real-time model checking [13] are currently supported for real-time statecharts.

In Section 2, we introduce an example and our modeling approach, with the corresponding notations. The analysis of the parameterized scenarios is then outlined in Section 3. Section 4 describes how the operational real-time behavior of a pattern can be derived. The application of synthesized patterns, including the systematic selection

---

[1] www.fujaba.de

of valid parameter sets and model checking their instantiations, is described in Section 5, followed by our final conclusion.

2 Modeling Approach

Our modeling approach is centered around the idea of composing complex software systems from domain-specific patterns describing component interaction. A pattern defines structure, by specifying and linking ports representing the roles the respective components play in that interaction, and behavior, by providing a statechart for each port. Additionally, it may provide constraints describing a set of desired properties that must hold for each individual pattern. Concrete components are derived by composing and refining the roles required by the applicable patterns. The overall system is ultimately created by simply connecting the components at the appropriate ports.

The extensions proposed in this paper pertain to the definition of the patterns and leave all other aspects of the development process unaffected. The manual construction of the statecharts for the pattern role protocols is replaced by scenario-based synthesis in order to make this step faster, cheaper and less error-prone. In the following subsections, we briefly introduce the concepts and notations that are relevant in this context. While we will provide some additional insight into the underlying ideas and assumptions, please refer to [1] for an in depth discussion of the basic approach.

As we present the notations, we introduce the running example used throughout the paper along the way. We model a watchdog, a well-known approach for monitoring safety-critical components. If the supervised controller (*DistanceController*) does not emit a heartbeat signal in a regular and timely manner, the watchdog (*SafetyController*) assumes that the controller has failed and resets it in order to return it to a valid state.

2.1   Real-Time Components and Patterns

Real-time components and the patterns that link them provide the structure around which our approach is organized. Even though the design process is usually not linear and new components and patterns may be introduced as it progresses, identifying potential components is the basis of every iteration. Their relevant interactions can then be described and formalized as patterns.

When discussing patterns, we abstract from the actual components and represent them by the roles they perform in the interaction. These are manifested in dedicated, named ports that provide the corresponding interfaces. If two roles communicate directly, their ports are linked by a connector. The precise behavioral semantics of the pattern are provided by attaching real-time statecharts to each of the ports and, in case they represent asynchronous communication channels, the connectors. Finally, the pattern may be completed with constraints in order to ensure that certain properties hold for individual ports or the overall pattern. Due to the limited number of implicated components, verification by means of model checking is feasible for isolated patterns, asserting whether the constraints may be violated. The central claim is that, by virtue of a well-defined context and structures that limit side effects, the verified properties are carried over to the system as a whole.

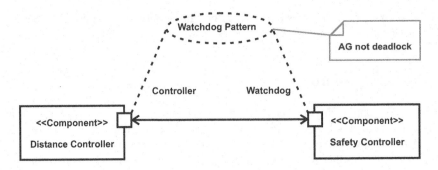

Fig. 1. The Watchdog Pattern modeled using the CASE Tool Fujaba

In order to achieve this, we need to restrict our notion of a component to the composition of a fixed number of role behaviors with well-defined, simple communication behavior. Though the composition is parallel, behaviors are usually not independent of each other; i.e. composite behavior that simultaneously and correctly implements all role specifications needs to be derived by appropriate refinement of the individual role behaviors. As local verification resolves or at least detects conflicts between roles within a component, a syntactically correct composition of verified components, using the provided ports, guarantees correctness of the whole system.

An additional advantage of the approach is that patterns, due to their modular nature and the abstraction provided by the role concept, promote reuse. If the identified components correspond to a previously encountered case, the appropriate, already verified pattern can simply be applied. In our example, we can easily identify the SafetyController and the DistanceController as the relevant components. They interact according to the Watchdog Pattern, which we will define from scratch. As a simple example for a required property, we specify that no deadlock may occur anywhere in the pattern. See Figure 1 for an illustration of the pattern, using standard UML notations.

2.2   Real-Time Scenarios

Now that we have defined the structure of our pattern, we can proceed to formalize our expectations concerning role behavior. Scenarios lend themselves to this purpose, as identifying a sequence of events for each concrete case comes more naturally to most people than reasoning in abstract state spaces.

A number of notations for scenario description techniques with timing constraints exists, such as UML 1.4 sequence diagrams [6], message sequence charts with timing constraints, [14], life sequence charts (LSC) with timers [9], or action diagrams (timing diagrams) [15]. In the different notations, timing constraints are described in quite different ways (cf. [14, 9]). Timers with reset and timeouts, delay intervals for events and activities, drawing rules, or timing markers in form of boolean expressions that constrain particular events or the whole diagram are possible options.

In this paper, we consider only a restricted subset of UML 2.0 sequence diagrams [16–p. 444] to describe parameterized timed scenarios. UML 2.0 sequence diagrams permit a duration observation of the form d = duration, which can be used to measure the time required for a specific message transfer. In-between two points on the lifeline of a UML sequence diagram, a duration constraint {l .. u} with a lower and an upper bound can be specified. Additionally, we can store the current time within a time observation t = now and later reference this measurement using a timing constraint {t .. t+3}. To enable the checking of constraints later, we further restrict the supported annotations for parameters $v \in V_p$, constants $A \in \mathrm{CONST}$, and expressions in form of arbitrary sums over parameters and constants $\exp \in \mathrm{SUM}(V_p \cup \mathrm{CONST})$ as follows: a duration constraint must have the form $\{A \ldots \exp\}$ and a timing constraint must have the form $\{\mathrm{to} + A \ldots \mathrm{to} + \exp\}$ for a related time observation to = now.

Techniques for conditional behavior such as triggers for sequence diagrams are another relevant aspect of scenarios. They have first been proposed for life sequence charts (LSC) [9]. Another proposal are triggered message sequence charts (TMSCs) [17]. In this paper, we use the **assert** block of UML 2.0 sequence diagrams [16–p. 444] to describe the conditional behavior of parameterized timed scenarios. An **assert** block indicates that a specific part of the scenario is mandatory once the preceding sequence of steps has been observed, which in turn may or may not occur at all. To resolve conflicts between different asserted behaviors, we further assign priorities to each scenario.

To describe the relationship between the scenarios and states of the participating roles, we use state labels. We restrict the labels to a single state or sets of possible states. * denotes all states of a role that are explicitly defined outside the present scenario. Explicit states can be added to or removed from state sets using + and -, respectively.

For the Watchdog Pattern, we identify four typical behaviors: the normal life cycle consisting of initialization, regular operation, and shutdown, plus the reaction of the watchdog when the heartbeat is not received in time.

In first scenario, the controller goes online and initializes the watchdog, as depicted by the topmost sequence diagram, Initialization, in Figure 2. The regular behavior, which essentially describes how the controller periodically sends its heartbeat (sane message) to the watchdog, is depicted in the sequence diagram Regular. To shut down the watchdog, a stop message is sent to the watchdog, which subsequently goes offline as shown by Shutdown, the third sequence diagram. As the last scenario of Figure 2, the sequence diagram Reset specifies that the watchdog will send a reset message to the controller if no sane message is received within the time frame {WTL .. wtu}.

2.3   Real-Time Statecharts

A formally defined pattern requires an operational description of the real-time behavior of its roles by means of statecharts. UML 2.0 statecharts do, however, not provide appropriate modeling concepts to realize real-time constraints. The when- and after-constructs permit only to refer to absolute time and relative to the point in time when entering a state, respectively. If more complex timing constraints which involve a whole sequence of states are considered, these concepts are not sufficient any more. Furthermore, the semantics of the when- and after-constructs of UML 2.0 statecharts require that the related transitions are executed exactly at the specified point in time. As such a behavior cannot be implemented on a real physical machine, we require a more appropriate state machine notation which ensures realizability. Finally, UML 2.0 statecharts do not allow combinations of event triggers and timeguards on the same transition.

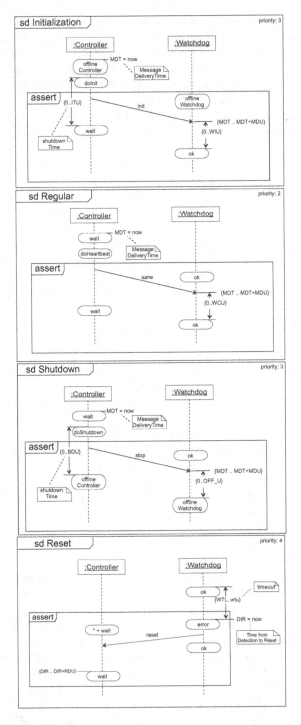

Fig. 2. Scenarios of initialization, regular operation, shutdown, and reset

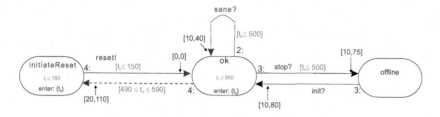

Fig. 3. Possible behavior of the watchdog role

Thus, we use the extensions of standard UML statecharts provided by real-time statecharts (RTSC) [11]. The first extension is an advanced time model which provides clocks which can be reset when firing transitions or entering/leaving states. The clocks are used to measure time in relation to these points of time.

Each state has time-invariants which determine the permitted clock values. Let the set of clocks be denoted by C, a clock by $t_i \in C$. Invariants are any logically possible combination of simple expressions of the form $t_i \leq T_i$, $T_i \in N \cup \{\infty\}$. For example, the state initiateReset in Figure 3 has the time invariant $t_0 \leq 150$.

The transitions have additional time guards which denote the valid activation times w.r.t. the current values of the clocks. A timeguard consists of logical combined simple expressions of the form $a_i \leq t_i \leq b_i$, $a_i \in \mathbb{N}$, $b_i \in \mathbb{N} \cup \{\infty\}$, $a_i \leq b_i$. In the example, the time guard of the outgoing transition of state initiateReset is $[t_0 \leq 150]$.

A parameterized RTSC (PRTSC) is a RTSC whose clock constraints are not simple constants, but expressions containing parameters beside the constants.

Two different types of transitions exist. *Urgent* transitions (solid line) fire immediately when they are triggered. In contrast, *non-urgent* transitions (dashed line) can fire arbitrarily as long as they are enabled. Only when the source-state's invariant would otherwise be violated, the non-urgent transition must be executed.[2] The execution of transitions, unlike in standard timed automata models, consumes time. Therefore, the transitions are also equipped with deadlines which describe when the transition execution has to finish, and worst case execution times. The deadline can be relative to the point in time when the transition was fired and absolute by referring to clocks.

Operations are annotated with their WCETs, and transitions are extended by deadlines that describe when a transition's side-effect has to be executed. The deadline is split into a relative and an absolute part. The relative part is specified by an interval of the form $[d_{low}, d_{up}]$ that describes how long the switching, i.e. the execution of the transition, may take at least respectively most once triggered. The absolute part is of the form $\bigwedge_{t_i \in C} t_i \in [d^i_{low}, d^i_{up}]$ and specifies lower and upper bounds dependant on clocks. In the example, the transition of state ok which receives the sane event has to be finished after at least 10 and at most 40 ms.

Figure 3 is a manually constructed statechart for the Watchdog role. It would theoretically be possible to prove certain properties for a set of scenarios and then show that

---

[2] This property is used within our approach to denote underspecification of the timing behavior where required.

a statechart, which we can verify using model checking, is consistent with them. The problem is obtaining the latter representation, as transforming and combining several scenarios into a single statechart can lead to conflicts or inconsistencies and potentially generates a vast number of superfluous states. Constructing a minimal correct model yet remains a creative process. In the following sections, we will attempt to facilitate and support this process and automate it where possible.

3   Scenario Analysis

We begin by formalizing a method for analyzing scenarios. Unlike other approaches such as [18] that also attempt to extract a system's structure, we build upon our component model and limit ourselves to the extraction of behavioral information.

To formalize the timing constraints provided by a sequence diagram, we map it to a graph (N, E). Nodes $n \in N$ are used to denote the possible states of the roles, and edges $e \in E$ are used to describe how time passes on the lifeline with timing constraints expressed as sums of parameters from the set V_p and constants from the set CONST (SUM($V_p \cup$ CONST)). We further assume a set R containing every role present in any one of the scenarios. We then map the basic elements of a sequence diagram to this graph as outlined in the following:

State labels in form of rounded rectangles are used to denote one or multiple states which are possibly entered at this point in the lifeline of a role. We further assume that a state label denotes only the point in time when the state is entered, i.e. all time references to it refer to this unique point in time. Labelling for the nodes is used to denote the relation between nodes and roles as well as nodes and the related states with respect to the assigned role.

In sequence diagrams, *activities* are used to describe the execution of a side-effect. They are denoted by white rectangles placed on the role's lifeline. We assume that the specific execution time of an activity is usually unpredictable. However, lower and upper bounds (cf. worst-case execution times (wcet)) l and u can be assumed or explicitly specified. We use an edge $(n, l, u, \mathsf{a}, n')$ to represent an activity.

The *communication* in sequence diagrams can be asynchronous or synchronous. While using asynchronous communication within the sequence diagrams, we assume that the resulting behavior of each channel can be described by synchronous communication by adding an explicit model of channel behavior describing the internal buffering and possible blocking. Time bounds for a communication describe the earliest point in time when communication could occur (l) and how long the role will wait for this communication (u). Wait edges $(n, l, u, \mathsf{w}, n')$ leading to an extra synchronization node n' are used to represent the communication within both the role and the channel.

Besides these explicitly visible elements we additionally have *glue* behavior which represents the lifeline in-between the other elements. This could include several forms of time controlled activation such as immediate execution in zero time or a timeout. We use an edge (n, l, u, g) to represent such a glue behavior that may occur in-between any of the other elements. It is specifically used to connect the synchronization node after a communication with the successor element in both roles.

The restrictions concerning the supported forms of timing constraints, which have been formulated for the sequence diagrams in Section 2.2, ensure that only a single measurement is referenced within a timing constraint. We can therefore map it to a timing constraint with a uniquely determined starting point, when the measurement is made, and an end point denoted by the constraint itself. Across multiple roles, we interpret such a timing constraint as an implied *check*, which denotes an upper and lower bound (l and u) on the permitted execution time in-between the two specified points in time. A special edge $(n, l, u, \mathsf{c}, n')$ is used for this purpose. Within a single role, we employ more constructive timing constraints named *restrictions*. A restriction enforces the lower bound, only checks the upper bound, and is represented by an edge $(n, l, u, \mathsf{r}, n')$.

To reflect the assert blocks within the sequence diagrams, we will represent nodes which relate to a state within an assert block in the sequence diagram by assert nodes ($N_a \subseteq N$) if they have any predecessor node. All other nodes become possible nodes ($N_p \subseteq N$).

This formalization is summarized in the following definition:

Definition 1. *A* time constraint graph *(TCG) is a graph* (N, E) *with* $N = N_p \cup N_a$ *a set of nodes which are either possible (N_p) or asserted (N_a) and* $E = E_a \cup E_g \cup E_w \cup E_r \cup E_c$ *of the form* $(n, l, u, \mathsf{x}, n') \in E_x$ *with source and target node* $n, n' \in N$, *lower and upper bound expressions* $l \in \mathrm{CONST}$, $u \in \mathrm{SUM}(V_p \cup \mathrm{CONST})$, *and a flag* $\mathsf{x} \in \{\mathsf{a}, \mathsf{g}, \mathsf{w}, \mathsf{r}, \mathsf{c}\}$ *denoting whether it is an activity (a), glue (g), wait (w), restriction (r), or check (c) edge. Each node is either possible (N_p) or asserted (N_a). For the set of nodes we further distinguish state (N_s) and communication nodes (N_c). A surjective state labelling* $l_s : N_s \rightarrow \wp(S)$ *and role labelling* $l_r : N_s \rightarrow R$ *with* $l_s(n) \subseteq S_{l_r(n)}$ *must further assign roles and states to all state nodes. The role labelling implies the node sets* N_{r_i} *of all nodes relating to role* r_i. *We further require that each communication node is only connected with nodes of two roles and can only be the target of wait edges and the source of glue edges.*

A sequence of edges $e_1; \ldots; e_k$ with $e_i = (n_i, \ldots, n_{i+1})$ and $e_{i+1} = (n_{i+1}, \ldots, n_{i+2})$ is named a path. We write $n_1[e_1; \ldots; e_k]_* n_{k+1}$ and $n_1[e_1\rangle n_2$ for $k = 1$. For convenience, we may also skip the specific path and write $n[\rangle n'$ resp. $n[\rangle_* n'$.

Due to the outlined distinction between possible and asserted nodes, we distinguish the following cases for edges: An edge is *possible* iff its source and target nodes are possible. It is *asserted* iff its source node is asserted. An edge leading from a possible to an asserted node is a *trigger*.

The outlined mapping is done automatically in our prototype tool. An example for the mapping of the sequence diagrams to TCGs is presented in Figure 4 where the TCG of the **shutdown** scenarios of Figure 2 is presented. When visualizing the graph, we label the arc simply using the lower and upper bound expression as well as the edge type. The possible nodes are depicted by grey nodes while the asserted nodes are white (see Figure 4 for an example).

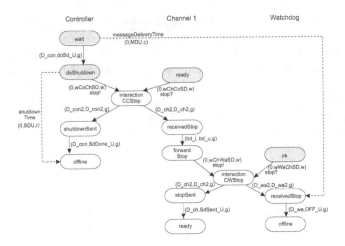

Fig. 4. The TCG for the watchdog shutdown

3.1   Checking Consistency and Locality

For a given evaluation $[\cdot]$: $\mathrm{SUM}(V_p \cup \mathrm{CONST}) \to \mathbb{R}_0$ for the expressions for the upper and lower bound l and u of an edge, we can determine the concrete lower bound as $[l]$ and $[u]$, respectively.

Definition 2. *A timed run of a given TCG (N, E) is a surjective function $\delta : E \to \mathbb{R}_0$ which assign a delay to each edge such that for all $e = (n, l, u, \mathsf{x}, n') \in E$ holds $[l] \le \delta(e) \le [u]$ (edge conform) and for any two $e = (n, l, u, \mathsf{w}, n'') \in E$ and $e' = (n', l', u', \mathsf{w}, n'') \in E$ holds $[l] = \delta(e)$ or $[l'] = \delta(e')$ (urgent).*

For timed scenarios, a first serious problem is *consistency*. A scenario is consistent if a time consistent behavior exists for it. In [19], an efficient decision procedure for this problem has been presented, which maps the question whether a timing behavior that fulfills all constraints exists to computing negative cost cycles and shortest distances in weighted digraphs. For the parameterized case we can define consistency as follows:

Definition 3. *A run r is consistent for an evaluation $[\cdot]$ iff for all two alternative paths $e_1; \ldots; e_n$ and $e'_1; \ldots; e'_m$ between two nodes holds $\sum_{i=1}^{n} \delta(e_i) = \sum_{j=1}^{m} \delta(e'_j)$. The set of all conform, consistent, and urgent timed runs for a given TCG and an evaluation $[\cdot]$ is denoted as $\Delta((N, E), [\cdot])$. We say that a parameterized scenario is consistent if an evaluation $[\cdot]_1$ exists with $\Delta((N, E), [\cdot]_1) \ne \emptyset$.*

Consistency alone, however, does not take into account that the timing of parallel tasks can in reality only depend on their interaction in the past. The notion of *causality* [15] thus demands that a realization exists that can ensure correct operation without global knowledge or knowledge about the future. A somehow closed fragment of a TCG which can be used to describe the history is an inital segment:

Definition 4. *A subgraph (N', E') of an TCG (N, E) is a segment iff $N' \subseteq N$, $E' \subseteq E$ with $E' = E \cap N' \times N'$, and for all $n, n' \in N'$ and $n'' \in N$ with $n[\rangle_* n''$ and $n''[\rangle_* n'$ holds $n'' \in N'$.*

An *initial segment* contains all initial nodes ($n \in N$ with $N \times \{n\} \cap E = \emptyset$).

While the general notion of causality assumes that the future behavior of each edge could depend on all preceding edges (the full history which could in principle be known), we further restrict the considered history to the explicitly defined states. Therefore, we assume for a given history all next activity or glue edges are behave randomly, but respect additional constraints in form of restriction edges as well as the state-specific bounds. We name this property, which implies causality, locality.

Definition 5. *A TCG respects* locality *for an evaluation* $[\![\cdot]\!]$ *iff for any initial segment* (N', E') *holds that any consistent and urgent timed run* $\delta \in \Delta((N', E'), [\![\cdot]\!])$ *can be extended respecting an arbitrary time annotation* $\delta_+ : ((E_a \cup E_g) \cap (N' \times (N - N'))) \rightarrow \mathbb{R}_0$ *for any* $N'' \supseteq N' \cup \{n \in N | \exists n' \in N' : (n', n) \in E_a \cup E_g\}$ *and* $E'' = E \cap N'' \times N''$ *to a consistent and urgent timed run* $\delta' \in \Delta((N'', E''), [\![\cdot]\!])$ *such that for all* $e = (n, \ldots, n') \in ((E_a \cup E_g) \cap (N' \times (N - N')))$ *holds* $\delta'(e) = \delta_+(e)$ *or* $\delta'(e) > \delta_+(e)$. *In the second case, an* $e' = (n'', l, u, r, n') \in ((E_r) \cap (N' \times (N - N')))$ *with* $\delta'(e') = [\![l]\!]$ *must exist.*

The definition ensures that for each history any possible local choice (maybe delayed due to local restriction constraints) leads again to a consistent behavior.

For the case of parameterized timing constraints, we even have to consider the dependencies which result from parameters which are present in the different scenarios which should be composed. To address the problem of consistency and locality, we use linear inequalities. For n variables $v_1, \ldots, v_n \in V$ over $\mathbb{R}$ a system of *linear inequalities* is defined by m inequalities with coefficients $\alpha_{i,j} \in \mathbb{R}$ of the form $\alpha_{i,1} v_1 + \ldots + \alpha_{i,n} v_n \leq b_i$. A set of linear inequalities is only *feasible* iff an assignment for all v_i exists which fulfills all m inequalities. When additionally a linear cost function $f : V \rightarrow \mathbb{R}$ is defined, we have a *linear optimization problem* which can be solved by the well known simplex algorithm.

To check for consistency, we have to derive a set of inequalities which describe the execution time dependencies. This includes all subgraphs of the TCGs which result from the start and end node of restriction and check edges. In addition, for each communication by means of two wait edges, the related preceding subgraphs (which start with a single node and reach this node without ever having a front with less than two nodes) has to be considered to detect possible timing problems.

We then have to determine the timing dependencies for each *non separatable segment* (N', E') with unique start and end node. They are characterized at first by a pair of nodes $n, n' \in N'$ such that n has no predecessor and at least two successors ($|\{n'' \in N' | n[\rangle n''\}| \geq 2$) and n' has no successors and at least two predecessors ($|\{n'' \in N' | n'[\rangle n''\}| \geq 2$). In addition, (N', E') cannot be separated into two unconnected subgraphs by eliminating a single node (there exists no $n'' \in N'$ such that for $(N' - \{n''\}, E' \cap (N' - \{n''\}) \times (N' - \{n''\}))$ holds $n \not{\rangle}_* n'$).

For each of these subgraphs, we start the propagation by assigning $(0, 0)$ as the upper and lower bound to the initial node n. Note that due to the occurrence of the same parameters within the different subgraphs the resulting inequalities are also related.

To propagate the minimal and maximal execution times, we use constants, variables, and sums over variables which are assigned to each node. Such an assignment (A, b) determines an upper bound described by the constant A and a term b describing a sum over variables. We further have variables representing scenario parameters (V_p) and temporary variables (V_t) which are employed to propagate the timing dependencies. For each specific edge leading from a node n with the assigned bounds (A, b) to a node n', we proceed as follows to describe the propagation of the minimal and maximal execution times:

(P1) In case of an activity edge $(n, L, u, \mathsf{a}, n')$ or glue edge $(n, L, u, \mathsf{g}, n')$, we assign $(A + L, b + u)$ to n'. We simply propagate the minimal resp. maximal value plus the minimal resp. maximal delay.

If two edges lead from nodes n and n' with assigned bounds (A, b) and (A', b') to a node n'', we proceed as follows:

(P2) For two waiting edges $(n, L, u, \mathsf{w}, n'')$ and $(n', L', u', \mathsf{w}, n'')$, we add a new variable $v_t \in V_t$ and two inequalities $v_t \geq b + L$ and $v_t \geq b' + L'$ and finally assign $(\max(A + L, A' + L'), v_t)$ to n''. While the lower bound is obviously determined by the maximum of both lower bounds, the upper bound would have been correctly derived as the maximum of $b + L$ and $b' + L'$. As b and b' are terms rather than constants, we cannot determine the maximum directly. Instead, we use an additional temporary variable v_t for which we establish that $v_t \geq \max(b + L, b' + L')$ holds. By further adding only inequalities of the form $\ldots + v_t + \ldots \leq \ldots$ we can ensure that the ability of v_t to also become larger than $\max(b + L, b' + L')$ cannot result in false positives. It is noteworthy that the employed system of linear inequalities will not result in false negatives either, as any solution for v_t implies that $v_t = \max(b + L, b' + L')$ is also a correct solution.

(P3) In the case of an activity edge $(n, L, u, \mathsf{a}, n'')$ or glue edge $(n, L, u, \mathsf{g}, n'')$ and a restriction edge $(n', L', u', \mathsf{r}, n'')$ we assign $(\max(A + L, A' + L'), b + u)$ to n''. The lower bound is determined by the maximum of the lower bounds of both alternatives, as the restriction will enforce this lower bound. For the upper bound, the activity or glue edge is simply propagated.

(P4) Finally, for an activity edge $(n, L, u, \mathsf{a}, n'')$ or glue edge $(n, L, u, \mathsf{g}, n'')$ and a check edge $(n', L', u', \mathsf{c}, n'')$ leading from n resp. n' to n'', we only propagate the delays and assign $(A + L, b + u)$ to n''. We simply propagate the minimal resp. maximal value plus the minimal resp. maximal delay as in the case of a single edge.

Besides the propagation, we have to additionally include the following check for the final node n'' if it describes a communication:

(P2*) For two waiting edges $(n, L, u, \mathsf{w}, n'')$ and $(n', L', u', \mathsf{w}, n'')$ with (A, b) and (A', b') assigned to n resp. n', we additionally add $A + u \geq b' + L'$ and $A' + u' \geq b + L$ to the set of inequalities. We thus check that the timing of two participants of the synchronous communication cannot exclude the communication, e.g. because one side already has a timeout while the other one is not yet ready.

For restriction and check edges, we have the special case that the restriction or check edge can only have the final node as target node if they also have the initial node as source node.[3] We thus have:

---

[3] Otherwise, the considered subgraph can be separated into two unconnected subgraphs by eliminating the source node of the restriction or check edge, which contradicts the selection criteria for the subgraphs.

(P3*) In the case of a restriction edge $(n, L, u, \mathsf{r}, n')$ with $(0, 0)$ and (A, b) assigned to the initial node n resp. final node n', we additionally add $b \leq u$ to check the upper bound. As the lower bound is guaranteed by the restriction itself, we do not have to add any check for this case.

(P4*) Finally, for a check edge $(n, L, u, \mathsf{c}, n')$ with $(0, 0)$ and (A, b) assigned to the initial node n resp. final node n', we additionally add $A \geq L$ for the lower bound and $b \leq u$ for the upper bound.

Locality Checking Algorithm: We check whether a set of TCGs is consistent and respects locality as follows:

1. For all non-separable segments with unique start and end node of all TCGs do:
   (a) propagate the lower and upper bound using the rules (P1) – (P4) and,
   (b) add the checks (P2*) – (P4*).
2. Check the resulting system of inequalities for feasibility.

If such a feasible solution exists, we have found a witness for the consistency of the combination of all timed scenarios which also respects locality.

For our Watchdog Pattern example and its four UML sequence diagrams presented in Figure 2, the Java-based tool prototype requires only 300 ms on a standard PC to generate the linear inequalities for 7 subgraphs. Solving the resulting system of 89 inequalities took only 20 ms using a Java implementation of the simplex algorithm.

3.2 Excluding Conflicts

Another class of problem arises when we combine multiple scenarios. While the checks outlined above ensure that an evaluation exists which fulfills the requirements of all scenarios, the consequences of overlapping have not been taken into account. The analysis of such problems is restricted by the fact that model checking the overall synthesized parameterized behavior is not even possible.[4] We therefore restrict our attention to incomplete but feasible checks which do not take reachability into account. The checks only report problems which are relevant (no false negatives) but may result in false positives. These false positives are addressed later in the process by model checking when specific parameter settings are given.

We can further classify such problems as *behavioral conflicts* or *timing conflicts*. While the former two already result within an untimed behavioral model, the latter relates to the timing of alternative behaviors.

To address the outlined class of problems, alternative behaviors for a single state which contradict each other have to be detected and resolved. Each such state $s \in S$ relates to the TCG nodes with the corresponding state label (all $n \in N$ with $s \in l_s(n)$). As restriction and check edges only declare required timing constraints but do not result in transitions, we can restrict our further considerations to operational edges, which leaves only the activity, glue, and wait edges.

---

[4] Emptiness for parameterized timed automata with more than 2 parameters has been proven to be undecidable by reducing the halting problem of 2-counter machines to it [20]. By a similar encoding via scenarios with related state labels, the same problem can be reduced to the synthesis problem which excludes time-stopping deadlocks.

Respecting priorities and assertions, the combination of the scenarios implies that asserted operational transitions exclude any other operational transition with lower priority. The same holds for any activity edge or send edges.

(C1) If a state $s \in S$ exists with one asserted operational edge, one activity edge, or one send edge and an additional edge which has a lower or equal priority, we have a *behavioral conflict*. The designer has to modify the scenario priorities and state labelling of all TCGs thus that the conflict is resolved. It is to be noted that such modifications can result in a node without any valid state label which disables the respective scenario. If no set of modifications that does not disable any of the scenarios can be found, we have an unresolvable conflict.

Besides the outlined problems which arise independently from the time dimension in the abstract model, we have to ensure that the timings of the different edges preempt each other as specified by the priorities.

(C2) If we have a trigger wait-edge $(n, L, u, \mathsf{w}, n')$ which additionally requires an event e, for all edges $(n'', L', u', \mathsf{w}, n''')$ with $s \in l(n) \cap l(n'')$ and lower priority that also require the event e, we have to check $L' \leq L$ directly. If it is fulfilled, we replace the wait-edge by two alternative edges $(n'', L', L, \mathsf{w}, n''')$ and $(n'', u, u', \mathsf{w}, n''')$ such that the preemption is respected. If it is not fulfilled, we replace the wait-edge by the edge $(n'', u, u', \mathsf{w}, n''')$ and add $u \leq u'$ to the the set of inequalities to ensure that $(n'', u, u', \mathsf{w}, n''')$ can occur.

(C3) For a trigger glue-edge $(n, L, u, \mathsf{g}, n')$, for all edges $(n'', L', u', \mathsf{x}, n''')$ with $s \in l(n) \cap l(n'')$ and a lower priority, we have to add $u' \leq L$ to the the set of inequalities in order to ensure that they are preempted by the first edge, which will in turn ultimately be enforced by the corresponding state invariant (cf. Section 4).

If we have multiple edges with the same priority or possible edges, the outlined conflict resolution rules result in non-deterministic behavior which simply includes all alternatives.

Conflicts Resolution Algorithm: For each state $s \in S$, we store all edges in a dedicated list, sorted by the priority. We then proceed as follows:

1. Apply the rules (C1), (C2), or (C3) to the first element of the list.
2. Remove the element and return to step 1, until all edges are processed.

This results in an extended system of linear inequalities which must then be checked to ensure that the specified trigger edges of one scenario are not fully disabled by another scenario due to the timing constraints. Additional inequalities $L + \Delta \leq u$ for all operational edges and a minimal triggering time Δ further ensure that every edge can still be triggered. We can then use the systematic exploration of the set of inequalities to detect which edges are excluded by timing conflicts.

As our example contained no conflicts, the additional processing resulted in merely two additional equations. Generating these additional equations took 10 ms, and solving the extended system of linear inequalities took 25 ms. The new equations thus only result in an extra effort of 15 ms.

4   Pattern Synthesis

For a consistent set of TCGs without conflicts we can also derive the synthesis result for the watchdog pattern (cf. Figure 1).

Like most approaches proposed for the synthesis of a distributed implementation (cf. [2, 4, 5]), we only consider the local knowledge present for each role in the scenarios. Therefore, our synthesis algorithm is efficient but incomplete. If the logical flow of events of a given timed scenario can be observed for the synthesized set of RTSC, we can ensure that the specified timing constraints of the scenario are met. We have, however, to check additionally whether the synthesis results excludes time-stopping deadlocks and whether implied behavior emerges due to the interaction of the synthesized RTSCs (cf. [21]).

The synthesis algorithm starts with the TCGs which result from the analysis of potential conflicts outlined in Section 3.2. The mapping to states is simply derived for each node $n \in N$ using the state labelling $l_s(n) \subseteq S_{l_r(n)}$. For glue edges, we add corresponding non urgent transitions, while the activity edges become urgent ones. The communication expressed by a wait edge, a synchronization node, and a local processing step is collapsed into a single urgent communication transition in both related processes. For a local edge, the time conditions simply result in a time guard and deadline such that the specified timing behavior is possible. In a similar fashion, the mapping for the wait edges results in a time guard which ensures the lower and upper time bound.

The timing restrictions of the edges, which are described by the upper and lower time bounds on the TCG edges, are addressed by referring to a special clock t_0 which is reset when entering any state. For the transition of an activity edge $(n, L, u, \mathsf{a}, n')$, the lower and upper bound simply become the relative deadline $[L, u] \rightarrow$. The guard becomes true and is thus omitted. For any transition $(n, L, u, \mathsf{g}, n')$ which represents a glue edge, the role specific fixed execution time d is used as relative deadline $[d, d] \rightarrow$ and the guard becomes $[L - d, u - d]$. A wait edge $(n, L, u, \mathsf{w}, n')$ results in a transition with the related event, guard $[L, u]$ and deadline $[d, d] \rightarrow$.

Another aspect of the synthesis is the treatment of timing checks and restrictions. Timing checks are established by the consistency checks as outlined in the preceding sections. The restrictions limit the possible timing of the lower bound and therefore have to be ensured by the synthesized real-time statecharts. A restriction $(n, L, u, \mathsf{r}, n')$ which runs in parallel to a single activity, glue, or wait edge simply results in using the specified bounds for that transition. In the more complex case of restrictions which do affect a series of TCG edges, we use an additional clock t_r which is set to zero when the initial node of the restriction edge is entered $(\{t_r\})$. This clock is used to adjust the time guards of the last transition of this series of TCG edges such that the overall restriction is enforced for the lower bound by adding $t_r \geq L$ to the time guard. Due to space constraints, only a one-edge restriction occurs in the presented example.

To ensure progress within the statechart for the non-urgent transitions, we finally derive the state invariant for each state. We store the edges for every specific state $s \in S$ in a list sorted by the priority and start with an empty upper bound list. We then proceed as follows:

1. While the edge list is not empty, enqueue the first edge and process it as follows:
   (a) If case (C1) can be detected, report an error and quit.
   (b) If rule set (C2) can be applied, then add the upper bound to the upper limit lists and erase all wait edges with the same event from the edge list.
   (c) If rule set (C3) can be applied, then add the upper bound to the upper limit lists and empty the edge list.
2. Assign the or-combination of all elements of the upper bound list as the state invariant.

Due to the outlined construction of the state invariant, each state is eventually left, if the required communication is offered or a timeout is reached.

We can further reduce the synthesis result using the following syntactic rules: (R1) If two states s and s' exists such that the set of outgoing edges is equal (always an edge with the same time constraints and target states exists), we can unite both states. (R2) If a non-empty subset S' of the state set S and a non-empty subset E' of all edges E exists such that all elements $s \in S'$ have the same outgoing edges within E' w.r.t. all states $s' \in S - S'$ outside this state set, we introduce a superstate for all states $s \in S'$ such that all edges of E' are are realized by this superstate and can consequently be erased for the single states of S'. (R3) If a state s with a single urgent transition t with deadline $[L, u]$ and without time guard and event exists (which may result from an activity edge) that leads to a state s', we can erase the state s and adjust all transitions t' leading to s by adding the side effect of t, updating their deadlines $[L', u']$ simply to $[L + L', u + u']$, and redirecting them to s'. (R4) If a state s with a single non urgent transition t with deadline $[L_d, u_d]$, time guard $[L_g \leq t_0 \leq u_g]$, and without event exists (which may result from an glue edge) that leads to a state s', we can erase the state s and adjust all transitions t' leading to s by adding the side effect of t, updating the deadline $[L', u']$ to $[L' + L_g + L_d, u' + u_g + u_d]$ and pointing them at s'. (R5) If no transitions leaving a state s requires the special clock t_0, we can remove the enter: $\{t_0\}$ action for that state.

The application of these syntactical rules erases four states from the watchdog's real-time statechart and results in the model depicted in Figure 5.

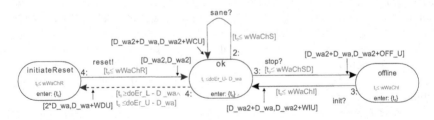

Fig. 5. Synthesized parameterized real-time statechart of the watchdog

5   Applying a Pattern

When a pattern realizing the required real-time coordination has been constructed, what remains to be done is (1) to adapt the parameters to the concrete requirements, (2) to check the resulting non-parameterized real-time behavior for anomalies, and (3) to realize the component-specific behavior by refining the applicable roles as required.

The analysis outlined in Section 3 further supports the identification of a valid parameter set for a given pattern. For example, an upper bound for the detection of the timeout and initiation of a controller reset by the watchdog of the form $RDU + wtu \leq 1000$ may be added. We can then check whether a consistent solution for the pattern and this constraint in form of a linear inequality exists.

In Figure 3 earlier in the paper, the RTSC which results from the RTSC in Figure 5 for the parameter setting $d_wa = 10.0$, $wWaChR = 150.0$, $wWaChSD = \infty$, $wWaChI = \infty$, $wWaChS = \infty$, $WDU = 100.0$, $doEr_U = 600.0$ $doEr_L = 500.0$, $WCU = 40.0$, $OFF_U = 75.0$, and $D\_wa2 = 0$ is depicted.

Once an appropriate and valid parameter setting has been determined, we use the model checking capability of the real-time version [13] of the Fujaba CASE Tool to ensure that the synthesis result for the given parameter values is free from deadlocks or time stopping deadlocks.

After the pattern is successfully model checked, the component behavior can be derived. The real-time statecharts for each pattern role are underspecified as they describe all possible correct behaviors of the role with respect to synchronization and timing. To derive the final operational behavior we are, however, free to reduce the non-determinism still present in the model where useful. For example, the rather large time frame between a possible detection of the timeout and the latest point in time when the timeout has to be detected may be subject to refinement.

6   Conclusion

We present how our approach for the development of correct real-time systems with components and patterns, which enable the compositional verification of real-time properties, can be supplemented by a scenario-based synthesis techniques for parameterized timed sequence diagrams with conditional behavior.

Static analysis ensures consistency and locality (causality) for a given set of parameterized scenarios. Conflicts can be also detected by extending the analysis results. The synthesis of a parameterized real-time pattern and its real-time behavior in form of parameterized real-time statecharts for each role further completes our approach.

When applying the pattern, appropriate parameter setting can be derived using the outlined analysis approach. The developer can thus systematically study the trade-offs between different parameter sets. Problems due to the reachability remain to be proven using real-time model checking after setting all parameters.

Acknowledgements

The authors thank the students Sergej Tissen and Martin Hirsch for their implementation of the scenario analysis and synthesis prototype respectively model checking extension of Fujaba and their valuable comments and questions.

References

1. Giese, H., Tichy, M., Burmester, S., Schäfer, W., Flake, S.: Towards the Compositional Verification of Real-Time UML Designs. In: Proc. of the European Software Engineering Conference (ESEC), Helsinki, Finland, ACM Press (2003) 38–47
2. Krüger, I., Grosu, R., Scholz, P., Broy, M.: From MSCs to Statecharts. In Rammig, F.J., ed.: Distributed and Parallel Embedded Systems, Kluwer Academic Publishers (1999) 61–71
3. Mäkinen, E., Systä, T.: MAS - an interactive synthesizer to support behavioral modeling in UML. In: Proceedings of the 23rd International Conference on Software Engineering (ICSE 2001), Toronto, Canada. (2001) 15–24
4. Uchitel, S., Kramer, J.: A Workbench for Synthesising Behviour models from Scenarios. In: Proceedings of the 23rd International Conference on Software Engineering (ICSE 2001), Toronto, Canada. (2001) 188–197
5. Whittle, J., Schumann, J.: Generating statechart designs from scenarios. In: Proceedings of the 22nd international conference on on Software engineering June 4 - 11, 2000, Limerick Ireland. (2000)
6. Li, X., Lilius, J.: Timing Analysis of UML Sequence Diagrams. In France, R., Rumpe, B., eds.: UML'99 - The Second International Conference on The Unified Modeling Language Fort Collins, Colorado, USA. Volume 1723 of Lecture Notes in Computer Science. (1999)
7. Somé, S., Dssouli, R., Vaucher, J.: From Scenarios to Timed Automata: Building Specifications from Users Requirements. In: Proceedings of the 1995 Asia Pacific Software Engineering Conference (APSEC '95). (1995)
8. Salah, A., Dssouli, R., Lapalme, G.: Implicit integration of scenarios into a reduced timed automaton. Information and Software Technology **45** (2003) 715–725
9. Harel, D., Marelly, R.: Playing with Time: On the Specification and Execution of Time-Enriched LSCs. In: Proc. 10th IEEE/ACM Int. Symp. on Modeling, Analysis and Simulation of Computer and Telecommunication Systems (MASCOTS 2002), Fort Worth, Texas, USA (2002) (invited paper).
10. Giese, H., Burmester, S.: Analysis and Synthesis for Parameterized Timed Sequence Diagrams. In: Proc. of the 3rd International Workshop on Scenarios and State Machines: Models, Algorithms, and Tools (SCESM), Edinburgh, Scotland (ICSE 2003 Workshop W5S). (2004)
11. Burmester, S., Giese, H.: The Fujaba Real-Time Statechart PlugIn. In: Proc. of the Fujaba Days 2003, Kassel, Germany. (2003)
12. Henzinger, T.A., Nicollin, X., Sifakis, J., Yovine, S.: Symbolic Model Checking for Real-Time Systems. In: Proc. of IEEE Symposium on Logic in Computer Science, IEEE Computer Press (1992)
13. Hirsch, M., Giese, H.: Towards the Incremental Model Checking of Complex RealTime UML Models. In: Proc. of the Fujaba Days 2003, Kassel, Germany. (2003)
14. Ben-Abdallah, H., Leue, S.: Timing Constraints in Message Sequence Chart Specifications. In: Formal Description Techniques X, Proceedings of the Tenth International Conference on Formal Description Techniques FORTE/PSTV'97, Osaka, Japan, Chapman & Hall (1997)
15. Khordoc, K., Cerny, E.: Semantics and verification of action diagrams with linear timing. ACM Transactions on Design Automation of Electronic Systems (TODAES) **3** (1998) 21–50

16. Object Management Group: UML 2.0 Superstructure Specification. (2003) Document ptc/03-08-02.
17. Sengupta, B., Cleaveland, R.: Triggered Message Sequence Charts. In Griswold, W.G., ed.: Proceedings of the Tenth ACM SIGSOFT Symposium on the Foundations of Softare Engineering (FSE-10), Charleston, South Carolina, USA, ACM Press (2002)
18. Leue, S., Rezai, M.: Synthesizing Software Architecture Descriptions from Message Sequence Chart Specifications. In: Proceedings of the Thirteenth IEEE Conference on Automated Software Engineering. (1998)
19. Alur, R., Holzmann, G.J., Peled, D.: An analyzer for message sequence charts. In: Proc. of the 2nd Workshop on Tools and Algorithms for the Construction and Analysis of Systems (TACAS96). Volume 1055 of LNCS., Passau, Germany (1996) 35–48
20. Alur, R., Henzinger, T.A., Vardi, M.Y.: Parametric real-time reasoning. In: Proceedings of the twenty-fifth annual ACM symposium on Theory of computing, ACM Press (1993) 592–601
21. Uchitel, S., Kramer, J., Magee, J.: Detecting Implied Scenarios in Message Sequence Chart Specifications. In Gruhn, V., ed.: Proceedings of the Joint 8th European Software Engineering Conference (ESEC) and 9th ACM SIGSOFT Symposium on the Foundation of Software Engineering (FSE-9), Vienna, Austria, September 10-14, ACM Press (2001) 74–82

Partial Order Semantics of Sequence Diagrams for Mobility[1]

Piotr Kosiuczenko

Department of Computer Science, University of Leicester, Le1 7RH, UK
piotr@mcs.le.ac.uk

Abstract. There are many formalism for mobile system specification, but until very recently, there was no satisfactory graphical notation for modelling of such systems. In a previous paper, we have introduced the so-called Sequence Diagrams for Mobility (SDM), a graphical notations based on UML Sequence Diagram. This notation has been used in several case studies and proved very useful. In this paper we introduce a formal, partial order based semantics for SDM. We define the notion of run and show how to figure out the system topology from the information contained in a run. We formalize the zoom-out abstraction mechanism introduced in a previous paper and show that its application does not depend on the particular order it is applied. We formalise also the notion of lifeline introduced informally in the previous paper. We integrate our semantics with UML2.0 and show that they fit well together. We explain our approach using series of examples.

1 Introduction

The developments in areas of communication and information technology allow one to equip tools, with processors and software to facilitate their use. The tools used in everyday life are getting more and more smart due to build in electronic. One of the most important new concepts is the concept of mobile systems and of mobile computation. Code mobility, which emerged in some scripting languages for controlling network applications, is one of the key features of the Java programming language. Agent mobility has been supported by Telescript, AgentTcl, or Odyssey (cf. e.g. [7]). In addition, hardware can be mobile too: Mobile hosts such as laptops, handhelds and PDAs can move between networks. Moreover, entire networks can be mobile as well, such as for example IBM's Personal Area Network (PAN) and networks of sensors in airplane or trains. Mobile computations can cross barriers and move between virtual and physical locations. The goal is to turn remote calls into local calls to avoid the latency caused by communication. But there is a price to pay since the administrative barriers and multiple access pathways interact in very complex ways.

These developments lead to enormous challenge of designing and configuring mobile and distributed systems that interact to achieve expected tasks. At the moment, this is a field of a very active multi disciplinary research. There are several aspects of

---

[1] This research has been partially sponsored by the IST project Architectures for Mobility funded by the European Commission as a part of the Global Computing Initiative.

such systems requiring different approaches. Specification, modelling and design belong to the most challenging ones. There exist several formalisms for specification of mobile systems (cf. e.g. [5, 4]), but until very recently, there was no satisfactory graphical notation for modelling mobile systems. Graphical Modelling Languages are influencing a great impact on the software development, but in the case of mobile systems, this aspect was neglected. These systems require special means for the modelling, specification and implementation.

Recently the gap was filled by designing appropriate graphical UML based notations. The so-called Sequence Diagrams for Mobility (SDM) [10] is a trace based, Sequence Diagrams like notation for the specification of mobile computation. There exists also an extension of UML Activity Diagrams for modelling of mobile system behavior [2]. The idea is similar to the idea of Ambients [4], in that a mobile object can migrate from one host to another and at the same time such an object can host other mobile objects. Like a place, a mobile object can host other mobile objects; it can locally communicate and receive messages from other places. Objects can be nested in an arbitrary way, generalizing the limited place-agent nesting of most agent and place languages. This concept generalises the Use Case Maps [3] in that we graphically model an object moving from one location to another, but also we allow moving objects to play the role of locations. The SDM notation generalizes the notion of object lifeline as defined in UML Sequence Diagrams [12].

One of the most important principles in science is the principle of abstraction. Ideally, there should be a notation allowing for displaying relevant and hiding irrelevant information. It should provide the possibility to abstract from features, which are irrelevant at a given stage of development. In the previous paper we have introduced a powerful mechanism for hiding irrelevant information [10]; the so-called zoom-out mechanism allows us to abstract from internal details of selected objects; we call such objects boundary. In particular, it allows us to hide the objects located in boundary objects and their behaviour. Similarly, we have introduced the so-called zoom-in mechanism for displaying details of objects and their behaviour.

The extension of Activity Diagrams [2] is very close to its origin, it uses only few new primitives form modelling of mobility and extends the standard UML notation a bit. The new primitives are defined using stereotypes, the standard UML extension mechanism. The SDM notation extends UML Sequence Diagrams in much more radical way and cannot be reduced so simply to the standard UML. Therefore in this paper we introduce formal partial order semantics for SDM only. We formalize the temporal ordering of event occurrences using partial order relations, more precisely quasi orders. The information stored in messages is accessible via labelling functions defined on elements of the partially ordered set. We show how to systematically define such models for SDM diagrams. We formally define the notion of lifeline, introduced in [10]. We have given some examples of its use, but we were not able to define it precisely there due to lack of proper terminology. Our formal semantics allows us to define it now in precise formal terms. We define the notion of a run and show how to figure out the system topology from the information contained in a run.

The tricky part in our semantics is the definition of object's location. We define locations only for objects participating in an event occurrence. Locations of other objects not related to the event occurrence are not fixed. For example, if an event occurrence is not temporally related to a move, then the move can happen before or after the event occurrence and the location of the moving object should not be fixed during the move.

The definition of our semantics is based on well defined topological artefact such as cross points, arrow directions and the relation of being located inside. Let us point out that there exist some formal partial order based semantics of Message Sequence Charts (MSC) [6], a graphical notation analogous to UML Sequence Diagrams (cf. e.g. [9]). MSC are a subject of a very intense research (cf. e.g. [11]).

We define semantics of the abstraction mechanism. The idea is to abstract from the information concerning hidden objects but to keep the partial ordering on visible communication events. We show, that the order, in which this mechanism is applied, does not matter. The local definition of object's location works fine also for the abstraction mechanism.

We show that our semantics fits very well to the concept of interaction defined in UML 2.0. Interestingly enough, the concept of SDM fits well to UML 2.0, but it was really hard to integrate with earlier versions of UML. We integrate the notion of partial order and run with the notions of trace and `GeneralOrdering` from UML 2.0. We formalise also the notion of lifeline as it is defined in UML 2.0.

Our paper is structured as follow. Section two presents the basic ideas of Sequence Diagrams for Mobility. In section three we define the formal model, which is the base of our semantics; we show how to define the semantics for concrete SDM diagrams. In section four we formalize the notion of abstraction. We conclude our paper with some remarks on the applications of our semantics.

2   The SDM Notation

Mobility is the ability to cross barriers. In our approach, a mobile object is also a location where interaction may happen. Action boxes are indicated by different locations. The action boxes describe what is inside and what is outside; they allow one also to show in a transparent way message exchange and object's migration. Locations can be arbitrarily nested and form a tree structure, this is aimed at modelling firewalls, administrative domains networks and so on. For example, a personal area network may be located in a car, which is located in a ferry; the ferry may enter a harbour and so on. We assume that the nested structure has the form of forest, i.e. an object can be located in at most one object and there no cycles of objects such that one is contained in another.

In the paper [2], we have introduced the stereotype <<location>>and the stereotype <<mobile>> to specify objects which can play the role of locations and objects which can be mobile, respectively. Each object of a class having stereotype <<mobile>> possesses attribute `atLoc`; this attribute has values of a class having stereotype <<location>>. If an object is not mobile, it does not possess this attribute. The idea is that a change of location of a mobile object is modelled by the change of the attribute `atLoc`. Objects which are locations only, and in general objects, which are not stereotyped with <<mobile>>, do not possess this attribute.

Mobile objects may interact with other objects by sending messages and changing locations. In UML, objects can communicate in synchronous as well as asynchronous way. We stick to this principle. Unlike Ambients Calculus [4], in our notation it is possible to express actions at a distance even if many barriers are involved.

A description of a mobile object's behaviour starts with a box containing optionally the object name and/or its class. A mobile object may move into another object, or move out of an object. If an object moves into or out of another object, then the action box ends in the former location and the object is moved to another location. This move is indicated by a stereotyped message arrow which starts with a black circle; we call it move arrow.

A mobile object cannot continue its operation outside a host, if it is already inside another host; consequently, the arrow starts strictly at the end of the first action box to indicate that all action in the box must precede the move. The start of operation of a mobile object (and if this object was not active before elsewhere) is indicated by a box as in the case of sequence diagrams. We indicate the end of mobile object description by two horizontal lines, where the upper line is dashed. Let us point out that it does not mean that the object was terminated (cf. [10]).

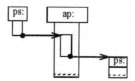

Fig. 1. Object mobility

Fig. 1 shows what a mobile object looks like. The passenger ps enters airplane ap. Since there is no conflict concerning the identity of objects inside ap; the corresponding action box does not bear any name. Than ps deplanes ap and starts its operation outside ap. The name in the last action box is not necessary either, since the identity of ps can be uniquely traced [10]. No message arrow is attached to the action boxes except of the move.

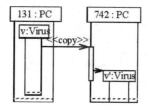

Fig. 2. Object copying and cloning

Fig. 2 shows a virus v located in PC 131. The virus proliferates attacking other PCs. We use here a message arrow with UML stereotype <<copy>>, the copied virus v' is assumed to behave as its origin would do inside the new location (cf. [12]).

3 Partial Order Semantics

In this section we introduce partial order semantics for SDM. We define a mathematical model containing a partially ordered set and a number of labelling functions, which allow us to extract information from the elements of this set. We present a general method of extracting such models from SDM diagrams. We show how to apply this method to concrete SDM diagrams. We formally define the notion of lifeline.

3.1 The Formal Model

In this subsection we define the formal model which will be the base of our semantics. The model is based on a partial order formalizing temporal relationship between event occurrences; it contains labelling functions for extracting information. This model is constructed in a similar to the partial order semantics of Message Sequence Charts (cf. e.g. [9, 11]). The tricky point in our semantics is the definition of object locations. We define locations only for objects participating in an event occurrence; locations of other objects not related to the event are not fixed. For example, if an event occurrence is not temporally related to a move, then the move can happen before or after the event occurrence and the location of the moving object should not be fixed during the move. If the object moves from location a to location b, then when the event occurs it can be in a or in b (see below).

According to UML 2.0 [12], an InteractionFragment consists of a number of so-called GeneralOrderings. A GeneralOrdering represents an ordering of two event occurrences; it specifies that one event occurrence must proceed the other in a valid trace. This concept provides the ability to define partial orders of event occurrences. In UML, a message is a specification of a particular communication between instances in an interaction. A communication can be raising a signal, invoking an operation, creating or destroying an instance. Message specifies not only the kind of communication, but also the roles of the sender and the receiver, the dispatching and the relative sequencing of messages within the interaction. A message may have two message ends corresponding to two event occurrences: sending and receiving of a message (cf. Fig. 3). Event occurrences corresponding to message ends can be ordered using GeneralOrdeing.

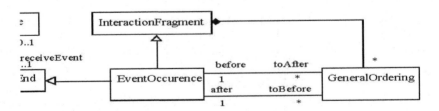

Fig. 3. UML event diagram

Our model is a tuple of the form: $(E, \leq, e_o, \text{lab}, p, IP)$. The binary relation $\leq$ is a quasi order, in particular a partial order. It corresponds to UML GeneralOrdeing.

Conceptually, E is the set of event occurrences. We consider here four kinds of events: send event, receive event, method or constructor return and cross event; the last one corresponds to the event of crossing objects boundary[1]. Further, we identify three kinds of send events: message send, method call, constructor call, object departure and send message. Similarly, we identify three kinds of receive events: message receive, method start, constructor start, object arrival and receive message. The relation $\leq$ defines temporal ordering of such event occurrences. We assume that, there exist an initial, auxiliary, event occurrence e_0, which we use to define the initial topology of a mobile system (see below). This event precedes all other event occurrences, i.e. for all $e \in E$, $e_0 \leq e$.

An event occurrence includes information about the values of all relevant objects at the corresponding point in time [12]. In our model, the information corresponding to an event occurrence can be accessed using labelling functions. There are three labelling functions: lab, p and lP.

The function lab labels elements of the set E specifying the corresponding communication kind; it can be sending or receiving of a message, method call or return and so on (we have listed the types of events above):

  lab : E $\longrightarrow$ EventKind

Every communication involves some objects; for example a message or a moving object may cross several object boundaries. The function p identifies objects participating in an event occurrence; it returns a finite set of event participants:

  p : E $\longrightarrow$ Fin(ObNames)

We assume that in the case of object departure and arrival, function p identifies the moving objects and all objects hosted in the moving object (see the next subsection).

Let MO be the set of mobile objects, i.e. objects whose class has the stereotype <<mobile>>. Similarly, let Loc be the set of locations, i.e. objects whose class has the stereotype <<location>>(see section 2). We define a partial function:

  lP : MO $\times$ E $\longrightarrow$ Seq(Loc)

lP(o, e) returns a sequence of locations, if oparticipates in event occurrence e. In the other case, the value is undefined. We call this sequence location path of object o (see below).

In UML 2.0 [12], the semantics of an interactions is given in the term of traces. A trace is a sequence of event occurrences of the form $<e_0, e_1,..., e_n>$. Two interactions are equivalent if their trace-sets are equal. Similarly, in our model, system behavior can be specified as a set of system runs. A partial run of model $(E, \leq, e_0, lab, p, lP)$ is an not empty sequence of elements $e_0, e_1,..., e_n$ such that the following conditions are satisfied:

- If $e_i \leq e_j$, then $i \leq j$.
- If $e \leq e_j$, then there exists an index $i \leq j$ such that $e_i = e$.

In other words, a partial run is a linearization, which preserves the temporal ordering; moreover for every event occurrence belonging to the run, all preceding event

---

[1] One could split such an event into to a send event and a receive one.

occurrences belong to the run as well. Let us observe, that any not empty prefix of a partial run is a partial run.

Partial runs define particular moments in system execution. For such moments we can determine system topology. Let $e_0,..., e_n$ be a partial run, we say that after this run object $o2$ is located in location $o1$ (inside $o1$, resp.) iff there exists an event occurrence e_i and an object o such that:

- The location path $lP(o, e_i)$ has the form $l_1,..., l_n$, contains locations $l_j = o1$ and $l_{j+1} = o2$(contains locations $l_j = o1$ and $l_k = o2$, such that $j < k$, respectively).
- For all event occurrences e_k, such that $i < k$, and for all objects $o \in p(e_k)$, the location path $lP(o,e_k)$ does not include $o2$.

The location of an object is determined by the most recent information concerning its location. Similarly, we can define location path of an object after a run. The topology of a mobile system at a particular moment of time is derived from the information contained in the events occurring in the corresponding partial run; it is the sum of object locations.

Models that are semantics of SDM diagrams have certain properties, which formal models in general may violate. We call such properties consistency conditions. For example the topology of a mobile system should not change during method call or return. The topology changes only in the case of object departure or arrival and constructor return. Moreover, departure and arrival change only the location (i.e. the atLoc attribute) of the moving object. Locations of all other objects remain unchanged. Constructor return doesn't change locations of already existing objects. As mentioned in section 2, we assume that the locations form a forest. Consistency conditions can be used when proving or model-check-ing properties of SDM diagrams.

3.2 Definition of the Partial Order Semantics

In this section, we introduce a generic method for defining a partial order semantics for a concrete SDM diagram. This method includes three steps: identification of event occurrences, derivation of the partial ordering and labelling of the occurrences.

We associate an element of the set E to every graphical artefact of the form: beginning and end of a message arrow (e.g. move message), a message arrow crossing an object box by going in or out as well as method and constructor termination indicated by a corresponding rectangle. Let us point out that if an arrow crosses an object box twice, then it does not interfere with the action box, such as for example a message arrow crossing a lifeline of an object in UML sequence diagram[2].

The definition below does not guarantee that we obtain a partial ordering. It yields only a quasi order, i.e. a reflexive and transitive relation. In fact, it depends on the SDM diagram being formalized, if we obtain a partial order or not. As in the case of general Sequence Diagrams, it is possible to draw diagrams with circular dependences. In such a case, the resulting quasi order is not a partial order.

---

[2] For simplicity, we do not consider cases when a message arrow crosses object boxes of the same object several times.

For simplicity, we do not talk about the topological artefacts, but about the corresponding event occurences (see above). The temporal ordering of event occurrences $\leq$ is defined as the smallest reflexive and transitive relation satisfying the following conditions:

- If event occurrence e_1 is located above event occurrence e_2 on a rectangle being a border of the same action box, then $e_1 \leq e_2$.
- If e_1 and e_2 are located on the same message arrow and e_1 proceeds e_2 in respect to the direction of the arrow, then $e_1 \leq e_2$.

For every element of E we define the values of functions lab, p and IP. The function lab returns the type of an event: message send, message receive, method or constructor call, method or constructor start, method or constructor return, cross event; method call, object departure and object arrival.

The function p identifies participants of a communication event e. If it is a send of a message, arrival of a message, method call, start of a method execution, method return, then p(e) includes only the sender, message receiver, caller, executing object, respectively. In the case of object departure and arrival, we assume that the event participants are the moving object and additionally all objects located directly or indirectly in the moving object; those objects can be identified by figuring out if the corresponding action boxes are located inside the action box of the moving object. The reason for including such object is that an object located in a moving object changes its location path when its host moves. The move is also a kind of caesura for the participating objects (see below).

The auxiliary element e_0 defines the initial topology of the system. $p(e_0)$ includes all objects which exist initially, i.e. objects whose object boxes start with a rectangle bearing a name of an object (see for example 131 on figure 4). If an event occurrence e corresponds to a message arrow crossing an action box of object o, then we assume that p(e) = {o}. If an event e corresponds to the moving of object o, then p(o) contains all objects with object boxes located in the object box of o before the move.

For every event e and every object o taking part in this event (i.e. for every o∈ p(e)), location path IP(e, o) is defined as the sequence of objects such that their object boxes contain the object box of o on which e is located; the objects are listed from the inner most to the outer most. If an object o' neither takes part in e nor occurs at a location path of an participating object, then the value of IP(e, o') is undefined. This is due to the fact that we do not want to restrain locations of objects not involved in an event. Concurrently executing objects may change locations independently. Let us observe that location paths are defined for all objects existing initially, since they belong to $p(e_0)$. Consequently, the initial topology is fully determined. Let us also observe that in the case of move, the locations of participating objects before and after the move are defined by the location paths corresponding to the departure and arrival event occurrences, respectively. In general the topology in different moments of time is determined by location paths. The location of an object is determined by the last relevant event.

3.3 Example

In this subsection we show how to define the partial order semantics for a concrete SDM diagram. For simplicity, we assume that all objects occurring in the diagrams are mobile, i.e. the corresponding classes have the stereotype <<mobile>> (see section 2). Fig. 4 makes explicit the event occurrences from Fig. 2: e_1 is a method call, e_1' corresponds to crossing the boundary of 131. e_2 is the start of the method execution, e_3 is a constructor call, e_4 is the termination of the method and e_5 is the start of constructor execution.

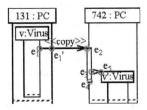

Fig. 4. Object copying and creation

There set of event occurrences has the form $E = \{e_0, e_1, e_1',..., e_5\}$. e_0 proceeds all other events. e_1 proceeds e_1' and e_1' proceeds e_2; this is due to the ordering of these occurrences on the corresponding message arrow. e_2 proceeds e_3 and e_3 proceeds e_4; this is due to the to down ordering of events on the object box of 742. Finally, e_3 proceeds e_5. The labelling function lab returns call for e_1, since it is of type call. It returns cross for e_1', start for e_2, call for e_3, start for e_5 and return for e_4.

Initially, there exist three objects: v, 131 and 742; therefore $p(e_0) = \{v, 131, 742\}$. The participants of occurrence e_1 are: v, 131. Similarly, $p(e_1') = \{131\}$, $p(e_2) = \{742\}$, $p(e_3) = \{742\}$, $p(e_4) = \{742\}$ and $p(e_5) = \{v'\}$. The topology is defined by the function IP: $IP(e_0, v) = <131>$ and $IP(e_0, 131) = IP(e_0, 742) = <>$. The location of object v during occurrence e_1 is 131, i.e. $IP(v, e_1) = <131>$. $IP(131, e_1)$ is an empty list and $IP(742, e_1)$ is undefined (see below).

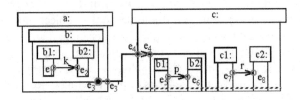

Fig. 5. Complex move

Fig. 5 shows communicating objects which change their locations. Object b moves from location a to location c. Objects b1, b2 communicate before and after the move. The communication between objects $c1$ and $c2$ does not depend temporally on the move. The initial topology is defined as follows:

$p(e_0) = \{a, b, b1, b2, c, c1, c2\}$,

$IP(b, e_0) = <a>$, $IP(b1, e_0) = IP(b2, e_0) = <a, b>$, $IP(c1, e_0) = IP(c2, e_0) = <c>$.

Object $b1$ is the only participant of occurrence e_1. When occurrence e_1 takes place, the location of $b1$ is b and the location of b is a. Consequently the location path of $b1$ during e_1 equals (b, a). There are three participants of the occurrence e_3, i.e. $p(e_3) = \{b, b1, b2\}$, and for participants of e_3', i.e. $p(e_3') = \{a, b, b1, b2\}^3$, this corresponds to the assumption that objects located in a moving object participate in the move. Similarly, $p(e_4') = p(e_4) = \{c, b, b1, b2\}$. The move is a kind of caesura for the involved objects. It separates events before the move and events after the move.

Let us observe, that we cannot infer from the diagram the temporal ordering of e_1 and e_7. Similarly, we cannot infer from the diagram where object b is located when occurrence e_7 happens; the location of object b during occurrence e_7 may be a or c or none of them. This explains why IP is a partial function.

There are several partial runs of the system shown on Fig. 5. For example, e_0, e_1, e_2, e_3, e_3', e_4', e_4, e_5, e_6, e_7, e_8 is a maximal partial run in the sense that it contains all event occurrences. Similarly, e_0, e_7, e_8, e_1, e_2, e_3, e_3', e_4', e_4, e_5, e_6 is another maximal partial run. Of course, all prefixes of these runs are partial runs. Let us consider the first run, the initial topology is not changed after e_1 nor after e_2. After occurrence e_3, object a does not contain any other object and object c contains objects $c1$ and $c2$ only. The topology changes once more after occurrence e_4: object c contains now additionally $b1$ and $b2$.

3.4 Lifelines

In this subsection, we formally define the notion of lifeline. We have introduced this notion in the paper [10] already. We have given some examples of its use there, but we were not able to define it precisely due to lack of proper terminology. Our semantics allows us to define the notion of lifeline in precise formal terms. This notion generalizes the notion of object lifeline as defined in UML Sequence Diagrams [12]. It generalizes also the idea of Use Case Maps [3]; this notation strictly separates mobile objects and locations. In SDM an object can be mobile, if its class has the stereotype <<mobile>>and at the same time it can play the role of location, if its class has the stereotype <<location>>.

Let in UML 2.0 "The semantics of the lifeline (within an interaction) is the semantics of the interaction selecting only event occurrences of this Lifeline." Our definition of object lifeline corresponds strictly to this definition: a lifeline of an

---

[3] Let us notice, that there is difference between $p(e_j')$, from figure 4 and $p(e_j')$ from figure 5. In the first case, the message causes an object creation, but the object does not exist when the message is sent. In the second case, the object move all together and therefore they are listed as event participants.

object is the set of all events the object participates in. Formally: let $(E, \leq, e_{\cdot}, \text{lab}, \text{p},$ IP) be a SDM semantics, and let o be one of the participating objects, the *lifeline* of the object o is the set

$$\{e \in E \mid o \in p(e)\}$$

The partial order relation on the set E orders the event occurrences belonging to a lifeline. So the temporal ordering of the lifeline is simply inherited from the superset E.

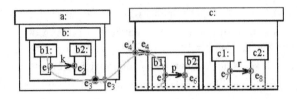

Fig. 6. Lifeline

As example let us consider the diagram in Fig. 6. The lifeline of object b1 has the form: $\{e_0, e_1, e_3, e_3', e_4', e_4, e_5\}$. The lifeline of object b consists of occurrences: $e_0, e_3,$ e_3', e_4' and e_4.

4   Abstraction Mechanisms

One of the most important principles in science is the principle of abstraction. Ideally, there should be a notation of abstraction allowing one for displaying relevant and hiding irrelevant information. In the previous paper we have introduced a powerful graphical mechanism for hiding irrelevant information [10]. The zoom-out mechanism allows us to abstract from internal details of so selected objects, called boundary. In particular, it allows us to hide the objects located in boundary objects and their behaviour. Similarly, we have introduced the so-called zoom-in mechanism for displaying details of objects and their behaviour.

In the first subsection we formalize the zoom-out mechanism. In the second subsection we explain how the formal machinery works using an example. In the third subsection we show how to formalize zoom-in to a move.

4.1   Formalization of the Zoom-Out Mechanism

In this subsection, we formalize the zoom-out mechanism. This mechanism allows us to abstract from the internal structure and behavior of selected objects, which we call boundary. We define which event occurrences are visible and which not. The zoom-out mechanism can be applied to whole models, but it can be applied as well to selected time intervals. The definitions prove to be simple, thanks to the local definition of object's locations.

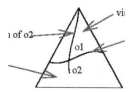

Fig. 7. Boundary objects

Fig. 7 shows the basic idea of boundary objects. The objects located in a selected object can be seen as a tree. The objects located in boundary objects are invisible, i.e. an object is invisible, if its location path contains a boundary object, in the other case it is visible. The objects located above boundary objects are visible. For example, let o1 and o2 be two objects participating in an event occurrence; o1 is visible, but o2 not. Similarly, we can define visible and invisible events.

Formally, let BO be a set of boundary objects, and let e be an event occurrence, we say that e is *not visible* in respect to BO iff one of the following conditions is satisfied:

- For all objects $o_1 \in p(e)$, the location path of o_1 contains a boundary object.
- e is a send event, the initiating object (i.e. the caller, the departing object or the sender), respectively is a boundary object and the target object (i.e. the receiver, the target location or the receiver, respectively) is located within the caller.

A *event occurrence is visible* if it is not invisible. In other words, an occurrence is not visible, if all objects participating in the occurrence are invisible or it is a send event, the initiating object is a boundary object and the target object is not visible. Partial runs correspond to points of execution. We say that an *object is visible after a partial run*, if this object is not located within a boundary object (see subsection 3.1).

Let us observe, that in the case of formal models satisfying the consistency conditions, for every two partial runs ending with the same event occurrence e, the sets of visible objects participating in this event occurrence are the same. In other words, for every occurrence and every object participating in the occurrence the fact whether the object is visible or not, does not depend on run the event is part of. More generally, if two event occurrences concern the same object, then they are temporally related. This follows from the fact that event occurrences on the same object box are temporally related. If an object moves or if its host moves then the object is involved and the move is a kind of ceasura.

We define an abstraction function F. This function has two arguments: a set of boundary objects and a model:
$F(BO, (E, \leq, e_0, lab, p, lP)) = (E', \leq', e_0, lab', p', lP')$, if the following conditions are satisfied:

- $E' = \{e \in E \mid e$ is visible in respect to BO$\}$.
- $\leq'$ is the restriction of $\leq$ to E'.
- lab' is the restriction of lab to the set E'.
- $p'(e) = \{o \in p(e) \mid lP(o, e)$ does not include objects from BO$\}$.

- IP'(o, e) is defined as IP(o, e), if e is a visible event occurrence and $o \in p'(e)$; IP' is undefined for other pairs of objects and occurrences.

E' is the set of visible events. p' contains objects visible during occurrence of e. IP' is defined as IP for objects visible during event occurrence, for other objects it is undefined. Let us observe, that by definition, for all visible event occurrences e and all $o \in p'(e)$, IP'(o, e) does not contain boundary objects.

We may perform abstraction several times; the result should not depend on the order we apply the zoom-out mechanism. The following statement says that this requirement is satisfied. It is due to associativity and commutativity of set theoretical union.

Statement

$F(BO_1, F(BO_2, (E, \leq, e_0, lab, p, IP))) = F(BO_1 \cup BO_2, (E, \leq, e_0, lab, p, IP))$

The statement follows from the fact, that it does not matter whether we abstract from event occurrences invisible in respect to BO_1 first and then from occurrences invisible in respect to BO_2, or we abstract from occurrences invisible in respect to $BO_1 \cup BO_2$ in one step. Consequently, the resulting set of visible occurrences depends only on the union. The resulting partial order is just the restriction of the initial partial order. The resulting participation function and the function returning location paths depend only on the union $BO_1 \cup BO_2$.

We may apply the zoom-out mechanism in a much finer way. It can be applied not only to whole lifelines of objects, but also to particular time intervals when the behaviour and internal structure of selected objects is unimportant.

Let $(E, \leq, e_0, lab, p, IP)$ be a partial order semantics of a mobile system and let N be a subset of E. We say that N is convex iff for every three occurrences e_1, e_2, e_3, if $e_1, e_2 \in N$ and $e_1 \leq e_2 \leq e_3$, then the element e_2 belongs to N as well. The definitions above can be formulated for convex sets of occurrences N:

An event occurrence is invisible relative to N iff it belongs to N and it is invisible in the above defined sense. We can redefine the functions lab, p, IP for event occurrences from N in an analogous way.

4.2 Zoom-Out: Examples

In the first example we show how to gradually abstract from the details of the interaction shown on Fig. 2. We present two views on the interaction. The left hand side of Fig. 8 shows the receiver view. The receiver of a virus usually cannot see the structure of the virus sender, but it may figure out who the sender of the virus was. A network observer can see only the communication over the network, but not the internal structure of the communication participants.

In the case of the first diagram, 131 is the only boundary object, i.e. $BO_1 = \{131\}$. e_1 is the only invisible event, consequently $M' = \{e_0, e_1', ..., e_5\}$. There are initially two objects: 131 and 742; therefore, $p'(e_0) = \{131, 742\}$. 131 is the only participant of the occurrence e_1', i.e. $p'(e_1') = \{131\}$. $p'(e_2) = \{742\}$, and so on. The the function IP' $(\_, e_0)$ is defined for objects 131 and 742.

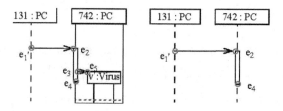

Fig. 8. Abstracting from internal details

In the network view, the set of boundary object is equal $\{131, 742\}$. There are only three event occurrences in this view: e_1', e_2 and e_4. Only the visible objects participate in these events.

The next example concerns partial zoom-out. We can abstract from internal structure and behavior of selected objects during certain time intervals. Fig. 9 abstracts from the behaviour and internal structure of b after it moves.

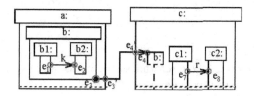

Fig. 9. Partial zoom-out

Objects b1, b2 communicate before and after the move. The initial topology is defined as follows: $p'(e_0) = \{a, b, b1, b2, c, c1, c2\}$, $lP'(b, e_0) = \text{<a>}$, $lP'(b1, e_0) = \text{<a, b>}$, $lP'(b2, e_0) = \text{<a, b>}$ and so on. There are four participants of occurrence e_4: $p'(e_4) = \{c, b, b1, b2\}$. $lP'(\_, e_4)$ is defined only for objects b and c.

4.3 Zooming into Move

In this subsection we formalize the zoom-in mechanism allowing us to display and to hide the details of object's move. It is possible to zoom into the object's move arrow to see the behavior of the participating objects. The top part of Fig. 10 shows the move of object bfrom location a to location c. All objects hosted by b participate in this move. In the top of the figure, the move is shown in the zoom-out view. The second diagram in Fig. 10 shows the move details, i.e. the zoom-in view. It displays the communication between b1 and b2during this move. The zoom-in version of the move arrow has only one black circle and one sharp end. We introduce this notation in order to make explicit that the communication happens between start of the move and the end of the move.

The zoom-out view can be seen as an abstraction of the detailed view. In this case the convex set is the interval $(e_3, e_4) = \{e \mid e_3 \le e \le e_4\}$, and the boundary set contains

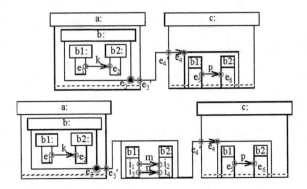

Fig.10. Zooming into a message

the object b only. The set of event occurrences corresponding to the first class diagram has the form $\{e_0, e_1,..., e_6\}$. The temporal order is linear: $e_1 \leq ... \leq e_6$. In the detailed view new occurrences are added and the temporal ordering is extended:

$$e_0 \leq e_1 \leq e_1 \leq e_3 \leq e_3' \leq i_1 \leq i_2 \leq i_4, i_1 \leq i_3 \leq i_4 \leq e_4' \leq e_4 \leq e_5 \leq e_6.$$

Concluding Remarks

The formal, partial order based semantics, presented in this paper explains the meaning of Sequence Diagrams for Mobility. It allows us also to formalize the abstraction mechanism introduced in the previous paper [10]. This semantics is well integrated with UML 2.0. Let us observe that it is possible to have a bit different semantics of SDM which assigns events only to send and receive actions (cf. [10]). For example, when an object located in another object sends a message, the message may cross the object box of the outer object; we may skip event occurrences corresponding to crossing of those boxes.

In the future, we are going to use this semantics to implement tools for graphical modelling of mobile systems. We are also going to investigate to what extend the decidability results and algorithms concerning Message Sequence Charts (cf. [11]) apply to SDM.

Acknowledgments

The author expresses cordial thanks to Martin Wirsing and the PST-research group at University of Munich for their helpful remarks on this semantics. He is also thankful to the anonymous referees whose critical comments helped to improve this paper.

References

1. Amyot D., Mussbacher G.: On the Extension of UML with Use Case Maps Concepts. In: Evans, A., Kent S. (eds.). The 3rd International Conference on the Unified Modeling Language, UML 2000, LNCS 1940, Springer, Berlin, 2000.

2. Baumeister H., Koch N., Kosiuczenko P., Wirsing M.: Extending Activity Diagrams to Model Mobile Systems. M. Aksit, M. Mezini, R. Unland (eds.): Objects, Components, Architectures, Services, and Applications for a NetworkedWorld, NetObjectDays Conference, LNCS 2591, Springer 2002, pp. 278 -293.
3. Buhr R., Casselman R.: Use Case Maps for Object-Oriented Systems, Prentice-Hall, USA, 1995.
4. Cardelli L.: Mobility and Security. Bauer, F., Steinbrüggen, R. (eds.): Foundations of Secure Computation. Proc. NATO Advanced Study Institute. IOS Press, 2000, 3-37.
5. Durán F., Eker S., Lincoln P., Meseguer J.: Principles of Mobile Maude. In: Kotz, D., Mattern, F. (eds.). Agent Systems, Mobile Agents, and Applications. 2000, LNCS 1882, Springer, Berlin, 2000, 73-85.
6. ITU-T. Telecommunication Standardization Sector. Message Sequence Charts, Z.120. 11.1999.
7. Jing J., Helal A., Elmagarmid A.: Client-Server Computing in Mobile Environments. ACM Computing Surveys. Vol. 31(2), 1999, 117-157.
8. Klein C., Rausch A., Sihling M., Wen Z.: Extension of the Unified Modeling Language for Mobile Agents. Idea Publishing Group, 2001.
9. J.P. Katoen, L. Lambert. Pomsets for MSC. Proc of FBT'98, H. König and P. Langendörfer (eds.): Formale Beschreibungstechniken für verteilte Systeme, Shaker Verlag, Aachen, 1998.
10. Kosiuczenko P.: Sequence Diagrams for Mobility. Krogstie J. (ed.): Advanced Conceptual Modeling Techniques: ER 2002 Workshops, Tampere, Finland, October 7-11, 2002, LNCS 2784, Springer, Berlin, 12 pages, 2003.
11. A. Muscholl, D. Peled, Z. Su. Deciding properties of message sequence charts, Proc. of FoSSaCS'98, LNCS 1378, pp. 226--242, 1998.
12. OMG: Unified Modeling Language. Version 2.0. Superstructure Final Adopted specification. 03-08-02.

From MSC to SDL: Overview and an Application to the Autonomous Shuttle Transport System

Ferhat Khendek and Xiao Jun Zhang

Electrical and Computer Engineering Department,
Concordia University, 1455, de Maisonnneuve W.
Montréal (Québec), Canada H3G 1M8
{khendek, xjzhang}@ece.concordia.ca

Abstract. We have developed an approach for generating automatically an SDL specification from an MSC specification and a given target architecture. The approach has been implemented in the *MSC2SDL* tool. In this paper, we give an overview of our approach and discuss several issues encountered during this research, before applying our approach to the Autonomous Shuttle Transport System and discussing this experience.

1 Introduction

MSC (Message Sequence Charts) [10, 11] and SDL (Specification and Description Language) [12] are two languages developed and maintained by the International Telecommunication Union (ITU-T). They are widely used within the telecommunication industry. MSC is used to express the behavioral requirements in terms of trace scenarios the system is required to exhibit. SDL is mainly used during the design phase, where an SDL specification consists of the architecture of the system as well as the behaviors of the different components in the system. SDL specifications can range from very abstract to very concrete specifications. Several commercial tools, such as ObjectGeode [16] and Tau [18], are available nowadays to translate automatically an SDL design specification into a (C, C++ or Java) implementation.

Our research goal was to bridge the gap between the requirement phase and the design phase. In this paper, we give an overview of our approach for automatic generation of SDL design specifications from behavioral scenarios specified with MSC. The architecture of the target design is given as an input parameter and taken into account during the translation. The generated SDL design specification conforms to the MSC specification. In other words, it has the same traces as the MSC specification. Moreover, the generated SDL specification is free of deadlocks or distributed choices. In this paper we will also discuss a few issues encountered during this research. The main contribution of this paper is an application of our approach to the Autonomous Shuttle Transport System (ASTS) described in [8].

The remainder of this paper is structured as follows. Section 2 introduces briefly the MSC and SDL languages as well as the concepts of consistency between MSC

S. Leue and T.J. Systä (Eds.): Scenarios, LNCS 3466, pp. 228–254, 2005.

and SDL specifications. In Section 3, we give an overview of our basic approach for translating an MSC specification into an SDL specification with a given architecture. In Section 4, we discuss the evolution of our approach and the main issues encountered during this research. The application to the ASTS case study is described in Section 5. In Section 6, we discuss related work, before concluding in Section 7.

2   MSC and SDL Languages

2.1   Message Sequence Charts (MSC)

The MSC language has two equivalent forms: one is graphical and the other one is textual. The graphical representation is widely used. The MSC'96 standard has introduced the high level MSCs (HMSC) where MSCs can be composed using a set of operators [10]. The MSC-2000 standard [11] includes time constraints and data.

A basic MSC (bMSC) is composed of a set of concurrent process instances that exchange messages asynchronously in a pairwise manner. Each process instance is represented by an axis that is delimited by a start and end symbol or a termination symbol. A simple bMSC is shown in Fig. 1 where process *P1* is sending message *a* then *c* to process. *P2*, while process *P3* is sending message *b*. In addition to message exchanges through sending and reception events, a bMSC may contain conditions, which describe the state of a subset of processes in the MSC, actions, timers and instance instantiation and termination as illustrated in the bMSC GET_ORDER_DELIVER of the case study in Fig. 11. Within each instance, events are totally ordered according to their positions from the start to the end symbols on the instance axis. All events are atomic and do not consume time.

Inline expressions define events composition in bMSCs. The parallel, alternative composition, iteration, exception and optional regions represent the inline operators. A parallel inline expression defines a parallel behavior in a bMSC. No ordering is defined between events in different sections. An alternative inline expression defines alternative behaviors in a bMSC as shown in Fig. 12. An iteration inline expression defines a repeated execution of a section in a bMSC. Events in the iteration area will be executed several times (0-inifinite). An exception inline expression defines exceptional behaviors in a bMSC.

Timers may be defined within a bMSC to express timing constraints (timer expiration and time supervision). For each timer-setting event, a corresponding time-out or/and timer reset has to be specified and has to follow it in order. However, corresponding timer events may be split among different bMSCs in cases where the whole scenario is obtained from the composition of several bMSCs (see HMSCs). Such as situation happens for instance in Fig. 9 and Fig. 10.

Time constraints have been introduced in the MSC-2000 standard [11] to support the notion of quantified time for the description of real-time systems. Time constraints can be specified in order to define the time at which events may occur. The progress of time is represented explicitly in a quantified manner, i.e. the traces of events are enhanced with a special event, which represents the passage of time. Timing in MSC enhances the traces of an MSC with quantitative time values. The time progress (i.e. clocking) is equal for all instances in an MSC. Also, a global clock is assumed. Time constraints can be absolute or relative. Absolute time constraint relates to an event and states a time interval or point at which the event is required to occur. A relative time represents a time distance between a pair of events. Furthermore, time can be measured and also be used as constraints for pairs of events. MSC-2000 provides constructs for the definition of data and for variables manipulation.

HMSCs give an overview of the system specification in terms of the composed MSCs, which could be bMSCs or HMSCs. HMSCs provide four operators to connect MSCs to describe sequential, alternative, iteration and parallel execution of MSCs. Global conditions in HMSCs represent global system states.

Sequential HMSC operator defines the sequential execution of MSCs. The MSCs will be executed one after the other in the order specified by the HMSC and according to the weak sequential composition semantics. Alternative HMSC operator defines alternative executions of MSCs. Only one of the alternative MSCs will be executed for each execution trace. Iteration HMSC operator defines iterative execution of MSCs. Parallel HMSC operator defines the parallel execution of MSCs. In Section 5 (case study) , we model the ASTS with an HMSC that contains sequential composition, alternative MSCs and iterations as shown in Fig. 6.

2.2 Specification and Description Language (SDL)

SDL [12] also has two equivalent forms: a graphical and a textual form. As for the MSCs, the graphical representation is widely used. The architecture of an SDL specification is described as a *system* that is represented as a structure of *blocks*, which may be, decomposed recursively into sub-*blocks*, until the basic components, namely *processes*, are reached. *Blocks* are interconnected through *channels* for communications between *blocks*. Communication between processes is asynchronous. SDL allows for multiple *channels* between processes (blocks), in each direction. However, each SDL process has a single *FIFO queue* for arriving messages, regardless of the source. Messages sent to a process by different processes are merged into the process single input queue, in the order of their arrivals. The SDL architecture for the ASTS is discussed in Section 5, where we can see the how the system is decomposed into blocks, which are also decomposed into processes.

The behavior of an SDL system is defined by the parallel composition of the behaviors of the *process instances* in the system. The process behavior is described by a diagram, which is an extension of the Extended Finite State Machine model. A process is modeled as a set of *states* and *transitions* connecting the states. Each transition consists of a series of actions, such as *local actions, procedure calls, timer set and reset, signal output*, etc. An SDL process, in a given state, initiates a transition by consuming an expected signal from its input queue. An input signal, which is not taken care of in a state (a signal, which does not initiate any transition) is implicitly consumed by the process. In this case, the signal is simply discarded and the process remains in the same state. In order to retain signals in the queue for later consumption, SDL provides a *save* construct. In a given state, signals mentioned in a *save* are neither removed from the queue nor consumed in that state. In other words, the *save* construct is used to change the order of signal consumption. Simple SDL process behaviors are given in Fig. 3, where process *P2*, for instance, goes from its initial state to state *s1* where it can consume signal *a* and save signal *b* if it is ahead of *a*, and move into state *s2*. From state *s2*, *P2* can consume signal *b* and move into state *s3*. In state *s*, if signal *c* is in front of signal *b*, it will be saved. From state *s3*, *P2* consumes signal *c* and terminates. Other SDL constructs are shown later on with the case study.

2.3 Consistency Between MSC and SDL Specifications

In any software process, the requirement specification has to be validated against the user requirements. Our approach assumes that the MSC specification has been validated against the user requirement and is used as a reference for the subsequent phases.

In this paper, we say that an SDL specification is *behaviorally consistent* with respect to an MSC if and only if the set of traces defined by the MSC is equal to the set of traces of the SDL specification. Our goal is to exactly capture and implement in SDL the behavior specified with the MSC.

We also define the concept of *architectural consistency* between the MSC and the SDL architecture as follows:

- all processes described in the MSC are present in the SDL architecture, and
- for each message *m* sent from an instance *I* to an instance *J* in the MSC, there is a channel *ch* in the SDL architecture that can convey *m* from process *I* to process *J*.

The SDL architecture may consist of more processes and channels than what is required for the implementation of the MSC.

3 From MSC to SDL

In this section, we give an overview of our basic approach for handling bMSCs by focusing mainly on communications and message exchanges between processes. Messages in MSCs are explicitly specified, and the order of the sending/consumption events with respect to their instances is explicitly specified. However, MSCs do not specify the actual arrival order of the messages into the input queue of the destination processes. Rather, the order depends on the underlying architecture and the processes interleaving. On the other hand, SDL instances implicitly discard signals, which are in the front of their input queues, and are not expected at the current state. These discarded signals, which may be required in the next states, may lead to a deadlock. In Fig. 1 for instance, *P2* has to consume specified messages in the following order: *a*, *b* then *c*. However, the actual arrival order of messages to *P2* input queue might be different from the consumption order, depending on the target architecture and processes interleaving. For the target SDL architecture, Architecture 1, given in Fig. 2, because messages *a*, *b* and *c* are conveyed through different channels, the possible message interleaving for *P2* are: *a*, *b* then *c*; or *a*, *c* then *b*; or *b*, *a* then *c*.

A straightforward translation of the processes P1, P2 and P3 into SDL will lead to a process P2 that consumes signal a first, then b and finally c without paying any attention to the arrival order of these signals into the input queue. For this SDL specification, there is no problem with the first order since signals a, b and c, arrive according to the consumption order. However, the other two arrival orders will certainly lead to deadlocks. In the second order (a, c then b), after P2 consumes signal a, signal c is discarded since I2 is expecting signal b not c. Consequently, P2 will never reach completion. For the last case, (b, a then c), signal b is discarded since P2 is expecting to consume a. After consuming a, signal c is discarded and P2 will wait for the previously discarded signal b. More deadlock scenarios can arise, if the SDL architecture allows signals a and c to travel through different paths as in Architecture 2 in Fig. 2.

In order to prevent deadlocks in the SDL specifications, our approach adds an SDL *save* construct for each signal that may arrive in the input queue earlier than expected. The need for a *save* construct can be determined by checking the order relation of each specified input event against the order of all successive input events for the same instance. The order relation between each pair of events, according to the MSC standard [10, 11], can be determined with the following rules and the transitive closure:

- events are totally ordered for each instance axis, and
- the output event of a message precedes the corresponding input event.

In [17, 13, 1] we have introduced an approach and the *MSC2SDL* tool for generating an SDL specification from an MSC and a target SDL architecture of the system. The automatically generated behaviors for the processes depend on the architecture of the system, i.e. the communication channels between the processes in the architecture.

As input the *MSC2SDL* tool takes an MSC specification as shown in Fig. 1 for instance and an SDL architecture, Architecture 1 or Architecture 2 for instance, as shown in Fig. 2. The *MSC2SDL* tool checks for the architectural consistency between the MSC specification and the SDL architecture, i.e. for each MSC process there is a corresponding SDL process and there is a channel to convey each message between the communicating processes in the MSC.

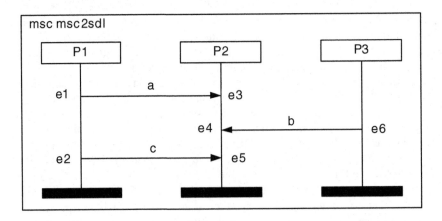

Fig. 1. A bMSC Example

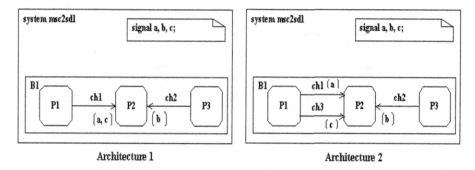

Fig. 2. SDL Architectures

After checking the architectural consistency between the given bMSC and the SDL architecture, the algorithm builds an *Event Order Table*, which captures the order relation between the events of the bMSC according to the two basic rules aforementioned and the transitive closure. In this table an entry (e_i, e_j) is set to T *(True)* if and only if e_i *precedes* e_j. The *Event Order Table* for the MSC in Fig. 1 is shown in Table 1.

Table 1. Event Order Table for MSC in Fig. 1

	e1	e2	e3	e4	e5	e6
e1		T	T	T	T	
e2					T	
e3				T	T	
e4					T	
e5						
e6				T	T	

The Event Order Table for an MSC is independent from the target architecture. In a second step, the algorithm builds Occupancy Tables. An Occupancy Table maintains the order relations between input signals of the corresponding SDL process. The number of tables is equal to the number of MSC processes that have input events. The rows of each table represent only the input events of the corresponding MSC process. The columns of each table represent the incoming routes that convey signals from other processes. The table is filled with all input signals that may exist in the input queue when the process is ready to execute the row event. This is done using the Event Order Table and following a simple rule: for a reception event e, a signal s might be in the queue, if and only if the reception of s does not precede e and e does not precede the sending of s. The Occupancy Table for MSC in Fig. 1 with Architecture 1 in Fig. 2 is shown in Table 2, while for Architecture 2 it is shown in Table 3. As we can see it from these two tables, for Architecture 1 c will always arrive after a, while for Architecture 2 c may arrive before a.

Table 2. Occupancy Table for MSC in Fig. 1 and Architecture 1 in Fig. 2

input events for P2	input message	Route Ch1	Route Ch2
e3	a	a, c	b
e4	b	c	b
e5	c	c	

Table 3. Occupancy Table for MSC in Fig. 1 and Architecture 2 in Fig. 1

input events for P2	input message	Route Ch1	Route Ch2	Route Ch3
e3	a	a	b	c
e4	b		b	c
e5	c			c

After building the *Occupancy Tables*, the last step in the algorithm consists of generating the SDL processes. For each MSC process, the tool automatically generates the corresponding SDL process. Each MSC process is handled separately and MSC constructs are translated into SDL constructs on a one-to-one basis without any intermediary representation. Several MSC constructs such as actions and timer events are translated in a straightforward manner into equivalent SDL constructs. An SDL process progresses from a state to another state by consuming an input signal. The approach inserts a new SDL state before each MSC input event. The approach adds an SDL *save* construct for each message in the corresponding *Occupancy Table* row, except for messages that are sent by the same instance and travel on the same channel as the input message.

In the case of the MSC given in Fig. 1 and for each of the Architecture given in Fig. 2, the tool generates the SDL processes shown in Fig. 3. The only difference between the SDL specifications for Architecture 1 and for Architecture 2 is in process P2, where we can see the usage of the SDL *save* construct to prevent the implicit consumption of messages that may arrive earlier than expected because of the architecture.

4 MSC2SDL Evolution and Issues

In order to handle HMSCs, we build an *Event Order Table* for each referenced MSC, and then generate a *global Event Order Table* by combining them properly according to the order relations between the referenced MSCs and weak sequential composition semantics. The order relation between any two HMSC nodes can be determined by finding a path from one to the other. If a path from node A to node B can be found, then node A precedes node B. The events in different referenced bMSCs respect the weak sequencing order. Then, a *global Event Order Table* is obtained by combining individual tables with the events respecting the weak sequencing order.

For handling time constraints, the *Event Order Table* has been enhanced to record not only the orders between events, but also their absolute time constraints and relative constraints. During the generation of SDL process behaviors, an absolute time constraint for a sending event is translated into a *continuous SDL signal* with the appropriate parameters and usage of SDL global clock *now*, while for a reception event it is translated into a (time) *conditional input*. Relative time constraints are handled in a similar manner. We have also extended the approach to handle the data part and variables.

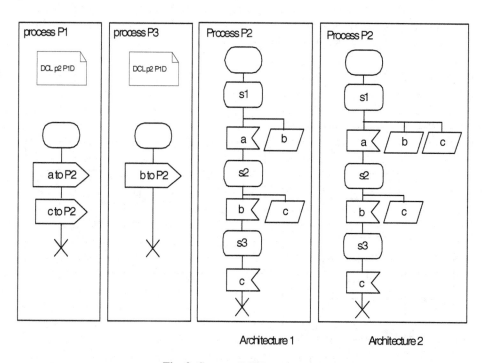

Fig. 3. Generated SDL processes

While working on the translation we have came across several issues, such as non-local choice, non-implementability of a given MSC in a given SDL architecture. The second problem is more general than the first one. In this case, for a given MSC and given SDL architecture, there is no SDL specification with such architecture and which exhibits exactly the behavior described by the MSC. The problem of implementability, also referred to as realizability in [2], comes from the inline expressions, especially the alternative. For instance, the MSC given in Fig. 4 cannot be implemented in the SDL architecture given in the same figure. We cannot find an SDL specification with this architecture and where process *Receiver* will always know which alternative has been taken by process *Sender*. The reason for that is messages *a* and *b* are conveyed through two different channels and they can arrive in any order and the process *Receiver* cannot guess which alternative has been taken.

The problem of implementability comes from the fact that the MSC specification says one alternative and only one can be taken, but when the behavior is distributed into processes according to the architecture, there is no way for some of the processes to find out which alternative has been taken. In [2], Alur et al. refer to this as the problem of implied scenarios. In our case, we call it non-implementability in a given architecture, because we cannot find a trace equivalent SDL specification with the given target architecture. In our approach, we check for implementability by verifying that every alternative in the MSC is controlled by one and only one instance and the architecture allows for every instance to distinguish which alternative has been taken. Our current *MSC2SDL* tool checks for the implementability of bMSC with inline expressions, but does not handle yet the full HMSC.

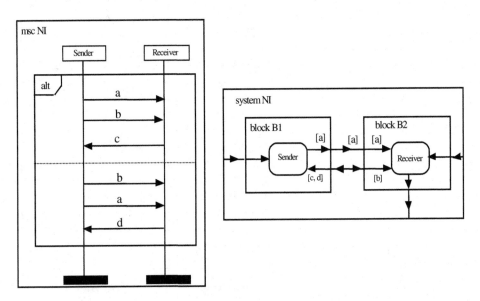

Fig. 4. Example of non-implementability

Timed MSCs may be non-implementable because of the aforementioned reasons and moreover because of the specified time constraints. For instance, it is not possible to implement the timed MSC given in Fig. 5 in a distributed architecture. This MSC states that either event *e1* or *e2* can be performed first, but the second one should be performed between 1 and 3 units of time later. This constraint cannot be enforced in a distributed architecture. Such a situation can be detected easily with a scanning of the Enhanced Event Order Table in the case of bMSCs. In the case of HMSCs, we are still investigating the set of HMSCs we can handle properly.

Timed MSCs have also brought some other challenges. Time constraints specify temporal orders between events. These orders have to be consistent with the causal orders between events. However, this is not always the case. A timed MSC may be inconsistent, because an absolute time constraint violates relative time constraints for

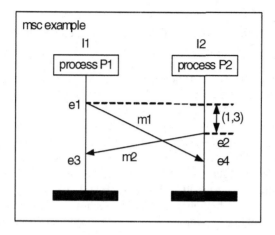

Fig. 5. Non-implementable timed MSC

instance. Our approach checks for time consistency of MSCs as discussed in [21]. While the time consistency of a bMSC can be checked in a polynomial time when relative time constraints between causally independent events are not allowed. The case of HMSC is more complex. In this case, the algorithm for checking time consistency is exponential, even when we do not allow for relative time constraints between events in different MSCs in the HMSC. In [21], we have characterized a subset of HMSC we can handle more efficiently.

The current version of *MSC2SDL* tool used for this case study handles all the constructs of MSC-2000, except the parallel operator, instance creation, multiple instances of the same process type, and from an HMSC we can only refer to bMSCs. We also have the abovementioned limitations for timed MSCs.

5 Case Study: Autonomous Shuttle Transport System

The Autonomous Shuttle Transport System (ASTS) [8] is a transportation system where shuttles transport goods between stations. Orders are announced by the broker and offers are made by shuttles. Once a shuttle has obtained an order, it delivers the order from the source station to the destination. Upon completion of delivery, a shuttle may get paid or will have to pay a penalty if the delivery deadline has not been respected. All the figures referred to in this section are given in the appendix of the paper.

5.1 MSC Specification of the ASTS

The MSC specification of the ASTS is given by the MSCs from Fig. 6 to Fig. 12. The system consists of seven actors. In our modeling we focused on the communication between the broker and one shuttle only. In other words, we only model one shuttle. The HMSC in Fig. 6 gives an overall view of the system specification. After initialization, *BrokerAgent* generates and announces orders to *Shuttle* as shown in Fig. 8. *Shuttle* then decides to bid for an order (see bMSC MAKE_OFFER in Fig. 9) or not (see bMSC NO_OFFER in Fig. 10.). In the later case, *Shuttle* does not do anything, i.e. does not respond to the announce made by *BrokerAgent*. In the case where *Shuttle* has made an offer, *BrokerAgent* may not select this offer from *Shuttle* (see bMSC NO_ORDER in Fig. 10), or grant this order to Shuttle. In this later case, *Shuttle* must deliver and report to *BrokerAgent* (see bMSC GET_ORDER_DELIVER in Fig. 11 and Fig. 12). Toward the end of this bMSC, we can see the interactions between *Bank*, *Shuttle*, *BrokerAgent*. If the delivery deadline has passed, *Shuttle* will pay a penalty. Otherwise, *Shuttle* gets paid for completing the order on time.

As the reader can see, in the bMSCs of Fig. 8 to Fig. 11, we have used timers. Timer *TBA* is used by *BrokerAgent* to guard against waiting forever for an offer from *Shuttle*, while timer *TS* is used by *Shuttle* to guard against waiting forever for an assignment from *BrokerAgent*.

Our current MSC2SDL tool does handle the HMSC parallel operator. So, in order to allow for concurrent behaviours for *Shuttle*, such as getting order announcements and making offers, and delivering goods, we have decomposed it into two processes, *Shuttle* and *ShuttleExt*. *Shuttle* bids and takes orders only, while *ShuttleExt* delivers goods. For the same reasons, we have also decomposed *BrokerAgent* into *BrokerAgent* and *BrokerAgentExt*. *BrokerAgent* generates, announces and assigns them, while *BrokerAgentExt* monitors the delivery of each order. With this, *Shuttle* may take more than one order at a time and the orders are delivered sequentially. When delivering an order, *ShuttleExt* contacts *TopologyAgent* to get the latest connection map of the railway. *ShuttleExt* also requires process *Simulator* to enable its moving, loading and unloading.

As we can see in the HMSC of Fig. 6, the repeated behavior is straightforward in the case of unsuccessful negotiations between *Shuttle* and *BrokerAgent* (i.e. NO_OFFER or NO_ORDER). The system loops back to the ANNOUNCE_ORDER bMSC. In the case of a successful negotiation, the iteration is achieved with MSC setting conditions. Each actor goes back to its initial state by using MSC conditions after one round of operation is completed. Notice that *Shuttle* and *BrokerAgent* can start negotiation of the next order before the completion of the current order by *ShuttleExt*.

In our modeling, we have made the assumption that the delivery deadline of each order is the absolute time of 10 times the order *ID x*. The order *ID x* is incremented by 1 for each new order. The completion time of each order is measured and compared with its deadline. The result is used to decide whether the shuttle should be paid for on time delivery or pay a penalty for late delivery.

5.2 An SDL Architecture for the ASTS

As discussed in the previous section the ASTS modeling in MSC is structured into seven processes. For the design of the SDL architecture, we propose to group these processes into four (logical) blocks as shown in Fig. 13 to Fig. 17. Block *Shuttle_blk* contains process *Shuttle* and *ShuttleExt*. Similarly, *BrokerAgent* and *BrokerAgentExt* are in the same block *Broker_blk*. Process *Bank* is in block *Bank_blk*. As for the other two components of the system, processes *TopologyAgent* and *Simulator* are grouped into the same block for the reason of simplicity. Processes communicate with each other through channels. There is one bi-directional channel between each pair of blocks where processes need to communicate with each other.

5.3 Generated SDL Process Behaviors

The generated SDL process behaviors are shown in Fig. 18 to Fig. 26. All SDL processes repeat their behavior indefinitely. This repeated behavior is modeled using SDL states. In the case of MSC, the repeated behavior is modeled using setting conditions. Our *MSC2SDL* approach/tool translates MSC setting conditions into SDL states. For example, process *Bank* has such a repeated behavior, when it goes from state *idle* and back to *idle*. Loops in HMSC are also implemented with SDL states. The approach keeps track of the initial states of each bMSC, it is able to direct the process behavior using the state names. An example of that is when the *Shuttle* does not make an offer; it loops back to its initial state *listening*.

As mentioned earlier for the MSC specification, there are timers in processes *Shuttle* and *BrokerAgent*. They are set for each of the two processes to wait for the interaction from the other one for a certain period of time. Therefore in both process behaviors, there are two branches for *timeout* and *reset timer*. Actually, these two timers and the decisions made by *Shuttle* and *BrokerAgent* (different input signals) control the alternative behaviors.

There are *loop* and *alt* inline expressions in bMSC GET_ORDER_DELIVER of Fig. 11 and Fig. 12, our *MSC2SDL* tool handles them properly. The controlling process for the *alt* is *BrokerAgentExt*, which makes the decision with a Boolean expression on the absolute time measurement result. Other participating processes follow the choice by consuming incoming signals. The *MSC2SDL* tool has a general SDL design for loop inline expressions in MSC, which has a four branches in the SDL behavior and controlled by a loop counter, loop lower bound, upper bound and guarding condition of the loop inline expression. This behavior can be found in the SDL behavior for process *ShuttleExt*, where guarding condition does not exist, and Boolean value "true" represents this situation. When the loop boundaries are the default values, our *MSC2SDL* tool uses 0 as the lower bound and 65536 as the upper bound.

One interesting point in the HMSC specification is that at each alternative point, only process *Shuttle* and *BrokerAgent* participate in the choice. If one assumes that all processes in one system appear in all referenced bMSCs by default, then a non-local choice would appear for processes other than *Shuttle* and *BrokerAgent*. However, since process *Bank*, *TopologyAgent*, *ShuttleExt*, *BrokerAgentExt*, and *Simulator* only appear in bMSC *GET_ORDER_DELIVER* in Fig. 11 and Fig. 12, which is in one branch of the HMSC and only appear at the bottom of the specification, the behaviors for these processes remain local, which actually does not lead to any non-local choice.

Notice that there is only very few usages of the SDL *save* construct in the generated processes. This is mainly due to the SDL architecture we have chosen for the system, *"mono-channel"*, i.e. at most one channel between each pair of communicating processes.

6 Related Work

Several research groups have been working on the translation of MSCs into other notations, more suitable for design specification, simulation and verification.

In [19, 20], Somé and Dssouli have considered the translation of timed scenarios to timed automata and check automatically the compatibility of the scenarios. However, the architecture of the system under consideration is not taken into account and the approach generates only the global automaton of the system.

In [14], Leue et al. have considered the translation of MSC specifications into ROOM specifications. Similarly in [15], Mansurov et al. have considered the generation of SDL specifications from MSCs. In these approaches, the architecture of the system is generated automatically and not taken as a parameter of the synthesis algorithm. We believe that the architecture of the system is an important and a creative parameter of the design that has to be provided by the user. Also, the issue of implementability of MSCs has not been considered. In other words, for a given MSC, the existence or not of a *behaviorally consistent* specification in SDL or ROOM is not considered during the translation. In [15], the generated SDL specification may have more behaviors than the MSC specification, which is not the case of our approach.

In [3], Alur et al. have investigated race conditions in MSCs, and discussed visual orders vs. "actual" orders. Our synthesis approach does a similar analysis according to a given SDL architecture. In [2], Alur et al. have also investigated the problem of synthesis and realizability of MSCs. This work focuses on the concept of implied scenarios, i.e. scenarios which are not specified in the MSC but which are possible in a distributed implementation with finite state machines. It handles only bMSCs with the alternative inline operator, but without time constraints. As discussed earlier in Section 4, implied scenarios happen when two instances or more can take different (alternatives) scenarios, and therefore ending with a scenario not allowed in the original MSC specification. The implied scenario is a combination of two allowed scenarios. Our approach is able to detect such situations in the case of bMSCs with inline expressions. In this case, we stop and inform the user that the given MSC cannot be implemented in the given architecture. We point out the alternative construct and/or the architecture as the problem for the implementation.

In [7], Hélouët and Jard investigated the necessary conditions for the synthesis of communicating automata from HMSCs under some specific communication assumptions. As for SDL, every communicating automaton has an associated input queue. However, this queue does not follow any specific policy for the consumption of messages. An automaton can consume any message present in its input queue when needed. On the other hand, automata are not allowed implicit transitions contrarily to SDL processes. These assumptions simplified the problem of implementability and render these results unusable in our framework.

In [6], Engels et al. have considered the implementability of bMSCs in given communication models, which can be seen as SDL architectures. The results in [6] are not applicable for HMSCs as shown in [13] or timed MSCs. In [5], the authors have designed an approach and a tool for the validation of MSCs against some errors, such as deadlocks, and distributed choices, etc., but this approach does not discuss the more general problem of implementability.

More related and recent work and discussions can be found in [4] and [9]. In [4] for instance, the authors have categorized the construction approaches into two groups: analytic vs. synthetic. They have assessed the approaches with respect to a certain number of criteria, such as source scenario notation, target construction model, automatic vs. interactive, etc.

7 Conclusion

In this paper we have described our approach for translating MSC specifications into SDL specifications with a given architecture. Our approach bridges the gap between behavioral requirements and design specification. It ensures, by construction, *behavior consistency* between the SDL specification and the MSC specification, and no further validation of the SDL specification against the MSC specification is required.

We have seen some of the thorny issues we are dealing with in our approach. Several of them are very hard and complex problems in the case of full HMSC. We have applied our approach to a simplified version of the ASTS. The generated SDL specification of the ASTS has been simulated with commercial tools.

We have spent some time on the modeling of the ASTS with MSC, which was not an obvious task. We wanted to avoid the usage of parallel composition operator of MSC, which is not handled by our tool. The HMSC roadmap of the ASTS looks intuitive but because of the concurrent behaviors the shuttle has to exhibit, we have to look inside the bMSC GET_ORDER_DELIVER and achieve some of the repeated behavior using MSC setting conditions. Also, the fact that the current *MSC2SDL* tool does not allow for referencing other HMSCs from an HMSC in a recursive manner has led to larger bMSCs, like bMSC GET_ORDER_DELIVER.

We have tried other MSC specifications of the ASTS, but some of them have led to the non-implementability problem. From this case study and several other ones, we found out that it is very easy to run into the non-implementability problem with MSCs. MSCs provide a global view of the system. One can very quickly write an MSC specification, which captures the global behavior of the system with several alternatives controlled by different processes for instance. At the MSC level, such alternatives do not cause any problem, because only one of them can be taken anyways according to the MSC semantics. However, these behaviors have to be distributed over different processes and the global meaning is lost and every process has only a local behavior, which may lead to implied (or inferred) scenarios. One of the constraints of our approach is therefore to design the right MSC specification, which can avoid all the aforementioned problems. In other words, more effort has to be devoted to the design of the MSC in order to take advantage of the automatic SDL code generation.

For this case study, we have considered only a *"mono-channel"* SDL architecture for the ASTS, i.e. at most one channel between each pair of communicating processes, which has also made the translation simpler and the generated SDL processes more intuitive.

Acknowledgements

During the course of this project, several students have worked on different aspects. We would like to acknowledge here the contributions of Robert Gabriel, Musa Abdalla, Stephan Bourduas, Umer Waqar, Tong Zheng and LiXin Wang. We would also like to acknowledge the contributions of Daniel Vincent and Benoit Parreaux from France Telecom R&D and the financial support provided by France Telecom R&D.

References

1. M. M. Abdalla, F. Khendek and G. Butler, "New Results on Deriving SDL Specification from MSCs", in Proceedings of SDL Forum'99, Montreal, Canada, June 22-25, 1999
2. R. Alur, K. Etessami, M. Yannakakis, "Inference of Message Sequence Charts", IEEE Transactions on Software Engineering, Vol. 29, No. 7, July 2003, pp.623-633
3. R. Alur, G. J. Holzmann, and Peled, "An Analyzer for Message Sequence Charts" Proceedings of 2nd International Workshop on Tools and Algorithms for the construction and Analysis of Systems, (TACAS'96), LNCS 1055, pp.35-48
4. D. Amyot, A. Eberlein, "An Evaluation of Scenario Notations and Construction Approaches for Telecommunication Systems Development", Telecommunications Systems Journal, Vol. 24, No.1, September 2003, pp. 61-94
5. H. Ben-Abdallah and S. Leue, "Syntactic Analysis of Message Sequence Chart Specifications", Technical Report 96-12, University of Waterloo, Electrical and Computer Engineering, Nov. 1996
6. G. Engels, S. Mauw, and M.A. Reniers, "A hierarchy of communication models for Message Sequence Charts", Science of Computer Programming, Vol. 44, No.3, September 2002, pp.253-292
7. L. Hélouët, C. Jard, "Conditions for synthesis of communicating automata from HMSCs", 5th International Workshop on Formal Methods for Industrial Critical Systems (FMICS), Berlin, April 3-4, 2000
8. http://wwwcs.upb.de/cs/ag-schaefer/CaseStudies/ShuttleSystem/
9. http://www.dagstuhl.de/03371/
10. ITU-T, "Recommendation Z.120 - Message Sequence Charts (MSC'96)", 1996
11. ITU-T, "Recommendation Z.120 - Message Sequence Charts (MSC-2000)", Nov. 1999
12. ITU-T, "Recommendation Z.100-Specification and Description Language (SDL-2000)", November 1999
13. F. Khendek, R. Gabriel, G. Butler and P. Grogono, "Implementability of Message Sequence Charts", Proceeedings of the first SDL Forum Society Workshop on SDL and MSC, Berlin, Germany, June 29 - July 1, 1998
14. S. Leue, L. Mehrmann, M. Rezai, "Synthesizing ROOM Models from Message Sequence Charts Specifications", Technical Report 98-06, University of Waterloo, Canada, 1998. Also in proceedings of the 13th IEEE Conference on Automated Software Engineering, Honolulu, Hawaii, October 1998
15. N. Mansurov and D. Zhukov, "Automatic Synthesis of SDL models in Use Case methodology", in Proceedings of SDL Forum'99, Montreal, Canada, June 22-25, 1999.
16. ObjectGeode, Verilog, Toulouse, France, 1999
17. G. Robert, F. Khendek and P. Grogono, "Deriving an SDL Specification with a Given Architecture from a Set of MSCs", in A. Cavalli and A. Sarma (eds.), SDL'97: Time for Testing - SDL, MSC and Trends, Proceedings of the eight SDL Forum, Evry, France, Sept. 22 - 26, 1997
18. SDT Tau , Telelogic, Sweden, 2002
19. S. Somé and R. Dssouli, "An Enhancement of Timed Automata generation from Timed Scenarios using Grouped States", The Electronic Journal on Networks and Distributed Processing,1997, URL: http://rerir.univ-pau.fr
20. S. Somé, R. Dssouli and J. Vaucher, "Toward an Automation of Requirements Engineering using Scenarios", Journal of Computing and Information, Vol. 2, No.1, 1996, pp.1110-1132
21. T. Zheng, F.khendek, "Time Consistency of MSC-2000 Specifications", Computer Networks, Vol. 42, No. 3, June 2003, pp. 303-322

Appendix: The ASTS Case Study

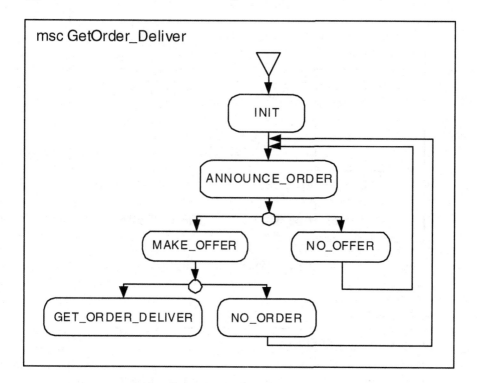

Fig. 6. HMSC for the ASTS

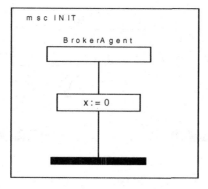

Fig. 7. bMSC INIT

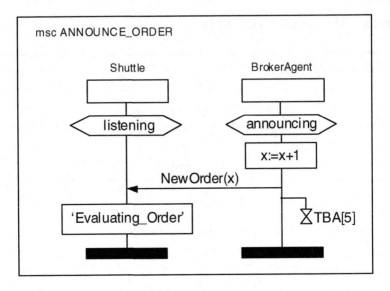

Fig. 8. bMSC ANNOUNCE_ORDER

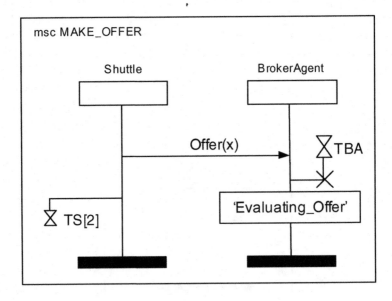

Fig. 9. bMSC MAKE_OFFER

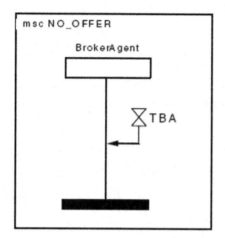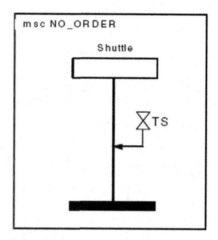

Fig. 10. bMSC NO_OFFER and bMSC NO_ORDER

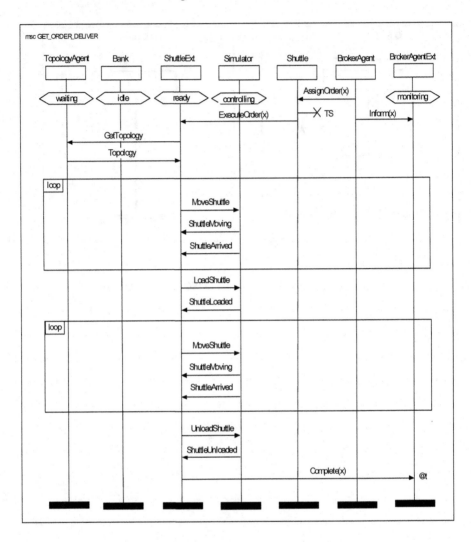

Fig. 11. bMSC GET_ORDER_DELIVER

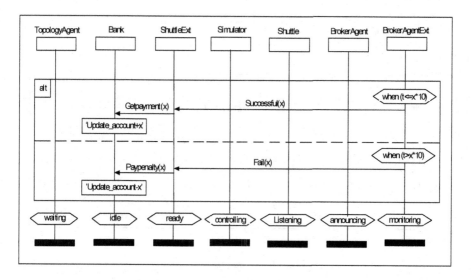

Fig. 12. bMSC GET_ORDER_DELIVER Con't

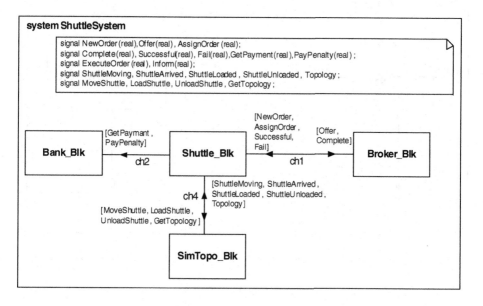

Fig. 13. ASTS Architecture

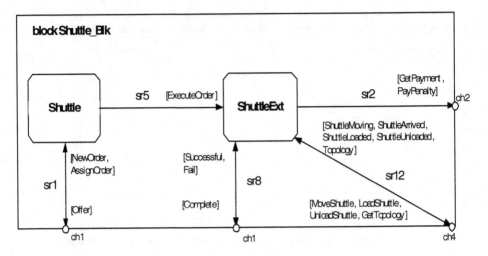

Fig. 14. The *Shuttle* block

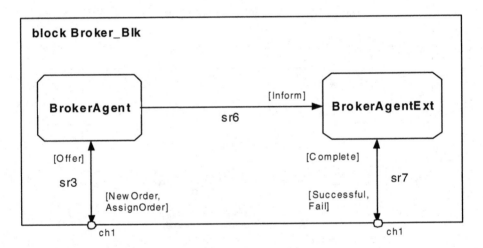

Fig. 15. The *Broker* block

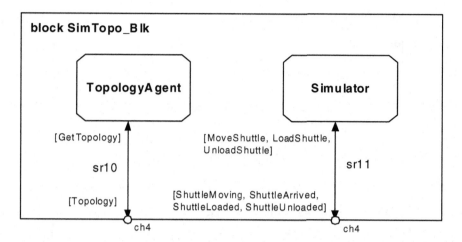

Fig. 16. The *Simulation* and *Topology* block

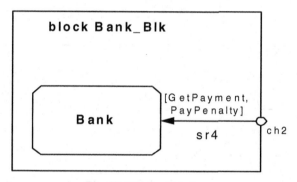

Fig. 17. The *Bank* block

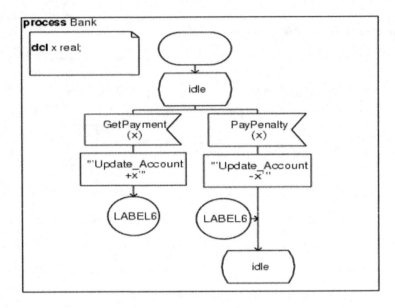

Fig. 18. Process *Bank*

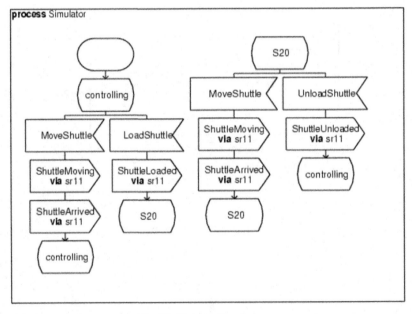

Fig. 19. Process *Simulator*

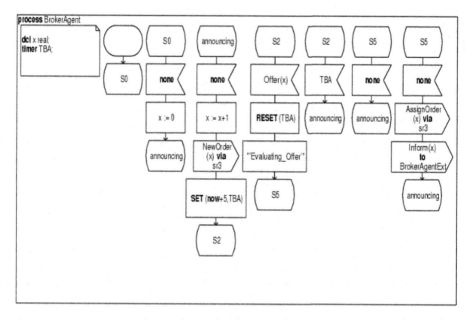

Fig. 20. Process *BrokerAgent*

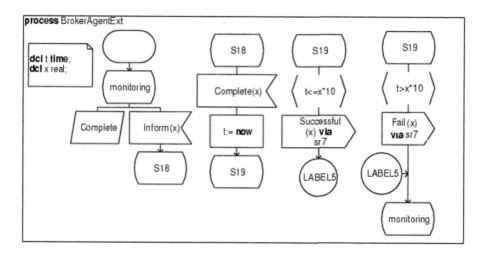

Fig. 21. Process *BrokerAgentExt*

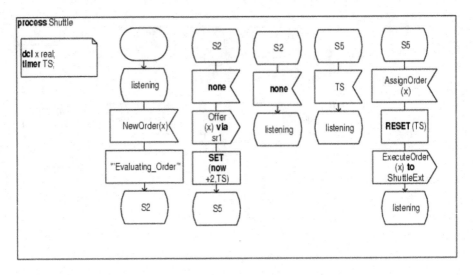

Fig. 22. Process *Shuttle*

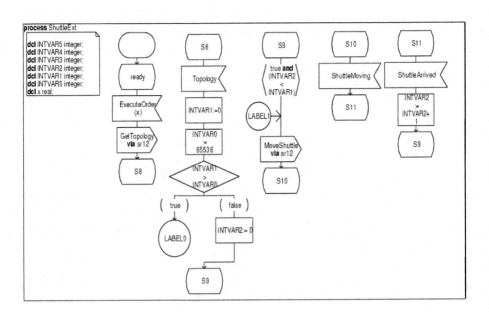

Fig. 23. Process *ShuttleExt*

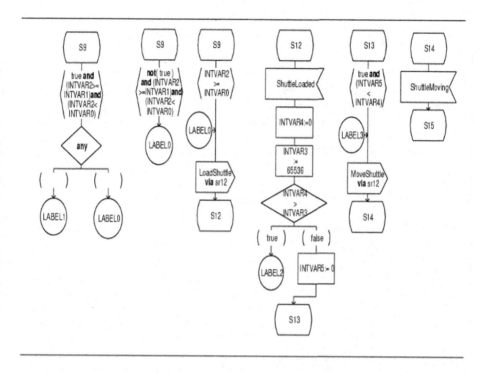

Fig. 24. Process *ShuttleExt* Con't

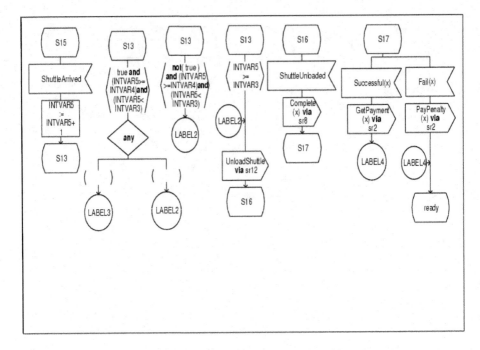

Fig. 25. Process *ShuttleExt* Con't

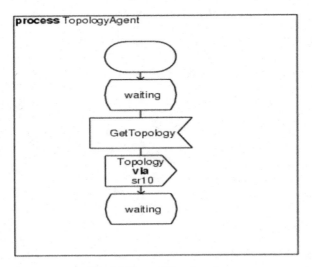

Fig. 26. Process *TopologyAgent*

Component Synthesis from Service Specifications

Ingolf H. Krüger and Reena Mathew

Computer Science & Engineering Department,
University of California, San Diego,
La Jolla, CA, 92093-0114, USA
{ikrueger, rmathew}@ucsd.edu

Abstract. Correct component models for distributed, reactive systems are difficult to construct. Typically, the services provided by such systems emerge from the interaction and collaboration of multiple components; each component, in general, contributes to multiple services. Consequently, services and their defining interaction patterns are key elements in the development process for distributed system: they contain the cross-cutting aspects of collaboration, which are only poorly captured on the component level. Typical modeling and development methods and associated notations, such as the UML, however, focus on the specification of complete information about components, instead of on the partial view provided by services. In this contribution, we give a precise definition of the term service, based on patterns of interaction. Using the CTAS case study, we demonstrate systematic development steps leading from service specifications to component implementations; we also show how to automatically synthesize prototypic state machines from interaction patterns defining services.

1 Introduction

Distributed, reactive systems consisting of concurrently operating and communicating components are notoriously difficult to develop. Increasingly, such systems are composed from individual *services*. Driven by the success of technologies such as "web services" (i.e. functions that can be accessed over the Internet) [31] in the business domain, the notion of service is also becoming more and more prominent in the embedded systems domain. Efforts such as AutoSAR [20], and AMI-C [21] base entire automotive software architectures on the notion of service to reduce the development and code complexity of next-generation vehicles [22].

Given the strong interest in the notion of service across application domains, important questions from a software engineering perspective are: What are services? How do the notions of service and component relate? What does a service-oriented development process look like? How to transit from service specifications systematically to component specifications?

In the remainder of this text we address these questions by (1) providing a precise definition of services, based on interaction patterns among concurrent components, (2) providing a specification language for services, (3) showing, in

S. Leue and T.J. Systä (Eds.): Scenarios, LNCS 3466, pp. 255–277, 2005.

the context of the CTAS case study[7], how this service notion gives rise to a service-oriented development process leading from interaction pattern specifications to service-oriented software architectures, and (4) showing how correct component specifications can be synthesized (semi-)automatically from a service specification.

The treatment of services as presented here is based on the corresponding presentation prepared for the Dagstuhl Seminar No. 0337 "Scenarios: Models, Transformations, and Tools", and influenced by the fruitful discussions at the seminar, as well as by subsequent further investigations into the topic, documented in [16, 14, 15]. Novel in this text is a presentation of the entire CTAS case study using the service-oriented development approach.

1.1   Services, Roles and Components

Services (sometimes also called features) are one of the cornerstones of applications in the telecommunications domain; see [27] and the references therein for an overview. Similarly, services play an important role in both established and evolving technologies and implementation infrastructures such as CORBA [26], Jini [25], .NET[24], and JXTA[23]. However, the definitions found in these references are shallow in the sense that they typically consist only of the *syntactic* signature of the function that implements the service. While this may be enough to know about a service on the implementation level, this is certainly insufficient for a systematic service-based development process. If we aim at using services for the development of high quality, highly dependable systems, we better associate the service definition also with *semantic* content. Only then can we make precise statements about the composition of services to yield new services, about refinement, and correctness of implementations.

We work with the following intuition for defining a precise service notion: in "real" systems, implementation components are involved in the execution of *multiple* services. Consider, as an example, a typical web client application, providing facilities for (a) browsing web pages, (b) downloading files via FTP, and (c) streaming of music and other media. While from the outside this web client may appear to be one monolithic application, we may as well think of it as the composition of three largely separate services (a), (b), and (c). In fact, in building service (c) we may need little or no knowledge about service (a).

This example is illustrative also in another regard. The services (a) through (c) emerge from the collaboration of the web client with multiple other components, which are distributed over the Internet; they also make use of other local services, say, provided by the underlying operating system. To a large extent, therefore, these services are determined by the interactions required for their implementation.

In this sense, we can understand services as a *partial* view on sets of interacting components. Combining the various services a component is involved in we obtain a *complete* behavior specification for that component. Therefore, we use *interaction patterns among distributed components* as the defining element for our service notion. We will formalize this concept in Sec. 3. Note, however, that the "traditional" notion of a "call/return" relationship between a service user and a service provider emerges as special case of this definition.

Another observation concerns the level of abstraction on which a service can be specified. Ideally, a given service should be implementable on a wide variety of target implementation architectures, as long as the implementation guarantees the correct execution of the interaction pattern defining the service. Therefore, we *decouple* the specification of the interaction pattern from the notion of implementation components. To that end, we introduce the notion of a *role*, which describes the contribution of any component that plays this role to a given interaction pattern. As an example for this decoupling, consider *peer-to-peer* networking systems; here, each node in the network is capable of playing both the client and the server role. These roles, and interaction protocols among them, can be specified separately from any concrete deployment on target components.

Together, the use of interaction patterns for defining services, and the abstraction introduced by roles leads to a powerful approach to service-oriented software development as we will demonstrate in the remainder of this text.

1.2   Towards a Service Oriented Software Development Process

The complementary nature of services as interaction and collaboration specifications raises interesting questions regarding the methodological handling and positioning of services within the overall development process for distributed and reactive systems. Services can be thought of as cross-cutting interaction aspects throughout the development process.

As a consequence of the partiality of the service definition, service development is necessarily a highly iterative process. The whole idea of service-oriented development rests on the premise that when developing one service we may not necessarily have available complete information about all other services that might also exist in the system. The mapping from a service specification to a set of components implementing the services is a design step: it is quite likely that a certain set of services needs to be implemented on a wide variety of target architectures.

The key questions from a developer's point of view are: how to identify services in the first place, how to identify a potential target architecture, and how to map sets of services to a given component architecture? To address these questions we propose the development process [14] outlined in Fig. 1.

This iterative process mainly involves two phases: (1) Define the set of services of interest; (2) Map the services to component configurations to define deployments of the architecture. Phase (1) starts by identifying the relevant use cases and their relationships in the form of a use case graph. From these use cases the roles and their interactions are derived as defining elements of services. This gives rise to a domain model for the roles involved. In phase (2) the role domain model is refined into a component configuration, onto which the set of services is mapped to yield an architectural configuration.

In Sec. 2 we apply this process to the CTAS case study; for further details on the process we refer the reader to [14, 15].

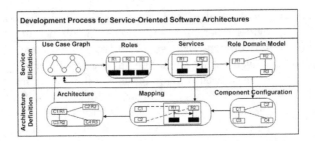

Fig. 1. Service-Oriented Development

1.3   Challenges, Contributions, and Outline

Traditional software development approaches and corresponding notations treat components, not services, as first-class modeling entities; consequently, these processes and notations focus mainly on complete behavior specifications, and provide little or no means for composing components from partial, let alone overlapping, behavior specifications.

In the service-oriented development approach we advocate here, we overcome this limitation by introducing services as first-class modeling entities; a central element of a service specification is the interaction pattern defining service behavior.

The remainder of this text is structured as follows. In Sec. 2 we explain the service-oriented software development process outlined above in more detail. To that end, we model a large part of the CTAS case study using our service notion. In Sec. 3 we provide a precise model for defining the semantics of service specifications. This model is the basis for discussing the synthesis from service specifications to state machines defining complete component behavior in Sec. 4. Sec. 5 contains our conclusions, related work, and an outlook.

2   CTAS Services: A Case Study in Service-Oriented Development

To further motivate and explore the service-oriented development process outlined in Sec. 1, as well as the notation we use for service specifications, we have modeled a significant subset of the Center Tracon Automation System (CTAS [28]) starting from a purely textual requirements document[7]. This case study is particularly appealing for our purposes for two reasons. First, the requirements are provided on a very detailed level, including interaction properties of the relevant components. Second, the document lacks a specification of the overall collaboration of the individual components; thus, the "big picture" is missing from the requirements specification.

The CTAS system requirements[7] identify the following types of components in the system. There is a Communications Manager (CM) and two types of clients that communicate with the CM - Weather Aware Clients (WAC) and Weather Unaware Clients (WUC). CTAS is responsible for two main processes: *initialization* of a WAC and *distribution* of weather updates to all the WACs. The initialization of a WAC is triggered when a WAC attempts to connect to CM, or tries to re-initialize itself. The weather updates occur when the CM detects that there is new weather information available for distribution to the clients. For this example we will be considering only the interactions of the CM and the Weather Aware Clients related to these two processes.

The CTAS components communicate by means of message exchange. Some of these messages contain parameter flags to indicate success or failure of an operation. Various constants used in the system, such as weather sources, weather modes, weather cycle status, weather cycle client status are also defined in the requirements documentation. Process requirements are explained in terms of how a component reacts when it is in a certain state, and receives a message from another component.

In this section, we describe the CTAS system using an architecture definition language (ADL) we have defined for service oriented software architectures [14]. This ADL defines the system under consideration in terms of *services* supported by the system. The services are defined as a set of *interactions* between the different *roles* identified in the system to accomplish a specific objective.

For reasons of brevity, we will introduce only the elements of the ADL needed for the specification of client initialization and weather update distribution. For a more detailed presentation of the elements of the ADL, including the mapping from roles and services to component architectures, we refer the reader to [14].

2.1 Use Cases

The first step in our service-oriented development process is to elicit the key use cases of the system under consideration. This provides "high-level" insight into the services the system needs to support.

In our example, we can identify use cases based on the features supported by CTAS. A client component may need to connect to the CM, or inform the CM that it needs to restart itself. In both cases, if CM is not busy, it will proceed to initialize the client. Furthermore, when the CM is not busy, it will continue to check for new weather updates to be distributed to the WACs; if there are new updates, they will be delivered. The use cases identified for the CTAS system are shown in terms of a graph in Fig. 2 (using UML notation for use cases).

2.2 Roles

The CTAS system requirements define the interactions between the different components of the system – clients (such as processes for airplane route analysis, aircraft and weather panels, as well as graphical user interfaces for simulation purposes) and the communications manager(CM). All clients execute the same protocols in communicating with CM, and can act as WUCs and WACs. Recall that we capture the commonalities of components within interaction patterns by

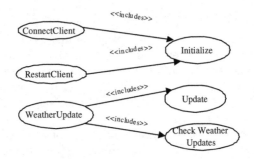

Fig. 2. CTAS Use Case Graph

means of *roles*. Each role describes the contribution of any component playing that role to an interaction pattern. The underlying assumption is that components can play multiple different roles, even at the same time.

For CTAS we have identified the following roles: *Aware Client* (Weather Aware Client), *Manager* (Centralized Manager), and *Button* (a user interface element that can be either enabled or disabled, but not both). These different roles will be played by the actual CTAS implementation components.

The services defined in the next section identify the interactions between these roles.

2.3   Services

Now we turn to the specification of the services CTAS supports for accomplishing the initialization and update processes. The requirements for the CTAS system are described in terms of how the CM and WACs react to messages received from each other. The services are defined from the perspective of the CM or client, respectively. These overlapping perspectives have to be combined to generate the service for a complete process; we will return to this point, below.

The services defined in this section show how the roles played by the CTAS components interact with each other. This helps us to isolate the design from the actual implementation for the system. In a later phase of the development process, we can map these services to the components we have defined for the system implementation. This mapping will involve assigning the roles a component plays in a service execution. For the CTAS system, for instance, we could map the Manager role to the CM component, and the AwareClient role to the PGUI and RAP client components mentioned in the requirements specification.

We use an extended version of Message Sequence Charts (MSC) to describe the interaction patterns defining services; we will introduce this notation "by example" using the CTAS services. The semantics of the notation is outlined in Sec. 3.

ClientGetNewWeather. This service explains how an AwareClient will react when it receives a CTAS_GET_NEW_WTHR message from the Manager. The client

will return back a CTAS_WTHR_RECEVIED message with a success or failure flag. The flag is determined by some internal operation for the AwareClient
indicated by the operation GetNewWeather. This service will be referred to in
the initialize and update CTAS services defined later on. Fig. 3(a) shows the
syntax we use for service specifications; it introduces a name for the service,
allows a verbal description, names all relevant roles, and provides an interaction
specification using an extended MSC.

MSCs have emerged in the context of SDL[29] as a means for specifying communication protocols in telecommunication systems. A basic MSC consists of
a set of axes, each labeled with the name of a component. An axis represents
a certain segment of the behavior displayed by its corresponding component.
Arrows in basic MSCs denote communication. An arrow starts at the axis of the
sender; the axis at which the head of the arrow ends designates the recipient.
Intuitively, the order in which the arrows occur (from top to bottom) within
an MSC defines possible sequences of interactions among the depicted components. In our extended MSC notation we use axes to indicate roles (instead of
components). Rectangular boxes labeled with **alt** express alternative interaction
patterns. The alternative chosen in Fig. 3(a) depends on the value of "Success",
a local variable of Aware Client.

ClientUseWeather. This service is similar to the service ClientGetNewWeather
as it defines how an AwareClient should respond when it receives either a

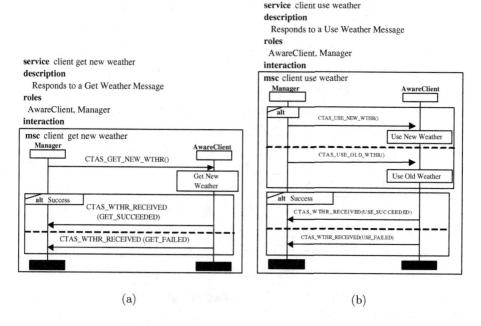

(a)   (b)

Fig. 3. Service: Client Get/Use New Weather

CTAS_USE_NEW_WTHR or CTAS_USE_OLD_WTHR message from the Manager. The AwareClient will send a CTAS_WTHR_RECEIVED message with a success or failure flag determined by a local operation. This service will also be referred by other CTAS services. The service specification is shown in Fig. 3(b).

InitializeCM. This service specifies the interactions involved when the Manager has to initialize a specific client. This service is defined from the Manager's perspective and so is named as InitializeCM. This service does not show the complete behavior of the AwareClient during this initialization. The states of

service initializeCM
description
    Manager initializes a weather client
roles
    AwareClient, Manager, Button
interaction

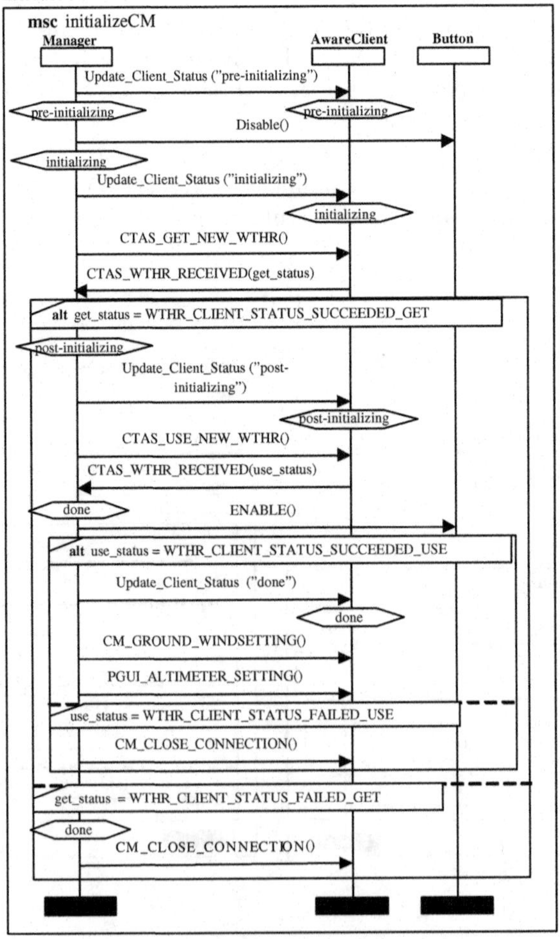

Fig. 4. Service - InitializeCM

the Manager and AwareClient will change as the service execution proceeds. In MSCs we denote state markers by means of labeled hexagons on role axes. Depending on the success or failure flag value returned by the AwareClient, the Manager reacts differently. The alternate options are shown in the service specification with the help of the **alt** operator. One thing to note is that at the end of this service, the Manager will return back to the *done* state. The service specification is shown in Fig. 4.

CTAS_Initialize. The CTAS_Initialize service captures completely the Manager and Client behavior when a Manager initializes an AwareClient. To achieve this we need to define this service in terms of the services IntializeCM, ClientGet-NewWeather, and ClientUseWeather.

Note that these services are *overlapping*; each one specifies a partial view on a segment of the interactions between the different roles. To compose these services we need to synchronize the common interactions of the respective services, depending on what alternative route is chosen. To that end, we have introduced an MSC operator **join**[5, 30], which synchronizes common messages in its operand MSCs; all other interactions specified in the operands are treated as being independent.

In InitializeCM, the Manager sends a CTAS_GET_NEW_WTHR message to the AwareClient. The AwareClient's behavior when it receives this message is captured in the ClientGetNewWeather service. We can see this for the CTAS_USE_NEW_WTHR message as well. The service specification is shown in Fig. 5(a).

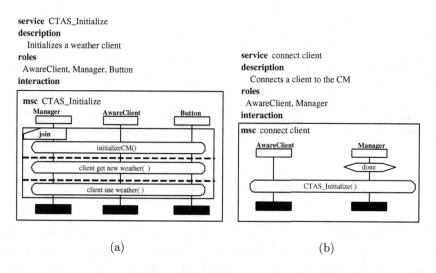

(a)   (b)

Fig. 5. Services: CTAS_Initialize and ConnectClient

ConnectClient. This service defines what interactions should occur when an AwareClient attempts to connect to the Manager. In this state of affairs, the CTAS_Initialize service is triggered. In fact, as we will see in detail below, triggered by a *Connect* message from a client, the ConnectClient service interrupts any other ongoing service in which the Manager may be involved. The service specification is shown in Fig. 5(b).

Restart Client. This service defines what interactions occur when an Aware-Client sends a CTAS_WTHR_REINITIALIZED message to the Manager to reinitialize itself. The response to this message depends on whether the state of the Manager is *done* or not (indicated as *!done* in the graphical notation). If the Manager is in the *done* state, the interactions for the CTAS_Initialize service are executed. Otherwise, the manager sends a CM_CLOSE_CONNECTION message to the AwareClient. Again, as we will see in detail below, triggered by a CTAS_WTHR_REINITIALIZED message from a client, the RestartClient service interrupts any other ongoing service in which the Manager may be involved. The service specification is shown in Fig. 6(a).

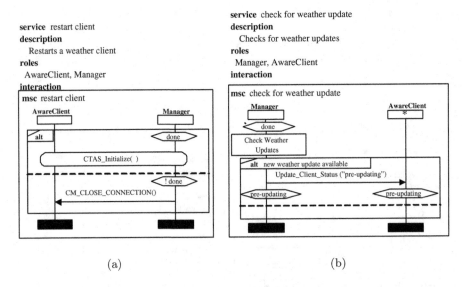

(a)   (b)

Fig. 6. Services: RestartClient and CheckForWeatherUpdate

CheckForWeatherUpdate. This service is defined for checking whether there are any new weather updates that have to be distributed to all AwareClients. The Manager role is responsible for performing this check. If an update is available, the Manager will update its state and that of *all* the AwareClients to *pre-updating.* We can see that this will trigger the service *updateCM* as the initial state for the Manager in the *updateCM* service is the Manager being in the *pre-updating* state. The definition for this service is shown in Fig. 6(b). The corresponding MSC shows another extension we use for service specifications. Role axes labeled with an asterisk ("*") refer to *all* components playing that role. This means that the Manager role actually broadcasts the message Update_Client_Status to all AwareClients.

UpdateCM. Whenever the Manager role changes its state to *pre-updating* this service is triggered; it shows the interactions involved during the update process from the Manager perspective. The asterisk shown for AwareClient role again indicates all instances of the role AwareClient. A message from the Manager axis to the AwareClient axis indicates a message sent from the Manager to all instances of the AwareClient role. Similarly, a message from the AwareClient role axis to the Manager role axis indicates the responses from all the AwareClients. This service shows how the Manager updates the weather information for all the weather aware clients for the CTAS system. The definition for this service is shown in Fig. 7. To discriminate between alternatives in this extended MSC we use the syntax "ALL get_status = v" to indicate that all "get_status" flags received by the Manager have the value "v", and "EXISTS get_status = v" to indicate that at least one of the "get_status" flags received has the value "v". We use these abbreviations here to avoid lengthy predicate logic specifications, which would clutter the MSC.

CTAS_Update. The *UpdateCM* service does not capture all the client behaviors during the update phase. The client's behavior when it receives the following messages: CTAS_GET_NEW_WTHR, CTAS_USE_NEW_WTHR, or CTAS_USE_OLD_WTHR is not captured in the *UpdateCM* service. It is, however, captured in the services *ClientGetNewWeather* and *ClientUseWeather*. Thus, these behaviors need to be combined together in one service as we had done for the *CTAS_Initialize* service using the *join* operator. The definition for this service is shown in Fig. 8(a).

CTAS_System. The overall CTAS service can be expressed in terms of the services we have already defined. This defines, in particular, the overall execution cycle. For this purpose we use a High-Level MSC (HMSC). An HMSC is a graph whose nodes are references to other (H)MSCs. The semantics of an HMSC is obtained by following paths through the graph and composing the interaction patterns referred to in the nodes along the way. We have extended the HMSC notation to introduce a "preemption operator" [30]. This operator is graphically denoted by a labeled, dotted arrow; the arrow is directed from the MSC reference specifying the interaction pattern to be preempted to the MSC reference specifying what happens when the preemption occurs. The label on the dotted arrow indicates the condition (a message that occurs, or a state that is reached) that causes the preemption to happen. If the preemption condition is met any time during the execution of the interactions of the source reference, that execution is immediately stopped, and followed by execution by the interactions of the target reference.

service updateCM
description
   Manager updates weather aware clients
roles
   AwareClient, Manager, Button
interaction

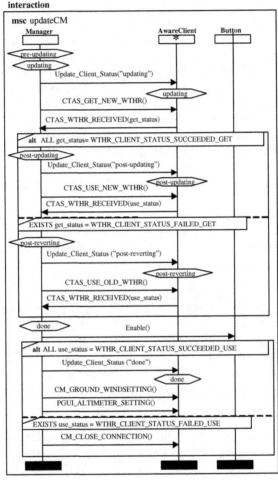

Fig. 7. Service - UpdateCM

For our example, we have defined that the service *CheckForWeatherUpdate* will be executed repeatedly until a weather update is available. This service will be preempted if a client attempts to send a *Connect* or a *CTAS_WTHR_ REINITALIZED* message to the Manager. Thus, after the system completes the execution for the *Connect Client* or *Restart Client* service, the system will again execute the *CheckForWeatherUpdate* service. The definition for this service is shown in Fig. 8(b).

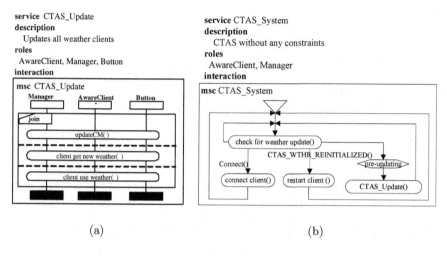

Fig. 8. Services: CTASUpdate and CTASSystem

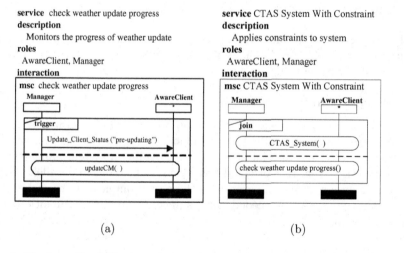

Fig. 9. Services: CheckWeatherUpdateProgress and CTASSystemWithConstraint

CheckWeatherUpdateProgress. So far, we have not placed any restrictions on the progress of the system as specified; in particular, the system could never actually transmit a weather update, if at least one of the clients were to pre-empt the *CheckForWeatherUpdate* service just before the system transits into the *CTAS_Update* service. In our extended MSC notation we can specify progress conditions using the **triggers** operator[30]. For two MSCs A and B we write A **triggers** B to denote that whenever an interaction pattern according to A occurs in the system under consideration, then the interaction pattern specified by B is inevitable.

One of the main conditions for the CTAS system to continue executing successfully is for the Manager role to return to the *done* state after executing a specific process. In this service we have defined a trigger for the updateCM() service. If the system ever has an *Update_Client_Status("pre-updating")* message, then the updateCM() service must execute eventually. The definition for this service is shown in Fig. 9(a).

CTASSystemWithConstraint. Now we can apply the constraint defined in the service CheckWeatherUpdateProgress to the system using this service. This can be done by using the *join* operator. In this case the two services CTAS_System and Check Weather Update Progress have been joined. Thus, the constraint defined in service CheckWeatherUpdateProgress will cross-cut the whole execution of the CTAS_System. The definition for this service is shown in Fig. 9(b).

This concludes our informal presentation of the notation and process we advocate for service specifications. Now we turn to the formalization of the underlying concepts.

3   Service Specification Using MSCs

In this section we introduce the formal model for the semantics definition of services and extended MSCs. This model serves as the basis for defining the synthesis of component implementations from MSCs in Sec. 4.

3.1   System Model

We prepare our precise semantics definition for services and MSCs by first introducing the structural and behavioral model (the *system model*) on which we base our work. We pay special attention to providing a system model that enables interaction- *and* state-oriented behavior specifications in parallel. This is a prerequisite for a seamless integration of these two complementary architectural aspects; this integration is needed, for instance, to provide a semantic foundation for the mapping from MSCs to individual component behavior as presented in Sec. 4. Along the way we introduce the notation and concepts we need to describe the model.

System Structure and Behavior. Structurally, a system consists of a set P of components, objects, or processes[1], and a set C of named channels. Each channel $ch \in C$ is directed from its source to its destination component; we assume that channel names are unique. Channels connect components that communicate with one another; they also connect components with the environment. Communication proceeds by message exchange over these channels.

---

[1] In the remainder of this document, we use the terms components, objects, and processes interchangeably.

With every $p \in P$ we associate a unique set of states, i.e. a component state space, S_p. We define the state space of the system as $S \stackrel{\text{def}}{=} \Pi_{p \in P} S_p$. For simplicity, we represent messages by the set M of message identifiers.

Now we turn to the dynamic aspects of the system model. We assume that the system components communicate among each other and with the environment by exchanging messages over channels. We assume further that a discrete global clock drives the system. We model this clock by the set $\mathbb{N}$ of natural numbers. Intuitively, at time $t \in \mathbb{N}$ every component determines its output based on the messages it has received until time $t - 1$, and on its current state. It then writes the output to the corresponding output channels and changes state. The delay of at least one time unit models the processing time between an input and the output it triggers; more precisely, the delay establishes a strict causality between an output and its triggering input (cf. [2, 1]).

Formally, with every channel $c \in C$ we associate the histories obtained from collecting all messages sent along c in the order of their occurrence. Our basic assumption here is that communication happens asynchronously: the sender of a message does not have to wait for the latter's receipt by the destination component.

This allows us to model channel histories by means of *streams*[2]. A stream is a finite or infinite sequence of messages. By X^* and X^∞ we denote the set of finite and infinite sequences over set X, respectively. $X^\omega \stackrel{\text{def}}{=} X^* \cup X^\infty$ denotes the set of streams over set X. We identify X^* and X^∞ with $\bigcup_{i \in \mathbb{N}}([0, i] \to X)$ and $\mathbb{N} \to X$, respectively, and use function application to write $x.n$ for the n-th element of stream x (for $x \in X^\omega$ and $n \in \mathbb{N}$).

We define $\tilde{C} \stackrel{\text{def}}{=} C \to M^*$ as a channel valuation that assigns a sequence of messages to each channel; we obtain the timed stream tuple $\tilde{C}^\infty$ as an infinite valuation of all channels. This models that at each point in time a component can send multiple messages on a single channel.

With timed streams over message sequences we have a model for the communication among components over time. Similarly we can define a succession of system states over time as an element of set S^∞.

With these preliminaries in place, we can now define the semantics of a system with channel set C, state space S, and message set M as an element of $\mathcal{P}((\tilde{C} \times S)^\infty)$. The existence of more than one element in the semantics of a system indicates nondeterminism. For notational convenience we denote for $\varphi \in (\tilde{C} \times S)^\infty$ by $\pi_1(\varphi)$ and $\pi_2(\varphi)$ the projection of φ onto the corresponding infinite channel and state valuations, respectively; thus, we have $\pi_1(\varphi) \in \tilde{C}^\infty$ and $\pi_2(\varphi) \in S^\infty$.

3.2 Services

Based on our observation that the key to understanding a service is to understand the interplay of the components involved in delivering the service, we define our service notion to be a projection of the overall system behavior on a certain period of time. More precisely, we define a set

$$Q \subseteq (\tilde{C} \times S)^\infty \times \mathbb{N}_\infty$$

to be a *service (specification)* with respect to the system model introduced in Sec. 3.1.

Given a service Q, every element $(\varphi, t) \in Q$ describes one nondeterministic alternative of the system's behavior until time t. This service notion captures in an abstract way what happens in the system under consideration until a certain time point; it refers to two major aspects of system behavior: component interaction and state change. Components are referred to only indirectly as the sources and destinations of channels, and as the locations for program state in this model.

A service specification Q defines only what the system must satisfy *at least*. Because of its "looseness" this service notion readily supports the partiality that we have identified as critical for service specifications.

3.3   From MSCs to Services

In earlier work [1, 5, 30] we have introduced a semantic mapping from an extended MSC notation into the semantic domain $(\tilde{C} \times S)^\infty \times \mathbb{N}_\infty$. For reasons of brevity, we do not repeat the entire mapping here, but give the basic idea behind it. Intuitively, we associate with a given MSC a set of channel and state valuations, i.e. a set of system behaviors according to the system model we have introduced in Sec. 3.1. Put another way, we interpret an MSC as a constraint at the possible behaviors of the system under consideration. More precisely, with every MSC α and every $u \in \mathbb{N}_\infty$ we associate a set $[\![\alpha]\!]_u \in \mathcal{P}((\tilde{C} \times S)^\infty \times \mathbb{N}_\infty)$; any element of $[\![\alpha]\!]_u$ is a pair of the form $(\varphi, t) \in (\tilde{C} \times S)^\infty \times \mathbb{N}_\infty$. The first constituent, φ, of such a pair describes an infinite system behavior. u and the pair's second constituent, t, describe the time interval within which α constrains the system's behavior. Intuitively, u corresponds to the "starting time" of the behavior represented by the MSC; t indicates the time point when this behavior has finished. Hence, outside the time interval specified by u and t the MSC α makes no statement whatsoever about the interactions and state changes happening in the system.

This mapping supports all the operators on MSCs introduced above, including join, preemption, trigger composition, and HMSCs. We refer the interested reader to [5, 30] for the details.

Roles can be handled in multiple ways in this framework. The most straightforward approach is to identify roles and components; this way we obtain a system model where each role defines exactly one implementation "role component". That role component would represent all instances of the role. If we start from a *given* target component architecture, then we may be interested in mapping multiple roles to one of the components, say T. Then, we can treat roles as subcomponents of T. Cases where MSCs contain "multi-axes" (axes labeled with an asterisk), can be elegantly handled by preprocessing the underlying system architecture, as we will discuss in detail in Sec. 4.

3.4   Mapping MSCs to Service Specifications

The only remaining task is to associate MSCs with service specifications. Given the preparations in the preceding subsections this is a simple task. Given an MSC α we immediately obtain a service specification Q_α as follows:

$$Q_\alpha \stackrel{\text{def}}{=} [\![\alpha]\!]_0$$

This definition facilitates the use of MSCs as a graphical description technique for service specifications. Clearly, as defined here, MSCs help capture the interaction part of a service specification.

4   From Services to Components

Once we have obtained a sufficiently detailed service specification we are interested in deriving a set of components that exhibit the interaction behavior captured by means of the defining MSCs. Here, we establish the formal relationship between components, their interaction behavior, and MSC specifications. Moreover, we describe an algorithm for obtaining state machines syntactically from a given MSC specification.

4.1   Preliminaries

To state the synthesis problem precisely, we define first what the (black-box) behavior of individual components is. To that end, for a component F we introduce the sets $I_F \subseteq C$ of input channels, and the set $O_F \subseteq C$ of output channels. We define $\overrightarrow{I}_F \stackrel{\text{def}}{=} (I_F \to M^*)^\infty$ and $\overrightarrow{O}_F \stackrel{\text{def}}{=} (O_F \to M^*)^\infty$ as valuations (*histories*) of these channel subsets. A *component specification* is a relation between the input and output histories of the component under consideration. More precisely we define a relation $F : \overrightarrow{I}_F \to (\overrightarrow{O}_F \to \mathbb{B})$ as the component specification for F. For a set J of indices, and a family $\{F_j : j \in J\}$ of component specifications we require that for $i, j \in J$ we have $o \in O_{F_i} \cap O_{F_j} \Rightarrow i = j$, i.e. output channels of components are unique. We call a component specification F *causal*, if at any time point $t \in \mathbb{N}$ the output of F depends at most on the inputs F has received before t.

Our next step is to define the notion of component composition. We base our composition operator on logical conjunction. For an index set J and a family of component specifications $\{F_j : j \in J\}$ we define the semantics of their composition $\bigotimes_{j \in J} F_j$ by requiring that a given behavior fulfills the conjunction of all component specifications:

$$[\![\bigotimes_{j \in J} F_j]\!] \stackrel{\text{def}}{=} \{\psi \in \tilde{C}^\infty : \bigwedge_{j \in J} F_j.(\psi|_{I_{F_j}}).(\psi|_{O_{F_j}})\}$$

In this definition we denote by $\psi|_D$ the projection of $\psi \subseteq \tilde{C}^\infty$ on the channels in $D \subseteq C$.

Based on these preliminaries we can define the notion of *realizability* and formulate the synthesis problem for MSCs. Let a set of channel valuations *Spec* $\subseteq$ $\tilde{C}^\infty$ be given. We call *Spec realizable*, if there exists a family $\{F_j : j \in J\}$ of causal component specifications, such that

$$[\![\bigotimes_{j \in J} F_j]\!] \subseteq Spec$$

holds. Realizability of a specification implies that we can find a set of components implementing this specification.

For a given (H)MSC α, the task of finding a family $\{F_j : j \in J\}$ of causal component specifications, such that[2]

$$[\![\bigotimes_{j \in J} F_j]\!] \subseteq \{\psi \in \tilde{C}^\infty : \langle \exists (\varphi, \infty) \in [\![\alpha]\!]_0) :: \psi = \pi_1.\varphi\rangle\}$$

holds, is the *synthesis problem* for MSC α.

4.2   Algorithm for Automaton Synthesis

In [1, 5] we have shown that the MSC dialect introduced above yields realizable specifications; therefore, component synthesis is possible for the MSCs we consider. In the interest of space we give only a brief account of the key steps for synthesizing component prototypes from the MSCs we have elicited from the CTAS requirements document.

Basic Algorithm. To avoid overly general solutions, we take into account state information provided by the MSCs' author using guards. We assume given a set of MSCs that describe all the interaction sequences among a set of components, i.e., we make a closed world assumption with respect to the interaction sequences that occur in the system under development. We translate each guard that appears in any of the MSCs into a corresponding automaton state. We assume further that we try to obtain an automaton for exactly one of the components, say $p \in P$, occurring in the MSCs. The second input we expect is the name of the initial state for p's automaton. We derive an automaton for an individual component specification from a given set of MSCs by successively applying four transformation steps: 1. *projection* of the given MSCs onto the component of interest, 2. *normalization* of the MSCs, i.e. adding missing start and end labels (state markers), and splitting MSCs with more than two labels at an intermediate label, 3. *transformation* into an automaton by identifying the MSCs as transition paths, and by adding intermediate states accordingly, and 4. *optimization* of the resulting automata. This synthesis algorithm [10] works fully automatically for *causal* MSCs [9], and can handle choice, repetition, and

---

[2] For reasons of simplicity and without loss of generality we assume that α describes infinite behavior.

concurrency/interleaving [5]. Because the algorithm is based on syntactic manipulation of the given MSCs it is oblivious to the underlying MSC semantics – as long as the semantics of the target component model matches the one used for the MSCs serving as input to the algorithm.

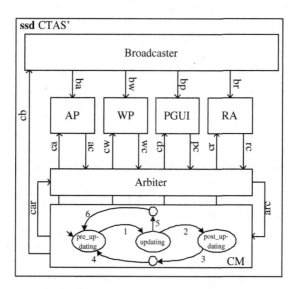

Fig. 10. Modified CTAS SSD including a broadcasting and arbiter component

Extensions for Handling Roles. Our basic synthesis algorithm deals only with point-to-point message exchange. To address role axes labeled with an asterisk we observe that an incoming message to such an axis denotes *broadcasting*. A message emanating from such an axis (a "multi-message") denotes the "collection" of all the responses by all instances of the role at the recipient of this message, i.e. the *inverse* of broadcasting. To adapt the algorithm to deal with such situations we introduce two separate component types: a "broadcaster", and an "arbiter", for each occurrence of a multi-axis. The "broadcaster" is responsible for relaying all messages it receives to all instances of the role it corresponds to. The arbiter is responsible for collecting messages from all instances of the role it corresponds to, and for forwarding a "cumulative" answer to the receiver of the multi-message. We show an example of this approach in Fig. 10; it depicts an architecture containing the following components: the communications manager (*CM*), the aware clients: Aircraft Panel (*AP*), Weather Panel (*WP*), Planview GUI (*PGUI*) and Route Analysis (*RA*), as well as the *Broadcaster* and *Arbiter* components. This allows us to also update the original MSCs accordingly; the newly added component *Broadcaster* receives broadcasting messages from *CM*, and forwards them to all other components. Similarly, to handle multi-messages, we introduce a component *Arbiter*, which receives the *yes* and *no* replies from all components and only relays the aggregate result (*all_yes* or *some_no*) to *CM*. As a consequence in the state automaton for *CM* we only need one transition for sending a broadcasting message, and for receiving a multi-message, respectively. In particular, we can directly reuse the basic synthesis algorithm without the problem of incurring cluttered automata. A second advantage of this approach is that it directly supports hierarchical component refinement, and thus scales nicely [11]. In a hierarchical component model the explicit broadcaster component (and similarly an arbiter) can also be introduced as a sub-component of *CM*, thus hiding it from *CM*'s environment.

The components *AP*, *WP*, *PGUI*, and *RA* are all instances of the AwareClient role and implement the corresponding automata. Fig. 10 shows *one* possible mapping of the services to components; another one emerges if we map the roles of Broadcaster, Arbiter, and Manager *together* onto the *CM* component.

5   Conclusions, Related Work and Outlook

Service-oriented software development is a promising alternative to traditional object- and component-oriented development approaches. We understand services as partial interaction patterns within the system under consideration. Components, on the other hand, emerge from the composition of services as complete behavior specifications. Exploiting this duality between partial and complete behavior specifications is a challenge for existing development processes; by introducing services as first-class entities of *both* design and implementation increases the traceability of the central interaction patterns of complex, distributed and reactive systems.

We have shown that, using an extended version of MSCs, we can specify the CTAS case study in a service-oriented manner. Besides a demonstration of the practical utility of our approach we also obtain a comprehensive collaboration specification for CTAS *beyond* the original, textual and component-centric requirements documents.

The notion of service is used with different meanings across application domains and abstraction levels [33]. In the realm of requirements capture and modeling, where our work is positioned, the idea of using services as "orchestrators" for the interactions of multiple components and objects is gaining popularity [32]. We support this view by *defining* services as interaction patterns among roles, and – as a separate step – mapping services to target architectures. This distinguishes our approach also from others [34, 35, 36, 37] where components and connectors, not services, are the center of concern.

Often the notion of service-oriented architectures is identified with technical infrastructures for *implementing* services, including the popular web-services infrastructure [31]. Our work, in contrast, supports *finding* the services that can later be exposed either as web-services, or implemented as "internal" services of the system under consideration.

The role concept introduced in [19] and the activities of [18] are related to our concepts of roles and services. Our approach, however, is more general and abstract than either of these approaches, as our role concept decouples services from target implementation architectures *using* roles as abstractions of components within interaction patterns. Baresi et al. discuss modeling and validation of service-oriented architectures [17]; here, however, interaction scenarios are treated as a means for validation only, not as the defining element of services. As we have argued above, we believe that using interaction patterns as the defining element for services does better justice to their cross-cutting nature in complex systems.

Clearly, there is ample potential for further extensions and elaborations of the service concept introduced here. Note, for instance, that the sets of components and roles need not be fixed over time (although they are in the CTAS example); addressing this issue will result in support for dynamic and mobile service configurations, which have many practical applications. A thorough investigation of the benefits of services and service-oriented software architectures, as compared to object- and component-oriented approaches is also a promising area of future research.

Acknowledgments

The author is grateful to the participants and post-proceedings reviewers of Dagstuhl Seminar 03371, as well as to Manfred Broy and Michael Meisinger for insightful comments on the topics presented here. This work was partially supported by the UC Discovery Grant and the Industry-University Cooperative Research Program, as well as by funds from the California Institute for Telecommunications and Information Technology.

References

1. M. Broy and I. Krüger: Interaction Interfaces- Towards a scientific foundation of a methodological usage of Message Sequence Charts. In J. Staples, M. G. Hinchey, and Shaoying Liu, editors, Formal Engineering Methods (ICFEM'98), IEEE Computer Society, 1 (1998) 2–15
2. M. Broy and K. Stølen: Specification and Development of Interactive Systems: Focus on Streams, Interfaces and Refinement. Springer New York (2001) ISBN 0-387-95073-7
3. The Action Semantics Consortium: Response to OMG RFP as/98-11-01. Action Semantics for the UML (2001)
4. ITU-TS. Recommendation Z.120: Message Sequence Chart (MSC). Geneva (1996)
5. I. Krüger: Distributed System Design with Message Sequence Charts. PhD thesis, Technische Universität München (2000)
6. J. Ellsberger, D. Hogrefe, and A. Sarma: SDL. Formal Object-oriented Language for Communication Systems, Prentice-Hall (1998)
7. SCESM 2003 Case Study, 2nd international workshop on scenarios and state machines: Models, algorithms, and tools, CTAS Case Study Overview, Requirements, http://www.doc.ic.ac.uk/ su2/SCESM/CS/requirements.pdf (2002)

8. Dagstuhl Seminar No. 03371, Scenarios: Models, Transformations and tools, Case Study, http://tele.informatik.uni-freiburg.de/dagstuhl03371/CaseStudy.html (2003)
9. B. Finkbeiner and I. Krüger: Using Message Sequence Charts for Component-Based Formal Verification. In Specification and Verification of Component Based Systems (SAVCBS). Workshop at OOPSLA (2001)
10. I. Krüger, R. Grosu, P. Scholz and M. Broy: From MSCs to statecharts. In Franz J. Rammig, editor, Distributed and Parallel Embedded Systems, pages 61-71, Kluwer Academic Publishers (1999)
11. I. Krüger, W. Prenninger, R. Sandner and M. Broy: From Scenarios to Hierarchical Broadcasting Software Architectures using UML-RT, International Journal of Software Engineering and Knowledge Engineering (IJSEKE) (April 2002)
12. S. Uchitel, J. Kramer and J. Magee: Implied Scenario Detection in the Presence of Behavior Constraints, Electronic Notes in Theoretical Computer Science, 65(7) (2002)
13. D. Harel and H. Kugler: Synthesizing State-Based Object Systems from LSC specifications. In Sheng Yu and Andrei Paun, editors, Implementation and Application of Automata, 5th International Conference, CIAA 2000, volume 2088 of LNCS, pages 1-33, Springer (2001)
14. I. Krüger and R. Mathew: Systematic Development and Exploration of Service-Oriented Software Architectures. in: Proceedings of WICSA'04 (2004).
15. I. H. Krüger, Diwaker Gupta, Reena Mathew, Praveen Moorthy, Walter Phillips, Sabine Rittmann and Jaswinder Ahluwalia: Towards a Process and Tool-Chain for Service-Oriented Automotive Software Engineering. In: Proceedings of SEAS Workshop at ICSE 2004 (2004)
16. I. H. Krüger: Service Specification with MSCs and Roles. in: IASTED International Conference on Software Engineering, Innsbruck (2004)
17. L. Baresi, R. Heckel, S. Thne and D. Varr: Modeling and Validation of Service-oriented Architectures: Application vs. Style. Proceedings of ESEC/FSE 2003 (2003)
18. B.B. Kristensen and D.C.M. May. Activities: Abstractions for Collective Behavior. In ECOOP'96, volume 1098 of LNCS, pages 472–501. Springer (1996)
19. Barbara Paech: A framework for interaction description with roles. Technical Report TUM-I9731, Technische Univerität München (1997)
20. AutoSAR. http://www.autosar.org/.
21. AMI-C. http://www.ami-c.org/publicspecrelease.asp.
22. M. Broy and I. H. Krüger (eds.): Pre-Procceedings of the Automotive Software Workshop San Diego 2004, available at: http://tharkun.ucsd.edu/aswsd/ (2004)
23. JXTA Project Homepage: available at http://jxme.jxta.org/ (2001)
24. D. S. Platt and K. Ballinger. Introducing Microsoft .NET. Microsoft Press (2001).
25. Sun Microsystems, Inc.: Jini Architecture Specification, Version 1.1. available at http://wwwwswest.sun.com/jini/specs/jini1_1.pdf (2000).
26. OMG: Real-Time CORBA Specification. Version 1.1, formal/02-08-02, available at: http://www.omg.org/docs/formal/02-08-02.pdf (2002)
27. P. Zave: Feature-oriented description, formal methods, and DFC. In Proceedings of the FIREworks Workshop on Language Constructs for Describing Features, pages 11-26, Springer-Verlag, London (2001)
28. CTAS homepage, available at http://www.ctas.arc.nasa.gov/
29. J. Ellsberger, D. Hogrefe, and A. Sarma: SDL. Formal Object-oriented Language for Communicating Systems. Prentice Hall (1998)

30. I.H. Krüger: Capturing Overlapping, Triggered, and Preemptive Collaborations Using MSCs. in: Mauro Pezz (Ed.): Fundamental Approaches to Software Engineering, 6th International Conference, FASE 2003, Lecture Notes in Computer Science 2621, Springer (2003)

31. J. Snell, D. Tidwell and P. Kulchenko. *Programming Web Services with SOAP.* O'Reilly (2002)

32. E. Evans: *Domain-Driven Design: Tackling Complexity in the Heart of Software.* Addison-Wesley (2003)

33. D. Trowbridge, U. Roxburgh, G. Hohpe, D. Manulescu and E.G. Nadhan: *Intergration Patterns. Patterns & Practices.* http://download.microsoft.com/download/a/c/f/acf079ca-670e-4942-8a53-e587a0959d75/IntPatt.pdf (2004)

34. D.C. Luckham, J.J. Kenney, L.M. Augustin, J. Vera, D. Bryan and W. Mann:*Specification and Analysis of System Architecture Using Rapide.* IEEE Transactions on Software Engineering. Vol. 21, No. 4 (1995)

35. J. Magee, N. Dulay, S. Eisenbach and J. Kramer: *Specifying Distributed Software Architectures.* in: 5th European Software Engineering Conference (1995)

36. A.J. Allen and D. Gralan: *A Formal Basis for Architectural Connection.* ACM Transactions on Software Engineering and Methodology (1997)

37. R.N. Taylor, N. Medvidovic, K.M. Anderson, E.J. Whitehead, J.E. Robbins, K.A. Nies, P. Oreizy and D.L. Dubrow: *A Component and Messages Based Architectural Style for GUI Software.* IEEE Transactions on Software Engineering. Vol. 22, No. 6, pp. 390-406 (1996)

Author Index

Lecture Notes in Computer Science

For information about Vols. 1–3449

please contact your bookseller or Springer

Vol. 3503: S.E. Nikoletseas (Ed.), Experimental and Efficient Algorithms. XV, 624 pages. 2005.

Vol. 3502: F. Khendek, R. Dssouli (Eds.), Testing of Communicating Systems. X, 381 pages. 2005.

Vol. 3501: B. Kégl, G. Lapalme (Eds.), Advances in Artificial Intelligence. XV, 458 pages. 2005. (Subseries LNAI).

Vol. 3500: S. Miyano, J. Mesirov, S. Kasif, S. Istrail, P. Pevzner, M. Waterman (Eds.), Research in Computational Molecular Biology. XVII, 632 pages. 2005. (Subseries LNBI).

Vol. 3499: A. Pelc, M. Raynal (Eds.), Structural Information and Communication Complexity. X, 323 pages. 2005.

Vol. 3498: J. Wang, X. Liao, Z. Yi (Eds.), Advances in Neural Networks – ISNN 2005, Part III. L, 1077 pages. 2005.

Vol. 3497: J. Wang, X. Liao, Z. Yi (Eds.), Advances in Neural Networks – ISNN 2005, Part II. L, 947 pages. 2005.

Vol. 3496: J. Wang, X. Liao, Z. Yi (Eds.), Advances in Neural Networks – ISNN 2005, Part II. L, 1055 pages. 2005.

Vol. 3495: P. Kantor, G. Muresan, F. Roberts, D.D. Zeng, F.-Y. Wang, H. Chen, R.C. Merkle (Eds.), Intelligence and Security Informatics. XVIII, 674 pages. 2005.

Vol. 3494: R. Cramer (Ed.), Advances in Cryptology – EUROCRYPT 2005. XIV, 576 pages. 2005.

Vol. 3493: N. Fuhr, M. Lalmas, S. Malik, Z. Szlávik (Eds.), Advances in XML Information Retrieval. XI, 438 pages. 2005.

Vol. 3492: P. Blache, E. Stabler, J. Busquets, R. Moot (Eds.), Logical Aspects of Computational Linguistics. X, 363 pages. 2005. (Subseries LNAI).

Vol. 3489: G.T. Heineman, I. Crnkovic, H.W. Schmidt, J.A. Stafford, C. Szyperski, K. Wallnau (Eds.), Component-Based Software Engineering. XI, 358 pages. 2005.

Vol. 3488: M.-S. Hacid, N.V. Murray, Z.W. Raś, S. Tsumoto (Eds.), Foundations of Intelligent Systems. XIII, 700 pages. 2005. (Subseries LNAI).

Vol. 3486: T. Helleseth, D. Sarwate, H.-Y. Song, K. Yang (Eds.), Sequences and Their Applications - SETA 2004. XII, 451 pages. 2005.

Vol. 3483: O. Gervasi, M.L. Gavrilova, V. Kumar, A. Laganà, H.P. Lee, Y. Mun, D. Taniar, C.J.K. Tan (Eds.), Computational Science and Its Applications – ICCSA 2005, Part IV. XXVII, 1362 pages. 2005.

Vol. 3482: O. Gervasi, M.L. Gavrilova, V. Kumar, A. Laganà, H.P. Lee, Y. Mun, D. Taniar, C.J.K. Tan (Eds.), Computational Science and Its Applications – ICCSA 2005, Part III. LXVI, 1340 pages. 2005.

Vol. 3481: O. Gervasi, M.L. Gavrilova, V. Kumar, A. Laganà, H.P. Lee, Y. Mun, D. Taniar, C.J.K. Tan (Eds.), Computational Science and Its Applications – ICCSA 2005, Part II. LXIV, 1316 pages. 2005.

Vol. 3480: O. Gervasi, M.L. Gavrilova, V. Kumar, A. Laganà, H.P. Lee, Y. Mun, D. Taniar, C.J.K. Tan (Eds.), Computational Science and Its Applications – ICCSA 2005, Part I. LXV, 1234 pages. 2005.

Vol. 3479: T. Strang, C. Linnhoff-Popien (Eds.), Location- and Context-Awareness. XII, 378 pages. 2005.

Vol. 3478: C. Jermann, A. Neumaier, D. Sam (Eds.), Global Optimization and Constraint Satisfaction. XIII, 193 pages. 2005.

Vol. 3477: P. Herrmann, V. Issarny, S. Shiu (Eds.), Trust Management. XII, 426 pages. 2005.

Vol. 3476: J. Leite, A. Omicini, P. Torroni, P. Yolum (Eds.), Declarative Agent Languages and Technologies. XII, 289 pages. 2005.

Vol. 3475: N. Guelfi (Ed.), Rapid Integration of Software Engineering Techniques. X, 145 pages. 2005.

Vol. 3474: C. Grelck, F. Huch, G.J. Michaelson, P. Trinder (Eds.), Implementation and Application of Functional Languages. X, 227 pages. 2005.

Vol. 3468: H.W. Gellersen, R. Want, A. Schmidt (Eds.), Pervasive Computing. XIII, 347 pages. 2005.

Vol. 3467: J. Giesl (Ed.), Term Rewriting and Applications. XIII, 517 pages. 2005.

Vol. 3466: S. Leue, T.J. Systä (Eds.), Scenarios: Models, Transformations and Tools. XII, 279 pages. 2005.

Vol. 3465: M. Bernardo, A. Bogliolo (Eds.), Formal Methods for Mobile Computing. VII, 271 pages. 2005.

Vol. 3464: S.A. Brueckner, G.D.M. Serugendo, A. Karageorgos, R. Nagpal (Eds.), Engineering Self-Organising Systems. XIII, 299 pages. 2005. (Subseries LNAI).

Vol. 3463: M. Dal Cin, M. Kaâniche, A. Pataricza (Eds.), Dependable Computing - EDCC 2005. XVI, 472 pages. 2005.

Vol. 3462: R. Boutaba, K.C. Almeroth, R. Puigjaner, S. Shen, J.P. Black (Eds.), NETWORKING 2005. XXX, 1483 pages. 2005.

Vol. 3461: P. Urzyczyn (Ed.), Typed Lambda Calculi and Applications. XI, 433 pages. 2005.

Vol. 3460: Ö. Babaoglu, M. Jelasity, A. Montresor, C. Fetzer, S. Leonardi, A. van Moorsel, M. van Steen (Eds.), Self-star Properties in Complex Information Systems. IX, 447 pages. 2005.

Vol. 3459: R. Kimmel, N.A. Sochen, J. Weickert (Eds.), Scale Space and PDE Methods in Computer Vision. XI, 634 pages. 2005.

Vol. 3458: P. Herrero, M.S. Pérez, V. Robles (Eds.), Scientific Applications of Grid Computing. X, 208 pages. 2005.

Vol. 3456: H. Rust, Operational Semantics for Timed Systems. XII, 223 pages. 2005.

Vol. 3455: H. Treharne, S. King, M. Henson, S. Schneider (Eds.), ZB 2005: Formal Specification and Development in Z and B. XV, 493 pages. 2005.

Vol. 3454: J.-M. Jacquet, G.P. Picco (Eds.), Coordination Models and Languages. X, 299 pages. 2005.

Vol. 3453: L. Zhou, B.C. Ooi, X. Meng (Eds.), Database Systems for Advanced Applications. XXVII, 929 pages. 2005.

Vol. 3452: F. Baader, A. Voronkov (Eds.), Logic for Programming, Artificial Intelligence, and Reasoning. XI, 562 pages. 2005. (Subseries LNAI).

Vol. 3450: D. Hutter, M. Ullmann (Eds.), Security in Pervasive Computing. XI, 239 pages. 2005.